Anything Can Happen

Interviews with
Contemporary American Novelists

Anything Can Happen

Conducted and edited by
Tom LeClair and Larry McCaffery

Thomas
"
1944–

UNIVERSITY OF ILLINOIS PRESS
Urbana   Chicago   London

This book is printed on acid-free paper.

Library of Congress Cataloging in Publication Data

LeClair, Thomas, 1944–
  Anything can happen.

  1. Novelists, American—20th century—Interviews.
I. McCaffery, Larry, 1946–   II. Title
PS129.L36   813'.54'09   82-2867
ISBN 0-252-00970-3   AACR2

For Kathy and Sinda

Acknowledgments

Our thanks to all the interviewees for their patience with the spoken word, to the transcribers who labored to turn it into print, and to the following who helped along the way: the National Endowment for the Arts, the San Diego State University Foundation, and the University Research Council and Taft Foundation of the University of Cincinnati. Special thanks of a more personal nature go to Dan Boone, Carolyn Forche, Tom Held, Kathy Sagan, and Ann Lowry Weir.

We thank, too, the editors of the journals where some of these interviews or parts thereof first appeared: *Chicago Review, Contemporary Literature, Genre, The New Republic, New York Times Book Review, Partisan Review,* and *Paris Review.*

Contents

Introduction

"Anything can happen. Everything is true." That's the way Stanley Elkin summed up his heaven and earth in *The Living End*, and it describes American fiction now. Editors don't become famous by announcing unpredictability or collapsing categories, but after reading and listening to novelists of the 1970s, we think (even insist) that what characterizes the fiction of our writers is syncretism—a healthy ecology for art, one that supplies open space for excess and protection for miniatures, supports differences without the threat of domination by some "fittest," and encourages hybrid species.

When we began interviewing, we had some writers presorted into familiar slots—realist, experimentalist, feminist, metafictionist, neoconservative—but our tapes and their art wouldn't fit. Some of our problems: William Gass, aesthetician of the nonreferential, is writing a novel about nazism. His antagonist John Gardner, defender of moral seriousness, plays autobiographical and textual games in *Freddy's Book*. John Barth, reported lost in the experimental regresses of Greek mythology, returns to write *Letters*, a book full of real American news and history. The new conservative John Irving gives us a polished autobiographical metafiction in *The World According to Garp*. Raymond Federman, who flooded his early novels with delirious prose and typographical hijinks, writes *The Voice in the Closet*, a "twenty-page novel" of absolute verbal compression and rigid typographical structure. Don DeLillo and Joseph McElroy orbit the world with science fictions—*Ratner's Star* and *Plus*—then follow up with novels about women and men in New York City.

There's no telling what a novelist will do from one book to the next. No accounting, either, for the imaginative writer's ability to desert an aesthetic position, mock a critical category, or transform the terms used to name his methods. Some examples from our interviews: Donald Barthelme, current Borgesian master, claims social relevance for his surreal thingums. Robert Coover shuffles stories like magic cards but thinks of himself as a realist; E. L. Doctorow works close to fact and calls himself a fabulator. Toni Morrison, Rosellen Brown, and Diane Johnson write about women, yet none cares to be called a women's writer. Tim O'Brien says his Vietnam novel, *Going after Cacciato*, is about the imagination.

This isn't exactly confusion, but to the namer of schools who is browsing in a Latin dictionary, looking for a new prefix to fit the fiction of the decade, we suggest only "omni-" will do. Every age has its diversity, different kinds of writers working simultaneously. Now, though, we have novelists shifting among different modes, merging traditional forms and experimental energies, redefining the methods we've used to keep them separate. Fiction is not only alive; it's mutating.

Variety and vitality turned out to be our discoveries because we went looking for quality—quality of art, quality of talk—in whatever style or place or personality we could find it. Interviews should consist of talk about work well done, no matter what it is or is about; talk that preserves, against the consumer and the critic, the creator's views. When writers are gathered for unity, they are viewed like oranges picked for juice. Academic syllabi, critics working from galley proofs, and quarterly essays too often put together groups of novelists who have a common feature and an uncommon diversity of talent. The original and the imitator, the profound and the facile are forced together like a necessary foursome for bridge.

The eighteen novelists included here were not selected because of critical reputation, popularity, elusiveness, influence, representativeness, or even diversity. We can't deny they possess these traits, but it's quality we began with. And it's quality, not similarity to some this or difference from some that, that we think readers should first consider when they reflect upon and reread recent fiction. Our guides to quality were the now generally ignored Jamesian dicta—grant the *donnée*, judge the execution—principles we think are consistently confirmed as worthy by the novelists' discussions of their very different *données*, intentions, and methods of execution. If Toni Morrison writes what she calls "village literature" and Raymond Federman does "improvisational fiction," we need to understand why and how, not necessarily to accept or praise, but to judge. The result is not critical relativism but the close scrutiny of individual art. Denied a literary strip map, a ride down the obliterating pipeline of generalization, yet presented with authoritative if sometimes eccentric local guides, readers of this collection should go back to the territory itself, the individual books. Not book biz; not schools of writers, unstable as schools of fish; not authors, those convenient tagging concepts for men and women made phantoms by their work; not even books in some sequence—but the single book, one after another after another, discrete and resistant, that makes our literature.

One safe generalization: these are writers of the 1970s. About half began publishing during the decade, most of them saw their reputations emerge during that time, and almost all have done their best work in the last few years. Some are more widely known than others. Several writers we would like to have included were either unavailable or talked out, but we think the novelists interviewed here represent the range of possibilities and the quality of recent fiction. A one-sentence literary history of the decade would state that the innovation that proliferated in the early '70s was gradually displaced by late '70s conservatism. But this recent "conservatism" is deceptive. While it is true that several influential older writers—Barth, Gass—were working in historically referential modes during the decade, and that several younger writers—Irving, O'Brien—received attention for novels strong in narrative and representation, the kind of conservatism vocally espoused by Gardner in *On Moral Fiction* seems not to have converted any of the writers we interviewed. Their work is, as it should be, deeply their own, issuing from very personal interests and limitations, little affected by critical fashions or other writers' opinions. Rather than a displacement of innovation, we see in the work and talk of some writers here a sophisticated defense of traditional forms. Giving the old equal theoretical status with the new provides an environment where hybrids of tradition and innovation such as Doctorow's *Loon Lake*, Barth's *Letters*, Morrison's *Song of Solomon* or Elkin's *The Living End* can be produced and appreciated. The decade's aesthetic disagreements, many of which are summarized in the Gass-Gardner debate included here, did not develop into a dialectical struggle in which writers faced off along strict theoretical lines. Instead, we found a refractive effect, with writers using the extremes articulated by Gass and Gardner as an occasion to define their own individual, even idiosyncratic aesthetics. Venn diagrams, not battle lines, are needed to chart the eighteen positions here. Plenitude, rather than ideological limitation, is the effect of the age's arguments.

Of these arguments, the moral issue engaged few of our novelists. The writer "has no social obligations," said Elkin, "unless his wife has accepted a dinner date for Thursday." Representation was a concept atomized by multiple interpretations. Story was held dear by writers who would never read each other's fictions. If there is an issue over which most of the interviewees diverged, one that they considered essential, it is the opposition between invisible and visible art—fiction that conceals its illusionary methods versus fiction that calls attention to its creator. The Gass–Gardner debate furnishes basic statements of the opposition. Gardner's ideal fiction is a "vivid and continuous dream" in which the reader is "living a virtual life, making moral judgments in a virtual state." For Gass, a book is a construct, "more like a building which you're trying to get someone to go through the way you want him to. . . . The kind of attention the reader is expected to pay to the page transforms the way the work exists." In Gass's aesthetic space, the reader is always aware of reading a book *made* of language; here character becomes concept and plot is pattern. In Gardner's dream, the reader forgets the artist and the language; character is person, plot is behavior. Gass's fiction insists upon itself as an object. Gardner's is transparent.

Visible artists have two rather different purposes and methods. Because Gass, Hawkes, and Elkin wish to make each page, each sentence a performance for the reader's pleasure, they create a heavily foregrounded and metaphoric literary language that asks to be read aloud. Style is a physical presence and reason for being. Barth, Coover, Federman, Ron Sukenick, and Steve Katz want to expose fiction's illusions because these illusions have become formulaic, no longer means but assumptions that readers accept as necessities. Barth and Coover are visible behind their texts as manipulators and parodists; Federman, Sukenick, and Katz are present in the texts as characters. Although both kinds of visible artists are often charged with self-indulgence, their baring of artifices usually functions (like a Brechtian alienation effect) to make the reader critically conscious, not just of the artist and his craft, but also of the thematic materials. Invisible artists, on the other hand, are accused of self-deception, of clinging to methods of organizing experience that distort reality. The defenders of invisible art—Irving, Brown, Doctorow, Johnson, O'Brien—collectively reply that language is inherently referential, that story remains a natural and effective way of ordering experience, and that their artifices have the useful function of vicariously connecting the reader with other lives and subjects. Their method is to use materials that have a built-in substance or significance—war, historical curiosities, social anxieties, or, as John Irving says, "soap-opera stuff." But the artful arrangements and imaginative perspectives they give these materials separate their work from a naive or journalistic realism.

In this opposition we would seem to have an index to innovation and conservatism, a descriptive way of keeping the decade straight. But what's to be done with Barthelme and McElroy? They are known as innovative writers, yet both say they have little interest in self-conscious fiction. Where are DeLillo and Morrison to be aligned? Although they are usually called traditional novelists, DeLillo finds the self-referentiality of his fiction, its turning back upon itself, one of its qualities worth remarking.

Morrison says she achieves her effects by creating an authorial presence to hold the reader's hand in the text. Our conclusion, once again, is that achievement, however it is accomplished, is more important than theory or similarity.

The most common complaint about fiction of the '70s asserts that the novel has become a whirligig, bright and aimless. Alfred Kazin magisterially sums up this attack in a census of the unworthy called "American Writing Now" (*The New Republic*, October 18, 1980). Peering mournfully into the recent past, Kazin finds writers confused and abstracted, corrupted by commerce, unable to imagine the impact of science, business, history, and the media on the American present. Reading and listening, we found just the opposite to be true: both visible and invisible artists are confidently creating imaginative worlds wide with history and politics, dense with commerce, media, and technics. When Joe David Bellamy introduced his collection of interviews with innovative writers, *The New Fiction*, in 1974, he hazarded that fiction "may suddenly be in the process of catching up with the age." This, contra Kazin, is exactly what distinguishes the best novels of the '70s: imagination equal to the complexities of the time, innovations used to capture the spirit and argots of the age. The inventive energy and substance of the decade are most obvious in its encyclopedic novels—*Gravity's Rainbow*, by the absentee Mr. Pynchon, Coover's *The Public Burning*, McElroy's *Lookout Cartridge*, DeLillo's *Ratner's Star*, and Barth's *Letters*—each of which has all of Kazin's subjects in artful collaboration. Not one of these massive books would be called realistic, any more than a telescope or microscope or kaleidoscope offers "realistic" ways of seeing light. Yet the books are at once rigorously empirical and powerfully abstract, finding, measuring, and expressing in all our contemporary lingoes the experience that realism sometimes misses with its naked eye and common tongue. In these novels the midrange of ordinary life has been narrowed to show how codes and signals, myths and formulas, gravity and fancy—all the invisible realities, sure as air and DNA—surround and engrave our lives. To illustrate their readiness in the world, the books find their forms outside literature—in information systems, ecology, pure mathematics, and the three-ring circus.

There's also mastery of the world in less excessive novels: Johnson's *The Shadow Knows*, Barthelme's *The Dead Father*, Sukenick's *98.6*, Gardner's *October Light*, O'Brien's *Cacciato*, Elkin's *The Dick Gibson Show*, Hawkes's *The Passion Artist*. Some of these are achieved works of conventional realism; others employ folktale and fairytale, dream, parody, gothic nightmare, fantasy, and virtuoso linguistic performance to possess our time and place. Even the militantly experimental writers Katz and Federman see their books attaching themselves to the world. In Katz's *Moving Parts* and Federman's *Take It or Leave It*, familiar distinctions be-

tween fact and fiction, author and character, reality and invention are jug-
gled into blurs by the "real fictitious discourses" the writers offer as models
for the imaginative processes we all use to establish meaning and self-
understanding. The works mentioned here, as well as the popular successes *Ragtime* and *Garp*, have impedance, some resistance to readerly
consumption. But their difficulties and demands, their deformations,
mass, or eccentricities, seem to us methods for discovering and de-
familiarizing important subjects. Algebra and fire, says Barth with
Borges, are the elements of quality. Elegant form and passionate matter
have a Siamese connection in the fiction of the '70s. Old assumptions
about the effeteness of innovation and the simplicity of imitation are
destroyed by our new experimental realists. Whatever the causes — the
insistence of the world, the writers' education and work outside the
university, a lust for the new languages specialists have created, the
natural progress of experiment from hypotheses to results—this engagement with large cultural themes is good news for the novel as a continuing
form. It is also good news for the world, which is now so much a fiction—beyond verifiability and the ordinary imagination—that only fiction can adequately represent it.

While shuffling through our question cards or cuing up our tapes, we'd
be asked why we did these interviews. Easy enough to answer "Because I
respect your work" or "I like to travel," but not so easy to tell some
novelists that we felt they were writing from assumptions misunderstood
by most readers, or to say to the lesser-known that we hoped to bring more
readers to their work, or to tell writers with popular reputations we
thought their fiction deserved more serious attention. Since our purpose
was never a scheme or sequence but a collection, our approaches to the interviews were dictated, we'd like to think, by each writer's work and
temperament. Ranging across the writers' lives and careers, stocking
material for biographers, we've asked the usual questions about personal
motives, literary influences, and publishing problems. But we have
centered, as much as the novelists would allow us, on the books, taping for
understanding and appreciation. How does a novel begin? How does it
grow? How does it change? These are some questions used to uncover
craft and meaning without asking the writer to be his or her own interpreter. We assume the reader's knowledge of and interest in the texts, but
we also include spools of aesthetic theory that don't require that
knowledge.

The two exchanges—Barth and Hawkes, Gass and Gardner—introduce
large issues that the interviewees consider in their own work. Barth and
Hawkes are the aesthetic grandfathers of this generation, both beginning
their remarkable careers in the 1950s. They bring us up to date and supply
their present positions on the imagination and the world: where imagina-

tion finds its sources, how it creates or represents, the risks it takes with the work and the audience. Because novels of the '70s are a wide-angle lens on the times, we've often asked about extraliterary influences on subjects and methods of composition. How does imagination take in and transform computers, minimal art, jazz, games, television, pure mathematics, terrorism, and all the other materials of the fiction? How do the writers imagine that their often risky and unusual books might be read? The general appeal of the Gass-Gardner debate has been related to their differences over the novel's function, but their argument about the medium of fiction is just as important to creators. We've asked most of our writers about both issues, once again probing for the constituents of quality. Our questions about the writers these eighteen respect were posed to give readers an elaborate triangulation of worth. Readers can begin with the interviews by novelists whose work they know, proceed to the others included here, and then move on to the work of writers our interviewees have mentioned, thus constructing their own networks of achievement. That there was not space to include in this collection interviews with all of the accomplished writers of the '70s mentioned in it illustrates, we think, that the decade offered readers a whole country of fiction, large, diverse, and surprising.

In our editing, we've tried to preserve the writer's voice, the print of personality that often tells as much about the work as does the utterance itself. Language spills from Irving, Federman, and Gass; it is squeezed from Barthelme and DeLillo, pondered by Coover, and acted out by Morrison. Once again, there are variety and quality: good talk, lucid and honest, worthy of the art it's about. Not the exchange of index cards that Nabokov called an interview, but talk: tape turned into type with few elisions or erasures. Individually, the writers reveal much about their work that the closest readings have missed, intricacies and intentions that have helped us and our students appreciate the fictions. Taken together, the interviews furnish readers (and interviewers) with ways of reading and thinking about literature that no single critic or artist could express, conflicting and overlapping versions of art that sharpen our knowledge of the present. We hope this syncretism is as useful and—why not?—as pleasurable for readers as it has been for us.

A Dialogue
John Barth and John Hawkes

Before American fiction was liberated by the publication of *Lolita* in 1958, John Hawkes and John Barth were writing the kind of novel that would be called Nabokovian in the 1960s and '70s. Hawkes's *The Cannibal* (1949) was a construct of metaphors giving both humorous and elegant expression to sexual aberration. In *The Floating Opera* (1956) Barth made narrative unreliability a parodic game of doubles, reflections of reflections on the craft of fiction. In the years since, they have created militantly original bodies of work, fictions that have demanded from readers a retooling of expectations and from critics an appreciation of artifice. Although they are two of the most influential practitioners of innovative fiction, Hawkes and Barth have written little criticism that would help the reader understand the aesthetics from which their novels are composed. In the following exchange they turn back to their early work and, with their most recent books—*The Passion Artist* and *Letters*—in mind, discuss their current ideas about what fiction should be and do.

The discussion took place before five hundred people during a Fiction Festival at the University of Cincinnati in November, 1978. Reading their fiction earlier in the festival, Barth and Hawkes resembled their artistic models—God and Satan respectively. Tall, thin, with a balding head that reflected light makes larger than it is, Barth performing is both remote and beneficent looking. He seems to float above the platform, acting every part, throwing every voice, filling empty space with a complete, full-

blooded world. Barth takes no breaths you can hear; it is the ease of creation. Hawkes is short, wide-eyed, uncertain in voice, anxious before his
audience. Alternately reading grotesque passages from his fiction and telling anecdotes that sound like the fiction, Hawkes replies to propriety,
gives dreams words, offers an anti-creation, a well-made hell.

Sitting together on stage before a tangle of microphones, feet showing
beneath the table, they lack the creator's presence. Barth is more professional than godlike. Relishing intellectual talk, he's drawn up close to the
table where he can use his notes. Hawkes pushes back and slumps a little in
his chair, the better to assume the role of outsider, "illiterate" craftsman.
After preliminary congratulations, they test each other's loyalty to the
risky aesthetic of creation rather than representation. Surprisingly, Barth
the formal experimentalist speaks passionately about the passions in fiction, while Hawkes the artist of the unconscious talks philosophically
about the imagination.

Barth's books before the publication of *Letters* in 1979 have come, he
notes, in pairs: *The Floating Opera* (1956) and *The End of the Road* (1958),
realistic and philosophical; *The Sot-Weed Factor* (1960) and *Giles Goat-
Boy* (1966), mythic and allegorical; and the story collections *Lost in the
Funhouse* (1968) and *Chimera* (1972). Between *The Cannibal* in 1949 and
The Passion Artist in 1979, Hawkes has published novels entitled *The Beetle Leg* (1951), *The Lime Twig* (1961), *Second Skin* (1964), and his triad of
sex, death, and the imagination—*The Blood Oranges* (1971), *Death, Sleep
and the Traveler* (1974), and *Travesty* (1976). Hawkes has also published a
collection of plays, *The Innocent Party* (1966), and a collection of short
fiction, *Lunar Landscapes* (1969).

—*Edited by Tom LeClair*

Barth: For between fifteen and twenty years, starting long before I
knew John Hawkes, I have been reading with sustained awe and admiration stories written by this man: outrageous situations and unforgettable
scenes refracted through a lens of rhetoric that transfigures them into
something as strange and as beautiful as anything I know of in our contemporary literature. They wear me out, Hawkes's books; they hurt my head.
They provoke, though, the kind of love that one feels only for amazing
things that could not come out of one's own imagination at all. One loves
them the more for that fact.

Somewhere along the road of those novels and those years Jack Hawkes
and I became friends, but a very peculiar kind of friends. We almost never
see each other. We don't exchange very many letters, and they are almost
all of a kind—the Hawkeses inviting the Barths to join them please in Pro-

vence or Greece, and the Barths saying, "No, we're sorry, we have to stay here in Baltimore for one stupid reason or another."

I suspect that we write novels to each other instead of letters. At least it's true that Hawkes is one of the readers whose displeasure in anything I wrote would most dismay and distress me. It was enough for him, for example, to say on one occasion that some of the voices in my novel *Giles Goat-Boy* did not ring right in his ears to make that novel the one I recall with the least pleasure among my books. There is no writer among our contemporary Americans whose new work I read with more immediate interest, to find out what is going on in that extraordinary imagination. But we've never had a literary conversation; today we're going to see if we can do it.

Hawkes: The things Jack Barth is saying about me really apply to himself and more. He is, for me, nothing less than a comic Melville.

The first work of Jack's that I read was *The Floating Opera*, when I had just finished *Second Skin*. It was his first novel, written long before, and in it I suddenly saw a marvelous, fiendish imagination that I felt great kinship to. Just as when I first read Nathanael West and Flannery O'Connor, I was shocked and amazed by that imagination. Now Barth has outdone even those two fine writers. The next novel of his I read was *The Sot-Weed Factor*. I picked it up one day when I was tired, and found I couldn't read it. Then one summer I was sick, depressed, whatever, and the weeks stretched ahead. I had time. I read *The Sot-Weed Factor*. It's the staggering fiction of our century. As for Jack Barth himself, his boundless imagination is so life-filled and so full of danger as well, that it's quite wonderful to be anywhere near him.

Barth: Our reciprocal esteem established, my first question is the kind I always wish my students would ask visiting writers who come through the seminars that I preside over at Johns Hopkins. The following short question: Jack, when did you get the call? Why do you write prose fiction, especially short novels? Why have you never perpetrated a long novel? Who or what specifically was of great or little help to you, and how? What was in your way that you had to get out of your way? What was the darkest hour in your professional life thus far? The brightest hour in that same professional life? Against whose works do you measure your own, and how does the measurement come out?

Hawkes: Now we hear Barth, as the storyteller, obviously putting me on the spot, making me feel very peculiar. I am tempted to talk about my athlete's foot. I began to write fiction at the moment I met the woman who became my wife, Sophie, when I was still an undergraduate. Her father was in the army in the middle of Montana. One summer she had to go home to him, and I followed her, trying to persuade her to get married. And we did, much against everybody's better judgment except ours; we knew what we were doing. In the middle of that Montana wasteland I suddenly realized that I could no longer write poetry, which I had aspired to do. I got athlete's foot. I wanted cowboy boots more than anything in the world. I couldn't afford to buy them, so somebody told me where I could find a pair. If we would just drive fifty miles out into the buttes, we would come to a little hut and in the middle of the hut was an old wrinkled pair of cowboy boots. I put them on and they gave me athlete's foot.

While I was sitting with my feet in a bucket of potassium permanganate, someone gave me a book called *The Thinking Reed*, an abominable work, which made me think I could do something better. So I asked for paper and pencil and spent the summer sitting with my feet in the solution trying to write a novel (*Charivari*) in which I made fun of her parents and mine. That is how I began to write fiction. A few months later I was accepted into Albert Guerard's writing class, and the conjunction of new wife, new teacher and, very quickly, publisher (James Laughlin of New Directions) all contributed to my life as a writer.

Dark moments are being put on the spot by Barth. I can't describe the agonies. I can say, though, that I am illiterate; I always was; I've never read enough and I can never catch up. But I do remember when I first went to Harvard from a little country town in upper New York state, a true innocent, knowing nothing, totally vulnerable. In Grolier's Book Shop in Cambridge, Mass., I found a slender green volume called *Pomes Penyeach* by Joyce; those little poems were so lyrical, so marvelous that, thanks to them, I first became interested in language.

Now, Jack, I'd like to ask why you consistently repudiate your first two novels, which I think are extraordinarily fine books. And how on earth did you make the leap from *The Floating Opera* and *End of the Road* to *The Sot-Weed Factor*?

Barth: One does, now and then, look back over the old bibliography for what one of Saul Bellow's characters speaks of as "the axial lines," lines that one sometimes can't see until they're extended far enough. One day I realized to my delight (I'm an opposite-sex twin) that all my books come in pairs. I had not realized that until there were enough pairs there for somebody to see the pattern and point it out to me. But I don't repudiate that first pair. One moves on. John Updike made the lovely remark once that he thinks of his own past productions as skins that a snake sheds on his way somewhere. The first books are what I was, what my imagination was, when I was twenty-four years old: young, ambitious, discovering that literature existed and trying to find my own voice in it. In some humors—when one's marriage, metabolism, and the weather are all simultaneously in good shape, one looks back and says, "That's not bad at all for a twenty-four-year-old." Other times one blushes for what one was.

That's the way I feel about my books. I don't reread them, but I think about them. I try to imagine in them an organicity or continuity. It would be presumptuous to call it growth, but it certainly is related change. I look for cues; I monitor in retrospect the things I've set down on paper in the past to see what signals they may have for me now about the thing I want to do next. This mitigates in some degree the emptiness of the blank next page that comes after the last page of the book you've just finished writing.

As for the leap, if leap it was: it was the birth of the next set of twins. Two short novels, relatively realistic and contemporary, then two very long novels, both of them irrealistic and non-contemporary. Your early ambition, Jack, was to be a poet. My early ambition was to be a musician; not a composer or a performer, but an *orchestrator*. I believe that just as being a twin has been important to my imagination in certain basic ways, so too this early ambition to be an orchestrator. It's been my career, in general, to take something received—a melody line, let's say, from narrative or some other literary convention—and re-orchestrate it to my purposes.

In my late twenties, I was reading the big eighteenth-century novels for the first time, and I set myself the double task of writing a novel that would be thick enough so that the publisher could print the title across instead of down the spine and cooking up a plot that would be more complicated than the plot of *Tom Jones*. I think I succeeded in both those objectives. Although I would not presume to compare *The Sot-Weed Factor* with Henry Fielding's novel, I do think my plot is more complicated. But I forgot, after the four years I took to write it, to instruct the publisher to put the title across the spine.

Your work, on the other hand, Jack, shows the astonishing continuity of voice and preoccupation that I associate with a writer such as Kafka. Just as there is no "early Kafka," really, that I know of, so there is no early Hawkes. The imagination at work in *The Beetle Leg* and your other early stories seems to be the very same imagination at work now. When you hear John Hawkes tell an anecdote, about athlete's foot or whatever, the anecdote is vintage, palpable Hawkes. Everything that happens to John Hawkes seems to be John Hawkesian, just as everything that happened to Kafka seems to have been Kafkaesque. But much happens to Barth that doesn't remind me of Barth at all. I'm reminded of Borges's remark that he recognizes himself at least as often in the writings of somebody else, or in the strummings of a milonga on a guitar, as he does in his own work. I feel that way, too.

Hawkes: Something I've never been able to understand is why you have such strong feelings for Borges, Beckett, and Nabokov, but not for Faulkner. Do you really think that Faulkner's comic visions are so terribly different from those of the other three writers? I love Faulkner and I'm disappointed that you seem not to.

Barth: My literary fathers have been foreigners. I read Faulkner with proper astonishment and instruction when I was graduate-student age. I do not remember him with great pleasure. But when I reread him I do so with even less pleasure than I remember him with. Yet there's a wonderful thing about Faulkner—the way European and South American writers learn from him. The most incantatory mumbo jumbo in Faulkner—"the outraged wagonwheels going down the immemorial something or other"—taken far *enough* south, below the Rio Grande, comes to interest me. I watch Gabriel García Márquez learning from Faulkner, and all the things that bother me in Faulkner I admire when I see them in Márquez.

Let's get to some other questions about fiction where we don't quite agree. You've made some remarks about literature that seem untenable, to my way of thinking, and nondescriptive of your own practice as a writer. One was your infamous obiter dictum that plot, character, setting, and theme are the natural enemies of fiction. This sounds like the aesthetic of an author who would write novels without characters and plots. But I find your novels to be dramaturgically whole. And I do remember characters — Skipper in *Second Skin*, the narrator of *Travesty* — as real as any characters in Faulkner, for example.

Hawkes: I made that remark about the enemies of fiction when I was very young. I wasn't trying to be different. I didn't set out to contribute to the development of the form of the novel; I simply wrote very small, peculiar, nightmarish books. But when people began to talk about my fiction, I got the idea that conventional fiction was in fact odious and that these terms lent themselves to use by pedantic and dull teachers of literature. They are the simplest kinds of schemes with which to talk about fiction, and I don't like them. On the other hand, I will recant and say that plot is of course necessary, even though I cannot create a plot and still do not know what a plot is.

Barth: Permit me, my friend: A plot is the incremental perturbation of an unstable homeostatic system and its catastrophic restoration to a complexified equilibrium. But what is that, between friends? A rejection that dismayed me no less than your statement about plot was that you were abandoning comedy because it was too safe.

Hawkes: I turned deliberately to comedy in about 1960; I thought I had begun as a comic writer but nobody knew it. So I set out to write a comic novel, which was *Second Skin*. However, a few years ago, with the coming of age, depression, and discomfort, I began to think that, at least in certain writers, comedy is too comforting. Nobody can truly suffer or be truly obscene in Saul Bellow's work, for example, because he has a humane comic vision. Perhaps his vision is sustaining. But for me everything is dangerous, everything is tentative, nothing is certain. I think the writing of fiction involves enormous anxiety and enormous risk. And I want fiction always to situate us in the psychic and literal spot where life is most difficult, most dangerous, most beautiful. Which leads me, Jack, to ask you if risk means anything to you in writing fiction? And how you feel about being called "a great American experimenter?"

Barth: Experimentation is a word with a bad press. Just as nobody, in the days when we were all called black humorists (a term that described only one splendid thing—Hawkes's novels), wanted to be called a black humorist, because that was a name to be whacked over the head with, nobody wants to be called an experimental writer now. Of course, all risks are a kind of experiment, and there are many sorts of literary risks. There is a risk in doing a sort of fiction which may not repay its publisher your advance, no matter how penurious. There is a risk in committing yourself to a project which may take years and years of prime writing time and then turn out to be not worth that investment. But risk has never been a theme in my work as it has in yours. For example, the hazard of driving the car in *Travesty*.

Hawkes: There is a risk in your work in creating enormous fictions that are self-contained. The voice, the language, the mentality involve considerable risk because they insist on creating their own reality. I also think you take risks when you reverse the thoughts that are closest to you. For me John Barth's fiction has the enormous power it does partly because it is always positing nothingness, because it is so "created" that it also insists on that which is vacant. To me this is frightening. I think of your work as an enormous poetic cerebration. It must have to do with the word "plot": it's conceiving more and more; it's gargantuan; and that's dangerous, because some people could think you were cut off from life and because you always make us aware of what we are most afraid of, which is nothingness. Out of the nothingness that is our context you create the fabulous. Do you want to talk about that?

Barth: I'm going to agree with it and not talk about it. We remember Beckett: "that silence out of which the universe is made." Plot and perhaps over-ingeniousness are a shore against that silence Beckett speaks of. There is another order of risk which I take seriously: By doing a work of great length, with complex permutations, one may lose the reader. A written object that is not read is in a strange ontological state indeed. You yourself write short novels, and they have almost everything to be said for them. But long novels, which I personally deplore (and sometimes write), have almost nothing to be said for them. Yet as a writer I agree with a remark of William Gass's: the artist's loyalty is not to the audience, certainly not to himself—that would be contemptible indulgence—but, finally, to the object. One can find that, at the risk of losing the reader or doing some strange thing to oneself and one's "career," there are objects that will demand to be done at such and such a length. And one finds, with a tisk of the tongue and roll of the eyes, that one goes along with what the object demands, hoping all the time that one can somehow hedge it here and trim it there. But even if the limiting can't be done, one must remain loyal to the object.

Hawkes: I think readers associate the term "literature of exhausted possibility" with John Barth. Is it your idea that literature has all been done in one form or another?

Barth: That is what I *don't* mean, but it's a phrase that obviously invites intelligent and honorable misinterpretation. It's an axiom with me, as it is with Borges (on whom "The Literature of Exhaustion" was my essay), that literature is inexhaustible because no one literary text can be exhausted. I immediately say yes to that; yet there is an apocalyptic feeling about literature in our century. Here's a curious thing about written literature: It is about four thousand years old, but we have no way of knowing whether four thousand years constitutes senility or the maiden blush of youth.

Incidentally, the text of one of the earliest literary documents is a complaint, much to our purpose: The scribe Khakheperresenb, in a papyrus from 2000 B.C., writes, "Would I had phrases that are not known, utterances that are strange, in new language that has not been used, free from repetition, not an utterance which has grown stale, which men of old have spoken." Sounds like Don Barthelme in *Snow White*, doesn't it?

Now, obviously this is encouraging: Literature has been "exhausted" for a long time and may go on being "exhausted" for millennia before it dies, along with our sun and our stars. Your sentences and mine contribute to the exhaustion, but there remains a large (though finite) number of things that can be said. My metier being orchestration, exhaustion is just an invitation to administer artificial resuscitation to the apparently dead. But I want the result to be real life, not some Lazarus-like life. What one finds in the biographies of writers is that they exhaust their *own* possibilities, which is quite different from exhausting the possibilities of literature.

Looking at the curve of your own work, Jack, what do you see in the future for yourself? What do you want to get done before the gods descend in a rosy cloud and carry you off to Mount Helicon for keeps?

Hawkes: I have time, I think, to write three more fictions before I retire from teaching. And I'm looking forward to retirement; I don't want to stay on in the university. I love the university, but I want to go to a Greek island or the south of France and eat grapes and olives and swim, or at least float in the ocean, and get clean again if I can. I want to get sex or the eroticized landscape out of my system once and for all.

Last year, while I was writing a novel called *The Passion Artist*, I thought of the next novel I would write. Out of my own literal and spiritual exhaustion while I was writing one novel I managed at last to think of another, and that was a tremendous experience for me; it had never happened before. I want to write a novel called *The Amorous Lives of the Gauls*, which is a title of an actual seventeenth-century book written by one Bussy-Rabutin (that name alone is enough to send one into erotic hysteria). Bussy-Rabutin wrote a gossip book about court life and got himself exiled for twenty years; I want to redo his book as a parody of a pornographic novel with a woman as the narrator. I hope I'll manage it. And you?

Barth: I have the ambition to become simpler, simpler, simpler. There is a kind of mentality—I'm afflicted with it—which delights in setting itself increasingly complicated tasks to see if one can bring them off: raising the bar ever higher on the jump to see if one can clear it with some brio and grace, and perhaps passion as well. For that kind of mentality, there can be no more complicated task than to become simpler. I thought surely that with the novel I just finished, *Letters*, I would achieve that simplicity. I did not. It will have to wait for the next. But I guarantee that if it doesn't happen in the next, it will in the one after that. Since I intend to reach my peak only as an octogenarian, and then go into a *very* slow decline, I shall be very patient with myself in that regard.

Hawkes: You're never going to get simpler. When you're a hundred, you'll be working on a six-volume version of your most elaborate fiction. And the better it will be for us, too.

Audience: *John Barth has quoted Thomas Mann's statement that what the writer is writing about is seldom the main point. It's what he is doing with his left hand that really matters. What do writers think they are doing with their left hands?*

Barth: The remark is from *Tonio Kröger* (1903), somewhat garbled, but never mind. This is early high modernism, and like many another writer who makes remarkable obiter dicta, Mann didn't practice what he preached. Mann is writing *about* things all the time, and often frontally: hence Nabokov's disdain of him. But the remark interests me because I have at times gone farther than I want to go in the direction of a fiction that foregrounds language and form, displacing the ordinary notion of content, of "aboutness." But beginning with the *Chimera* novellas—written after the *Lost in the Funhouse* series, where that foregrounding reaches it peak or its nadir, depending on your aesthetic—I have wanted my stories to be *about* things: about the passions, which Aristotle tells us are the true subject of literature. I'm with Aristotle on that. Of course form can be passionate; language itself can be passionate. These are not the passions of the viscera, but that doesn't give them second-class citizenship in the republic of the passions. More and more, as I get older, I nod my head yes to Aristotle. I want my fictions to be not only passionately formal, not only passionately "in the language," as Theodore Roethke used to say about poems he liked, but passionately about things in life as well. That I think I'm achieving; simplicity, maybe not.

Hawkes: My work is so saturated with unconscious content anyway that I've got about five left hands all digging in the mud someplace. I have a hard time just trying to maintain consciousness and struggle along through the well-lighted mire.

Audience: *Has fiction usurped the place of poetry?*

Hawkes: I think that in a large way fiction has usurped the place of poetry. I think there are many more of us who are sustained by fiction, made to grow, made able to survive through language used in narrative form. But there are also certain poets whose works are very much alive. Roethke and Galway Kinnell are two I admire.

Barth: The kind of fiction that Jack Hawkes seemed to be describing when he made that wrong-headed statement in his youth about getting rid of plot and character — that would leave a lyrical fiction which foregrounds language. He doesn't write that kind of fiction, and neither do I, and neither of us would approve of it. But it may be statistically the case that more and more American poets are writing a kind of prose poem, and in many cases—witness my departed colleague Anne Sexton, and William Merwin—even narrative poetry. I think narrativity—the interposition of the teller between the tale and told—differentiates what most fiction writers still do from lyric poetry. Narrativity and plot.

Audience: *Can you describe the difference between creating reality and representing reality?*

Hawkes: It's a question of mind, temperament, and vision. There are certain fictions that are transparent: you see through them, you read through them. You're interested not in the fiction but in the "life" the fiction seems to be about. Such writers think they are reflecting or reproducing reality. They must think they know what reality is; they must think that "out there" is reality, which I don't think at all. As a writer, I'm not interested in "life." Fiction that insists on created actuality is its own reality, has its own vitality and energy. The writer wants the reader to speak it, to hear it, to see it, to react to the various aspects of its reality as art. Perhaps something Barth once said has to do with this question; he said, "God was a pretty good novelist; the only trouble was that he was a realist."

Barth: It seems to me that all fiction — including the fiction of experimental groups, such as OULIPO, that generate literary texts by algorithms without reference to the ordinary denotation of the words — both creates reality (for any literary text is a new thing in the world) and renders reality, if only in the sense that nonsense takes its sense from sense. The key would seem to me to be Plato's old notion of participation.

Consider the nonsense of an OULIPO text such as the opening two sentences of *Moby-Dick* changed by the algorithm "substantif plus sept": "Call me islander. Some yeggs ago, having little or no mongol in my purulence and nothing particular to interest me on shortbread, I thought I would sail about a little and see the watery partiality of the worriment." Even this renders reality, since whatever meaning its nonsense has comes from its participation in two orders of reality—the world and the literary text it is derived from. It is a spooky simulacrum of sense. The spookiness comes from its being just far enough removed to be strange, but not so far removed as to be utterly unintelligible—which is a lot like the way metaphors work. In "Tlon, Uqbar, Orbis Tertius," Borges says that in his imaginary land, objects can imagine themselves into real existence. These objects are called "hronir"; not only are they in the world, but they can displace prior reality. Now there is no better example of a "hron" than a literary text, a John Hawkes novel, for example—a piece of imagined reality that you can hold in your hand. It can do work in the world, even though it came out of my dear friend's formidable head.

A Debate
William Gass and John Gardner

John Gardner and William Gass had been arguing in private and sniping at each other in print for years before they got together at the University of Cincinnati in October, 1978, to debate publicly their aesthetic differences. Their two-hour panel was not, as one listener alleged, an academic exercise; rather, it was just the public and polite segment of a two-day conversation. They contended late into the night after Gass's reading, at lunch before the panel the next day, after the panel, and again at a reception following Gardner's reading—hours and hours of unfortunately untaped talk, Gardner jabbing away with folk wisdom and thrusts of his pipe, Gass countering with repeated "But Johns" and a playful aestheticism. In these unmoderated sessions Gardner sometimes seemed the renegade student seeking recognition from a former teacher who was willing to tolerate but never to approve or accept the student's militantly argued ideas. At other times Gardner seemed the elder, a concerned editor worried about his friend's misuse of talent. Occasionally impatient, Gass was most often bemused by Gardner's insistence.

When the two writers sat down in front of their audience of three hundred, you could see before they said a word that theirs was a nature/art quarrel. Gardner, a heavyset man with shoulder-length hair, a round boyish face, and agitated bearing, was wearing heavy workboots and slightly rumpled casual clothes. Gass is small, neat, not exactly formal, but he did sit almost primly erect with his toes on a chair rung. The impression is similar when they read their fiction. Gardner is an enthusiastic but nervous performer, hurrying his suspenseful stories to their conclusions as though he, like the audience, wants to find out what happens. Gass's reading seems rehearsed, the language elegant and musical, its delivery an actor's. However, once the two began to articulate their ideas during the panel, accidental associations and personal traits were forgotten as two lucid, well-stocked minds engaged each other and some of the most important issues in fiction today.

That Gardner and Gass should come to be known as spokesmen for two opposing kinds of writing is ironic for several reasons. While Gass has published four books that develop his aesthetic theory—the essays in *Fiction and the Figures of Life* (1970) and *The World within the Word* (1978), the mixed-genre discourses *Willie Masters' Lonesome Wife* (1971) and *On Being Blue* (1976)—his novel, *Omensetter's Luck* (1966), and the stories in *In the Heart of the Heart of the Country* (1968) do not always manifest very directly his theoretical notions. Gardner is a much more prolific novelist, yet he is most widely known now for his single book of criticism, *On Moral Fiction* (1978). While Gardner has published scholarly studies of Chaucer—*The Poetry of Chaucer* and *The Life and Times of Chaucer* (1977)—and several realistic novels—*The Resurrection* (1966), *The Sunlight Dialogues* (1972), *Nickel Mountain* (1973)—his achievement lies in highly imaginative narratives that are sometimes at odds with his positions in *On Moral Fiction*. These works include the epic poem *Jason and Medeia* (1973); the historical novels *The Wreckage of Agathon* (1970), *Grendel* (1971), and *Freddy's Book* (1980); and a combination realistic/pulp novel, *October Light* (1976). Gardner has also published two collections of stories—*The King's Indian* (1974) and *The Art of Living* (1981)—four books for children, and a narrative entitled *In the Suicide Mountains* (1977) that can be read by children and adults.

—Moderated and edited by Tom LeClair

Is there a use of language in fiction which is inherently moral?

Gardner: When I wrote *On Moral Fiction*, I was talking about a particular kind of fiction which I think is consciously moral, fiction which tries to understand important matters by means of the best tool human beings have. Many of the most academically popular writers of our time are completely uninterested in understanding these matters. They are more interested in understanding juxtapositions than in understanding how we should live. They are concerned with making beautiful or interesting or ornate or curious objects. As for language—when I talk to you, I speak English and try to choose words, from all the possible words in the world, which seem most likely to say what I mean. If I am writing and find that one of the words that I choose is wrong, I put in a better word for my precise meaning. While English is just noises that we make with our mouths, teeth, throat, lungs and so on, fiction is an enormously complicated language. It has much more discreet, much more delicate ways of communicating. When I create a character, I want to make a lifelike human being, a virtual human being. Maybe by using the right kind of weather, I can give you a hint of what this person is. By comparing him to a bear or a rhinoceros or a spider, I can give you another hint. In other words, everything I choose in writing a piece of fiction is aimed at communication. I think that beauty in fiction is finally elegant communication, where the very form of the work helps to say what I'm trying to say. If I'm writing about an ordered universe, I write an ordered novel. If I'm talking about a tension between order and disorder, I write a novel in which the form expresses that tension. But always I'm using the tool of language to dig a hole. Other people sometimes use the tool of language to chew on.

Gass: John's saying that a number of contemporary writers are really not interested in solving problems is a little misleading. I think the difference lies in whether they believe one can understand important human issues by writing novels; they might be so concerned with these problems that they would rather not trust the solution of them to novelists. My own feelings are, of course, that moral issues surround us everywhere, that they are deeply important, and that the survival of the human race is necessary so that parasites like myself can diddle away in corners. The question that lies between John and me here is whether or not writing fiction, rather than, for instance, doing philosophy, is a good method for such an exploration. Philosophy has its own disciplines, its own methods of coming to clarity about these issues, so the way one talks about them won't twist the conclusions. Because fiction is a method which, by its very nature and demands, deforms, I am suspicious of it.

John goes on to say that in writing he faces the problem of revision and getting his best words by constantly asking, "Is this really what I believe?" I think that's fine. I don't care how the right words get on the page as long as they're the right words. But my condition is much bleaker. I don't know, most of the time, what I believe. Indeed, as a fiction writer I find it convenient not to believe things. Not to disbelieve things either, just to move into a realm where everything is held in suspension. You hope that the amount of meaning that you can pack into the book will always be more than you are capable of consciously understanding. Otherwise, the book is likely to be as thin as you are. You have to trick your medium into doing far better than you, as a conscious and clearheaded person, might manage. So one of the problems that I face is exactly the opposite of John's. John's concern is to communicate; I have very little to communicate. I'm not sure I understand what little I do have. I think it would be thin and uninteresting and hardly useful. If I did want to communicate, I would move over to philosophy and submit to the rigors that are concerned with the production of clarity, of logical order, truth, and so on. In fiction, I am interested in transforming language, in disarming the almost insistent communicability of language. When you are not asserting, you are not confusing, and I would be happy to avoid that.

Does this kind of purity of creation have a moral value in the world, as well as an aesthetic one?

Gass: Sure, John wants a message, some kind of communication to the world. I want to plant some object in the world. Now it happens to be made of signs, which may lead people to think, because it's made of signs, that it's pointing somewhere. But actually I've gone down the road and collected all sorts of highway signs and made a piece of sculpture out of these things that says Chicago, 35,000 miles. What I hope, of course, is that people will come along, gather in front of the sculpture, and just look at it—consequently forgetting Chicago. I want to add something to the world which the world can then ponder the same way it ponders the world. Now, what kind of object? Old romantic that I am, I would like to add objects to the world worthy of love. I think that the things one loves most, particularly in other people, are quite beyond anything they communicate or merely "mean." Planting those objects is a moral activity, I suppose. You certainly don't want to add objects to the world that everybody will detest: "Another slug made by Bill Gass." That's likely to be their attitude, but you don't hope for it. The next question is, why is it that one wants this thing loved? My particular aim is that it be loved because it is so beautiful in itself, something that exists simply to be experienced. So the beauty has to come first.

Gardner: There's no question that an object made simply to be beautiful is an affirmation of a kind, and any affirmation of that which is good for human beings is moral. But Bill and I, in our writing, are concerned with different kinds of affirmation. When I write, I try to find out, by honest thought, moment by moment, psychological response by psychological response, what it is that I can affirm as true and good. I think, for example, it's better to be an American democratic person than a headhunter. I think I think that. When I work it out in a novel, I might change my mind a little. But in the process of discovering what I really believe, what I can say yes to: "Yes, I affirm that, that's good, that's helpful to people, that makes it possible for individuals to live in society," in the process I create an effect.

By telling a moving story, I've led the reader to an affirmation of the value I have come to find that I can affirm. The difference between what I am doing and what a philosopher is doing is that my activity leads to a feeling state, whereas the philosopher has only cold clarity. I'm after an affirmation of how to live, but it's a difficult affirmation. Again and again people read my books and misunderstand the endings; they think the end of *Grendel* is a curse. It's such a marginal affirmation that maybe it might as well be a curse. There isn't an awful lot one can affirm, but I try to get to the affirmation that I can really believe and that will move people. I'm trying for an affirmation that has something to do with how to live; Bill and other writers like him are trying for an affirmation of just living. A guy walks along the street and sees this magnificent sculpture made out of signs and his day is better for it. But what I want the guy to do is continue past the signs and go do his job.

Gass: One of the problems that I find with John's view is that it might lead you to say harsh things about great writers, a terrible thought. Suppose you have a writer who clearly inspects what he believes and ends his great long work by saying, "You must go on, I can't go on, I'll go on." That's about as affirmative as Beckett gets, and there are other writers who, in following a process of being honest about what they can affirm, find only "going on" left and are not even sure of that without writing another book to make sure they're still going on. Gaddis hasn't made a habit of hooray. Since I think, quite independently of any theory, that Beckett is one of the greatest writers of his period, I'm wondering, John, if your view allows you to regard him in that way?

Gardner: I don't think that's a problem because one is terribly moved by Beckett and one does go on, and one even feels he has a reason for going on, although the reason may be in the technical sense absurd. There are other writers who would persuade you not to go on, that everything is nonsense, that you should kill yourself. They, of course, go on to write another book while you have killed yourself. If we look back through the history of literature, those writers have not been the ones who have been loved and who have survived. Again and again we're moved by Achilles, we're moved by the best of Shakespeare, Chaucer, and the others we keep going back to. Writers who give us visions to which we say, with all our unconscious minds as well as our conscious minds, "That's just not so," we don't read.

I'm not saying that other people shouldn't make wonderful sculptures; I'm saying they shouldn't be mistaken for the big tent, the most important kind of work. The theory that I'm proposing says, fundamentally, that you create in the reader's mind a vivid and continuous dream. The reader sits down with his book just after breakfast, and immediately someone says, "Hermione, aren't you coming to lunch?" One instant has passed although two hundred pages have passed, because the reader has been in a vivid and continuous dream, living a virtual life, making moral judgments in a virtual state.

. . . The real problem with this argument is that Bill Gass is a sneaky moralist. His books end in magnificent affirmation. I'm arguing against his theory, but his books don't follow it.

Bill, what about this vivid and continuous dream?

Gass: It's rather imaginary. In music, let's say, the motion of the work comes from the performance. That's true also in the theater. So if there's an interruption, or your mind goes blank, or someone rattles a bag, you miss something and that's too bad, it's lost. In reading fiction, however, the motion that moves the text comes from the reader. Now the writer can indicate or try to indicate how that motion should go and at what rate. But I don't think that anyone writes a book now supposing that the reader will sit down and read two hundred pages through in a continuous dream. He's going to, in fact, stop, brush a fly off his nose, go back to the first page, read it over, skip, look around for the juicy parts. The book is more like a building which you're trying to get someone to go through the way you want him to. The experience of a novel can occasionally be what John describes. I remember it happening when I was twelve or so, reading *Boy Scout Boys on the Columbia River*.

Gardner: You're right if you're talking about the concert hall, but with a record you can go back. And when you go back, you remember what came before, you know where you are, and you know where you're going. If a novel is plotted, if you have the actualization of the potential that exists in a character in a certain situation, then the argument of the novel—the movement of the plot, the development of the characters in their response to problems—leads you through the novel. What argument is to philosophy, plot is to fiction. Most philosophers set up a syllogism and move steadily through it. You have a feeling of profluence, of forward flowingness. When a novel has a plot, it doesn't matter if the reader goes to chapter eight, then ducks back to chapter five, and then goes forward again. Finally, the ultimate apparition, the ultimate dream of the novel, is a continuous one. When you decide as a writer that the novel is just a house you're trying to get somebody to go through in various ways, you have broken faith with the reader because you are now a manipulator, as opposed to an empathizer. If the novelist follows his plot, which is the characters and the action, if he honestly and continuously proceeds from here to here because he wants to understand some particular question, the reader is going to go with him because he wants to know the same answers. On the other hand, if the writer makes the reader do things, then I think he puts the reader in a subservient position which I don't like.

Let me elaborate with the plot of a story someone told me once. A woman has had a perfect marriage. After her husband dies, she finds a walnut box of perfectly labeled feathers in the garage. She finds out that all his life he has had a secret hobby, and at that moment she begins to wonder how come he didn't tell her? The next time she hears a conversation about her husband, she's going to listen in a different way. The next time her kids talk about him, she's going to listen in a different way. The next time she meets his thirty-year-old secretary, she'll look at her a different way. We're onto a real problem, which is human doubt, human faith, and as long as we're on that, we don't want the author pushing us around. We want someone honestly, gently taking us through an exploration of this situation. There is an act of faith, whereas when the author manipulates the reader he is solipsistic in the worst sense: he's not in a love relationship with the reader.

Gass: I didn't mean the manipulation of the reader when I compared reading to going through a building. The kind of response to novels that John is talking about certainly was appropriate two hundred years ago, when there were lots of novels written in that form. There are just not many of them being written that way anymore. When Fielding comes to the end of *Tom Jones*, for example, I suspect that he expects us to remember about as much of the first chapter as we would of that early part of our life, if we were thinking back. Not every detail, not every adjective attached to a noun in a certain way. In someone like Joyce, quite the contrary is true. He wants an experience that can happen only when the reader moves constantly about the book. The notion of the space in which this kind of book is constructed is quite different from the notion of the time through which the Fielding work moves. While I don't mind Fielding's having written the way he wrote, John begrudges some people writing in this newer or different way, in which the kind of attention the reader is expected to pay to the page transforms the way the work exists.

Gardner: I think we both agree that we're trying to create something that the reader will love. Is it possibly the case that the fiction you're advocating, Bill, is simply not lovable, that it simply doesn't hook readers? You can quickly say, "But the most sophisticated reader. . ." I'm not sure that's true. In the academy we teach Pynchon instead of Trollope. About Trollope there's nothing to say because it's all clear. On the other hand, every line of Pynchon you can explain because nothing is clear. So the academy ends up accidentally selecting books the student may need help with. They may be a couple of the greatest books in all history and twenty of the worst, but there's something to say about them. You get an artificial taste in the academy. The sophisticated reader may not remember how to read; he may not understand why it's nice that Jack in the Beanstalk steals those things from the giant.

Gass: I suspect, John, that you want not things that will be loved but things that will be promiscuous. If you had a daughter to send into the world, would you want everybody to love her? I might be at my winery turning out bottles of Thunderbird which everybody loves. It wouldn't give me much satisfaction. It's not just that books are loved, but why they're loved. If you've given them the properties that make them worthwhile, then it doesn't matter if no one does love them. Frequently very few people do, or a work will go unobserved for years.

Do the two of you write from different motives? We've heard love mentioned several times. I know that Bill Gass has used the word anger. Do the motives for your writing produce the differences in the kind of fiction that you write?

Gass: I have a view I'm sure John wouldn't agree with. Very frequently the writer's aim is to take apart the world where you have very little control, and replace it with language over which you can have some control. Destroy and then repair. I once wrote a passage in which I had the narrator say, "I want to rise so high that when I shit I won't miss anybody." But there are many motives for writing. Writing a book is such a complicated, long-term, difficult process that all of the possible motives that can funnel in will, and a great many of those motives will be base. If you can transform your particular baseness into something beautiful, that's about the best you can make of your own obnoxious nature.

Gardner: I agree with almost everything Bill says except the nonsense about human nature. I think human beings are a little lower than angels and a hell of a lot more important. One does take the world apart and put it back together, but I would express it differently. You write the book to understand and get control of in yourself things that you haven't been able to control and understand in the world. When you have the kind of problem that will come to you in repeated dreams, you work it out on the page. Maybe it's an illusory understanding, but I think it helps you live. I think with each book you write you become a better person. It's certainly true that a great many famous writers, Marcel Proust for instance, were awful human beings, were much better in their writing. The reason is, I think, that when one is writing a book one gets to think over a nasty crack, and to gentle it and put it in a way that's not quite so cutting. Bill might say it's more elegantly expressed. "I want to rise so high that when I shit I won't miss anybody" is so well said that the meanness is partly muted. It becomes a joke, a kind of self-mocking, so it's not saying the same thing that the writer might say if drunk and angry. I believe that we revise our lives in our work, and with each revision we find a mistake we don't have to make again. I also think people become gradually slightly better people as they write books. That may not be true, but that's my conviction.

Gass: Do you think Alexander Pope got better as a person?

Gardner: I think that Bill values a great deal of literature that I don't value. Alexander Pope expresses a mood that we all have—meanness—and he expresses it very well. But one ultimately says, "I don't feel like reading Pope tonight. 'Kojak' is on; I'll get my meanness quick." One always reads through the mean writers with a certain amount of fascination, the same way you watch the female praying mantis eat the male. But that doesn't mean you go home every day and watch the praying mantises.

Gass: Some of us do.

The concept of character in fiction is one you differ on. Would you talk about your notion of character?

Gass: It's complex. I'll try to simplify it very quickly. A character for me is any linguistic location in a book toward which a great part of the rest of the text stands as a modifier. Just as the subject of a sentence, say, is modified by the predicate, so frequently some character, Emma Bovary for instance, is regarded as a central character in the book because a lot of the language basically and ultimately goes back to modify, be about, Emma Bovary. Now the ideal book would have only one character; it would be like an absolute, idealist system. What we do have are subordinate locales of linguistic energy—other characters—which the words in a book flow toward and come out of. A white whale is a character; mountains in *Under the Volcano* are characters. Ideas can become characters. Some of the most famous characters in the history of fiction are in that great novel called philosophy. There's free will and determinism. There's substance and accident. They have been characters in the history of philosophy from the beginning, and I find them fascinating. Substance is more interesting than most of my friends.

Now why would one adopt such awkward language—why not just talk about character in the traditional sense? The advantage is that you avoid the tendency as a reader to psychologize and fill the work with things that aren't there. The work is filled with only one thing—words and how they work and how they connect. That, of course, includes the meanings, the sounds, and all the rest. When people ask, "How are you building character?" they sometimes think you're going around peering at people to decide how you're going to render something. That isn't a literary activity. It may be interesting, but the literary activity is constructing a linguistic source on the page.

Gardner: I obviously don't agree with Bill on all that. It seems to me a character is an apparition in the writer's mind, a very clear apparition based on an imaginative reconstruction or melding of many people the writer has known. The ideal book has to have more than one character, because we know a character by what he does: what he does to other people, and what they do back to him. Bill wants to avoid the reader's "filling in," but when we read J. D. Salinger, for instance, we understand many things about his characters that aren't in the book because we know what people mean when they make the gestures that Salinger's made-up people make. So we're all the time seeing more of the picture than is given. In the good novel, the reader gets an apparition, a dream, in which he sees people doing things to each other, hurting each other or exploring each other or loving each other or whatever, and a tiny linguistic signal sets off a huge trap of material which gives us a very subtle sense of these imaginary people. It's true that one can analyze them as words on a page, but I have never cried at the fate of free will or determinism in a good philosophy book.

Bill has argued that it's wrong to be frightened by a character in a book or to cry at the death of a character. I say it's not. I say a book is nothing but a written symbol of a dream. If someone jumps at me with an ax in a nightmare, I scream, and I have every right to scream because I believe that person is real. In the same way, when the dream is transported to me by words and I see the character leap out at me with an ax, I have every right to believe that my head is going to be knocked in. I think it's very useful to talk about character in the traditional ways. Contemporary philosophy has reconstructed the world into its own words while distrusting the words that we've used over and over and over. Meaning exists in literature because of the way thousands of generations of people have used words. With just the slightest tap, you ring the whole gong of meaning. I'm more interested in the gong than the tap. I think Bill concentrates on the technique of the tap.

. . . First it matters to him that [a novel] is elegant and well done and that it has other characteristics I think are perhaps secondary. But given two well-done books, one of which strikes him as absolutely truthful while the other is not what he would affirm in his life, Bill would take, he says, the one that he thinks is true.

Gass: Yes, but that's just wanting thickness to experience. If, for instance, I play golf for my health and to persuade some client and because I'm hooked on the symbolism of getting a ball into a hole, that's better than playing golf just to have a good score. But ultimately, whether you play golf well or not is determined by how well you score—your performance—and that's what ought to be used as the aesthetic measure. If a beautiful book is a source of virtue and a source of truth—fine. That's jolly. The composer of such a work would be a fine philosopher, a noble saint, and an artist. But he's not a good artist because he's a fine philosopher or a noble saint.

. . . There is a fundamental divergence about what literature is. I don't want to subordinate beauty to truth and goodness. John and others have values which they think more important. Beauty, after all, is not very vital for most people. I think it is very important, in the cleanliness of the mind, to know why a particular thing is good. A lot of people judge, to use a crude example, the dinner good because of the amount of calories it has. Well, that is important if you don't want to gain weight, but what has that got to do with the quality of the food? Moral judgments on art constantly confuse the quality of the food. I would also claim that my view is more catholic. It will allow in as good writers more than this other view will; John lets hardly anybody in the door.

Gardner: I love Bill's writing, and I honestly think that Bill is the only writer in America that I would let in the door. For twenty-four years I have been screaming at him, sometimes literally screaming at him, saying, "Bill, you are wasting the greatest genius ever given to America by fiddling around when you could be doing big, important things." What he can do with language is magnificent, but then he turns it against itself. Our definitions of beauty are different. I think language exists to make a beautiful and powerful apparition. He thinks you can make pretty colored walls with it. That's unfair. But what I think is beautiful, he would think is not yet sufficiently ornate. The difference is that my 707 will fly and his is too encrusted with gold to get off the ground.

Gass: There is always that danger. But what I really want is to have it sit there solid as a rock and have everybody think it is flying.

Gardner: Bill Gass is quoted as saying that his ambition in life is to write a book so good that nobody will publish it. My ambition in life is to outlive Bill Gass and change all of his books.

Audience: *Should moral issues be left to the philosophers to clarify?*

Gass: When I put on my other hat, that's what I want to do. Of course, a great number of philosophers feel that the purpose of philosophy is primarily cleansing of the intellectual apparatus, rather than solving these issues. There is a great dispute about just this in philosophy, but that is exactly where it should take place. But I don't want to sound as if I actually thought that philosophers got very far. I think that it is also a great and glorious game, and it would be a grievous disappointment if we ever solved anything.

Gardner: I would say only that philosophers deal abstractly with what novelists deal with concretely. When you deal with abstractions, you can go a lot farther a lot faster, but you are also wrong more of the time.

Audience: *Is the affirmation John Gardner speaks of momentary or longer lasting?*

Gardner: I think chaos gets overadvertised. We are all sitting here politely in this room. If we were orangutans, we might not be quite so polite. If we were baboons from four different tribes, we would be very impolite. I think it is through storytelling that we achieved what we have now. People sat in caves and made up stories about sitting down and listening. Gradually we learned to be kind to animals. Gradually we learned to vote, rather than hit it out with sticks. The affirmations that we make are based on an assumption of general order. What we do in fiction is revitalize affirmations that we've made all along. I don't think fiction teaches you anything; it reminds you of things in a moving way.

Audience: *Is the function of the artist to make up a way to live?*

Gardner: That's the business of ministers, priests, and rabbis. The business of the artist is to find out, in the process of telling the story, what story he can honestly tell. If he has an idea, he's radically open to persuasion as he tells the story. When I started to write *October Light*, I wanted to celebrate tough Vermonters. But I put those values under pressure, and as I pushed and pushed I ended up with a tragic story in which I took back much of what I thought I would say. And I found some other things I could say. In the process of writing the fiction, I found out what I had to write.

Audience: *What is John Gardner's view of a fiction which has been produced by the moral process but ends up nihilistic and has immoral effects on the audience?*

Gardner: It's still moral fiction. A novel which ends up nihilistic after a rigorous and honest pursuit is probably a neurotic novel. No writer can control whether he's sane or not. If the writer comes to a conclusion about which most of humanity, in its wisdom and its history, would say, "That's nuts," you have an interesting species of honesty that we just watch but don't live by.

Audience: *Is there an analogy between games and fiction?*

Gass: Not for me, because I am interested in the finished product. In a game there is no finished product except the scorecard. But there are lots of writers, many of whom I admire, who regard the finished work as simply a byproduct of the activity of composition. Valéry felt that way. The danger is that, by emphasizing process over product, you escape judgment.

Photo by Thomas Victor

An Interview with
Donald Barthelme

My arrival in New York City to interview Donald Barthelme coincided almost exactly with the beginning of a transit strike. So it was that on April 4, 1980, I found myself taking a leisurely walk south from 63rd Street, heading for the lower West Village where Barthelme lives. It was a hot spring day, and since I had given myself over an hour for my jaunt, I zigzagged my way in the general direction of my destination, the teeming energy of the city made perhaps even more evident since so many people had been forced to join me on the streets.

Barthelme says in the interview that follows that he likes cities, and despite the fact that most of his literary sensibilities were already formed when he arrived there in 1962, the name Donald Barthelme will inevitably be connected with New York, if only because of his association with *The New Yorker*. At any rate, as I was walking I was struck by the profusion of words that bombarded me as I passed newsstands, sweating delivery men, hand-held radios, college students pretentiously discussing Sartre or the upcoming Picasso exhibit, taxidrivers yelling obscenities. These are the same words that find their way into Barthelme's fiction, along with the jargon of academics, the argot of television commercials, newspaper straighttalk, and the ongoing mysteries of current teenage slang. Barthelme has been building his surreal, collage-like literary arrangements out of these words for over twenty years now, and if there were certain critics who found a waning of freshness in Barthelme's work of the mid-1970s—this was heard after the publication of *Amateurs* (1976) and *Guilty Pleasures* (1974)—he firmly put such talk to rest in 1979 with the publication of *Great Days*, a witty and strangely moving collection that is surely the work of a mature writer who continues to open up new narrative possibilities.

Barthelme greeted me attired in blue jeans. Now in his late forties, the brown hair has flecks of gray in it, but his face retains much of the youthfulness and intensity of the early dust-jacket photographs from *Come Back, Dr. Caligari* (1964) and *Unspeakable Practices, Unnatural Acts* (1968). His apartment was spacious and decked with greenery; on the walls were several large prints. After each of us had opened a beer and sat down, I realized that Barthelme's accent was the least expected aspect of his presence—an honest-to-God Texas accent was occasionally creeping into his East-coast inflections. Once the interview proper began, Barthelme's answers came slowly and thoughtfully, the familiar one-liners emerging from protracted periods of silence. He had warned me in a letter that he had an aversion to tape recorders, that he needed to type in order to think—"an impediment in the modern world," he apologized. Still, I enjoyed our interview and found a warmth and humor that most writers don't provide on a first meeting.

Barthelme is the author of two novels, *Snow White* (1967) and *The Dead Father* (1975); however, he is probably best known for his seven collections of short fictions, many of which appeared originally in *The New Yorker*. The collections are *Come Back, Dr. Caligari* (1964); *Unspeakable Practices, Unnatural Acts* (1968); *City Life* (1970); *Sadness* (1972); *Guilty Pleasures* (nonfiction, 1974); *Amateurs* (1976); and *Great Days* (1979).

—*Larry McCaffery*

You've published two novels but most of your work has been in short fiction. Do you have an explanation for this tendency?

Barthelme: Novels take me a long time; short fiction provides a kind of immediate gratification — the relationship of sketches to battle paintings.

Didn't I see somewhere your claim that you're always working on novels?

Barthelme: Over a period of years I can have a dozen bad ideas for novels, some of which I actually invest a certain amount of time in. Some of these false starts yield short pieces; most don't. The first story in *Sadness*—"La Critique de la Vie Quotidienne"—is salvage.

Do you have a routine in your work habits, a daily schedule?

Barthelme: I get up very early, read the *Times*, and then work until lunchtime, sometimes a bit after. If I'm particularly involved in something, I work at night.

Do stories typically begin for you by landing on you, like the dog in "Falling Dog"?

Barthelme: Well, for about four days I've been writing what amounts to nonsense. And then suddenly I came across an interesting sentence—or at least interesting to me: "It is not clear that Arthur Byte was wearing his black corduroy suit when he set fire to the Yale Art and Architecture Building in the spring of 1968." I don't know what follows from this sentence; I'm hoping it may develop into something.

Do most of your stories begin in this way—from the sound or texture of a sentence, rather than from a plot idea or a character?

Barthelme: In different ways. I did know someone who was at Yale teaching in the architecture department at the time of that notorious fire; I'm not sure if the date was 1968, I'd have to check. I don't believe they ever found out who set it. I certainly have no idea. But I'm positing a someone and hoping that tragic additional material may accumulate around that sentence.

At the end of your story "Sentence," your narrator says that the sentence is "a structure to be treasured for its weaknesses, as opposed to the strength of stones." Am I right in assuming that one of the things that interests you the most about the sentence as an object is precisely its "treasured weaknesses"?

Barthelme: I look for a particular kind of sentence, perhaps more often the awkward than the beautiful. A back-broke sentence is interesting. Any sentence that begins with the phase, "It is not clear that . . . " is clearly clumsy but preparing itself for greatness of a kind. A way of backing into a story—of getting past the reader's hardwon armor.

Can you describe what's happening once you've found this initial impulse? Obviously you aren't aiming at developing characters or furthering the plot or whatever else it would be that most writers would say.

Barthelme: A process of accretion. Barnacles growing on a wreck or a rock. I'd rather have a wreck than a ship that sails. Things attach themselves to wrecks. Strange fish find your wreck or rock to be a good feeding ground; after a while you've got a situation with possibilities.

Have you ever studied philosophy of language in any kind of systematic way? Critics are always suggesting that your stories read like "glosses on Wittgenstein" and so forth . . .

Barthelme: No. I spent two years in the army in the middle of my undergraduate days at Houston. When I came back to the university, which must have been about 1955, there was a new man—Maurice Natanson—teaching a course entitled "Sociology and Literature" that sounded good. I enrolled and he was talking about Kafka and Kleist and George Herbert Mead. I wasn't a particularly acute or productive student of philosophy, but in that and subsequent classes I got acquainted with people Mauri was interested in: Husserl, Heidegger, Kierkegaard, Sartre, and company.

You were originally interested in journalism, weren't you?

Barthelme: It seemed clear that the way to become a writer was to go to work for a newspaper, as Hemingway had done—then, if you were lucky, you might write fiction. I don't think anybody believes that anymore. But I went to work for a newspaper while I was still a sophomore and went back to the newspaper when I got out of the army. I was really very happy there, thought I was in high cotton.

By the late '50s, when you became editor of the Forum, *you were obviously already interested a great deal in parody and satire as literary forms. What so attracted you to this type of writing, as opposed, say, to the standard, realistic narrative forms?*

Barthelme: People like S. J. Perelman and E. B. White—people who could do certain amazing things in prose. Perelman was the first true American surrealist—of a rank in the world surrealist movement with the best—and Nathanael West was another. Wolcott Gibbs—all those *New Yorker* writers. Hemingway as parodist, *The Torrents of Spring.*

And you've already mentioned Kafka and Kleist . . .

Barthelme: Kleist was important to Kafka, something I didn't find out for a while.

Somewhere in here you got involved as a director of an art museum. What was the background of that?

Barthelme: A peculiar happenstance. I was entrusted with a small museum for a couple of years—the Contemporary Arts Museum in Houston. They had just lost the director, didn't have a prospect. I'd been on the board. They asked me to fill in temporarily, which I did for a while, and then they made me director—probably more fun than anything I've done before or since. For two years I mounted shows and developed programs in music, theater, and film. In consequence I met Harold Rosenberg in 1962. At that time Harold had in mind starting a new magazine which he and Thomas B. Hess would edit. They needed someone to be the managing editor—that is, someone to put out the magazine—and they hired me.

This was the now-legendary magazine Location?

Barthelme: Yes. It was meant to be not just an art magazine but an art-literary magazine. We were able to publish some wonderful material—some early Gass, some of John Ashbery's work, Kenneth Koch's stuff. It was supposed to be a quarterly, but in fact we published only two issues. Tom and Harold were not worried about putting the magazine out on time and certainly never put any pressure on me. We waited until we had enough decent stuff for a good issue. That experience was a great pleasure—listening to Tom and Harold talk.

This must have been about the time you first started selling pieces to The New Yorker.

Barthelme: Yes. Also, once in a while when I was low on cash I'd write something for certain strange magazines—the names I don't even remember. Names like *Dasher* and *Thug.* I do remember picking up five hundred bucks or something per piece. I did that a few times. Kind of gory, or even Gorey, fiction.

Have any of these things ever resurfaced?

Barthelme: No. Nor shall they ever.

I've always suspected that your experience in working for the museum must have had at least as much impact on your sensibility as any literary influences.

Barthelme: It was a very small place. My responsibility was to put some good shows together, mildly didactic, modestly informative. So I had to study quite a lot very fast to be able to do this—to make intelligent or useful shows. Luckily I've always gotten along quite well with painters and sculptors, mostly by virtue of not asking the wrong questions of them. There's a style of conversation . . .

It's been my experience that it's always in bad taste to ask a painter what his work "means." Now that I think of it, this seems to hold true for writers as well.

Barthelme: It's a separate study, "How to manifest intelligent sympathy while not saying very much." The early '60s were, as you know, an explosive period in American art, and I learned on the job, nervously. Just being in the studio teaches you something. I'll give you an example: when we were doing *Location* I went over to Rauschenberg's studio on lower Broadway with Rudy Burkhardt, the photographer, to take some pictures. Rauschenberg was doing silk-screen pieces and the tonality of these things was gray—very, very gray. I looked out the windows and they were dirty, very much the tonality of the pictures. So I asked Rudy to get some shots of the windows and we ran one of them with the paintings. They were very much New York Lower Broadway windows. A footnote.

Your narrator in "See the Moon?" comments enviously at one point about the "fantastic metaphysical advantage" possessed by painters. What was he referring to?

Barthelme: The physicality of the medium—there's a physicality of color, of an object present before the spectator, which painters don't have to project by means of words. I can peel the label off that bottle of beer you're drinking and glue it to the canvas and it's there.

Like a lot of painters in this century, you seem to enjoy lifting things out of the world, in this case words or phrases, and then . . .

Barthelme: And then, sung to and Simonized, they're thrown into the mesh.

But what you're doing—this rearrangement of these "real" elements into your own personal constructions—is related to collage, seems to partake of some of that metaphysical advantage you're describing.

Barthelme: This sort of thing is of course what Dos Passos did in the Newsreels, what Joyce did in various ways. I suppose the theater has the possibility of doing this in the most immediate way. I'm on the stage and I suddenly climb down into the pit and kick you in the knee. That's not like writing about kicking you in the knee, it's not like painting you being kicked in the knee, because you have a pain in the knee. This sounds a bit aggressive. Forgive me.

Another aspect of painting that seems relevant to your fiction is the surrealist practice of juxtaposing two elements for certain kinds of effects—in fiction or poetry, different sorts of language.

Barthelme: It's a principle of construction. This can be terribly easy—can become cheapo surrealism, mechanically linking contradictions. Take Duchamp's phrase, in reference to *The Bride and the Bachelors*, that the Bride "warmly refuses" her suitors. The phrase is very nice, but you can see how it could become a formula.

How do you avoid falling into this trap in your own work? Is there a formula for avoiding the formula?

Barthelme: I think you stare at the sentence for a long time. The better elements are retained and the worse fall out of the manuscript.

One last aspect of painting that I'd like you to comment upon in relation to your own work is the tendency of painting in this century to explore itself, its own medium—the nature of paint, colors, shapes, and lines— rather than attempting to reproduce or comment upon something outside itself. This tendency seems relevant not only to your work but also to that of several other important writers of the past fifteen years. Is this a fair analogy?

Barthelme: It is. I also think that painting—in the '60s but especially in the '70s—really pioneered for us all the things that it is not necessary to do. Under the aegis of exploring itself, exploring its own means or the medium, painting really did a lot of dumb things that showed poets and prose writers what might usefully not be done.

What sorts of things are you thinking of?

Barthelme: I'm thinking mostly of conceptual art, which seems to me a bit sterile. Concrete poetry is an example of something that is, for me, not very nourishing, though it can be said to be exploratory in the way that a lot of conceptual art is exploratory. I can see why in some sense it had to be done. But perhaps not twice.

What about some of the "New-New-Novelists" in France—Pinget, Sollers, Baudry, LeClezio? They seem to be trying to push fiction to the same limits of abstraction that conceptual artists have been searching for.

Barthelme: A work like Butor's *Mobile*—after a time there's nothing more you can say of this than "I like it" or "I don't like it"—the stupidest of comments. A more refined version is "I know this is good but I still don't like it." And I think this is a fair comment. There are more *recherché* examples of this kind of thing. *TriQuarterly* did an issue a while back entitled "In the Wake of the Wake"—published several gallant Frenchmen whose work I'd seen in scattered places. The emphasis was toward "pure abstraction." For me this is a problem, since they get further and further away from the common reader. I understand the impulse—toward the condition of music—but as a common reader I demand this to be done in masterly fashion or not at all. Mallarmé is perhaps the extreme, along with Gertrude Stein. I admire them both.

Don't we find this kind of metafictional self-inquiry about language and fiction-making surfacing quite often in your works? I'm thinking about stories like "Daumier" and "See the Moon?" or Snow White, *which even has a questionnaire for the reader appearing in the middle of it.*

Barthelme: Wouldn't "metafiction" be "fiction-about-fiction"?

Yes, although I personally like to use the word "fiction" in a fairly broad sense.

Barthelme: I don't have any great enthusiasm for fiction-about-fiction. It's true that in 1965 I put that questionnaire in the middle of *Snow White*. But I haven't done that much in that direction since. I think I've actually been fairly restrained on that front. Critics, of course, have been searching for a term that would describe fiction after the great period of modernism—"postmodernism," "metafiction," "surfiction," and "super-fiction." The last two are terrible; I suppose "postmodernism" is the least ugly, most descriptive.

What do you think about Philip Roth's famous suggestion back in the early '60s that reality was outstripping fiction's ability to amaze us?

Barthelme: I do think something happened in fiction about that time, but I'd locate it differently—I think writers got past being intimidated by Joyce. Maybe the reality that Roth was talking about was instrumental in this recognition, but I think people realized that one didn't have to repeat Joyce (if that were even possible) but could use aspects of his achievement.

One of your most evident abilities is your gift at mimicking a wide range of styles, jargons, lingoes. Where do these voices come from?

Barthelme: I listen to people talk, and I read. I doubt that there has ever been more jargon and professional cant—cant of various professions and semi-professions—than there is today. I remember being amazed when I was in basic training, which was back in the early '50s, that people could make sentences in which the word "fucking" was used three times or even five times.

How did your relationship with The New Yorker *begin?*

Barthelme: I sent them something in the mail and they accepted it. Agented by probably a nine-cent stamp.

It wasn't long before The New Yorker *began publishing a story of yours almost every month. You didn't develop a specific understanding with them about regularly accepting your work?*

Barthelme: I had moved to New York to work with Tom and Harold doing *Location,* and since I was only working half-time on the magazine, I had more time to write fiction. I had and have what they call a first-reading agreement.

Have you had a specific editor working with you at The New Yorker?

Barthelme: Yes; Roger Angell.

Do your stories usually require much in the way of editing?

Barthelme: Roger makes very few changes. If he and the magazine don't like a piece that I've written, they'll turn it down. The magazine sometimes turns down a piece I don't think should be turned down—but what else can I think? Roger is a wonderful editor, and if he objects to something in a story he's probably right. He's very sensitive about the editing process, makes it a pleasure.

Do you see yourself working out of some kind of New Yorker *tradition?*

Barthelme: The magazine in recent years has been very catholic. Anybody who publishes Singer, Merwin, Lem, Updike, Borges, and Márquez has got to be said to be various in terms of taste. Plus Grace Paley and Susan Sontag and Ann Beattie and who knows who else.

I've noticed that in your last few books you seem to have dropped the interest in typographical or graphic play that was so evident in City Life *and* Guilty Pleasures. *What got you interested in this sort of thing in the first place?*

Barthelme: I think I was trying to be a painter, in some small way. Probably a yearning for something not properly the domain of writers.

Surely this opinion doesn't derive from a belief in the need to keep aesthetic categories separate . . .

Barthelme: Maybe I was distracted by the things that painters can do. Look here and over there [pointing at an Ingres poster and a Richard Lindner poster on his living room walls]—an ambition toward something that maybe fiction can't do, an immediate impact—a beautifully realized whole that can be taken in at a glance and yet still be studied for a long time. There's a Flannery O'Connor quote where she says, very sourly, very wittily, that she doesn't like anything that looks funny on the page. I know what she's talking about, but on the other hand, I'm intrigued by things that look funny on the page. But then there was the flood of concrete poetry which devalued looking funny on the page.

I recall a comment of yours that you not only enjoyed doing layout work but that you could cheerfully become a typographer. Did you do all your own visual work?

Barthelme: They're mostly very simple collages, Ernst rather than Schwitters.

Have you tried your own hand at drawing?

Barthelme: Can't draw a lick.

At the end of the title story of City Life, *Ramona comments about "life's invitations down many muddy roads": "I accepted. What was the alternative." I find a similar passivity in many of your characters—an inability to change their lot. Does this tendency spring from a personal sense of resignation about things, or are you trying to suggest something more fundamental about modern man's relationship to the world?*

Barthelme: The quotation you mention possibly has more to do with the great world than with me. In writing about the two girls in *City Life* who come to the city, I noticed that their choices—which seem to be infinite—are not so open ended. I don't think this spirit of "resignation," as you call it, has to do with any personal passivity; it's more a sociological observation. One attempts to write about the way contemporary life is lived by most people. In a more reportorial fiction one would, of necessity, seek out more "active" protagonists—the mode requires it, to make the book or story work. In a mixed mode, some reportage and some part play (which also makes its own observations), you might be relieved of this restriction. Contemporary life engenders, even enforces passivity, as with television. Have you ever tried to reason with a Convenience Card money machine? Asked for napkin rings in an Amtrak snack-bar car? Of course you don't. Still, the horizon of memory enters in. You attempt to register change, the color of this moment as opposed to the past or what you know of it.

Is it because you're dealing with this common kind of modern life that your characters so often seem concerned with coping with boredom?

Barthelme: I don't notice that so much. I think they're knitting lively lives—perhaps in subdued tones. Are you asking for T. E. Lawrence?

Hmmm. Maybe I should call this aspect of modern life "the cocoon of habituation that covers everything, if you let it," as your narrator in "Daumier" says.

Barthelme: Recently I've come to believe that, as one of the people in *Great Days* says, "Life becomes more and more exciting as there is less and less time." True, I think.

Related to what we're talking about is a criticism I've heard directed at your fiction. It's been claimed that your fiction isn't "relevant" enough—to use that ugly word—to be really significant. That is, it has been said that rather than dealing with the "big issues" in a direct way—the Vietnam war, political scandals, minority rights, violence, the Holocaust, and so on—your fiction has tended to deal with what one critic has called a "range of minor, banal dissatisfactions . . . no anomie or accidie or dread but a muted series of irritations, frustrations, and bafflements." How do you respond to such criticisms which, as you know, are regularly leveled at Barth, Gass, Nabokov, and other postmodernists?

Barthelme: I'd argue that this was a misreading. I would not attempt the Holocaust, but aside from that I think a careful reading of what I've written would disclose that all the things you mention are touched upon, in one way or another—not confronted directly, but there. The Vietnam war colored a lot of pieces. It's found in "The Indian Uprising" and very much in "Report," where the narrator endeavors to persuade a group of engineers to abandon their work in exotic military technology; also in other odd places.

Do you recall the germinating idea for The Dead Father?

Barthelme: A matter of having a father and being a father.

In some basic sense the book deals with the notion that we're all dragging around behind us the corpses of our fathers, as well as the past in general.

Barthelme: Worse: dragging these *ahead* of us. I have several younger brothers, among them by brother Frederick, who is also a writer. After *The Dead Father* came out, he telephoned and said, "I'm working on a new novel." I said, "What's it called?" and he said, "*The Dead Brother*." You have to admire the generational wit there.

Was "A Manual for Sons" originally conceived as being part of the novel? It seems like a marvelous set piece.

Barthelme: Originally it was distributed throughout the book as a kind of seasoning, but in time it became clear that it should be one long section. My German publisher, Siegfried Unseld, said rather sternly to me one evening, "Isn't this a digression?" I said, "Yes, it is." He was absolutely right, in technical terms.

In The Dead Father—*and even more obviously in the recent series of structurally related stories in* Great Days—*you strip the narrative almost completely of the old-fashioned means of story development. In fact, by the time we get to the stories in* Great Days *what we find are simply voices interacting with one another. I recall in "The Explanation" one of your characters speaks of the "many valuable omissions" certain narrative formats allow. What advantages do you find in pursuing this type of narrative strategy?*

Barthelme: In *The Dead Father* there are four or five passages in which the two principal women talk to each other, or talk *against* each other, or over each other's heads, or between each other's legs—passages which were possible because there is a fairly strong narrative line surrounding them. It's a question as to whether such things can be made to fly without the support of a controlling narrative. As, for example, in the final story in *Great Days* which is, I think, more or less successful.

Do you worry about losing your hard-won audience in moving in this direction?

Barthelme: There's always the tension between losing an audience and doing the odd things you might want to try. The effort is always to make what you write nourishing or useful to readers. You do cut out some readers by idiosyncrasies of form. I regret this.

Was Beckett an influence in this recent form of experimentation your fiction has been working with?

Barthelme: Beckett has been a great influence, which I think is clear. But the effort is to not write like Beckett. You can't do Beckett all over again, any more than you can do Joyce again. That would waste everyone's time.

Have you ever tried writing poetry, as such?

Barthelme: No. Too difficult. I can't do it. A very tough discipline, to be attempted by saints or Villons.

Are you alarmed by reports of the death of the novel?

Barthelme: A form of this strength and capacity can't expire—it may emphasize new aspects of itself.

We've talked about the influence of painting on your work. What about the cinema?

Barthelme: I was bombarded with film from, let us say, my sixth year right up to yesterday, when I saw Wiseman's *Basic Training*. There's got to have been an effect, including the effect of teaching me what waste is—as with painting, film has shown us what not to pursue. The movies provide a whole set of stock situations, emotions, responses that can be played against. They inflect contemporary language. One uses this.

I noticed that you were writing movie reviews for The New Yorker. *Is this likely to develop into a habit?*

Barthelme: This was just a short stint to fill in—six weeks. They had several of us lend a hand when Pauline Kael left for a sabbatical. I enjoyed it, wouldn't want to make a habit of it.

Your fiction has often drawn materials from the realm of pop culture—Snow White, Batman, the Phantom of the Opera, King Kong, and so forth. What do you find useful in this kind of material?

Barthelme: Relatively few of my stories have to do with pop culture, a very small percentage really. What's attractive about this kind of thing is the given—you have to do very little establishing, can get right to the variations.

What initially intrigued you about using the Snow White mythology in your novel?

Barthelme: Again, the usefulness of the Snow White story is that everybody knows it and it can be played against. The presence of the seven men made possible a "we" narration that offered some tactical opportunities—there's a sort of generalized narrator, a group spokesman who could be any one of the seven. Every small change in the story is momentous when everybody knows the story backward; possibly I wasn't as bold in making these changes as I should have been.

It's very obvious in Snow White—*and in nearly all your fiction—that you distrust the impulse to "go beneath the surface" of your characters and events.*

Barthelme: If you mean doing psychological studies of some kind, no. I'm not so interested. "Going beneath the surface" has all sorts of positive-sounding associations, as if you were a Cousteau of the heart. I'm not sure there's not just as much to be seen if you remain a student of the surfaces.

Let me ask you about a specific feature of your work that I've always admired—your lists, which rank with those of William Gass and Stanley Elkin as the best around. What function would you say these serve?

Barthelme: Litanies, incantations, have a certain richness per se. They also provide stability in what is often a volatile environment, something to tie to, like an almanac or a telephone book. And discoveries—a list of meter maids in any given city will give you a Glory Hercules.

Who are some of the contemporary writers you find most interesting?

Barthelme: Along with the South Americans, who everyone agrees are doing very well, I think the Germans: Peter Handke, Max Frisch, certainly Grass, Thomas Bernhard, who did *Correction*. I think the Americans are doing very well. The French perhaps less so.

Who are some of the American writers you admire?

Barthelme: Gass, Percy, Jack Hawkes, Grace Paley, Ralph Ellison. Barth, Bellow and Updike, Vonnegut and John Sayles, Susan Sontag, Peter Taylor, Pynchon. Barry Hannah and Ann Beattie—the spectrum is quite large, as you can see. A dozen people I can't think of at the moment. There seems to be considerable energy in American writing at the moment; it seems a fruitful time.

Do you read much poetry?

Barthelme: Not as much as I should. I read Ashbery and Koch and Schuyler with great pleasure, Merwin with great pleasure, and there are others.

Raymond Federman recently made a comment to me that I found very relevant to what's been happening in fiction during the past few years. He says that while Samuel Beckett had devised a means of taking the world away from the contemporary writer, Márquez had shown writers a way to reconnect themselves with the world.

Barthelme: I don't agree with Ray that that's what Beckett has done; the Marquez portion of the comment seems more appropriate. I think they've both opened things up, in different ways. Márquez provided an answer to the question of what was possible after Beckett—not the only answer, but a large and significant one. Robert Coover, among American writers, seems to be doing something parallel, to good effect.

What are you working on right now?

Barthelme: I'm working on three things: the story I mentioned earlier, a novel, and a filmscript someone's asked me to do.

Have you worked on filmscripts before?

Barthelme: Richard Lester asked me once to write one years ago. I was unable to do it, so I had to give him his money back. Painful but necessary.

Do you feel that New York City has helped shape your sensibility over the years?

Barthelme: I think my sensibility was pretty well put together before I came here. Although I've now lived here close to twenty years, I've also lived in other places in the meantime—Copenhagen for a year, Paris, Tokyo. I like cities. But this is a tiny corner of New York, very like a real *village*-village. Once I was walking down Seventh Avenue with Hans Magnus Enzensberger. We'd just finished lunch, and we bumped into my daughter, who was then about eight, and I introduced them and she went home and told her mother she'd just met Hans Christian Andersen. And, in a way, she had.

Do you see any changes having taken place in your approach to writing over the past twenty years?

Barthelme: Certainly fewer jokes. Perhaps fewer words.

Photo by John Fensterwald

An Interview with
Rosellen Brown

Rosellen Brown lives with her husband and two daughters in a rambling, beautifully preserved and antique-filled 1789 farmhouse in Peterborough, New Hampshire, the town of Thornton Wilder's *Our Town* and the Mac-Dowell artists' colony. The ordinary and the artful in her house and place are the qualities Rosellen Brown joins in her work and in her talk. When we taped the following interview in late August, 1981, on the sunny front lawn where she writes when weather allows, her comments on her work and the kind of fiction she values were direct, more open than those of any other writer I've interviewed, and also finished, rich with concrete comparisons and ordered in paragraphs. With her long, jet-black hair, often quizzical expression, and jeans and pullover, she appears to be no more than five (rather than twenty) years out of Barnard College. Her voice is earnest, but also quick to laugh and wonder. When we broke for lunch, she showed me the large garden she keeps and the two short-lived New Hampshire women's gravestones that she found in her barn. On this day her kitchen is crowded with family, both resident and visiting, and the evidences of family—photos, children's artwork, an old lobster pot full of shoes. But it's also a writer's kitchen: the cover of the new paperback edition of *The Autobiography of My Mother* is hanging on the refrigerator door; galleys and magazines are around, and there's the phone that keeps her in touch with local literary friends and New York magazines for which she reviews fiction. During lunch, talk moves back and forth between the difficulty of heating in New Hampshire winters and the difficulty books have in finding an audience, between good high schools for her daughter and good criticism. Though it might not seem right for a novelist, Rosellen Brown is comfortable in her life and family, happy.

Both her fiction and poetry, often about traumatic experiences, have moved toward what Brown calls "amplitude," an earned serenity. Her first book of fiction, *Street Games* (1974), is a set of stories about different ethnic groups and variously troubled individuals in Brooklyn. Her first novel, *The Autobiography of My Mother* (1976), is a powerful family debate between women of two generations, an immigrant achiever and her hippie daughter. The effect of their antagonism is measured on a third-generation girl, whose accidental death ends the novel. *Tender Mercies* (1978) begins with an accident and tells with subtlety and discipline the story of a woman's recovery from the mutilation of her body by her husband. Brown has also written two volumes of poety: *Some Deaths in the Delta and Other Poems* (1970) and *Cora Fry* (1977), a series of short poems about one woman's life. Rosellen Brown's novel in progress, *Civil Wars*, returns to some of her experiences in Mississippi during the civil rights struggle in the 1960s.

—Tom LeClair

Where did you grow up, and what effect did it have on your writing?

Brown: That's one of my favorite questions because, in fact, I didn't grow up anywhere. We lived in a great number of places for no particular reason, chance included. We left Philadelphia when I was ten weeks old, went to Allentown and Reading, Pennsylvania; then to Mt. Vernon, New York, and to Los Angeles, and back to New York, where I was a teenager in Queens. I've always thought a major determinant of my personality was my forever having to begin again. The influence on my writing is that I'm very preoccupied with *place*. That was not at first conscious, but now it has recurred enough times for me to see it. Not just locale, but characters of, from, and made by the place they live in. My first book of poems, *Some Deaths in the Delta*, was set in—that is, the poems were palpably *about*—Mississippi and New York City.

Did your three books of fiction begin with place, or was this something you worked toward?

Brown: My first fiction, *Street Games*, is a linked series of stories that takes place on one block in Brooklyn. Not all the characters are natives, but they are the kinds of people one would find in that neighborhood. In these stories place is almost like a character. I had written about half the stories that appeared in *Street Games* randomly, with no larger scheme in mind; some, but not all, of them had their seeds in the lives of my neighbors in Brooklyn. I had also written a series of vignettes that was published under the title "Mainlanders" and, parenthetically, went into the O. Henry Prize Stories as a story only because the magazine which published it had neglected in that issue to differentiate between fiction and essays! I hadn't thought of it as fiction and I don't think they did, either. So much for form in our day! But when I had the idea that these stories could hold together as a set of variations on—well, not so much a theme as a vantage point, a specific place and time; when I discovered that the marvelously mixed neighborhood was a phenomenon in itself—I cannibalized "Mainlanders" (as I often do: my words are my words) and made four stories out of my sketchy little essays. Then I found another half-dozen probable voices—I could have kept going indefinitely—for neighbors, some of whom I'd never spoken to, some of whom didn't exist.

The Autobiography of My Mother is about the sense of exile. A character in that novel recites a long list of places where she has lived, then says, essentially, "After the first move, there is no other. That is what made me an exile." *The Autobiography* is less fixed on the place of its action (New York City) than either of the other books of fiction. That's probably because a lot of my energy went into a short (but to me satisfying) re-creation of Gerda's childhood in Alsace-Lorraine, where I once found myself accidentally for two days, just enough time to be intrigued, to feel an itch of curiosity but not to linger long enough to scratch it. That may be as good a motive for writing something as the typical one, which is a deep familiarity. That's writing as investigation, filling in the blanks by intuition and guesswork, not making a sure likeness.

I think I may be eager to write about people who have roots, to use the currently popular word, that I don't have. Both *Cora Fry* and *Tender Mercies* are about people who understand a place deeply, something I've worked toward. Not too surprisingly, my husband and I have managed to bring our sense of unrootedness to our children. Although my daughters have spent some of their childhoods here in Peterborough, they feel not entirely of this place. They are small-town girls; I was a no-town girl; and the sum for them is that they will never naturally and unselfconsciously "belong" here.

As a Vermonter, I wonder how you dared to write Cora Fry *without living here in New Hampshire for sixty years or so.*

Brown: I said when we first moved to New Hampshire that it would be a long time before I would write about its people. The only reason I did was that I had a good friend who lived nearby who allowed me to see into her life in a way that ten years of superficial neighborliness would not have accomplished. I began by writing about her and me, country woman and city woman, but along the way I dropped out. If I made it a poem of fragments, with lots of space between, I thought I could manage it. I never would have dreamed of writing a novel about Cora. I wasn't sufficiently steeped in the kind of life she lived. *Tender Mercies* is set in a town "coincidentally like" Peterborough. I believe that took some nerve because the novel is about a subculture—someone I know calls it "the chain-saw set"—that I didn't know very well. I worried more about getting the men wrong in *Tender Mercies* than I did about Cora because she was an individual, perhaps idiosyncratic. One editor who read the manuscript said the small-town material ought to go, but what I wanted—and what was published gladly by another house—was the relation between a small town and a flawed family. So the town constitutes half of the drama; the other half is the domestic drama, lived out in all the intimate spaces of home. And for that I used this house. The book is, thank God, not my life, but the beloved house is my house. It was a kind of song of praise to the builders who raised these unshakable posts and beams in 1789. I almost felt I was paying a debt, writing so lovingly about the arch that holds up my own hearthstone.

John Irving has recently observed that, to write, one should get obsessed and stay obsessed. How would you characterize your best creative process?

Brown: I'm not sure I can characterize my "best creative process," but I will say that whatever the quality of concentration is that lets me do my work, obsessive or not, keeps me—quite inconveniently—from doing anything else while I'm in the middle of something. No stories, no poems while this damn novel is gestating. Sometimes it's enough to make me feel buried alive.

I will say that I sail a lot by the vaguest of markers, discovering as I go just what it is that I am traveling toward. It's not automatic writing, not with my two words forward–three words back attention to the words. But I often feel myself following a step or two behind my characters, full of curiosity about what they're going to do next. I'm afraid that when I fall into a pit of uncertainty—I'm in one now, for example—I have nothing to blame but that "nondirective" method in which I trust that, if I have posited a plausible character, he or she will emerge in some recognizable place having resolved something of at least modest significance. At the same time, the obsessions, if such they are, tend to puddle up without the restraints of logic and that "irritable reaching after fact and reason" that Keats deplored.

You write about people quite different from you. Do you feel it your responsibility . . .

Brown: Yes, I admit with both pride and embarrassment to a political passion that could never find its expression in activism. I've never been able to commit myself wholly to an ideology or a movement, nor am I very good at activist "business," so writing about people with whom I deeply empathize is a way for me to try to give them voice when they are inarticulate or kept from speaking for themselves. If you can't *do* anything particularly useful, I thought in the mid-'60s when I was in Mississippi, you can at least make a kind of imaginary record. Not in the naive sense of a tape recording, but when I was feeling guilty in Mississippi about staying home and writing poetry while others were venturing their heads and their limbs, I would justify my poetry by trying to get down what certain lives in that time might have felt like. I thought such poems were more "useful" than love songs or lyrics about the sun rising. Of course, I'm suspicious of utility as a motive for writing. I'm not suggesting the morally pragmatic, the edifying, the work as an invention of object lessons or heroes-in-action. But I did, at that time, cast my lot, in a sense, with the *other*, rather than with *myself* as subject, almost as an act, however futile, however arrogant, of solidarity.

I get very tired of reading about writers. I don't even understand why people want to read novels about them. There's apparently some glamor, but I'll be damned if I can see it. I would much rather try to understand the lives of people who don't write letters to the *New York Review of Books*. I admire Updike, for example, for writing about Rabbit. A book I like very much for the same reason is Ernest Hebert's *Dogs of March*, about a man in a sour little armpit of a town outside of Keene, New Hampshire, whose beached cars on his lawn make him the outrage of the neighborhood. Hebert comprehends his characters' passions and gives them a language that is not stripped down, flat. He doesn't elevate the man, but he does assume there are complex thoughts taking place in there, even if the character might not articulate them aloud. I, too, want to hear and say what such a person might have said had he had the so-called advantages of the writer.

Is "Sally and Me," the story in Street Games *about an outsider and a young woman who speaks for him, an analogue for the role you choose as a writer? Is there any fear combined with the sympathy you feel for the people you write about?*

Brown: I don't know. That's an interesting question I never thought of asking myself. If so, and probably quite realistically, the writer takes one hell of a beating at the hands of the "outsider," whose life, in so many ways, goes on resisting her good offices. As for the "fear" I might feel—I'm not sure that I truly ever do know how my characters are going to comport themselves ultimately, and so I worry as I would over the behavior of real friends, as if they were flesh-and-blood people I love. You commented once that I—my characters—ask a lot of questions in my books, literally ask them in question form. The questions are real and open-ended for me, and I need to hear them asked outright and earnestly. (Because that is the voice in my novels, isn't it? Earnest.) Such answers as I arrive at are fairly inconclusive because, *pace* John Gardner, I don't believe we should be looking at novelists, head-on, as our moral guidance counselors. But that means I am liable to end up disappointed by my characters, or sorry to see what they've let befall them: fear for them, in other words. They are nominally within my control, but their autonomy, if they are honestly conceived, gives them the power to represent all the hazards and foolishness of "real," and therefore frail, men and women.

Is it possible that you choose characters for their language, for words that are not naturally your own?

Brown: Much more interesting than my own. I loved writing in the voice of Luis Beech-Nut, for instance, in *Street Games*. I've always been bored with my own autobiography, and I feel I have no accent anyone can identify—another effect of dislocation. So I am engaged by others' voices. In fact, I've promised myself that the next time anyone interviews me, I am going to give only false—imaginary—answers. *Autobiography of My Mother* is written in an accent almost wholly borrowed and fabricated. Even the epigraph on the first page is from a nonexistent source, in a pseudo-real voice. *Cora Fry* perhaps not quite so much, because the necessities of poetry changed some of the tonalities of Cora's voice. A language with its own color is much more engaging for me than transparent language. Neutral third-person is difficult because I continually find myself falling off the ridge of consistency. Assuming the voice of someone else, which readers think is difficult, is infinitely easier for me. The parameters of someone else's voice are clear to me; my own are not. I know just how far Luis Beech-Nut would go in analyzing the world, for example, and know what he wouldn't say. Third-person is also unrewarding because I feel that passing overt, or even tacit, judgment on the lives of characters in the voice of this faceless narrator is somehow arrogant, a lordly dictation. In making statements about my characters, I feel I'm sermonizing, which embarrasses me. Perhaps this abnegation of the authority of third-person could be a failure of nerve, a frailty of ego masquerading as a becoming modesty. Anyway, it's convenient for me that this narrative diffidence intersects with my delight in the language of others. My father, who paints, once did a ballerina with dreadful hands. He couldn't get them right; so he put them in an ermine muff and called this method the "Brown Muff Principle." Perhaps my speaking in others' voices is my Muff Principle.

Do you think this is an influence of the nonimperial self of the '60s?

Brown: Yes, I often wonder what I would be like had I come of age in the '40s or '50s. As a person who matured in the '60s, I dislike the cloak of Authority. SNCC used to say, "Anybody can do it." Of course, that wasn't true: everybody couldn't speak. But there was a certain kind of validity in anyone's testimony in his own words, or hers, to how something looked from *there*; a relative (not an absolute) authority, and surely not an official one. Third-person fakes a neutrality and posits a single truth. It seems more honest for me to say, "I'm Rosellen Brown writing in the voice of a sharecropper," because the reader knows, after all, that it's me, the writer as ventriloquist. And if I get the sharecropper's sound, then that's *one* voice, not the only one to comment on the proceedings. I declare myself as an outsider and try to make the best of it. I suppose I share this sense of limitation with the New Journalism: "I'm Tom Wicker at Attica. I don't know what's going on, maybe I'm just a honkie like they say. Writing for the *Times* doesn't confer a guarantee of truth on these words. But this is what these men are saying, and I am trying to hear them."

Could the self-reflexiveness of experimental writers whom Gardner charges with immorality be moral scrupulosity?

Brown: I'd like to think that, but I believe often it's a failure of interest in ordinary lives and distrust of the artifice and pleasure of the unsophisticated—that is, the natural—ordinary narrative. Another thing the '60s may have done is made us tired of hearing the insufficient voices of "ordinary people." Many writers have decided to replace those voices with scientific talk or deadened, distant, and consciously unrealistic styles. I continually try to confront and enjoy this shadow of the artist's hand across the page, but I keep coming back to hearing people speak, which is more interesting to me than watching the art of writing unfold. That "otherness" is deep and prevailing, yet I wish to pursue it because I still write for the same reason I wrote when I was nine years old: to speak more perfectly than I really can, to a listener more perfect than any I know.

The problem seems to me to be defamiliarization. How do you solicit interest in your "ordinary people"?

Brown: When my husband acted in a summer theater, the director would compliment him by saying, "Your character was *big* today." The character was slightly larger than life and could therefore carry across the footlights of the stage. What you're talking about is making language *big*: visible, heightened, capable of revivifying experience. Every day when I get up and look at what I've done the day before, I try to eliminate what I used to call "he said, she said writing." The dead circumstantial. I replace scenes in which things simply happen with language as vivid as I can make it, with ellipsis, metaphor, summary which makes a pattern, something which distinguishes the writing from the plodding prose one often finds in realistic fiction.

Is there a temptation to move away from the ordinary subjects in which you're interested in order to generate the kind of language you've mentioned?

Brown: I do feel that. One needs to be subtle enough to do what seems to be an ordinary subject—although there are, in fact, no subjects that must stay ordinary in fiction—and yet still light that fire. While I fear the slough of unimaginative, reportorial writing, when I pick a subject such as the quadriplegic woman in *Tender Mercies*, I do feel farther from the probable than I want to be. Such things happen, and frequently, but I wish I could have written about that marriage without the flamboyant premise, the precipitated crisis.

What about the novel you're working on now, in which you're returning to experiences of yours during the civil rights struggle in Mississippi?

Brown: It has at its center again an emotionally extravagant occurrence. I was having difficulty writing about a couple of superannuated civil rights workers trying to deal with the "ordinariness" of their lives after the excitement of their activist youth. Their reduced lives would not take fire on the page, so I introduced an element which I had thought was going to be my next book: the couple finds themselves guardians of two children whose parents were killed in an accident. I bring these kids from a very different life, a segregationist background, into this family to prod them to reflect on their post-movement life and political engagement. The mother remembers being thrown into dirty jail cells and being forced to plunge her dinner dish into boiling water up to her elbow, and she realizes now that in a different way it is more difficult, at least because it is less *satisfying*, to decide what to make for dinner for these new children. As in *Tender Mercies*, I use an extraordinary circumstance to push the characters to remember what their ordinary lives were like before everything was changed by a stroke.

Perhaps because I began as a poet, I make large narrative gestures; they vault me into lives in order to do what I really want: to examine character and write as beautifully as I can. The cataclysmic is reflected on but rarely seen, and it is assimilated, finally almost without motion, in tiny increments. I'm fascinated by the play of scale, large against small, as a painter might be intrigued by composition, placing different masses against one another, different weights of event. My favorite quotation about writing is Flaubert's comment that when he wrote *Madame Bovary* he was really trying to approximate the shade of gray, color of a wood louse, the molelike existence of the dreary town. The details of Emma's life engaged him so little that until the last moment she was going to be a spinster. It was the gray that interested him, and that I understand.

What were you doing before you went to Mississippi in 1965?

Brown: At Barnard I did almost nothing but write, which I regret because I sort of forgot to get an education. No one could have stopped me from writing at the time, but the history, botany, and all the rest that I missed makes me wince now. I majored in English, and at Barnard at that time one couldn't read anything that wasn't in the language of its composition. So I didn't read the Russians or Mann or . . . All I wanted to do was write. Before that, I had assumed I would go into journalism; I didn't dare anything more "creative." In my freshman English class I was told to write a sonnet. I did one called "On the Ghost of Thomas Wolfe," appropriate to a seventeen-year-old, and sold it to the *New York Times*. (That was when the paper was printing absolutely execrable poetry on the editorial page.) Later I had some good teachers, Robert Pack and George Elliott. I did learn to sit still and revise, but I ignored the substance of every other discipline. Then I went to Brandeis to get a Ph.D. I hated it. In my class, which was full of would-be writers, I was the last to drop out. Graduate school was mutilating. In order to learn method, we were told we should suspend our sentimental interest in the content of the work. I quit when I decided that, if I put the effort and time I would spend on my thesis into my poetry, I might actually be a writer. In those days you could let your husband support you without a great deal of self-consciousness, and that's what I did. It would probably be a lot harder to do that now.

What writers were important to you when you started?

Brown: That's very hard to answer. I was just doing the best I could. I was reading, amazed to be able to understand poetry at all, Yeats, Stevens, all the lesser models in the Hall-Pack-Simpson anthology, grave and iambic every one. In class we would belabor Empson's *Seven Types of Ambiguity*. I was learning a very self-conscious kind of writing, perhaps best for me at the time. I was a true child of the '50s—inhibited, self-absorbed, all too analytic. The buttoned-up and buttoned-down poetry I was practicing to write was bad for me in one way—it was overcontrolled—but it did play to my strong points. I had written a lot of jingles when I was a kid, I was famous for my yearbook doggerel, so it was fairly easy for me to work with a formal kind of poetry. I guess I also learned the habit of economy and compression, though, and an interest in the sound and rhythm sentences have, qualities I try to carry over into my prose. But when I was in school, I never thought I'd write fiction. I did love Henry James while I was in graduate school, and I suppose if I really let my prose go now it would come out full of Jamesian elaboration and thoroughly devoid of visible event.

Is this what you meant by the phrase "luxurious suavity of style" in your review of Marilyn French's Bleeding Heart?

Brown: Yes. I am satisfied to read the serviceable gray gabardine prose of, say, Doris Lessing, for the sake of her ideas and her penetrating vision. But there are so many other modes, so many kinds of sensuous style from Woolf to Updike to Bellow to Gass or Paley or even Edna O'Brien (whom Gass would perhaps not like to stand next to on a list). Or there is the pure and elegant style of, say, Elizabeth Bowen, whom I love, or Paula Fox or Nabokov. How can anyone be less than eclectic in appreciation of such richness and diversity?

Some of my stories are more verbally playful or resplendent than anything I've done since, when my concentration's been subverted by the structural challenges of putting a novel together. Gerda, in *The Autobiography of My Mother*, was a pleasure to create because, as an emigrée speaker, the language still bristled under her touch. It rolled away from her like mercury, precision always just out of reach: it was still a live medium. In *Tender Mercies*, as in *Cora Fry*, I chastened that language for my four-square New England characters, but I gave Laura her head. If she had no more motion, at least she had extravagance of language, a kind of extension of the senses, for what that was worth, as if in compensation.

Were you an only child?

Brown: The youngest of three, with two older brothers. Why do you ask?

I'm interested in your repeated concern with accident. It seems to me only children are more anxious about accidents.

Brown: As an only girl, I may bear some of the characteristics of only children. When I was at the Radcliffe Institute, I did an informal survey of women of some accomplishment and "determined" that high-achievers were usually either the first girl or the only girl. It may mean that some of the weight placed on an only child bears on an only girl. I am interested in accidents, fascinated by how much pure accident is possible, accident in which no component of personality is present. In *Tender Mercies* I wanted to explore how Dan's personality contributes to Laura's accident—not willfully, but as an outgrowth of his particular habits of action and passion. How much is he to blame? And then, if he is, because no one human is without fault, how much ought he to be punished? The same question occurs at the end of *Autobiography of My Mother*: How much are daughter and mother to be held responsible for the accident in which the granddaughter perishes? Our lives are full of accidents of varying kinds, and the discrimination between those kinds engages me.

Does this engagement make you primarily a moralist or metaphysician?

Brown: I'm most wary of attempting to kick my material a level higher toward abstraction. I don't wish to claim that you can solve a problem by reading fiction, or tell people how to live. I'm interested only in the investigation, not in a fixed set of results.

I have been criticized for not pursuing such issues. Cynthia Ozick was surprised that there was not more of the fist raised at God in *Tender Mercies*: it is a very secular book, which is a reflection not only of my characters' pragmatism but of my own. On the other hand, I got a letter and pamphlets from a woman in the Midwest who said my characters could have been happy had they found Christ. They are poles of the same question: What is the next level of extrapolation? But I'm not the one to move my characters there.

In Autobiography of My Mother, *you quote Sartre about how immorality is only the concrete made abstract. You have a large distrust of abstraction?*

Brown: Huge, huge. And the older I get, the more concrete I am. In *Civil Wars,* my novel in progress, my character contemplates the coffins of her wards' parents and thinks the thoughts those kids must be thinking: Are they buried with their shoes on?   . . .   She says to herself that finally the difference between useful truth and useless mystery turns out to be specifics. I have a bad head for philosophy; when I read it I tend to be utterly confused or else to simplify it, and then I wonder how this could be what people are spending their lives debating. When I was writing a talk for a local lyceum, I realized that I hate to follow certain kinds of thoughts out to their very logical conclusions, as you do when you're giving a speech with a subject that's gone out to the world on a thousand printed announcements. It made me long to get back to fiction, where logic is not exactly the point. You're following your intuitions out to their ends, where there may yet be a dozen surprises.

You can't leave this in the transcript. It makes you a bad feminist.

Brown: It certainly seems to. However, the *facts* of the lives of women are such that simply to record them as they are is to do a useful service to feminism. I am committed to being useful, if that's the word, as long as I don't have to compromise my sense of the complexity of an issue or a life.

Is there a way of remaining concrete and expanding material?

Brown: Metaphor is one way. In *Tender Mercies* that slash of accident cutting across the family's lives opened up possibilities for metaphor and an instant deepening or expansion. It allowed me to write the sections in Laura's voice, which are almost pure metaphor, poetic beyond her realistic capabilities yet still, I think, plausible. Ellipsis is another way. My book of poems, *Cora Fry,* is a fiction writer's poem, strung on a narrative frame, devoted to the construction of a character by an accretion of fragments, tiny increments of daily observation enlarged by imagery. Which means, of course, that all the ellipses of passed time and unremarked-upon action fall in the cracks between the poems. It's a sort of hobby-horse of mine that more prose writers ought to make themselves comfortable with poetry so that they can accommodate a greater range of experience.

What writers who are women do you enjoy reading?

Brown: Someone I like enormously is Alice Munro, who is a Canadian. She publishes some in *The New Yorker,* and she has written two books of linked stories that have the continuity of novels. These books about the lives of girls growing to be women in small Canadian towns are subtle, funny, detached, and thoroughly concrete. Munro brings us evidence of a lived life in a particular place which is illuminating and accurate without ever becoming sociology. By contrast, a book getting a lot of play now, Joyce Maynard's *Baby Love,* renders the lives of small-town women, but the novel has little in it beyond an extremely precise naming of brands, both of things and emotions. Marilyn French is also certainly accurate (if narrow) in her sociology, and useful to many people, but hers is not the kind of writing that interests me. There is not a single interesting sentence in her last book: no pleasure in words, no transformation of passionately held convictions into passionately worked prose.

You said once that the writer you'd respect most is one "who'd make a good gossip, a better small-time con man, a bad rabble-rouser, and a worse debater. And yet still be serious." Who else besides Alice Munro fits that bill?

Brown: Flannery O'Connor, Stanley Elkin, Margaret Drabble at her best, Anne Tyler when she's not being too ingratiating. Fred Busch, who's a wonderful writer full of deep feeling and care for language, and who's still waiting for the audience he deserves. Diane Johnson, Eudora Welty. Cynthia Ozick, though she has a cold cutting edge—she may be the Jewish sister-under-the-skin of Flannery O'Connor.

Does it bother you that Alice Munro is unknown and Marilyn French is widely read?

Brown: Yes, of course, but it continues to elude me what makes a popular book. It shouldn't concern me; I should be more noble, beyond such concerns for myself. But it bothers me that so many works of quality never reach the public eye, or don't penetrate the public's fixed gaze. No one seems to know what strange conjunction of writing and public interest makes certain books leap to the forefront. It's not simply quality or lack of quality; it's not subject matter. I don't know what it is. Sometimes it's lazy marketing, the self-fulfilling defeatism of publishers who don't expect anything of books they call, with a certain vaguely exasperated sigh, "literary" even though, in fact, they are quite accessible to a mass readership. Then every once in a while, one of those breaks through and ruins every theory.

You're familiar with the objections to realism. Do you have a theoretical rationale for your work?

Brown: No. I'm not abstract, remember? You can't get me to do it. I struggle every time I sit down to write; I fear an unleavened quality in my prose, and I fear the staleness of certain mechanics of narrative. People like you have done this to me. I may try some experiment as an agent for textured prose, but each time I find myself distracted by the method, find I'm not able to represent deeply enough the emotional lives of my characters. I think it took a long time to get *Civil Wars* off the ground because I spent time experimenting with odd perspectives and, after a good bit of wasted time, ended up saying, "Back to the usual." I understand there's a displacement of means in accomplishing an end in fiction. I just want to make sure the end is accomplished. I want to *move* you. I may do some sociological business, a little humor on the side, but I'm happiest when someone says to me, "I was moved by that book" or "I felt for that character." People who tell me they lost sleep, or were reduced to tears, well . . . sadist that I am, those are my dearest readers.

If you really take seriously that quote of Kafka's—"The book must be an ax for the frozen sea within us" — except in a very few cases, with people who have a rarefied sophistication, that frozen sea is not going to be cracked open by a writer who takes such an ironic view of human nature that no real people are allowed to exist or be respected on the page. Simpler means are a surer touch for the purpose that most writers begin with: reaching out to other people, not instructing them in the futility of taking their lives seriously. As I look back at my fiction, I see a movement away from experiment. *Street Games* was occasionally innovative, and the uncollected stories I wrote before those were even more so, I suppose, but I've come to feel that the best way I engage complexities of character is by really quite straightforward means.

For you, then, language is referential?

Brown: Yes, it is referential. Even when a story has an unconventional structure—a nonlinear narrative or a cryptic style—its intention, if it's going to mean anything to me, is to illuminate the way real lives are lived. I can only keep repeating that. Its language may not be realistic, but its exaggerations or energy do not exist reflexively for their own sake. Why don't we say that language for me is a kind of lens: it may clarify or it may enlarge, it may even distort for effect, but, however it works, it always works as a tool to bring the subject closer to the audience. What the writer whispers up close might be thoroughly subversive, but there is the understanding that real words are being heard, with reference to a real world or to an imagined one that reflects the qualities of this one rearranged. I love stylized or elliptical writing, vivid writing, but for me its ends are really fairly conservative. That is not to say that I think that writing should be anything but (as Elizabeth Bowen called it) "uncompromised by purpose." Perhaps you shouldn't be talking to me at all!

Do you think other writers in the last five years or so have begun to accept the artifices of fiction and to write again about reality?

Brown: I never understood who was reading self-conscious fiction in the first place. Maybe it's because I don't live in a university atmosphere. In fact, it's very important for me to live in a place where there are nonliterary people. They may not be the best readers of my work, but they're closer to me than to reading Barth. Most of the people I know—even most of the writers I know—don't read Pynchon, for example. Maybe fiction *is* changing. I have no theory on the matter. When four other writers and I did a benefit reading in Cambridge not too long ago, people afterward said with some surprise that we were all writing about our families. Retrograde, but true.

Why don't women write like Pynchon or Barth?

Brown: I don't want to get into the nurture/nature issue, but there is evidence that baby girls—young infants—are already more responsive to people, to faces and smiles, than are boys. That could suggest that women were biologically intended, however they may want to respond to that predisposition, to respond and nurture. All through their lives the emotional attachments of women are more bonded; we deal with separations from loved ones with greater difficulty than men. If all that is true, and I believe that for complex reasons it is, it wouldn't be surprising if women were more concrete, more concerned with audience. Art is an extension, after all, of one's whole emotional constitution. This means, possibly, that women will be more engaged by the social than by the reflexive function of writing.

How do you go about keeping your work your own when there are so many groups of readers willing to employ it for themselves?

Brown: Some writers would be delighted to think their work is "employable," enrolled in a good cause. They would see my indifference to being useful, or at least the qualifications I feel about fiction as tract, as evidence that I'm a moral laggard and would suggest that I not be proud of my frivolity. In any event, I don't think you "go about" keeping your work your own—either it is appropriated by some group or it is annexable by no one in particular, the way the birds in the air serve no party and accomplish no mission. That comes of hearing your own voice when you write, which respects the distinction between fiction and rhetoric, not those of the many proselytizers for worthy causes who are (except in rare cases, I think) like the Sirens leading one astray. Eudora Welty says somewhere that she doesn't write for friends or even for herself. I write, she says, for *it*, for the pleasure of *it*. Anyone who wants to claim the work when it's finished is free to do so; it's the solicitation of my attention before it's finished that I want to resist. Needless to say there's a fine line, often, between a worthy "relevance" and didactic heavyhandedness. Or, on the other side, the desire to cast a story about politics in engaging and illuminating human terms might result in a decline into triviality. I'm working on a novel now that has raised all these questions for me: Writing about characters who live for politics, how do I find a point of entry somewhere between the petty and the grandiloquent or the pedantic?

You want to move readers. How do you make sure you don't cheat, don't write melodrama?

Brown: I don't know. I do throw out a lot of pages along the way. I felt with *Tender Mercies* that if I took a cool enough tone at the outset and kept to it, I would be able to get through some potentially sentimental moments. What happened, though, was that now and then I've been criticized for not being close enough to the characters, for not allowing the reader to like them better. In that novel I may have gone to such lengths to protect against sentimentality that some readers did not feel invited into the book. It is a "rigorous" book, someone has said. The same thing may be true of *Autobiography of My Mother*: it is about a cold woman, legalistic and detached. I find her a sympathetic character, one capable of evoking emotion, because she is a victim of her own family and past; but she is no more easily "enjoyed" than a lot of real people who challenge our capacities for sympathy.

You mention "victim." Several reviewers have commented on your interest in victims. Do you feel that's true?

Brown: "Victim" is usually a word used from the outside to pronounce upon another person's life. It's easy for middle-class readers to call the denizens of *Street Games* "victims," but I don't think of them that way and I don't think the characters would see themselves as victims. Everybody suffers from something. "Victim" may be reviewers' shorthand for saying, "They are different from us."

Another theme seems to be recovery, both as a bringing back in memory and as getting well.

Brown: Only in that I think I see what I'm doing in a book like *Tender Mercies* as telling the ultimate scary story. One critic understood beautifully when he said that, to me, life is "always on the verge of paralysis—about to go still, with worry, guilt, fear and with death in the long run"—and then proving to myself (and anyone else who's still listening) that the really vital lovable parts of ourselves can always, though at great cost, be redeemed. There is no redemption at the end of *Autobiography*, except perhaps that cool, emotionally paralyzed Gerda begins to melt into feelings. I wanted *Tender Mercies* to affirm, against all odds, that our love for each other can exist independent of "function," or household service or physical accomplishment. It *persists*, on the human edge of a kind of purity. And so does memory as a record of a lived life.

As a way of summary, would you discuss the titles of your two published novels and Civil Wars?

Brown: I had the title for *The Autobiography of My Mother* before I had the book, and I didn't care whether the book fit it when it was finished or not. Or say that, like *Ragtime*, which Doctorow, I think, tells us actually gave him the rhythm of his prose, the Moebius-strip elusiveness of the subject in my title influenced my refusal to decide who was subject and who object in that book. Obviously the title really grew out of my conviction that the "reality" of the reader is relative, a function of vantage point, but I think the title may have helped to keep my intentions clear when I was in danger of forgetting them.

"Tender Mercies" was a harder title to find than the book was to write. Every day for months another two or three terrible titles went on my refrigerator in my kids' magnetic letters, to be scrutinized or tasted or whatever you do when you're trying to feel the weight and judge the color and flavor of a title. And finally I came upon "tender mercies," a common enough phrase which is actually from Psalms, when I was reading Beckett!

As for "Civil Wars," that too is an absolute title for me. It represents every conceivable rift between intimates that I can imagine—you understand that this novel is set in Mississippi during and after the civil rights period—every cross purpose at which friends and family can move. (Alison Lurie wrote a novel called *The War between the Tates*; her distance from her characters begins in the mocking pun of the title. Mine is more straightforward.) I love the feeling—anyone does—that aspects of writing are what Freud called "over-determined," that is to say, reiterated in different ways, underlined, as it were, with a thicker and thicker marking. That's what makes dramatic structure work, makes felicitous connections between words, lines, images in poems or richly written, inwardly allusive prose. So every time I discover another facet of family battle or struggle between old friends or allies who find themselves, now, with opposing ideologies, the more pleasure I take in the title "Civil Wars." It's as if I go on justifying it after the fact, like a critic gone sleuthing: "Oh, that's what she meant!" You can feel a real adrenalin high when you happen onto the title that ties things together. It releases an energy greater than that of the sum of the untitled parts.

Have you been taken to task by any feminist critics for not giving your female characters better lots?

Brown: To my surprise—no. Not for sending Cora Fry home to a less than sensitive husband; not for the mother in *Autobiography of My Mother*, a person of great intellectual achievement who doesn't know how to live a forgiving and flexible life. She's certainly not much of a role model. What has been said, fortunately not too often, is that *Tender Mercies* was a long drawn-out metaphor for the annihilation of women at the hands of men. The book, however, while it is about the body, is not about the body politic. Never was I writing without compassion for the man who found himself to blame in a way for the destruction of his wife's body. Never did I feel I was out to get him or to say to all men, "Here is what you do to your wives." Vivian Gornick in the *Village Voice* saw the entire novel so metaphorically that she entirely misrepresented the healing that goes on at the end. Laura does not walk into the sunset, does not walk anywhere; but her husband comes to her, and she back to him, with a very difficult and broad forgiveness. There seems to me a sense of the amplitude of all that is left to them. The husband who has not thought much before the accident realizes that he values his wife, not for the things she did with her body, but for who she was in some amorphous and satisfying way. When I was searching for that title I looked through my thesaurus for synonyms for amplitude, fullness, rightness—that's what I thought the book expressed, the ability of people to restitch the torn fabric and move on.

If I had reviewed Tender Mercies, *I would have said that I distrusted liking it—because the writer seems to be fair to men.*

Brown: I would have taken that as a compliment, because it's what I'm trying for in my fiction. *Autobiography of My Mother* is a less likable book than *Tender Mercies*—it is full of argument between mother and daughter—but what pleases me about responses to the book is that different readers pick different sides of the argument to support. For me that averages out to fairness and says, "You have done your job well," no simple judgments passed.

I can get as angry as anyone about men. But my sense of the ways lives are lived is that everyone is a product of a childhood, of a set of parents who did not choose their lives because they had a set of parents who did not choose their lives, and so on. This kind of sympathy makes me a poor politician—a bad feminist, a bad activist, a bad any-ist. This is not to say that I forgive what people do, but I have a difficult time in my writing blaming anyone. (I wish I were as evenhanded in my life.) In *Tender Mercies* Dan thinks about his father, who is a real bastard, a drunk who beats his wife, that he was a child too. He (the father) dreamed of growing up and having children. He could not have dreamed that he would abuse them the way he did. No one plans such mutilation, although to say that does not absolve anyone of responsibility for his actions. But a book is a good place to try for the whole story, the compassionate history of the interior, the invisible pain of the one who inflicts pain. In my story "A Letter to Ismael in the Grave," a wife forgives, or at least comprehends for a moment, her husband, his life and death, as a victim's victim. That is, it seems to me, what writing is for. You have a better chance of understanding people in your writing than you ever do in your life. You can be fair, more perfect, more forbearing on paper. My real fear as a writer is that some inadequacy of which I am not aware will be projected into the work and will limit its value in the final judgment. Because, ultimately, all of our work will be seen from a distance, like a view of the earth from above, and it will turn out that the shape and size of this or that body of writing will look wholly different from there. Skimpy. Stingy. Uninflected and unshaped. Or uninteresting except in relation to its surroundings. We are unintentionally responsible for the private qualities of these emanations of ourselves, and what they lack will, not coincidentally, be a judgment on our personalities and character in spite of all we try to control in them. Even biographers make statements about themselves, first by their choice of subject, then by the way they organize and interpret the life and work of another. The naked accounting will come later (perhaps too late to embarrass us or make us fall into a shamed silence), when we shall have to recognize in our work our own callowness, and by their absence all the thoughts we haven't thought, the imaginings we haven't dared, and the compassion we have not been able to summon. Some of us might even be proud that we found a way if not to display, then at least to embody, our virtues while our concentration appeared to be elsewhere. No sense thinking about it, though. If our life and work weren't spun of a single thread, where would the intimacy of insights—all those chancy shared secrets—ever come from? And why would anyone want to read them?

Photo by Lynn Swigart

An Interview with
Robert Coover

Robert Coover didn't want to do this interview. The '70s were a difficult period for Bob, both personally and creatively, mostly due to the enormous hassles and frustrations he suffered in connection with publication of *The Public Burning*. Having devoted nearly ten years and a great deal of his creative energies to its writing, he also lost quite a stretch of writing time in trying to see the work through to publication. At any rate, he was understandably reluctant to tie up any more of his writing time when I occasionally brought up the possibility of an interview during several years of correspondence. Finally he relented, and I flew to Providence, Rhode Island, where he had recently moved following almost fifteen years in England and Spain. Our interview took place on November 15, 1979, with a few minor follow-up questions handled by mail.

Robert Coover is one of the most intense literary figures anyone is likely to encounter. After an evening of drinking wine and exchanging anecdotes at his house with his close friends Robert Scholes, Jack Hawkes, and their wives, we met for our interview at the ancient lounge of the Brown University English department. Bob led the way through the labyrinthine corridors of this building to his office, with its unobtrusive, unmarked door. Coover is a rather short, slightly built man with thick brown hair and a quick, boyish smile that makes him look fifteen years younger than his forty-eight years. In answering questions, he spoke with passionate and confident conviction; although he chose his words carefully, Coover expressed his opinions forcefully. All around us—on his desk, the walls, even the floor—were note cards and manuscript pages, written in different colored inks, from his various works in progress.

Coover is the author of three novels: *The Origin of the Brunists* (1965), which won the William Faulkner Award for the best first novel by an American author; *The Universal Baseball Association* (1968); and *The Public Burning* (1977). His short fiction includes one collection, *Pricksongs and Descants* (1970), and five novellas, *After Lazarus* (1979), *Hair o' the Chine, Charlie in the House of Rue, A Political Fable*, and *Spanking the Maid* (all 1980). He has also written a series of plays, collected in *A Theological Position*. He is currently at work on several projects, including a major novel tentatively entitled *Lucky Pierre*.

—Larry McCaffery

You've done most of your writing during the past ten or fifteen years while living in England and Spain. Are there any advantages to being an expatriate writer?

Coover: Detachment mainly. A writer needs isolation, a cell of his own, that's obvious, but distance can also help. It has a way of freeing the imagination, stirring memory. Fewer localisms creep in, less passing trivia, transient concerns. Personally, I don't seem to be able to cut myself off very well here in the States. I get too engaged in things around me and end up having less time to write, less energy for it. It can work both ways, of course. If you're not careful you can stay away too long and lose touch. No easy answer.

You say in your "Introduction" to the Fiction Collective's Statements Two *that "in America, art, like everything else (knowledge, condoms, religions, etc.) is a product. The discovery of this is the capstone to the artist's alienation process in America." I take it from this that you feel that the commodity mentality of American culture makes it even more difficult to be an artist here than elsewhere—in Europe, for example.*

Coover: Yes—in fact, many Europeans have been shocked at their own transformations when they enter the American market. Of course, art's treated as a commodity throughout most of the Western world—and elsewhere, maybe even worse—but in America the market's so vast and impersonal. To most Americans the publishing industry is as strange and remote as Oz, but it's also true the other way around: to the industry, the American public is like a magical and unpredictable fairyland, "out there somewhere," complete with a fabulous buried treasure just waiting to be dug up. There is no common language or concern between them; their only exchange is barter. A writer exists as a kind of icon, or else as nothing. If this, or something like it, happened to a writer in Europe, he would at least have his own intellectual community to fall back on. Here we have no such communities—nor is there any real hope for one. There's no place for it, no physical way to work it out. The nearest thing we have is the academic circuit, where the steady flow of jobs, readings, conferences, visiting lectureships, and so on, brings people together, but it's very loosely strung, and many people have no access to it. And besides, it's been drying up. We have no gathering places, no forum, no national magazines, no cafés, no boulevards. We do not get together and talk about things on national TV or radio. P.E.N. is trying to do something about it now, setting up local chapters, but the effort is necessarily full of artifice—a kind of thinking man's Rotary Club. We have no natural center.

The Fiction Collective also seems to be trying to do what they can to change things. What do you think of their efforts to date?

Coover: Well, it also has to compete in the marketplace. It doesn't have much time for anything else. And its people are scattered and they lack the money for getting everybody together. It should be a more exciting phenomenon than it is, but it's still largely a publishing maneuver. As such, though, important. Probably, overall, they've put out the best list in town.

On the other hand, you've also said that you feel there's not much life in the fiction coming out of Europe today; yet American fiction, from my vantage point, has been enormously exciting during the '60s and '70s. Doesn't this seem contradictory to you?

Coover: No. A writer may or may not be discouraged by isolation and alienation. If he goes on, he may even benefit from it. Highly communalized groups of intellectuals like you have in Europe probably put more pressure on their members to conform to certain standards, discouraging too much eccentricity or adverturism. The standards are probably higher, though, letting less shit through. It's like going to a very good school: you must learn what's being taught at that school, rather than striking out on your own. You gain discipline, knowledge, historical perspective, and so on, but you may lose a little confidence in your own imaginative potential. Besides, we may have been underestimating the quality of European fiction during this period when writing in the Americas seemed to be enjoying such a renaissance. After all, not only are there all the masters of the old forms, there are writers like Tournier and Beckett and Grass, Calvino, Carter, Gombrowicz, and so on. Perhaps we've also had an exaggerated notion of our own uniqueness and importance and quality. Novelty can hide a lot of flaws.

But this renaissance you speak of—you've suggested that most of the important contemporary American writers weren't even aware of each other's works: so what was going on to generate this creative outburst?

Coover: Well, many reasons probably. The postwar appetite for change and newness, the college boom and the money that was around —

all those new English professors, for example, needing something to write about—and then little things like the Kafka phenomenon, Barney Rosset's Grove Press and the new paperback industry, the resurgence of interest in the surrealists, ease of travel, the explosion of all the new media, video especially. And then there was the general feeling, especially during the Cold War, of being stifled by dogma, the sense that so much of the trouble we found ourselves in was the consequence of not being imaginative enough about the ways out. Plus the threat of nuclear apocalypse: how could we go on thinking in the old trite ways when every day we had to imagine the unimaginable? All the disciplines were affected, not just writing. Physics, for example, had long since been leading the way . . .

You mentioned the media. Obviously your fiction has been influenced by television, cinema, and theater. Were you consciously aiming at integrating elements from these other media?

Coover: I think in part it was unconscious. Stories tend to appear to me, not as formal ideas, but as metaphors, and these metaphors seem to demand structures of their own: they seem to have an internal need for a certain form. Nevertheless, we've all been affected by film technology, the information bombardment of television, and so on, and certainly I've had a conscious desire to explore the ways all this makes our minds work.

Can you say something more about these metaphors that your fiction grows out of?

Coover: They're the germ, the thought, the image, the idea, out of which all the rest grows. They're always a bit elusive, involving thoughts, feelings, abstractions, visual material, all at once. I suppose they're a little like dream fragments, in that such fragments always contain, if you analyze them, so much more than at first you suspect. But they're not literally that—I never write from dreams. All these ideas come to me in the full light of day. Some, when you pry them open, have too little inside to work with. Others are unexpectedly fat and rich. Novels typically begin for me as very tiny stories or little one-act play ideas which I think at the time aren't going to fill three pages. Then slowly the hidden complexities reveal themselves.

Do you recall what this germinating idea was for The Origin of the Brunists?

Coover: Well, wholly fleshed out, of course, it's the book itself. But my first glimpse of it came one grim wintery day, just before Christmas, while I was sitting in the bleachers of a high school basketball gymnasium, eating a peanut butter sandwich and staring down on five grotesquely burnt and mutilated cadavers. There had been a mine explosion, and I was there helping the guy who edited the newspaper my father managed, getting identifications and so on. They'd expected a steady flow of bodies, there were over a hundred men still below, but after they'd brought up the first five—this episode is sort of in the book—they decided to push on and see if they could find anyone still alive. So, for the moment, there was nothing for me to do but watch as relatives came in to try to identify these five almost unidentifiable men, all of which left me, as you can imagine, quite shaken. There was a lot of tearful praying going on, and it led me to wonder what might happen if some guy did get rescued, and came up thinking he'd been saved for some divine mission? What might that lead to? As a matter of fact, a man did get rescued, but though he was a religious man, he had no messianic complex, he was just thankful. Anyway, I carried this idea around for a while after that, experimenting with different approaches, but it wasn't until nearly ten years later, after a lot of the fictions in Pricksongs had been written, that I married this idea to the desire I was feeling then that I wanted to pay my dues, as it were, to traditional fiction. The germinating idea, of course, was by now a folder full of elaborate notes, half-starts, experimental inventions, and so on. But no matter what the variations, they always had something to do with a coal-mine disaster, and it was this, more than the messiah story, that now made me want to try this story as a full-length mimetic fiction. In effect, I wanted to go down into the mine myself and come out of it, hopefully with some revelations of my own, new insights, more skill, discipline, all that. And that was pretty much how it turned out. It was a very valuable experience for me.

But if you're "paying your dues" to traditional narrative approaches in The Origin of the Brunists, *I sometimes sense that you're paying them with reservations; there seem to be a very large number of nonrealistic elements in the novel, at least on certain levels. Did you really conceive the novel to be a straightforward realistic presentation?*

Coover: Yes, it is, of course. Maybe I think that all my fiction is realistic and that so far it has simply been misunderstood as otherwise. There are paradoxes, of course. Though the varying perspectives may at times seem to disturb the "realism" of the book, the overview that embraces them all I think is wholly realistic—and yet this overview includes the book's design, and that design is born of, well, something else. That vibrant space between the poles of a paradox: that's where all the exciting art happens, I think.

In the Brunists—*and in your other novels as well—one of your main thematic intentions seems to be to expose the so-called objective reports of history, news reporting, theological dictims, and so forth. You suggest that such reports result largely from man's desire to shape random events into some kind of pleasing pattern or design. Do you mean to suggest that all these spring from a central artistic impulse?*

Coover: I wouldn't say "artistic." Art's not nature after all. But, yes, the human need for pattern, and language's propensity, willy-nilly, for supplying it—what happens, I think, is that every effort to form a view of the world, every effort to speak of the world, involves a kind of fiction-making process. Memory is a kind of narrative, as is our perception of what the future is apt to bring us, our understanding of anything going on out in the world—even our scientific understanding of the world has to be reduced to a narrative of sorts in order to grasp it. What's a formula but a kind of sentence, a story among other possible stories? Men live by fictions. They have to. Life's too complicated, we just can't handle all the input, we have to isolate little bits and make reasonable stories out of them. Of course, that's an artificial act and therefore, you might say, "artistic." But I would say the impulse was from necessity, and only some of the resulting stories are "artistic." All of them, though, are merely artifices—that is, they are always in some ways false, or at best incomplete. There are always other plots, other settings, other interpretations. So if some stories start throwing their weight around, I like to undermine their authority a bit, work variations, call attention to their fictional natures.

Is this your explanation for why we have had this outburst of self-reflexive fictions during the '60s and '70s?

Coover: Yes. If storytelling is central to the human experience, stories about storytelling, or stories which talk about themselves as stories, become central, too. For a while anyway. I think, as a fashion, it's passing, though more self-reflexive fictions will be written.

One of the frequent criticisms leveled against metafiction is that by concentrating on the act of writing, by becoming more involuted and self-conscious, it becomes narcissistic and evades the kinds of "moral issues" that John Gardner has recently championed. Do you feel that there is an inherent opposition between didactic and aesthetic aims in a work of fiction?

Coover: No, it's a phony issue. John's a moral fiction-writer—some of the time; probably not often enough—but he's an immoral moralist. He knows this debate about "entertainment" and "instruction" is a terribly old, seedy issue, a kind of political game at its worst, that goes back to the ancients. Who's to say, for example, that self-reflexive fiction, dealing as it assumes it does with a basic human activity, is not, by examining that activity as it celebrates it, engaged in a very moral act?

But you wouldn't insist that good fiction must be moral in the way that Gardner suggests it must—that is, by creating heroic models, proposing solutions to issues rather than simply raising them, or whatever?

Coover: I would not, myself, say that fiction *must* anything. Ever.

I find your fiction repeatedly returning to a central situation. We observe a character or characters engaged in this subjective, fiction-making process we have just been talking about. In their desire for stabili-

ty and order, however, they lose sight of what they have been doing and begin to insert these fictions into the world as dogma; this winds up entrapping or even destroying them. Is this a fair reading?

Coover: Yes. Why not?

Why do you return so often to this idea?

Coover: To the scene of the crime, you mean? A weakness, no doubt, a lack of moral fiber. Maybe the struggle I had as a young writer against the old forms made me overly aware of their restrictive nature, such that I found myself burdened with a vast number of metaphoric possibilities, all of which were touched by this sense of dogma invading the world and turning it to stone. But I have literally hundreds of ideas, virtually every day I think of another one, so maybe I'll get lucky next time, choose one with a different bloom. It's the choice that scares me. I mean, we only have so many lives to lead. The *Brunists* took me four years, *The Public Burning* longer. If I could work through all the ideas I have now without thinking up any more (and as I said that, damn it, I've just thought of another one), I'd need a couple of hundred years more at least. Like human seed: a billion kids eager to be born every minute, but you only get a few at best.

The first things you ever published were a series of poems in The Fiddlehead. *Since then you've worked with drama, movie scripts, translation, and various other literary forms. Which ones have you found the most interesting to work with, and what are the most important differences among them?*

Coover: The central thing for me is story. I like poems, paintings, music, even buildings, that tell stories. I believe, to be good, you have to master the materials of the form you're working in, whether it's language, form and color, meter, stone, cameras, lights, or inks, but all that's secondary to me. Necessary but secondary. I know there's a way of looking at fiction as being made up of words, and that therefore what you do with words becomes the central concern. But I'm much more interested in the way that fiction, for all its weaknesses, reflects something else—gesture, connections, paradox, story. I work with language because paper is cheaper than film stock. And because it's easier to work with a committee of one. But storytelling doesn't have to be done with words on a printed page, or even with spoken words: we all learned that as kids at our Saturday morning religious experience in the local ten-cent cinemas. Probably, if I had absolute freedom to do what I want, I'd prefer film.

What is it that excites you so much about film?

Coover: First of all, its great immediacy: it grasps so much with such rapidity. Certainly it's the medium par excellence for the mimetic narrative. And it has a relationship with time that is fascinating—we can take in centuries in an hour or two, even in a few minutes. All narratives play with time, but only film can truly juggle it. So: a mix of magic and documentary power. And I don't dislike the communal aspect of film, the bringing together of a lot of different talents to produce a work of art—it's healthier somehow than that deep-closeted ego involvement of the novelist, poet, or painter. But the problem, of course, is that it's so expensive and potentially so profitable. Too many non-creative types get in on the processes; more than one good film's been ruined by them. The tales of woe from writers misused by the film industry are beyond number.

What about your experiences with the theater?

Coover: Like film, it's terribly destructive of creative time. You find yourself working long hours over five or six lines that took you maybe fifteen minutes to write. And before that there's the casting, the designing of the set, struggles with producers and directors, costumes, music maybe—and if you're going to get seriously involved with theater, you've got to get involved with all of it. But there's something exhilarating about it, too—it's a kind of Pygmalion experience, seeing it come alive before your eyes. And all the performing arts have the excitement of ephemerality. Novelists sometimes get this sense of the weightiness of their task, as though they were chipping their work out of stone—one slip and it's all ruined forever. Contrarily, every night at the theater it's all brand new—and when it's over, it's gone, except as it exists in the memory, so long as that lasts. It gives me a sense of living in the present that I rarely get as a novelist.

Have you ever gotten involved in the productions of your plays?

Coover: Yes, several times, most intensely a few years ago in the New York production of "The Kid" at the American Place Theatre. Jack Gelber was the director, and working with him and with Wynn Handman, who ran the theater, was one of the happiest experiences in my life. We made a mistake in the casting which proved to be troublesome, and there were a few decisions made that maybe weren't wise ones, but there's always going to be this—if we did it again, there would be others, that's part of the fun of it. For the most part, it was a wonderful show, greatly enhanced by all the talents that contributed to it. Jack got an Obie for directing it and the production won several other awards. It was a real treat. I was also very modestly involved in a wonderful production of "Love Scene" in Paris, where it premiered, there called "Scene d'amour." It was directed by Henri Gilabert in a little Left Bank theater called the Troglodyte and with such intelligence and balance that it was like seeing before my eyes—and in French at that—exactly what I'd envisioned in my mind before. "Rip Awake" premiered out in Los Angeles where Ron Sossi played Rip, and his Odyssey group also premiered "A Theological Position."

I'm sure you heard of the scandal that surrounded "A Theological Position"'s production out there.

Coover: Yes, well, Ron probably asked for it by including it in what he called "An Evening of Dirty Religious Plays," but my work's had a long history of suppression or bowdlerization, so I'm used to it. Actually, I don't see it as a scandalous play—there's nothing new about talking cunts, after all. Probably, for some of the people on the council out there, the image struck too close to home. Anyway, it's a good theater group, and I hope to work more with them.

Those Western materials you used in "The Kid" you've also used in other stories, and you return repeatedly to fairytales, sports, and other elements that are usually seen as pop-cultural material. What's the source of your fascination with this kind of stuff?

Coover: It's all material that's close to the mythic content of our lives, and is therefore an important part of our day-to-day fiction-making process. The pop culture we absorb in childhood—and I'd include all the pop religions as well—goes on affecting the way we respond to the world or talk about it for the rest of our lives. And this mythology of ours, this unwritten Bible, is being constantly reinforced by books and newspapers, films, television, advertisements, politicians, teachers, and so on. So working inside these forms is a way of staying close to the bone.

What about your interest in another concept that recurs in your fiction—the concept of number and its inevitable companion, numerology? These both seem to be perfect examples of what you described earlier as fictions man uses to navigate through the world.

Coover: Yes, or to stumble through it. It's one way among many that the mind gets locked into fixed distorting patterns. Silly stuff. But it was an important element in the Christian apocalyptic vision, so it had to be part of the *Brunists*. Then, once I started working with it, I found it again in a lot of secondary and ironic ways. Especially in the formal design.

You mean like Calvino's use of tarot images in The Castle of Crossed Destinies? *He seems to be using tarot in that book as a generating formal design in much the same way that you use number theory in a story like "The Elevator."*

Coover: Mmm. Tarot exists in the *Brunists*, too. You remember the widows of the miners gathered at Mabel's and sat around her cards in the key chapter of the section called "The Sign." It's also in the structure. Number presents itself more directly; you recognize it more quickly.

What about your apparent interest in puns and wordplay? Freud maintains that one derives pleasure from the pun or the play on words by following the possibilities and transformations implicit in language. Gombrich describes this process as "the juxtaposition of concepts which one arrives at casually, unexpectedly, unleashes a preconscious idea." Does your fascination with puns have to do with this view of the transformational possibilities lying within the formal properties of languages?

Coover: I was more fascinated just now with the Gombrich quote. It's a painterly thought: the shock of strange juxtapositions. I like the pun for its intense condensation, but for me it's only a second-rate version of the more exciting idea of the juxtaposition of two unexpected elements —structural puns, you might call them. A lot of my stories begin this way. Again the use of seeming paradox, the vibrant space between the poles.

Is that how "The Panel Game" got started? It's obviously very much concerned with this business of wordplay.

Coover: Yes, but it's an early breakaway story for me, so it's more self-conscious than most. I was struggling to do something I had never done before, and it shows. All seven of the stories in that little "Exemplary Fictions" section of *Pricksongs* are discovery stories like that, blind launchings-forth as it were. I only selected those that seemed unique turning-points. "The Panel Game" is a mid-1950s story, and the next one in that group is already from the 1960s, with a lot missing in between.

You wrote me once that "The Panel Game" was an important early story for you, and when I looked back at it, it seemed to contain the seeds of a lot of the central motifs in your later work—the struggle with transformation, the attempt to unravel a structure encoded in symbols, the game metaphor, and so on.

Coover: Yes, well, Borges said we go on writing the same story all our lives. The trouble is, it's usually a story that can never be told—there's always this distance between the sign and the signified, it's the oldest truth in philosophy—and that's why we tend to get so obsessive about it. The important thing is to accept this unbridgeable distance and carry on with the crazy bridge-building just the same.

In The Origin of the Brunists *you say that "games were what kept Tiger Miller going." The same is obviously true of Henry Waugh in* The Universal Baseball Association *and, in a different sense, of Richard Nixon in* The Public Burning. *Why do you return so often to this concept of game in your fiction?*

Coover: We live in a skeptical age in which games are increasingly important. When life has no ontological meaning, it becomes a kind of game itself. Thus it's a metaphor for a perception of the way the world works, and also something that almost everybody's doing—if not on the playing fields, then in politics or business or education. If you're cynical about it, you learn the rules and strategies, shut up about them, and get what you can out of it. If you're not inclined to be a manipulator, you might want to expose the game plan for your own protection and ask how it can be a better game than it is at present. And formal games reflect on the hidden games, more so in an age without a Final Arbiter. So it's an important metaphor to be explored.

The game of writing not to be excepted, I assume. I mean, Henry's relationship with his baseball association seems to share a number of in-

*teresting parallels with the way a writer relates to a novel, and I believe
you've said somewhere that you intended the book to be primarily for
writers rather than for baseball fans. Do you mean that you intended the
book to be a sort of allegory of the writer's plight or situation?*

Coover: That statement had to do with the fact that when I was
working on that particular book I was convinced that it had no audience—it had become too eccentric an idea. But I felt that embedded in it
were a lot of ideas, notions about fiction and about the activity of the
imagination itself, its role in the world, the interplay of formal and informal fictions, and so on. And I thought that, if no one else did, at least other
writers would perceive this, would see what I was doing and would be
fascinated by how I worked out my problems. Seeing the way a little
metaphor slipped through here and there, working its way out, they'd
receive a kind of greeting, a recognition, a signal. Of course, it turned out
somewhat differently. The book has had an unexpectedly large readership. It turned out to be popular among athletes and other people involved
in sports, journalists especially. And, as it happens, there are a lot more
people playing table-top baseball games than I could ever have imagined.

*Once and for all, would you clear up exactly where Henry is in the last
chapter?*

Coover: No.

*OK, OK, leave that a mystery if you must. I only asked because my
students always ask me the question . . . But it's one of my favorite
chapters, and one of the things you seem to be doing is playfully tearing
down some of the mythic and religious parallels you had been establishing
earlier in the novel.*

Coover: Well, in that sense it might be seen as a gift to the unobser-
vant reader who had taken those parallels too seriously in the first place. I
believe it reinforces the central themes of the book, bringing it all into
focus without at the same time turning it off.

*Keeping things open-ended, you mean. Is that one of the reasons why
your last chapter is the* eighth *chapter, rather than the ninth—which we
might have expected, in keeping with your baseball metaphor?*

Coover: Yes. The design, the structure of the book is so self-
revealing—and it's not a gloss on the text from which it borrows its design,
in the sense of being a theologian's gloss; it's an outsider's gloss, an ironist's
gloss. The idea of an "eighth" chapter, the potential of it, the wonderful
ambivalences implied—all this came to me even before I knew what was
going to be in it.

*Part of what's in it I seem to see in all three of your novels: a crowd com-
ing together and in their interactions producing a significant collective
response of some sort. Am I right in seeing Durkheim's influence here?*

Coover: Yes, especially his image of "collective effervescence," which is his explanation, in part, for the invention of divinities.

Certainly it's important to The Public Burning *as well . . .*

Coover: Yes—where would Uncle Sam be without it?

And that whole final section there, that "dream time" experience as you call it—is that notion from the same source?

Coover: No, it's a primitive expression, but I first read it in the works of a French writer named Roger Caillois. "Dream time" is a ritual return to the mythic roots of a group of people. A tribe might set aside a time every year to do this, most often during initiation rites—to take the young who are coming into the tribe as adults and deliver them into an experience in which they relive the experiences of the civilizing heroes. If you go back to dream time, of course, you must first pretend that the tribe has not yet been civilized, that the rules you live by have not yet come into existence. So everything gets turned upside down, all the rules are upended, and then, through the mythic experiences of the civilizing hero, you re-create the society and discover your place in it. It usually involves dope, mock battles, sexual initiation, scarring, and so on, and is a very awesome and exciting experience, with the whole tribe involved. This idea of a ritual bath of prehistoric or preconscious experience was very attractive to me as I began developing the Rosenberg book, not merely for its contributions to the final section, but also because I realized that this was one of the great disruptive functions of art: to take the tribe back into dream time, pulling them in, letting them relive their preconscious life as formed for them by their tribe. So, though its function is more obvious at the end of the book, it is operative throughout. I think, for example, that many of the people who have remarked on the way they empathized with Nixon were, in fact, having this kind of experience. They were finding their way back to the formative elements of themselves that they had not suspected or questioned before.

Yes, critics and reviewers have often remarked on this surprising empathy they feel for Nixon. How did you choose him to be your central narrator in The Public Burning?

Coover: I'm not sure whether it was a matter of choice or necessity—he emerged from the texts, as it were. He has a way of doing that, fighting his way to the center stage; it's hard to stop him. Nevertheless, there were other possibilities. The book began as a little theater idea which grew into a series of rather raucous circus acts. I began to feel the need for a quieter voice to break in from time to time. I wanted someone who lived inside the mythology, accepting it, and close to the center, yet not quite in the center, off to the edge a bit, an observer. A number of characters auditioned for the part, but Nixon, when he appeared, proved ideal.

Why was that?

Coover: Well, for one thing he's such a self-conscious character. He has to analyze everything, work out all the parameters. He worries about things—and then there's his somewhat suspicious view of the world. He doesn't trust people very much—often for good reason. He lives in a world where trust is often misplaced, and he learned early to trust no one. And that included Eisenhower, J. Edgar Hoover, the whole government and judicial establishment. This attitude of his allowed me to reach skeptical conclusions through him about what was happening at the time of the Rosenberg executions, conclusions which would have been difficult from other viewpoints. For Eisenhower, if the FBI and the courts said so, then the Rosenbergs were guilty, they had to be. But Nixon could doubt this. He could imagine that his best ally, a man like Hoover, say, might not be letting him see everything. He could see the case in terms of who stood to gain what from it. And, of course, I also had it on faith from the beginning that any exploration of Nixon, this man who has played such a large role in American society since World War II, would have to reveal something about us all. It was another quality, though, that first called him forth in my mind—this was in 1969, just after he'd been elected president—and that was his peculiar talent for making a fool of himself.

You've spoken of seeing him as a kind of clown . . .

Coover: Yes. I was developing this series of circus acts—all these verbal acrobatics, death-defying highwire acts, showy parades, and so on—and I needed a clown to break in from time to time and do a few pratfalls. He was perfect for this. For a while, anyway. Eventually his real-life pratfalls nearly undid my own; I couldn't keep up with him. Had I been able to finish the book in time to publish it in 1972—as a kind of election-year gift to the incumbent, as it were—life would have been a lot easier. On the other hand, the Watergate episode forced me to work a lot harder, dig deeper, think beyond the pratfalls. So I probably ended up with a better book. Dearly as it cost me.

Your novella, "Whatever Happened to Gloomy Gus of the Chicago Bears," appeared in the American Review *during this period when you were working on* The Public Burning, *and it also deals with Nixon. Was it originally conceived as an integral part of your bigger project?*

Coover: No, it was completely separate, though there is a writerly connection in that I used it to work off some of my frustrations with *The Public Burning.* One of the peculiarities of *The Public Burning* was that it was made up of thousands and thousands of tiny fragments that had to be painstakingly stitched together, and it was not hard to lose patience with it. It was like a gigantic impossible puzzle. I was striving for a text that would seem to have been written by the whole nation through all its history, as though the sentences had been forming themselves all this time, accumulating toward this experience. I wanted thousands of echoes, all the sounds of the nation. Well, the idea was good, but the procedures were sometimes unbelieveably tedious. And at some low point I got a request from a popular magazine for a sports story. (That's what happens when you write a book with "baseball" in the title.) I turned them down, of course, but the idea stuck in my head somewhere and niggled at me. One of the most successful failures in Nixon's life had been his abortive high school and college football career, but I hadn't found much space for it in *The Public Burning*. In an idle moment I married this to his belief that if you just work hard enough at something you could achieve it, and considered an alternate career for him as a pro football player. As this would had to have taken place in the 1930s, it suddenly opened up for me the possibility of writing a good old-fashioned 1930s-style novella, full of personal material, thoughtful asides, and so on. Everything fell into place like magic, and I sat down at the machine and for the first time in years just banged happily away. It was the most joyful writing experience I ever had. It was very refreshing and probably helped me get on through to the end of *The Public Burning*.

There must have been some moments when you felt you'd never finish The Public Burning . . .

Coover: Oh yes, many times. The worst moment was probably when Hal Scharlatt, my editor at Dutton, died. Hal was a man with a lot of strengths and he was very supportive. He was the only man, I felt, who would ever publish this book. And he was a friend. When he died suddenly, a young man still, I went through a very sorrowful time. It was as though all the props had been pulled out from under this monstrous thing I was building, and I was about to be flattened by it. I no longer believed it would be published, and I had to write against this certainty. And I was very nearly right.

Your problems in getting the book published after you finished it are already nearly legendary. What happened, from your perspective?

Coover: It's a complicated story, but at its heart is a betrayal by my editor at Knopf, Bob Gottlieb. He failed to stand by me or the book when it counted, and so cost me a lot of harassment and a couple of years of my writing life. The book was finished in 1975. That summer, with a lot of seeming enthusiasm, Gottlieb wrestled the manuscript away from Dutton, promising to publish it in 1976, during the Bicentennial and the presidential election. I was living in England at the time and made a trip back to the States at my own expense that autumn in order to complete the editing with Gottlieb and with Ted Solotaroff of Bantam, the company involved in the paperback rights. But then, with the book going into production just after Christmas, the RCA and Random House corporation lawyers began putting pressure on Knopf, and Gottlieb soon knuckled under, even sug-

gesting to me on the phone that the book might after all be "immoral." I
understand that the final decision to suppress the book came from the Random House boss Bob Bernstein, who shortly thereafter won a Freedom of
the Press award. The book went from house to house then, amid a lot of
false rumors, getting rejected by one set of corporation lawyers after
another. I finally had to return to the States myself to sort it out. By then
I'd already lost over a year, the Bicentennial which might have cushioned
its publication had passed, and the book had become a kind of notorious
hot potato. Eventually Richard Seaver convinced Viking to do the book.
There were a lot of conditions. They refused to pay off Knopf, for example, on the reasonable grounds that Knopf had broken their contract with
me and were owed nothing—indeed, they had even made it more difficult
to get the book published successfully. Viking also held all my moneys due
in escrow for several years in case of legal costs, for which they held me
100 percent responsible. At the same time, the house lawyers did
everything they could to pressure me to emasculate the book, though in
the end, thanks mainly to Dick Seaver with support from Tom Guizburg,
the book did go through and was given a good production. As for Knopf,
they still held Bantam to the old contract and refused to let them go—and
thus, in effect, since Bantam's support was the key to Viking's willingness
to do the book, refused to let the book be published at all—until I signed a
separate statement saying that I owed them all advances paid. I am still
paying off that debt today. Finally, two-and-a-half disruptive years after I
had finished it, the book appeared.

*You just mentioned that the house lawyers tried to "emasculate" the
book. Did they succeed in directly affecting your aesthetic decisions—say,
in the final process?*

Coover: No. There were a lot of unpleasant pressures, but they were
resisted. Dick Seaver was a big help in this, acting as a buffer against the
worst of it. Both he and Solotaroff were very helpful editors, two of the
few good editors left in the industry. The book needed cutting and we
worked hard to do this, taking out maybe a quarter of the original
manuscript. Dealing with lawyers at the new house, Viking, was much
worse; we had some bad sessions, and I became very tenacious finally,
anxious to hang onto everything in fear that I was being asked for the
wrong reasons to take it out. The book's probably still informed a bit by
that anxious tenacity.

*As you were developing the book, did you see your role as being, in any
way, a vindicator of the Rosenbergs? I say this because it seemed pretty
evident to me in reading the book that you felt the Rosenbergs were, if not
completely innocent, then certainly not guilty enough to be executed.*

Coover: I originally felt back in 1966 that the execution of the
Rosenbergs had been a watershed event in American history which we had

somehow managed to forget or repress. I felt it was important to resurrect it and look at it again. By the time I'd finished researching the thing I was convinced, one, that they were not guilty as charged, and, two, even had they been, the punishment was hysterical and excessive. Indeed, given the macho arrogance of our military establishment, if anyone did contribute to the proliferation of information about the bomb, they probably did us all a favor. They were dead, there was no one to feel sorry for. I wasn't trying to vindicate them in that sense, but it was important that we remember it, that we not be so callous as to just shrug it off, or else it can happen again and again.

Various reviewers used the term "apocalyptic" in discribing the mood of this book. Is that accurate?

Coover: No. Apocalypse is a magical idea borrowed from Christian mythology and the notion of cyclical time and a purpose in history. But short of apocalypse there's always disaster, which we have visited upon us from day to day. We have had, in that sense, an unending sequence of apocalypses, long before Christianity began and up to the present. From generation to generation, whole peoples get wiped from the face of the earth, so for them the apocalypse has already happened. And we can be pretty sure there's more to come. I mean, who can stop it? And technologically it's so much more frightening today. So in a lot of contemporary fiction there's a sense of foreboding disaster which is part of the times, just like self-reflexive fictions.

Let's talk about what you are working on right now. When I met you seven or eight years ago, you were working on a long book called Lucky Pierre, *which you were very excited about. Are you still engaged in that project?*

Coover: Yes, but other things have intervened. I've been working on theater pieces, radio plays, things like that. And shorter fictions. After the gigantism of *The Public Burning*, this is the year of the small book. Five of them, in fact. Viking is publishing one, *A Political Fable*, which originally appeared in 1968 as "The Cat in the Hat for President," and the other four are being done by small presses. Two of them, *After Lazarus* and *Hair o' the Chine*, are in the form of filmscripts, written nearly twenty years ago. The other two are new novella-length fictions, *Charlie in the House of Rue*, from Penmaen Press, and *Spanking the Maid*, which Bruccoli-Clark is publishing. And there's another novel-length fiction, not loo long I hope, which is on my desk and walls right now, so *Lucky Pierre* will have to wait yet a bit longer. Impatient as he is, the restless fucker.

An Interview with
Don DeLillo

Of American novelists who began publishing in the '70s, Don DeLillo is one of the most prolific. He is also one of the most elusive. While his novels are located in America's fascinations—entertainment, big-time sport, intrigue—they are written with a detachment that causes reviewers to praise him for very different, sometimes contradictory intentions. The books are elusive because, for DeLillo, fiction draws its power from and moves toward mystery. Elusive, too, because DeLillo has not joined the literary auxiliary: he does not sit on panels, appear on television, judge contests, review books, or teach creative writing. He travels and writes.

DeLillo agreed to do this interview from what he thought was the safe distance of Greece. When I managed to get to Athens in September, 1979, and not long after I met him, he handed me a business card engraved with his name and "I don't want to talk about it." He does not like to discuss his work, but he is a witty conversationalist, an informed and generous guide, invaluable in Greek taxis and restaurants. At forty-three, DeLillo in his jeans and sneakers has the look of a just-retired athlete. He walks Athens' crowded streets like a linebacker, on his toes, eyes shifting, watching for crazed drivers among the merely reckless. When we taped in his apartment near Mt. Lycabetus, he spoke quietly and slowly, in a slight New York accent, searching for the precision he insists upon in his fiction. One soon understands from his uninflected tone, which sounds more like thought than talk, and from the silences between his short declarative sentences that Don DeLillo's elusiveness comes naturally, necessarily, from his concern with what he quotes Hermann Broch as calling "the word beyond speech."

DeLillo's books offer a precise and thorough anthropology of the present, an account of our kinship in myths, media, and conspiracies. His first novel, *Americana* (1971), begins in the television industry and moves cross country searching for relief from the image. The heroes of *End Zone* (1972) and *Great Jones Street* (1973) are football and rock stars trying to work free of their public mythologies. In *Players* (1977) and *Running Dog* (1978), DeLillo writes about up-to-date conspiracies prompted by the appeal of terrorism and pornography. The book DeLillo considers his best is *Ratner's Star* (1976), where he combines elements of children's literature, science fiction, and mathematics to create a conceptual monster. Like his more realistic fictions, *Ratner's Star* uses its bulk and abstraction to imply all that cannot be spoken in characters, words, and numbers.

—*Tom LeClair*

Why do reference books give only your date of birth and the publication dates of your books?

DeLillo: Silence, exile, cunning, and so on. It's my nature to keep quiet about most things. Even the ideas in my work. When you try to unravel something you've written, you belittle it in a way. It was created as a mystery, in part. Here is a new map of the world; it is seven shades of blue. If you're able to be straightforward and penetrating about this invention of yours, it's almost as though you're saying it wasn't altogether necessary. The sources weren't deep enough. Maybe this view is overrefined and too personal. But I think it helps explain why some writers are unable or unwilling to discuss their work. There's an element of tampering. And there's a crossover that can be difficult to make. What you write, what you say about it. The vocabularies don't match. It's hard to correspond to reality, to talk sensibly about an idea or a theme that originates in a writer's desire to restructure reality.

But here I am, talking.

Of your six novels, which one is closest to your own experience?

DeLillo: *Americana*, probably, in the sense that I drew material more directly from people and situations I knew firsthand. I was hurling things at the page. At the time I lived in a small apartment with no stove and the refrigerator in the bathroom and I thought first novels written under these circumstances ought to be novels in which great chunks of experience are hurled at the page. So that's what I did. The original manuscript was higher than my radio.

It's not an autobiographical novel. But I did use many things I'd seen, heard, knew about.

*Your work seems to me quite different in tone and in language from
most contemporary fiction. I wondered if you felt that you were onto
something different.*

DeLillo: When I was about halfway through *Americana*, which took
roughly four years to do, it occurred to me almost in a flash that I was a
writer. Whatever tentativeness I'd felt about the book dropped away. I
finished it in a spirit of getting a difficult, unwieldy thing out of the way, in
a spirit of having proved certain things to myself. With *End Zone* I felt I
was doing something easier and looser. I was working closer to my instincts. I paced things differently. Balances became important, starts and
stops. I approached certain things from unusual angles, I think. Some of
the characters have a made-up nature. They are pieces of jargon. They
engage in wars of jargon with each other. There is a mechanical element, a
kind of fragmented self-consciousness. I took this further in *Ratner's Star*,
where characters don't just open their mouths to say hello. They have to
make the action part of the remark. "My mouth says hello." "My ears
hear." The characters are words on paper. This isn't necessarily true of the
other books. *End Zone* and *Ratner's Star* are books of games, books in
which fiction itself is a sort of game.

My work also grew more precise. I began to study things more,
disassemble them. Possibly what I was studying was ways to use the
language. It may be the case that with *End Zone* I began to suspect that
language was a subject as well as an instrument in my work, although I'd
find it hard to say in what ways exactly.

Games are important in your fiction. Were they an early interest?

DeLillo: The games I've written about have more to do with rules and
boundaries than with the freewheeling street games I played when I was
growing up. People whose lives are not clearly shaped or marked off may
feel a deep need for rules of some kind. People leading lives of almost total
freedom and possibility may secretly crave rules and boundaries, some
kind of control in their lives. Most games are carefully structured. They
satisfy a sense of order and they even have an element of dignity about
them. In *Ratner's Star* someone says, "Strict rules add dignity to a game."
There are many games in *Ratner's Star*, and the book is full of adults acting
like children—which is another reason why people play games, of course.

In *Running Dog*, Selvy is playing a game when he leads his pursuers in a
straight line to southwest Texas, where he knows they'll try to kill him. In
End Zone, one of the games is football. There are others. Games provide a
frame in which we can try to be perfect. Within sixty-minute limits or one-
hundred-yard limits or the limits of a game board, we can look for perfect
moments or perfect structures. In my fiction I think this search sometimes
turns out to be a cruel delusion.

In *Players*, the rules become almost metaphysical. They involve inner restrictions. There's some of that in *Running Dog* as well. Empty landscapes seem to inspire games.

Your third novel, Great Jones Street, *is set in the empty landscape of its title. How did you happen to write about a rock star?*

DeLillo: It's a game at the far edge. It's an extreme situation. I think rock is a music of loneliness and isolation. The Doors work very well at the beginning of the film *Apocalypse Now*. A man with a half-shattered mind, alone in a rented room. Noise, electricity, excess, Vietnam—all these things are tied together in *Great Jones Street*, and a certain tension is drawn out of the hero's silence, his withdrawal. Bucky Wunderlick's music moves from political involvement to extreme self-awareness to childlike babbling.

Perhaps because of the game element, reviewers of your fiction have a hard time locating your attitudes toward your characters.

DeLillo: My attitudes aren't directed toward characters at all. I don't feel sympathetic toward some characters, unsympathetic toward others. I don't love some characters, feel contempt for others. They have attitudes; I don't.

Some people may have felt I disliked Pammy and Lyle in *Players*. Not true. I think these two characters are more typical of contemporary Americans than people want to believe. Lyle is an intelligent, high-strung, spiritually undernourished person. Pammy is more humane. She is also more prone to be affected by the shallow ideas drifting through her world, and she is constantly afraid. I can talk about them this way, but I can't talk about them as people I love or hate. They're people I recognize.

What writing means to me is trying to make interesting, clear, beautiful language. Working at sentences and rhythms is probably the most satisfying thing I do as a writer. I think after a while a writer can begin to know himself through his language. He sees someone or something reflected back at him from these constructions. Over the years it's possible for a writer to shape himself as a human being through the language he uses. I think written language, fiction, goes that deep. He not only sees himself but begins to make himself or remake himself. Of course, this is mysterious and subjective territory.

Writing also means trying to advance the art. Fiction hasn't quite been filled in or done in or worked out. We make our small leaps. This is the reason for the introduction to *Players*. All the main characters, seven of them, are introduced in an abstract way. They don't have names. Their connections to each other are not clear in all cases. They're on an airplane, watching a movie, but all the other seats are empty. They're isolated, above the story, waiting to be named. It's a kind of model-building. It's the novel in miniature. We can call it pure fiction in the sense that the characters have been momentarily separated from the storytelling apparatus. They're still ideas, vague shapes.

What do you think of the renewed interest in "moral fiction"? Anthony Burgess wrote that the term "evil" has no meaning in Running Dog. *Another reviewer complained that the book was reductive.*

DeLillo: Moll Robbins is the weathervane for all the avarice in the book, the maneuverings for power. Her own imperfections may frustrate the reader who is looking for a moral center. The evil, or whatever we call it, is there. We can't position these acts and attitudes around a nineteenth-century heroine. They float in a particular social and cultural medium. A modern American medium. Half-heartedness and indifference are very much to the point. People tend to walk away from their own conspiracies. Hitler is a fatigued and defeated man dressed up like Charlie Chaplin.

I'd say the style and language reflect the landscape more than they reflect the writer's state of mind. The bareness is really the bareness and starkness of lower Manhattan and southwest Texas. And since the book is essentially a thriller, I felt the prose should be pared down. But the reductiveness belongs to character and setting, not to the author's view of things. The author was amused, by and large. The author thought most of the characters were damned funny.

Glen Selvy, who was not one of the funny ones, believes that choice is a subtle form of disease. He feels he has to commit what is in effect a ritual suicide. He is leaving behind whatever is difficult about life, whatever is complicated. I try to understand what makes Selvy go. I don't patronize him or feel contempt for him because he leads a life that is simplified to an extreme degree. Selvy feels that knowing his weapons, how to take them apart and put them back together, is a form of self-respect. He finds his truth in violence. He is an adept of violence, a semi-mystic.

Is this the case with many of your main characters? They withdraw, reduce their relations, empty out, discipline themselves.

DeLillo: I think they see freedom and possibility as being too remote from what they perceive existence to mean. They feel instinctively that there's a certain struggle, a solitude they have to confront. The landscape is silent, whether it's a desert, a small room, a hole in the ground. The voice you have to answer is your own voice. In *End Zone*, Gary Harkness stops eating and drinking in the last paragraph. He goes on a hunger strike. He isn't protesting anything or reacting to anything specific. He is paring things down. He is struggling, trying to face something he felt had to be faced. Something nameless. I thought this was interesting. I couldn't give a name to it. He just stops eating. He refuses to eat.

In End Zone *you have a character taking a college course in "the untellable." That's not entirely facetious, is it?*

DeLillo: I do wonder if there is something we haven't come across. Is there another, clearer language? Will we speak it and hear it when we die? Did we know it before we were born? If there are life forms in other galaxies, how do they communicate? What do they sound like?

The "untellable" points to the limitations of language. Is there something we haven't discovered about speech? Is there more? Maybe this is why there's so much babbling in my books. Babbling can be frustrated speech, or it can be a purer form, an alternate speech. I wrote a short story that ends with two babies babbling at each other in a car. This was something I'd seen and heard, and it was a dazzling and unforgettable scene. I felt these babies *knew* something. They were talking, they were listening, they were *commenting*, and above and beyond it all they were taking an immense pleasure in the exchange.

Glossolalia is interesting because it suggests there's another way to speak, there's a very different language lurking somewhere in the brain.

Are you interested in specialized language?

DeLillo: Specialized languages can be very beautiful. Mysterious and precise at the same time. In *Ratner's Star* there's a dictionary definition of the word "cosine" that illustrates this, I think. Mathematics and astronomy are full of beautiful nomenclature. Science in general has given us a new language to draw from. Some writers shrink from this. Science is guilty; the language of science is tainted by horror and destruction. To me, science is a source of new names, new connections between people and the world. Rilke said we had to rename the world. Renaming suggests an innocence and a rebirth. Some words adapt, and these are the ones we use in our new world.

Then there is jargon, which I associate with television for some reason. The one was invented to deliver the other. But I'm interested in the way people talk, jargon or not. The original idea for *Players* was based on what could be called the intimacy of language. What people who live together really sound like. Pammy and Lyle were to address each other in the private language they'd constructed over years of living together. Unfinished sentences, childlike babbling, animal noises, foreign accents, ethnic dialects, mimicry, all of that. It's as though language is something we wear. The more we know someone, the easier it is to undress, to become childlike. But the idea got sidetracked, and only fragments survive in the finished book.

Would you name some writers with whom you have affinities?

DeLillo: This is the great bar mitzvah question. Probably the movies of Jean-Luc Godard had a more immediate effect on my early work than anything I'd ever read. Movies in general may be the not-so-hidden influence on a lot of modern writing, although the attraction has waned, I think. The strong image, the short ambiguous scene, the dream sense of some movies, the artificiality, the arbitrary choices of some directors, the

cutting and editing. The power of images. This is something I kept thinking about when I was writing *Americana*. This power had another effect.
It caused people to walk around all day saying, "Movies can do *so much*."
It's movies in part that seduced people into thinking the novel was dead.
The power of the film image seemed to be overwhelming our little world of
print. Film could do so much. Print could only trot across the page. But
movies and novels are too closely related to work according to shifting
proportions. If the novel dies, movies will die with it.

The books I remember and come back to seem to be ones that
demonstrate the possibilities of fiction. *Pale Fire, Ulysses, The Death of
Virgil, Under the Volcano, The Sound and the Fury*—these come to mind.
There's a drive and a daring that go beyond technical invention. I think it's
right to call it a life-drive even though these books deal at times very
directly with death. No optimism, no pessimism. No homesickness for lost
values or for the way fiction used to be written. These books open out onto
some larger mystery. I don't know what to call it. Maybe Hermann Broch
would call it "the word beyond speech."

There's an allusion to Wittgenstein in End Zone. *Do you find something
important in his work?*

DeLillo: I've read parts of the *Tractatus*, but I have no formal training
in mathematical logic and I couldn't say a thing about the technical aspects
of the book. I like the way he uses the language. Even in translation, it's
very evocative. It's like reading Martian. The language is mysteriously
simple and self-assured. It suggests without the slightest arrogance that
there's no alternative to these remarks. The statements are machine
tooled. Wittgenstein is the language of outer space, a very precise race of
people.

*There are references to Zen in most of your books. Would you consider
it an influence on your work?*

DeLillo: I may have used the word several times, but I think only in
Americana is there any kind of extended reference, and it has more to do
with people playing at Eastern religion than anything else. I know very little about Zen. I'm interested in religion as a discipline and a spectacle, as
something that drives people to extreme behavior. Noble, violent,
depressing, beautiful. Being raised as a Catholic was interesting because
the ritual had elements of art to it and it prompted feelings that art
sometimes draws out of us. I think I reacted to it the way I react today to
theater. Sometimes it was awesome; sometimes it was funny. High funeral
masses were a little of both, and they're among my warmest childhood
memories.

Are you interested in mathematics for the same reasons?

DeLillo: I started reading mathematics because I wanted a fresh view
of the world. I wanted to immerse myself in something as remote as possi-

ble from my own interests and my own work. I became fascinated and ended up writing a novel and then a play about mathematicians. Aside from everything else, pure mathematics is a kind of secret knowledge. It's carried on almost totally outside the main currents of thought. It's a language almost no one speaks. In *Ratner's Star* I tried to weave this secret life of mankind into the action of the book in the form of a history of mathematics, a cult history, the names of the leaders kept secret until the second half of the book, the mirror image, when the names appear in reverse order. This purest of sciences brings out a religious feeling in people. Numbers in particular have always had a mystical appeal. Numbers work in such surprising ways it's hard not to feel a sense of mystery and wonder.

Do you consider Ratner's Star *to be your best book?*

DeLillo: We're supposed to say the one I'm doing now is my best book. Otherwise, *Ratner's Star*, yes.

What were some of the influences on and intentions of Ratner's Star?

DeLillo: There's a structural model, the Alice books of Lewis Carroll. The headings of the two parts—"Adventures" and "Reflections"—refer to *Alice's Adventures in Wonderland* and *Through the Looking Glass*. The connection, as I say, is structural. It involves format, not characters or themes or story except in the loosest sense. It works from the particular to the general. What is real in *Alice* becomes an abstraction in *Ratner's Star*. The rabbit hole of Chapter One, for instance, becomes "substratum" — early or underground mathematics. There is also a kind of guiding spirit. This is Pythagoras. The mathematician-mystic. The whole book is informed by this link or opposition, however you see it, and the characters keep bouncing between science and superstition.

I was trying to produce a book that would be naked structure. The structure would be the book and vice versa. I wanted the book to become what it was about. Abstract structures and connective patterns. A piece of mathematics, in short. To do this I felt I had to reduce the importance of people. The people had to play a role subservient to pattern, form, and so on. This is difficult, of course, for all concerned, but I believed I was doing something new and was willing to take the risk. A book that is really all outline. My notes for the book interest me almost as much as the book does. This is an incriminating remark, but there you are.

I hadn't started out to do this. All I had in mind was a fourteen-year-old mathematical genius who is asked to decipher a message from outer space. Things started happening to this simple idea. Connections led to other connections. I began to find things I didn't know I was looking for. Mathematics led to science fiction. Logic led to babbling. Language led to games. Games led to mathematics. When I discovered uncanny links to Alice and *her* world, I decided I had to follow. Down the rabbit hole.

A friend of mine said it was like reading the first half of one book and the second half of a completely different book. It's true in a way. There's a strong demarcation between the parts. They are opposites. Adventures, reflections. Positive, negative. Discrete, continuous. Day, night. Left brain, right brain. But they also link together. The second part bends back to the first. Somebody ought to make a list of books that seem to bend back on themselves. I think Malcolm Lowry saw *Under the Volcano* as a wheel-like structure. And in *Finnegans Wake* we're meant to go from the last page to the first. In different ways I've done this myself. *Great Jones Street* bends back on itself in the sense that the book is the narrator's way of resurfacing. *Players* begins in darkness with an unidentified voice talking about motels. This is Lyle's voice, and the book ends with Lyle in a motel room in Canada, in blinding light. In *Ratner's Star*, Softly, who is a sort of white rabbit figure, leads Billy into the hole that will take him back to the beginning of the book. In Chapter One Billy had a bandage on his finger—the finger he cut near the end of the book.

In Ratner's Star, *in a much-quoted passage, you refer to a class of writers who write "crazed prose" and books that are not meant to be read. Is* Ratner's Star *in that category?*

DeLillo: No it isn't, although I think I felt some of the pull of crazed prose. There's an element of contempt for meanings. You want to write outside the usual framework. You want to dare readers to make a commitment you know they can't make. That's part of it. There's also the sense of drowning in information and in the mass awareness of things. Everybody seems to know everything. Subjects surface and are totally exhausted in a matter of days or weeks, totally played out by the publishing industry and the broadcast industry. Nothing is too arcane to escape the treatment, the process. Making things difficult for the reader is less an attack on the reader than it is on the age and its facile knowledge-market. The writer is driven by his conviction that some truths aren't arrived at so easily, that life is still full of mystery, that it might be better for you, Dear Reader, if you went back to the Living section of your newspaper because this is the dying section and you don't really want to be here. This writer is working against the age and so he feels some satisfaction at not being widely read. He is diminished by an audience.

Do you think about your readers?

DeLillo: I don't have a sense of a so-called ideal reader and certainly not of a readership, that terrific entity. I write for the page. My mail tells me nothing useful about what might be out there in the way of readers. It comes in driblets, much of it from crazy people.

Do you think they feel they have a sympathetic correspondent? There are crazy people in the backgrounds of your books.

DeLillo: Yes, they've crept in. The streets are full of disturbed people.

For a long time I wondered where they were coming from, so many, at once. We now learn they've been let out of asylums and hospitals and into halfway houses and welfare hotels. I've always thought New York was a medieval city and this is another sign of that. They speak a kind of broken language. It's part of the language of cities, really. In *Players* these people are always talking to Pammy. They talk to Diana in "The Engineer of Moonlight." In the subway arcades under Fourteenth Street you hear mostly Spanish and black English with bits of Yiddish, German, Italian, and Chinese, and then there's this strange broken language. The language of the insane is stronger than all the others. It's the language of the self, the pain of self.

Is obsession necessary to create fiction that's better than pedestrian?

DeLillo: Obsession is interesting to writers because it involves a centering and a narrowing down, an intense convergence. An obsessed person is an automatic piece of fiction. He has a purity of movement, an integrity. There is a kind of sheen about him. To a writer, an obsessed person is *right there*. He is already on the page.

When it comes to writers being obsessed, I have one notion. Obsession as a state seems so close to the natural condition of a novelist at work on a book that there may be nothing else to say about it. It's not possible to say whether an obsession can drive someone to do better work. He's probably not obsessed. If he is obsessed, it's probably beside the point.

How do you prepare to write?

DeLillo: By doing nothing. Keeping life simple. Giving ideas time to sort themselves out. I try to be patient. Time usually does the selecting for me. What I'm left with at the end of a given period is usually what I need to begin.

What about the actual mechanics?

DeLillo: In the beginning I work brief shifts. The important mechanics are mental. A lot of mental testing goes on. Promising threads develop out of certain ideas or characters, and some of these lines reach almost to the end of the book, or out into infinity, since the book doesn't have anything resembling an end at this point. Other lines are very short. Again, most of this is mental. It's stored. Some things I'll take right to the machine. Writing is intense concentration, and the typewriter can act as a focusing tool or memory tool. It enables me to bore in on something more strongly. It also enables me to see the words being formed. What the words look like is important. How they look in combination. I have to see the words.

Past the early stages I work longer periods. I find myself nearing the end of certain early lines of thought. This represents progress. It reminds me that the work doesn't actually go out into infinity. These identical, shapeless, satisfying days will come to an end somewhere down the line.

There's some very abstract spatial analysis of characters or situations in your fiction. Would you comment on its function?

DeLillo: It's a way to take psychology out of a character's mind and into the room he occupies. I try to examine psychological states by looking at people in rooms, objects in rooms. It's a way of saying we can know something important about a character by the way he sees himself in relation to objects. People in rooms have always seemed important to me. I don't know why or ask myself why, but sometimes I feel I'm *painting* a character in a room, and the most important thing I can do is set him up in relation to objects, shadows, angles.

Does place have any effect on your composition?

DeLillo: Sometimes things insinuate themselves onto the page. When I was working on *Great Jones Street*, there was dynamiting going on all the time, and eventually these construction noises turned up in the book. But place has more important meanings. So much modern fiction is located precisely nowhere. This is Beckett and Kafka insinuating themselves onto the page. Their work is so woven into the material of modern life that it's not surprising so many writers choose to live there, or choose to have their characters live there. Fiction without a sense of real place is automatically a fiction of estrangement, and of course this is the point. As theory it has its attractions, but I can't write that way myself. I'm too interested in what real places look like and what names they have. Place is color and texture. It's tied up with memory and roots and pigments and rough surfaces and language, too. I'm interested in what mathematicians say. No matter how pure their work is, it has to be responsive to the real world, one way or another, in order to keep its vitality and to cleanse itself of effeteness and self-absorption.

Would you comment on your play "The Engineer of Moonlight"? It seems to be a distillation of many of the ideas and voices in your fiction.

DeLillo: We talked earlier about people in rooms. The play is just that. People talking, people silent, people motionless, people juxtaposed with objects. There are four characters. What connects them is the awesome power of their loving. The main character is Eric Lighter, a once-great mathematician who is now a pathetic but compelling ruin. If the play has a line of development at all, it hinges on whether Eric's former wife will abandon a recent marriage and successful career to help the others transcribe and type Eric's half-insane memoirs, along with other day-to-day chores and obligations. The idea is absurd on the face of it. Diana ridicules the notion. Toward the end of the play she leaves the stage still denying that she'll stay. But we know she still feels a powerful love for Eric, for the aura of greatness that clings to him, and we feel uncertain about taking her at her word. The suggestion that she may stay is contained in a strange board game she'd played with the others earlier in Act

Two. A game involving words and logic used in unfamiliar ways. If we take this game as a play within the play, what we see is that Diana, who has never played before, gradually comes to understand the strange and complex nature of the game—an understanding the audience doesn't share. Toward the end she is elated; she is saying it all begins to fit, the colors, the shapes, the names. She wants to play.

An Interview with
E. L. Doctorow

On April 3, 1980, as I drove up the hill on Broadview Avenue in New Rochelle, New York, toward E. L. Doctorow's beautiful turn-of-the-century house, I sensed something familiar about the drive. But only after the author had greeted me and was fixing us some coffee did it strike me that we were sitting in the house described in the opening words of *Ragtime*: "In 1902 Father built a house at the crest of the Broadview Avenue hill in New Rochelle, New York. It was a three-story brown shingle with dormers, bay windows and a screen porch. Striped awnings shaded the windows." This realization produced in me that same peculiar sensation familiar to millions of *Ragtime*'s readers, who were repeatedly forced to consider the thin line which separates fact from fiction, history from storytelling. The street was the same street that Harry Houdini had cruised along in his black forty-five-horsepower Pope-Toledo Runabout. It was also the same road that Coalhouse Walker had traveled to see Sarah, before his fancy motorcar was ruined, Sarah died, and he set out to take his own ultimately tragic revenge. Here I was, sipping coffee and eating breakfast rolls in Father's very own kitchen . . .

Ed Doctorow is a handsome, distinguished-looking man in his early fifties. As we made small talk in preparation for the interview which follows, he quickly put me at ease with his humor and utter lack of pretentiousness. The telephone was ringing constantly during the several hours I was there—prepublication activities for *Loon Lake*, his novel which was due out in the summer. Somehow or other Ed easily managed to shift back and forth between his phone and my tape recorder.

Doctorow has had an impressive and meteoric career. After graduating from Kenyon College in the early 1950s and doing some graduate work at Columbia, he began his career as reader of fiction for television and film studios. This led him into editorial work, first at New American Library and then as editor-in-chief for Dial Press in the 1960s. As he explains, his reading of a succession of awful Western filmscripts helped inspire his first novel, *Welcome to Hard Times* (1960), a darkly humorous saga of the Wild West. *Big as Life* (1966), a semi-science-fiction work, proved to be Doctorow's biggest literary disappointment to date ("Unquestionably it's the worst I've done," he says). However, *The Book of Daniel* (1971), a fictionalized account of the Rosenberg case and its violent, radicalized legacy during the tumultuous 1960s, established Doctorow as one of America's most important writers. Nominated for the National Book Award, *Daniel* anticipated many of the innovative techniques that Doctorow would later employ in *Ragtime* (1975) and *Loon Lake* (1980): the mixing of fact and fiction; the use of various cinematic techniques, including the inter-cutting of various narrative levels; the use of rhythm and pacing in sentences to create specific effects. *Ragtime* is one of those rarest of books—a bold, experimental novel of great seriousness which also struck the public's fancy. It rode high on the bestseller lists for months and was made into a film directed by Milos Forman. *Loon Lake*, a book dealing with Depression-plagued America, is probably his most daring novel in terms of literary form; it has also been well received by critics and has made the bestseller lists.

—Larry McCaffery

You spent the first few years of your professional life as an editor, first with New American Library and then with Dial Press. What was the background of this involvement with editing?
Doctorow: I knew from a very early age that I wanted to write. The question was, How was I going to support myself while I was writing? Somehow I stumbled onto the profession of reader. There was a demand for expert readers on the part of television and film companies in New York during the 1950s. You'd read a novel and write a synopsis of it and tack on a critique in which you said whether you thought this story or novel should be adapted for film or television. I immediately declared myself an expert reader, did a couple of books on a try-out basis to establish my credentials, and I was off and running. I had myself a fairly active career.
How active is "fairly active"?
Doctorow: I was reading a book a day, seven days a week, and writing synopses of them—I suppose each synopsis was no less than 1,200

words. I was getting an average of ten or twelve dollars a book, so I was making pretty good money—anywhere between seventy and a hundred dollars a week.

This sounds pretty intense . . .

Doctorow: Yes, it was. No time to do my own work. But then I was offered a staff job as an inside reader for a film company. An inside reader worked on a salary, so this job paid me the same amount of money no matter how much work I did.

Did this staff job lead you directly to editing?

Doctorow: Well, I worked at it for a year, or a year and a half. Then one day the company I worked for found out about a book that had a good advance word. There's great competition among film companies, you know, to get an early look at these things. What my boss, the story editor, discovered was that there was a set of galleys over at the paperback house called NAL—New American Library. He had a friend there, the editor-in-chief, who agreed that we could have an early, clandestine look at this miraculous work, but he wouldn't let the galleys out of his office. So I went over there and quickly read the thing; the editor-in-chief, Victor Weybright, had said, "When you're through, come tell me what you think." I did, and eighteen months later he called up and asked if I'd like a job.

I began as an associate editor at NAL, became a senior editor, and stayed there for five years. It was a great life, publishing good books in big printings—and, in those days, selling them for pocket change. You could feel good about the way you made your living—reprinting a first novel that nobody knew about, working on everything from Ian Fleming to Shakespeare to books on astronomy and every other damn thing, and seeing those books go out with price tags of fifty or seventy-five cents. I felt very good.

Why did you change houses?

Doctorow: Mostly because the owners of this wonderful paperback house sold their company to the Times-Mirror Corporation of Los Angeles. Within the year it became quite clear that things were not the same, not as much fun. Publishing is a business of personal enthusiasms, hunches, instincts. The Times-Mirror brought in business consultants and personnel people who had no sympathy for this kind of work. The soul went out of the place. Along about then a man named Richard Baron, who was part-owner of the Dial Press with Dell Publishing Company, started to talk to me about coming to work there. Eventually I took that job as editor-in-chief, which I held for five years. I got to be vice-president and then publisher before I quit to write full-time.

As an editor, did you find yourself favoring any certain type of book—championing the kinds of nontraditional approaches that you yourself were developing during this period, for example?

Doctorow: No, not at all. The publishing mentality, ideally, is generous, expansive, catholic in taste. You have to be receptive to lots of things, to know the value of different things. This might mean loving a book because it's highly and seriously accomplished or because it's a good trashy novel with no literary pretensions whatsoever. Or to think up an idea for a book and find just the right writer to do it. The point is that you don't have a set of rules or preconceptions to restrict your availability to what comes along; you just have to be open to as much as possible and pick and choose from what flows by.

What sort of effect did your experiences as an editor have on your own writing?

Doctorow: I don't imagine I would have written *Welcome to Hard Times* if I'd not been working at that film company and reading lousy Western screenplays week after week. I had no affinity for the genre—I'd never even been west of Ohio. I thought Ohio *was* the West. Oh, as a kid I'd liked Tom Mix radio programs and maybe I went to see a few movies; but, really, I had no feeling for Westerns. But from reading all these screenplays and being forced to think about the use of Western myth, I developed a kind of contrapuntal idea of what the West must really have been like. Finally one day I thought, "*I* can lie better than these people." So I wrote a story and I showed it to the story editor, Albert Johnson, who was by now a friend, and he said, "This is good. Why don't you turn it into a novel?" And so I did.

Was this your first try at a novel?

Doctorow: No. I had been trying to write a book about a boy in college. I was actually working on that. *Welcome to Hard Times* was crucial for me for a couple of reasons. First, it showed me my strength, which was *not* autobiographical writing. Somehow I was the kind of writer who had to put myself through prisms to find the right light—I had to filter myself from my imagination in order to write. The second thing I learned was that all writing begins as accident. Eventually it will come around to who you are, it will find some essence, but the *start* of a book is necessarily contingent. You can't plan it. If I had not worked as a reader and gotten angry at what I was reading, I would not have written that particular novel.

You've said somewhere that Ragtime *began as a set of images that were related to this house we're sitting in. Is this the sort of accident you're talking about that gets you going on a novel?*

Doctorow: Yes, that's exactly the kind of thing. In the case of *Ragtime*, the creative accident occurred one day as I was staring at the wall; I started to write about the wall. This house was built in 1906. And I was off. The other element for me in this kind of creative accident is my own desperation. I've learned that each time around I have to reach a truly desperate moment. I need to really feel very keenly a crisis of despair in order to find the level of recklessness or freedom that allows me to write the book. This has happened time and again. In the case of *The Book of Daniel* I knew the subject, it interested me, and I thought I could hang an awful lot on it. I spent about six months' initial work on it—about a hundred and fifty pages. And those pages were terrible, awful. At this point I thought that if I could ruin a momentous subject like this, then I had no business writing. I threw away the pages and in a state of reckless, irresponsible, almost manic despair I sat down at the typewriter and started writing what turned out to be *The Book of Daniel*. The point is that it had to be done in his voice, not my own. And I had to really hit bottom to come to this realization. This terrible moment happens with every book, sometimes earlier and sometimes later. In the case of the book I just finished, *Loon Lake*, it happened fairly late, while the book was in its third draft.

You've mentioned that you knew very early that you wanted to be a writer, and yet you studied philosophy at Kenyon College as an undergraduate. How did these two things jibe?

Doctorow: I went to Kenyon to study with John Crowe Ransom. He was a wonderful teacher but also an Olympian presence. As much as I learned from him—I studied prosody with him, for instance—somehow I was inclined to a different kind of mental life. And I found it, I thought, in philosophy. I had a mind for philosophy, and although I kept taking English courses it was never with the same excitement I felt for my philosophy work. The philosophy department there was very small and I had some very fine teachers, but the man I responded to most was Philip Blair Rice, a brilliant philosopher and also the associate editor of the *Kenyon Review*—Ransom being the editor. I studied metaphysics and aesthetics with Rice and ethics and logic with his colleague, Virgil Aldridge. I loved it. During that four-year period I did relatively little writing and had little interest in the established English department requirements. Instead, I did philosophy and got into theater as a student actor. I had no plan; I just did what interested me. I was erratic, totally without discipline, full of longings, feelings of power, and not knowing what to attach them to. When I graduated, Rice said to me, "Doctorow, you're one of the five best students I've every had—and of the five, you're the least informed."

What made you turn away from an academic career in philosophy?

Doctorow: I don't think I ever intended to pursue it. On graduation day, Ransom introduced me to Robert Penn Warren, who was getting an honorary degree and who happened at that time to be teaching playwriting at the Yale Drama School. I had written a play at Kenyon and had acted in several. In my senior year I'd decided I wanted to be a playwright. Ransom said, "Red, I think this young man ought to go to Yale," and Warren said, "All right, Pappy." What a beautiful day in June. But this was during the Korean War, and my draft board told me I would have only one year for graduate studies before I'd get packed off—and the Yale M.F.A. was a three-year program. So I ended up going to Columbia for one year, studying English drama and acting and directing, and then I was drafted, just as they had promised. And I never went to Yale. But it's almost as good that Ransom spoke for me on my graduation day.

Welcome to Hard Times and Big as Life both obviously lie pretty far outside the realm of traditional, realistic fiction. Did you have any sense when you were starting out of reacting against a certain type of fiction, of trying to create your own special niche as a writer? I ask this because your early books are so startlingly different from the kinds of books that most other serious writers were producing during that period.

Doctorow: I think I've already almost answered that question by suggesting the accident of my involvement with *Welcome to Hard Times.* What happens is that you do something and only then do you figure out what it is. You write to find out what you're writing. It was only after I had written those first two books, for example, that I developed a rationale for the approaches I had taken—that I liked the idea of using disreputable genre materials and doing something serious with them. I liked invention. I liked myth.

I take it, then, that you were hardly under the spell of any particular writers at the time—you weren't relating, either positively or negatively, to the sorts of things you were seeing every day on your desk as an editor.

Doctorow: As an editor I spent a lot of time taking books and making them work. Structuring them. Cracking them open and putting them back together. Getting their authors to do more—or less. I liked doing that, and I suppose my own books have gained from the practice. But I've never related to my contemporaries on a competitive basis. Mailer, for instance, was a long-established writer when I started writing; I had read his first book in high school. That whole generation of writers—Mailer, Styron—they're not ten years older than I am, but they've been around a long time. They all flashed pretty early and got the hang of literary combativeness. I think this might have something to do with their going through World War II. When people fight in a war, it takes them a while—and society a while—to wind down afterward. If at all. The war keeps going on after the war is over. Different generations imprint differently, of course. It's the fate of my generation that we've never shared a monumental experience. We think of ourselves as loners.

So you've never seen yourself as part of a literary movement which reacted against the type of fiction being written in the '40s and '50s?

Doctorow: I don't think the real life of a writer has anything to do with literary movements. To the extent that it does, the writer may be in trouble. You're just singing, you're just doing what you can, discovering what you can, living and trying to do something sound and good.

One of the criticisms leveled against a lot of fiction written in the past twenty years—but not against yours very often—is that it is "too academic," too directly responsive to the analytic, critical train of mind. Do you think this type of thinking is actively harmful to the creative process?

Doctorow: I did a lot of criticism as an undergraduate. I know what that analytic faculty is; I saw it working in true splendor in Ransom, who had as nice a mind as I've seen. But I think this faculty works against you unless it's in balance with everything else. I like to affect a kind of ignorance about my work that might be a sham, an affectation. On the other hand, I'm really wary of being too critically informed.

It can't be just an accident that Big as Life *is rarely mentioned on your biographical dust-jacket summaries.*

Doctorow: Sometimes it's mentioned, sometimes not. Unquestionably it's the worst I've done. I think about going back and redoing it some day, but the whole experience was so unhappy, both the writing and the publishing of it, that maybe I never will. It's my *Mardi*—you know, Melville's *Mardi*?

Sure.

Doctorow: *Big as Life* is mine.

Except for Big as Life, *all of your books have used the past to explore not only the past but also certain parallel tendencies in the present. In* Welcome to Hard Times *your character expresses this idea as, "We can never start new," while in* The Book of Daniel *it goes, "Everything that came before is all the same." Could you discuss this inability of the present to escape from the errors of the past?*

Doctorow: Those lines came out of those particular books, and I'm uncomfortable talking about such things in the abstract. I would say that the fact that they're similar and express similar sentiments should not suggest that I started the books because of those ideas. In each case it came as a discovery to me as I was writing through the personality of the narrative voice I was using.

Obviously, then, you don't begin a work with a specific point to make or a thesis to illustrate. It sounds like you regard your work more as a kind of personal exploration, rather than as a vehicle self-consciously devised to develop a theme.

Doctorow: I like to quote a remark of Marcel Duchamp. He appeared to have given up painting. Someone said, "Marcel, why have you stopped painting?" and he said, "Because too much of it was 'filling in.' " That's a wonderful line. Anybody who finds himself in this situation of writing to a prescribed notion or to illustrate or to fill in what he already knows should stop writing. A writer has got to trust the act of writing to scan all his ideas, passions, and convictions; but these must emerge from the work, be *of* it. I think that's standard wisdom, at least among American writers.

Since all of your works, in one way or another, seem passionately committed to examining major social and political issues, I assume you would take issue with, say, William Gass's claims about art's "disconnection" from ordinary reality.

Doctorow: Yes, I'm opposed to that view. I think art and life make each other. Henry Miller said, "We should give literature back to life." I believe that. I believe more than that.

When you're intensely at work on a project, do you find yourself usually focusing on a specific aspect of writing—the plot movement, the language, the character development, fleshing out your own ideas?

Doctorow: I think it varies with the book. In *Ragtime* it was the historical imagery and the mock-historical or ironic-historical tone which most interested me. And the idea of composition at a fixed narrative distance from the subject neither as remote as history writing (which is very, very distant from what is being described) nor as close as modern fiction (which is very intimate with the subject). I was aiming for the narrative distance of the historical chronicle that you find, for instance, in Kleist, who, of course, was very important to me in the composition of that book.

In the case of *Daniel*, it was a far different feeling: it was the characters and their complexity that moved me—the historical intersection of social and personal agony, history moving in Daniel, powering his own pathology—all this had an enormous meaning and interest for me. So did his relationship to his sister and the parents' relationship to each other, and Daniel's relationship to himself as he sits in that library and does these historical essays and descriptions of himself in the third person, breaking down his own voice and transforming his own being to produce this work. Daniel breaks himself down constantly to reconcile himself to what is happening and what has happened to him. This kind of act that the book is—*Daniel's* book—is the central force that I felt in the writing of it.

With *Welcome to Hard Times* it was just a sense of a place which moved me tremendously. It was the place I found in the language. I had never been West. Halfway through the book, it occurred to me that maybe I ought to make sure it really was a possible terrain. I went to the library and read a geography book by Walter Prescott Webb—a marvelous book called *The Great Plains*. Webb said what I wanted to hear: no trees out there. Jesus, that was beautiful—I could spin the whole book out of one image. And I did.

What about your new book, Loon Lake?

Doctorow: It is more like *Daniel* in being a discontinuous narrative with deferred resolutions, and in the throwing of multiple voices that turn out to be the work of one narrator. So there are similarities with *Daniel;* but the subject is far different and the tone is also different. It takes place in the Depression, it's a sort of Depression *Bildungsroman.* But not with that form's characteristic accumulation of data. I have a lot of broken-line stuff in it—weighted lines. That's new for me. In *Loon Lake* the sound the words make is important—the sound of the words and their rhythm. I think a good many parts of it are better read aloud.

Was there an accident involved in your getting started with Loon Lake, *as there was with the others?*

Doctorow: Yes. I was driving through the Adirondacks a couple of years ago. We'd been visiting friends who have a place up there. I found myself incredibly responsive to everything I saw and heard and smelled. The Adirondacks are very beautiful—but more than that, a palpably mysterious wilderness, a place full of dark secrets, history rotting in the forests. At least that was my sense of things. I saw a road sign: *Loon Lake.* Everything I felt came to a point in those words. I liked their sound. I imagined a private railroad train going through the forest. The train was taking a party of gangsters to the mountain retreat of a powerful man of great wealth. So there it was, a feeling for a place, an image or two, and I was off in pursuit of my book.

You tend to develop rather peculiar narrative structures that several critics have labeled "cinematic." Did the cinema or television affect your notion of structure?

Doctorow: I don't know how anyone can write today without accommodating eighty or ninety years of film technology. Films and the perception of films and of television are enormously important factors in the way people read today. Beginning with *Daniel* I gave up trying to write with the concern for transition characteristic of the nineteenth-century novel. Other writers may be able to, but I can't accept the convention of realism anymore. It doesn't interest me as I write. I'm speaking now not of a manifesto, but of the experience of the writer, or at least this writer: you do what works. Obviously the rhythms of perception in me, as in most people who read today, have been transformed immensely by films and television.

I don't think, however, that this issue is primarily a matter of "writing visually" as opposed to not writing visually. I don't know what nonvisual writing is. I think all writing puts pictures in people's heads—pictures of different things, but always pictures of the moral state of the characters being written about. Good fiction is interested in the moral fate of its people. Who they are or how they look or what they do or how they live—these are judgments of character, finally. A poem too tries to define someone's moral existence. And that comes off the images. Poets are not alone in using imagery. So when someone says my prose is visual, I don't really know what that means. No, what we've learned from film is quite specific. We've learned that we don't have to explain things. We don't have to explain how our man can be in the bedroom one moment and walking in the street the next. How he can be twenty years old one moment and eighty years old a moment later. We've learned that if we just make the book happen the reader can take care of himself. You remember that television show *Laugh-In*? That was the big hit on television while I was writing *Daniel*. I told people when *Daniel* was published that it was constructed like *Laugh-In*. They thought I was not serious. But the idea of discontinuity and blackouts and of running changes on voice and character—it was that kind of nerve energy I was looking for. *Loon Lake* too is powered by discontinuity, switches in scene, tense, voice, the mystery of who's talking. Will people be able to understand it? I think they will. Anyone who's ever watched a news broadcast on television knows all about discontinuity.

Daniel *says something about life not being as "well plotted" as we would like it to be. Is this one of your problems with the conventions of realism?*

Doctorow: Life may have been better plotted at one time.

That's an interesting idea. Philip Roth suggested back in the early 1960s that it's more difficult for contemporary writers to create realistic fiction because reality is less realistic, more extravagant than any world the writer can hope to create. In fact, your character Harry Houdini in Ragtime *seems to be an artist figure who has a difficult time making his art more wondrous than that of the world. Do you share this sense of a world outstripping your ability as an artist to produce wonders?*

Doctorow: Certainly the clatter, the accelerated rate of crisis, the sense of diffusion of character, of disintegration of belief or social assumptions is reflected in the novelists who find the novel itself no longer convincing and who write anti-mimetic novels essentially about how it's impossible to write. That view explains a lot of stuff that's been done in the last twenty years, but it doesn't explain Roth, does it? Fortunately, he keeps trying. Whatever the difficulties are, the obstacles, that's the nature of the game.

I enjoy problems and I enjoy adversity, at least professionally, and if life as represented in the headlines of the paper makes the act of writing absurd, I accept that and I'll try to deal with it. That's the condition under which I'll do my work. And I may fail, probably will, probably have, probably always will fail. But that's a kind of occupational hazard—it's built into the trade. I can imagine Cervantes sitting there in jail tearing his hair while he wrote *Don Quixote*.

When Ragtime *came out, several critics expressed their surprise about the use of real historical figures. Obviously, though, real people and events appear in your earlier book,* Daniel—*sometimes disguised but sometimes not. What did you find so intriguing about the use of real facts and real historical people in your work?*

Doctorow: As my answer to the last question suggests, if you do this kind of work you can't finally accept the distinction between reality and books. In fact, no fiction writer has ever stood still for that distinction; that's why Defoe pretended that *Robinson Crusoe* was really written by Crusoe. I don't want to understand that distinction between art and everything else, so I don't. This is not merely an aesthetic position, you understand. I get impatient with people who are moralistic about this issue. Someone said to me, "Don't you think it shows a lack of imagination to use historical characters?" and I said, "Yes, it does. Of course, it was a terrible lack of imagination on Tolstoy's part, too, when he made a character out of Napoleon." In fact, he even made a character of Napoleon's General Doctorow, an ancestor of mine. Someone said another time, "What would *Daniel* be if there hadn't been a Rosenberg case?" I said, "You're absolutely right. And where would *The Red Badge of Courage* be without the Civil War?" What I think has happened is that people used to know what fiction was and now they've forgotten. It comes as a surprise when they're reading a novel and they find Harry Houdini saying things and carrying on. It could be that there's been such a total disintegration into specialist-thinking on the part of all of us in our trades and jargons that no one remembers what the whole life is. What is imagined and what is experienced? The imagination obviously imposes itself on the world, composes a world which, in turn, affects what is imagined. That's true even in science. Indisputable. I suppose this leans toward a kind of philosophical idealist's position, although it isn't really that exactly—I mean, I know that when I kick the rock I refute Berkeley. But I also know that a book can affect consciousness—affect the way people think and therefore the way they act. Books can create constituencies of consciousness that have their own effect on history; that's been proven time and again. So I don't see that distinction between facts and art. If you read a good social scientist, an anthropologist, a sociologist, I think you'll find they do everything we fiction writers do. These people who write sociology create composite characters. Anyone who represents a class or a kind of ethnic or economic group is dealing in characterization. That's what I do.

Gass has a line about Plato's soul being one of the greatest literary characters of all time.

Doctorow: Well, why not? And if you read the newspapers you see the creativity involved. Just deciding what to look at and write about is an immensely creative decision. As a newsman you're deciding what will exist and what won't exist.

I was intrigued by another remark you made once: "When you write about imaginary events in the lives of undisguised people, you are proposing that history has ended and mythology has begun." What were you trying to suggest in your distinction between history and mythology?

Doctorow: Just what we've been talking about. All history is composed. A professional historian won't make the claims for the objectivity of his discipline that the layperson grants him. He knows how creative he is. We used to laugh at the way the Russians knocked people out of their encyclopedias from one edition to the next, but we did the same thing. It turned out that American historians had written, for the most part, as an establishment—they had written out of existence the history of black people and women and Indians and Chinese people in this country. What could be more apparent than the creativity of that? That's part of what I meant when I said of the little boy in *Ragtime*, "It was evident to him that the world composed and re-composed itself constantly in an endless process of dissatisfaction."

As you've acknowledged on several occasions, the figure of Coalhouse Walker is based on Kleist's Michael Kohlhaas. What was the background of your decision to use this earlier fictional character in your own book?

Doctorow: Several years ago my wife related a true story she'd heard, about a housemaid in our neighborhood who bore a child and then buried it in a garden. I knew when I heard this that I'd use it someday. I found myself using it in *Ragtime*, where I never knew in advance what was going to happen. Suddenly there was Mother discovering the little brown newborn in the flower bed. There was Sarah coming to live in the house with this baby. Obviously she would have tried to kill her child only from some overwhelming despair or sense of betrayal. So there had to be a father. I had introduced Houdini driving up the Broadview Avenue hill in his car, and that was the way I decided to introduce the child's father. He came along in his shining Ford, an older man, and he said, "I'm looking for a young woman of color." Where had he been? I decided he was a musician, a man who lived on the road, going where he found work. Now he was back to make amends. He starts to court Sarah, and when she refuses to see him he plays the piano for the family in their parlor. And that's how I found the central image of the book. Then I began to think about the implications of a black man owning his own car in the early 1900s. I knew Sarah would forgive him and they would be reconciled. But that car: what would happen to that lovely car of his is what happened to Michael Kohlhaas's horses. I had always wanted to rework the circumstances of Kleist's story—I felt the premise was obviously relevant, appropriate—the idea of a man who cannot find justice from a society that claims to be just.

So there it was. I'd finally found the use for that legend I'd hoped to find—but not until the moment I needed it.

Both Coalhouse and the Younger Brother die in the pursuit of their radical ideas. And, of course, the Isaacsons are framed and eventually electrocuted. You seem to be opting for the view that history is on the side of compromise and cooperation—that idealism is rarely rewarded in our country.

Doctorow: I believe it's more complicated than that. The radical ideas of one generation make up the orthodoxy of subsequent generations, so the radical role is to be sacrificial. Certainly in the history of this country the radical is often sacrificed and his ideas are picked up after he himself has been destroyed. I believe Eugene Debs came up with the idea of social security and he really suffered for that. And among Emma Goldman's outrageous, radical ideas, for which she was deported, was that of a woman's right to her own body, her right to have an abortion if she chose. Hideous radicalism at the time, yet it's the law of the land, although there is some challenge to it right now.

Tateh is allowed to become a financial success even though he sells out his moral beliefs. Were you tempted to condemn him for abandoning his working-class ideals?

Doctorow: No. I love that character, but I also understand him. I was making an observation in my treatment of him that very often a man who begins as a radical somehow—with all his energy and spirit and intelligence and wit—by a slight change of course can use these gifts to succeed under the very system he's criticizing. Very often this happens without his losing his sense of himself as a radical. You can often find among the wealthy a conviction that they are unrestructured radicals—they give a lot of money to political causes of the left, and so forth.

Tateh's presence in Ragtime *seems to undercut some of the criticism your book received for being blindly sympathetic to its leftist characters.*

Doctorow: Yes. When people claim that I have this sentimental, simplistic approach to the characters on the left, they're not reading carefully. As compassionate as we feel for Tateh and as much as we love him, here's a man who has betrayed his principles and sympathies and gotten ahead that way. After all, he has gotten to enjoy his life by abandoning his commitment to the working class. So that's hardly an uncomplicated, simplistic view of one of the book's leftists. I think I also portray Emma Goldman as a person who stomps all over people's feelings, who just wreaks havoc with people's personal lives wherever she goes. This sort of thing is true of the radical idealist personality, though it's hardly a simplistic portrayal of her.

Do you recall what initially interested you in the Rosenberg case as a possible source for a novel?

Doctorow: When I started thinking about the case, the Rosenbergs had been dead fourteen or fifteen years. I think I was in the army serving in Germany when they were executed, and maybe that's why at the time it was a more remote horror to me than to many others. I was fully sensitive to the McCarthy period generally, but the case didn't propose itself to me as a subject for a novel until we were all going through Vietnam. Here was the New Left, the antiwar involvement, an amplification by a later generation of the torment of the 1950s. At any rate, it seemed to me that I could write about the case, that my imagination could find its corporeal being in those circumstances. I would not write a documentary novel but quite clearly and deliberately use what had happened to the Rosenbergs as the *occasion* for the book. I don't mean this as a comparison, only as an example: Defoe knew that Alexander Selkirk had been a castaway, and that the idea of the castaway was very important and alive in London. And that's all he needed to do *Robinson Crusoe*—the real phenomenon of the castaway. I felt people would know about the Rosenbergs, and that was all I needed to write a book about Paul and Rochelle Isaacson. Although I was perhaps a little older than Daniel, I was of an age when I could respond, symbolically or metaphorically, as a person of his era. So a lot of things came together around this idea. The relationship between radical movements of one generation and another. The idea of a radical family—all the paradoxes and contradictions of that family against whom the entire antagonistic force of society is directed. So I wondered, what is the nature of that experience? What happens to people under such circumstances? How does it feel? I found that I had a proprietary sense of recognition for the subject. Also I was angry. It seems to me certainly a message of the twentieth century that people have a great deal to fear from their own governments. That's an inescapable worldwide fact. Daniel has a line about every citizen being the enemy of his own country. It is the nature of the governing mind to treat as adversaries the people being governed.

Given your own personal sympathies, were you ever tempted to make Daniel a thoroughly sympathetic character, rather than giving him sadistic, almost monstrous qualities at times?

Doctorow: Suffering doesn't make people virtuous, at least in my experience. But I see his "sadism," as you call it, in a slightly different way. I see the scene where he abuses his wife, for instance, as being of the same kind as the scene in which he throws his son up in the air. The act has existential dimensions. Daniel is over-tuned to the world. He doesn't miss a thing. He's a hero—or a criminal—of perception. When he delivers his eulogy of his sister, Susan, he says there has been a failure of analysis—Susan could only survive by limiting the amount of reality in the situation insofar as her parents were concerned. She had to come to a very strict, defensive judgment, and eventually it broke her. But Daniel gives himself to the act of perception and opens himself to it—much as all writers must—and he survives that way, survives by however cold and frightening an embrace with the truth. That is perhaps his only strength. Of course, it would take a tremendous act of will to accept the very idea of a family after this kind of thing has happened to you as a child. Daniel recognizes this, and in acting out the terrible conflicts within himself between giving in and not giving in—his sister chose not to go on, and he's trying to go on—he is enduring, but letting in as much truth about himself and his life to his own perception as he can.

As you've implied, this openness to perception seems to make Daniel an especially interesting example of any artist . . .

Doctorow: Maybe the nature of fiction is that, unlike reporting for the *New York Times*, it has to admit everything—all aspects and forms of thought and behavior and feeling, no matter how awful they may be. Fiction has no borders; everything is open, you have a limitless possibility of knowing the truth. But there are always people telling you what you can't do, where you mustn't go. Every time you write a book someone says, "Oh, you shouldn't have done this or you shouldn't have done that." There's always a commissar who wants to tell you what the rules are. Yet when I'm writing out of a spirit of transgression, I'm probably doing my best work.

An Interview with

Stanley Elkin

If an interviewer could invent a novelist to talk with, the model would be Stanley Elkin. He's friendly, direct, funny, and he even enjoys talking about writing and his work. When my wife and I arrived in St. Louis in September, 1974, for our first meeting with Elkin, he immediately invited us to his home even though he was entertaining a boyhood friend from out of town. He roamed his living room, keeping two or three conversations in the air at once. The next day we talked in his office on the Washington University campus for four hours, with the only interruption coming when a tape broke. He immediately volunteered to repeat any lost answers. I've found him equally generous in subsequent meetings and have found, too, that his name mentioned in conversation with any other writer who knows him insures minutes of amusing Elkin anecdotes.

On the day of our first talk Elkin, then forty-six, was wearing corduroys and a white turtleneck sweater. If his voice had not been so rough, he could easily have been mistaken for a distinguished poet. Physically intense, he shifted about in his chair, sometimes hunching over the microphone like a body puncher, sometimes sitting back with his hands behind his head like a satisfied president. In more recent years, multiple sclerosis has reduced his physical vigor—he now walks with a cane—but his language and wit are as vital as when I first met him.

For many years Elkin was known as a writer's writer, creator of an extravagant prose like no other novelist's. Rooted in oral models and saturated with metaphor, Elkin's style in his first novels—*Boswell* (1964), *A Bad Man* (1967), and *The Dick Gibson Show* (1971) — often overwhelmed reviewers who complained about his omnivorous voice. His short stories were, however, widely anthologized and published in a collection called *Criers and Kibitzers, Kibitzers and Criers* (1966). With his collection of novellas, *Searches and Seizures* (1973), his novel *The Franchiser* (1976), and especially with his linked stories in *The Living End* (1979), Elkin has begun to reach a larger audience while solidifying his reputation as America's eminent vulgarian, the novelist who tells us most about life under the neon torches and golden arches that light up this land. Because Elkin has pressed his nose to the American showcase, has heard all the sellers of self and thing, all talk is available for his writing and speech.

—*Tom LeClair*

Your father was a salesman. I can't help but wonder if he was a master rhetorician—as many of your characters are—and if the passionate speech that characterizes so much of your fiction has its genesis in your early environment.

Elkin: If not a master rhetorician, at least a master salesman. He sold costume jewelry, and I went with him once on one of his trips through the Midwest. He had a vast territory. He had Michigan, Minnesota, the Dakotas, Wisconsin, parts of Indiana, Illinois, Missouri—an immense territory. I was with him in small Indiana towns where he would take the jewelry out of the telescopes, which are salesmen's cases, and actually put the earrings on his ears, the bracelets around his wrists, and the necklaces about his throat. This wasn't drag, but the prose passionate and stage business of his spiel. The man believed in costume jewelry, in rhinestones and beads, and sang junk jewelry's meteorological condition—its Fall line and Spring.

Is there something of your father in Feldman's father?

Elkin: Yes, and a great deal in Feldman. Probably more in Feldman than his father.

Your mother's name was Feldman. Do you bestow, like Nabokov does, details of your own life on your characters?

Elkin: No. There is little autobiography in my work. When I was growing up, we had a bungalow in New Jersey which we visited in the summers. Everybody in that small community was named Feldman and was either an aunt or cousin of mine. I just found it comfortable to use the name Feldman. For a long time before I ever published anything, all my characters were named Stephen Feldman. I hadn't read Joyce, I didn't know about Dedalus. But it didn't make any difference what story it was or what age the characters were. I named them all Stephen Feldman. And then, only later, years later, when I was writing *A Bad Man*, did the name come to mean anything to me—Feldman the felled man.

You've said that you spent just under 183 years going from freshman to Ph.D. at Illinois.

Elkin: Right.

Were you writing stories while getting your M.A. and Ph.D.? You were in the army too, weren't you?

Elkin: Yes, for a couple of years—1955 to 1957. The remarkable thing, remarkable for me anyway, was that I discovered that I could write only after I passed my prelims. I had been writing and chopping away at stuff, at this story or that. I took all the writing courses, but I had no style—or, rather, I *did* have a style but it wasn't mine. I had William Faulkner's style. I studied a year in bed—never got out of bed for an entire year, had all the books around the bed. I'd get up to teach my classes, of course, but I taught from eight to ten in the morning on Mondays, Wednesdays, and Fridays. Then I'd return to the apartment and get back into bed and not get up until it was time to teach my classes again. But at any rate, I decided to give myself some time to write, and I wrote a story called "On a Field, Rampant." It was the first story that I'd ever written which had what was to become my style.

How much influence does your academic training have on your writing? Do you work into your fiction the intricate patterns of imagery that much academic criticism is concerned with?

Elkin: Well, it depends upon the fiction. When I was about a hundred pages into *Boswell*, I suddenly discovered that I had Boswell in a lot of elevators, and because I had been trained in the New Criticism I decided, hey, this is pretty neat! Elevators. Makes a nice pattern. And so I was conscious of the elevator motif and kept moving him in and out of elevators. In a way it works because a great deal of novelistic fiction is about ascent. Since Boswell was a guy on the make and had this sort of excelsior personality, it was quite fitting for him to be in elevators, on up escalators and to climb stairs. There's one scene in *Boswell* where he's in a Jewish community in Brooklyn, as I recall, to meet a miracle rabbi, and he can't get past the front door. He is not permitted to climb those stairs and is stalled. Sure, I'm conscious of symbols and patterns in my work. But this is something I've sometimes come on to only after the fact and then made the most of.

You said in your dissertation on Faulkner that he sympathized with the "egocentric will pitted against something stronger than itself."

Elkin: Maybe that's what I admire, or what I came to admire, in Faulkner without knowing that it is what I was ultimately to be about myself. But I think it *is* what I am ultimately about. And I think it is true in Faulkner. I think it is truer of me, though, than it is of Faulkner. Faulkner's heroes are often nicer guys than mine.

You also commented on Faulkner's legendizing of character through hyperbole and his repetitive technique. These seem to show up in your fiction.

Elkin: My editor at Random House, Joe Fox, used to tell me, "Stanley, less is more." He wanted to strike—oh, he had a marvelous eye for the "good" stuff—and that's what he wanted to strike. I had to fight him tooth and nail in the better restaurants to maintain excess because I don't believe that less is more. I believe that *more* is more. I believe that less is less, fat fat, thin thin and enough is enough. There's a famous exchange between Fitzgerald and Thomas Wolfe in which Fitzgerald criticizes Wolfe for one of his novels. Fitzgerald tells him that Flaubert believed in the *mot precis* and that there are two kinds of writers—the putter-inners and the taker-outers. Wolfe, who probably was not as good a writer as Fitzgerald but evidently wrote a better letter, said, "Flaubert me no Flauberts. Shakespeare was a putter-inner, Melville was a putter-inner." I can't remember who else was a putter-inner, but I'd rather be a putter-inner than a taker-outer.

Are there philosophical, religious, or psychological traditions which are especially important to you?

Elkin: Like most people of my generation, I fell in love with the philosophy of existentialism. There is no particular religious tradition in my work. There is only one psychological assertion that I would insist upon. That is: the SELF takes precedence.

Are there particular existential writers?

Elkin: Camus. I think he was a wonderful writer. I ate his books up alive in the better restaurants.

Is there a system of ideas within which your fiction could be considered?

Elkin: No. I'm not a "thinker." For example, *The Franchiser* is about the man who makes America look like America. He owns a McDonald's franchise. He owns a Fred Astaire Dance Studio franchise. He owns a KOA campsite franchise. He owns perhaps thirty franchises. He trades them like a kid with Monopoly cards. What had appealed to me—what had instigated the novel and in a way has instigated almost everything I've ever written—was the *occupation*. I don't know what the thing is all about until I start to write it. Then, as I'm writing, I really do invent ideas, make ideas up.

Reviewers and critics often consider you with the black humorists or the absurdists and with the Jewish-American writers, who are also humorists. Would you care to comment on affinities you might have with writers like Barth, Donleavy, Vonnegut, Heller, Roth, Bellow?

Elkin: If I have any affinities at all, they are with men like Bellow—and, to a lesser extent, Barth. Certainly not to Roth, who is more a sociologist of the personal than anything else. And not really to Donleavy, whose work I admire very much—but who finally disappoints me because he not only writes the same book over and over again, but the same sentence over and over again or the same sentence fragment over and over again. He uses the same characters; he uses the same rhetorical patterns. I find that his best book is not *The Ginger Man* but *A Singular Man*, the book where he finally got it right. Everything else is redundant. Spin-offs from spin-offs, as if he learned to write at Mary Tyler Moore's knee.

Barth is wonderful, but the Barth I really admire is back there in the Golden Age of Barth. That is to say, the Barth of *The Floating Opera*, of *The End of the Road* and *The Sot-Weed Factor*. The Barth who takes himself seriously as a metafictionist is a Barth who bores finally. There's some great stuff in *Lost in the Funhouse,* and I suppose there are nice little pastiches in *Giles Goat-Boy,* but later Barth really is Barth for Barth's sake.

Bellow I think is a magnificent writer—probably, with Gass, the best writer in America. I just somehow feel on Bellow's wave length. I don't think that he has a reader in America who digs him more than I do. There has not been a single Bellow novel or story that I have not liked, including probably his weakest books—*Dangling Man, The Victim,* and *Henderson the Rain King. Henderson the Rain King* is not really in his mode—it's more in my mode than his—but I like *Henderson* for its ending, which it seems to me is a paradigm for the endings in a great deal of modern fiction. Henderson is carrying the kid in his arms in Newfoundland or wherever, and begins to run and dance—dancing, running, leaping, jumping, moving. I find that whole concept very, very exciting. It's the leap of faith; the only way finally to make any sense out of the world is simply by saying "yes" to it, and jump up and down in it.

Writers say yes or no?

Elkin: Yes, the binary system. What a writer's message is is totally unimportant. Either he is agreeing with life by affirming, or he is saying life is just a bowl of wormwood.

So you haven't changed anybody's life with your fiction?

Elkin: Certainly not. Nobody does.

What about Faulkner?

Elkin: He never changed anybody's life either. Auden went to his grave complaining that his poems never saved a single Jew from the ovens, and he was absolutely right.

In your collection Stories from the Sixties, *you include stories by Coover and Gass, who are often called experimental in their concern with form and language. Do you have affinities with experimental writers?*

Elkin: I think Gass is the best word-man in America. Coover is a very good friend of mine, and I think "The Babysitter" is a wonderful story, a very successful tour de force, and while a tour de force is its own excuse for being, a little goes a long way. Vintage Coover to me is not the Coover of *Pricksongs and Descants* so much as the Coover of *The Origin of the Brunists*, or *The Universal Baseball Association*, which are superb novels. Bob is such a good writer and has so many gifts to offer the traditional novel that it seems to me that he works against his own best interests when he goes off to play in his laboratory.

You mentioned tour de force. There seems to be a lot of localized tour de force in your work.

Elkin: But it's not tour de force in terms of fictive strategy; it's tour de force of language and that's, as far as I'm concerned, always legitimate. But look for the language in post-Coover Coover, and it's more difficult to find. There's marvelous language in *Pricksongs and Descants* but it's subsidiary to the experiment with structure. I tell you this for your own good, Bob. The reason I like Gass so much is that Gass is not fucking around with structure. He is fucking around with language. That to me is legitimate and acceptable, and the furthest out you can go is the best place to be. That's what's so magnificent about Shakespeare. Shakespeare wrote very conventional plays, but the language wasn't conventional.

Do you have a philosophy of language?

Elkin: It's a matter of feeling one's way. It is not instinctive. It's a question of using a pencil, erasing, creating a palimpsest of metaphor right there on the page. One gets a notion of the conceit and one is inspired to work with it as a draftsman might work with some angle that he is interested in getting down correctly. There's where all the fun of writing is for me.

I don't read much nonfiction because the nonfiction I do read always seems to be so badly written. What I enjoy about fiction—the great gift of fiction—is that it gives language an opportunity to happen. What I am really interested in after personality are not philosophic ideas or abstractions or patterns, but this superb opportunity for language to take place.

Do you have an impassioned statement about the function or purpose of the novelist?

Elkin: I just made it. He has no social obligations, it seems to me, unless his wife has accepted a dinner date for Thursday.

John Gardner has a good deal to say about your fiction in On Moral Fiction. *Do you have any remarks about his book or the issues he raises?*

Elkin: John Gardner is a bore, and he's never raised an issue in his life, merely resurrected some. Tolstoy did it better in "What Is Art?" and didn't have to bad-mouth his friends. Of course any work of art which is genuine is by necessity and definition moral.

Do you have some sense of an audience when you write?

Elkin: I do have an ideal audience in mind. That ideal audience is a man like Bill Gass, or someone like Howard Nemerov, or any other writer who respects language. But other than that, no notion at all of an audience. I don't think any writer does. I don't think that poor Jacqueline Susann had any notion of an audience. I think she was doing the best she could. There is no such thing as prostitution in writing. One writes what one can write. One writes *up*, though one man's up is another man's basement.

In a New York Times *review, Josh Greenfield said that you seem to write with the conviction that the world is winless. Do you agree with this?*

Elkin: Yes, well, we all die, yes? We suffer, correct? The score keeps changing, is it not so? And Mommy holds us on the teeter-totter before we can sit upright on chairs. I don't really care so much about the fact that the world is winless. It is simply a condition that seems true to me. It is just a condition the way a red light is a condition at a traffic crossing. Yet, quite marvelous books have been written about winner worlds. Other people write them.

Indeed, the novel is generally a kind of Christian device where people who are good get their just rewards and where people who are bad are punished. I don't believe that this is the case in life, but it might be a case the novelist wants to make, and great novels have been written making such cases. I don't care so long as the novel is written well.

You've said, "I don't write from memory. I imagine everything." Could you elaborate on the purposes of this approach?

Elkin: I used to think and I used to tell my writing students that the reason one can't write autobiographically is that one is too close to the material. But that's wrong. I was terribly humiliated when I was in the army, and I tried to get that down into fiction. I constantly failed, and I kept thinking that I was failing because I was too close to it, but that's not why I failed. The real reason I failed is that you cannot write autobiographically; you cannot write from memory. If you write from memory, the chances are that you will say, "Well, because this happened in just such a sequence I will use it in just such a sequence." Now, life is shapeless, but art, as everybody knows, is shaped. If one is writing from memory, one is writing ultimately a kind of shapeless, amorphous slice of lifeism. Besides, I don't remember anything all that exciting ever happening to me.

You've said that you believe in inspiration. Does inspiration work throughout the story in structure and form, or does it work mostly in the original conception?

Elkin: Mostly in the original conception. I think I said that stories come altogether all at once or they do not come at all, but that's rather an overstatement. I'll give you an example. I was reading Mike Royko's book, *Boss*, about Mayor Daley. Someplace in that book he talks about a saloon where cops, detectives, and bailbondsmen hang out. I saw the word "bailbondsmen" in the sentence, and suddenly it stood out—I don't know why. I had nothing to do with bailbondsmen, I had no memory of bailbondsmen, I had never met a bailbondsman. I'd never put up bail for anyone, but I started to think about the implications of the word "bailbondsman." Since I begin most stories or novels with an occupation, it struck me that there was a rich lode here, so I knew I was going to write a novella about a bailbondsman. What the novella was going to be about, what the plot was going to be, I had no idea; that was simply a process of inventing as I went along. But the original inspiration—seeing that word on the page and having it trigger the momentum in me—occurred in a swell fell swoop.

Of course, inspiration is an ongoing, continuing process in the composition of a book. One doesn't, for example, plot a joke. Like a lot of what happens in novels, inspiration is a sort of spontaneous combustion—the oily rags of the head and heart.

What is your response to reviewers who, although immensely entertained by your novels, end up saying that the whole is less than the parts? Are you concerned with structure and form the way someone like Nabokov or Barth is?

Elkin: Although I am immensely entertained by their reviews, I end up saying that the whole is less than the parts. As a matter of fact, I *am* concerned with structure and form and my novels *are* structured and formed. There isn't a novel I have written which does not have a very well-defined structure. *The Dick Gibson Show,* for example, is not a series of isolated episodes; it is a progress. *A Bad Man* is not a series of brouhaha speeches; it is a structure. *Boswell,* less so, although there is a structure there too. *Boswell* was the first long thing I wrote, and I really didn't know quite what I was up to. But I think all my work subsequent to *Boswell* has been rather tightly structured. Now, if people don't recognize the structure, that isn't my fault. Well, maybe it is my fault, but I *hope* it's their fault.

It seems to me that the plots of your novels develop through the protagonist's repetition of action. Do your novels develop largely out of what you have called the "physics of personality"?

Elkin: Yes, and the physics of obsession. Fiction is about obsession, but there is a distinction between obsession and madness. There is no successful mad fiction. Although I have written a story which *ends* in madness and suicide, it seems to me that novels *about* craziness are always unsuccessful. They become case studies. *The Bell Jar,* for example, is a terrible novel. The only thing that gives *The Bell Jar* any interest at all is the fact that it is autobiographical. We have this greasy interest in Sylvia Plath. If that woman had never killed herself, her books would sell less than mine.

Your characteristic style is, I think, distinguished by its oral quality. Could you comment on the sources of this style? Your father . . .

Elkin: I was a very attentive listener to my father's stories and to my father's shop talk . . . this may be the real source of my style. All shop talk, the specialized jargon of a closed universe, fascinates me. Whenever I hear it, wherever I hear it, I'm thunderstruck.

Do you put yourself in situations where you are likely to hear shop talk?

Elkin: No. Not really, but when I am fortunate enough to run across it, I recognize it and listen to it and try to duplicate it in my writing. Now, some of those rhetorical flourishes, of course, are beyond the shop talk of most people, but it's as though I were giving others free rein to talk as they would if they had my vocabulary. Passion is the secret of shop talk.

A friend of mine here in St. Louis, Al Lebowitz, who is a lawyer and a novelist, had to argue a case before the Missouri Supreme Court, and he asked me if I would drive him to Columbia, the state capital. I did and we went that evening to a restaurant in which there were all of these pols. We were sitting close enough to them so that we both stopped talking ourselves and just listened to these guys talking and it was marvelous. It wasn't just the language of anecdote but the language of impassioned partisan anecdote. Unbelievably beautiful—almost a kind of poetry. What other writers get from geography—regionalism—I get from shop talk.

It seems that your narrators or heroes are professional rhetoricians. There's con man Boswell, salesman Feldman, disc jockey Gibson, lecturer Preminger, and bondsman Main. Are they displacements of the artist?

Elkin: I wish I *could* talk like these characters—I can't. Sometimes in class, if I'm particularly good that day, I can go about twenty-seven seconds, not quite a sixth of a round. But it's the way I would like to be able to talk, and I guess the reason I write fiction—I hadn't ever thought of this before, but this is a true answer—is to give myself an opportunity to talk that way.

You said in some comments on Faulkner that comedy is a "quick inconsequential passion."

Elkin: "Inconsequential" is the operative word there. Consequence to me is when the bone doesn't heal, when the germ does not do what the penicillin wants it to. Consequence is pain. There can be no consequence in comedy. Tom and Jerry chase each other; Tom falls off the Empire State Building and shatters like a dish. In the next loop he has reconstituted himself. Now, I don't laugh at Tom and Jerry, but in a simplistic way, that's the model for all comedy. Nothing bad may happen. There is safety in comedy.

Would you discuss the function of the comic in your fiction?

Elkin: There is a night-club and television comedian named George Carlin. His routine is the Hippy Dippy Weather Man, and most of his jokes are jokes about the television industry. He makes fun of commercials; he makes fun of *format*. I have yet to laugh at George Carlin because his humor is institutional humor. It is backstage humor. Green Room. It seems to me—and this is a very difficult thing to phrase properly—that noses are funnier than the particular crotchets of network vice-presidents. I told you an anecdote yesterday about my friend Herbie Bogart. We were in Max, Indiana, a small town, stopped at a red light and this hick came down the street with a piece of straw in his mouth, and Bogart said to me, "Look at that Bozo," then opened the window and said, "Hiya Bozo." That, to me, is absolutely hilarious. I can't really explain *why* it's hilarious, but one thing it has going for it is that it's not institutional, not backstage. It's comedy of the streets. Not just of that red light and crossroads in Max, Indiana, but the vernacular comedy of street, avenue and U.S. 41. It's a rare joke that is funny. Only situations are funny.

What is black humor? Are you a black humorist?

Elkin: I can't even tell you what black humor is. Black humor is a term invented by *Time* Magazine. But I'll tell you what kind of humorist I am—and I don't think I am really a humorist. It seems to me that there is only one modern joke: the joke of powerlessness. And Charlie Chaplin me no Charlie Chaplins. The grand joke of modern fiction is the *Lucky Jim* joke of making faces *behind* the professor's back. Now, the grand jokes of *A Bad Man* or *The Dick Gibson Show*—whatever I've written—are the jokes where the character in trouble, confronted with a force much stronger than he is, mumbles *under* his breath something that is absolutely devastating to the authority which threatens him. But the fact that he has to mumble it under his breath, you see, is what makes it funny. Had he shouted it at the aggressor, at the warden, or what-have-you, it wouldn't be funny. I am thinking of a specific line. When Feldman is closeted with the girl, Mona, in the warden's party section of *A Bad Man*, he thinks Mona may be the warden's wife. Oh, God, he thinks, suppose they catch me with the warden's wife? Yet the woman is very attractive to him. She says to Feldman, "One of the things that always bothered me about you stick-up men and murderers and thugs is the fact that when you're driven up to the police station in a police car, you always hold your hats over your faces. Why do you do that?" And Feldman says, "Yeah, well, we like the way they smell." Feldman is not really answering her question: that is the answer of powerlessness.

Are there any conventions which especially appeal to you and that find their way into your fiction?

Elkin: No. But I believe in the big things, the traumas that no writer invents that change all preexisting alternatives for the character. Divorce: a guy goes home and sees his wife packing a suitcase. He says, "Going on a trip, are you?" She says, "Yeah, and I've already burned your suitcases so

you ain't coming with me. We are now not going to be married anymore."
This means that the guy has to change his priorities. Or he comes down to
the English office and Professor Madsen calls him in and says, "You were
going to teach at one o'clock today? Well, don't bother; you're fired." So
no matter what this guy's life has been before the world leaned on him, he
now has to make adjustments. Now, at the beginning of *A Bad Man*
Feldman is arrested for things that happened way before the novel began,
so he has to make certain kinds of adjustments. He is going to a place
where Feldman cannot be Feldman anymore. The same thing is true
—more or less—in every book written, not just by me but by anybody.

If these big things that change priorities come too quickly and too often,
the book will of necessity be a melodrama, a soap opera. On the other
hand, there are things which the writer invents. I am thinking of the bone
shop, for example, in Charles Dickens's *Our Mutual Friend*, where one of
the characters goes down into this subterranean old dark shop and there
are drawers all around the walls of the shop. He finds the knucklebone of
the third finger of the right hand and kneecaps and the left anklebone.
Every bone there is catalogued and stored. I am sure that no such shop existed in life, that Dickens invented it. If I were to use it, it would be a case of
pure plagiarism. That's something that is spontaneously generated by the
writer. If a book has nothing but those spontaneous generations, the result
will be not melodrama but chaos. That's why I criticized Coover before
because *Pricksongs and Descants* is nothing but invention piled upon invention with no—I don't like the word—trauma to give the thing stability.

*I have some questions now about themes or ideas I find in much of your
fiction. You have Dick Gibson say, "The point of life was the possibility it
always held out for the exceptional." The heroes in your novels have a
tremendous need to be exceptional, to transcend others, to quarrel with
the facts of physical existence. Is this a convention—which we've just been
talking about—or something very basic to your whole view of life?*

Elkin: It is something very basic to my view of life, but in the case of
that character it becomes the initial trauma which sets him going. It
becomes his priority. Dick Gibson goes on to say that he had believed that
the great life was the life of cliché. When I started to write the book, I did
not know that was what the book was going to be about, but indeed that is
precisely what the book gets to be about as I learned what Dick Gibson's
life meant. Consider the last few pages of the book:
"What had his own life been, his interminable apprenticeship which he
saw now he could never end? And everyone blameless as himself,
everyone doing his best but maddened at last, all, all zealous, all with explanations ready at hand and serving an ideal of truth or beauty or health
or grace. Everyone—everyone. It did no good to change policy or fiddle

with format. The world pressed in. It opened your windows. All one could hope for was to find his scapegoat . . . "

Now, everything that follows this is a cliché: "to wait for him, lurking in alleys, pressed flat against walls, crouched behind doors while the key jiggles in the lock, taking all the melodramatic postures of revenge. To be there in closets when the enemy comes for his hat, or to surprise him with guns in swivel chairs, your legs dapperly crossed when you turn to face him, to pin him down on hillsides or pounce on him from trees as he rides by, to meet him on the roofs of trains roaring on trestles, or leap at him while he stops at red lights, to struggle with him on the smooth faces of cliffs . . . " and so on. The theme of the novel is that the exceptional life—the only great life—is the trite life. It is something that I believe. It is not something that I am willing to risk bodily injury to myself in order to bring to pass, but to have affairs, to go to Europe, to live the dramatic clichés, all the stuff of which movies are made, would be the great life.

But what if one were aware that they were clichés? Isn't that what causes so much despair in contemporary fiction—that characters can't live a life of clichés?

Elkin: Dick Gibson is aware that they are clichés. What sets him off—what first inspires this notion in him—is his court-martial when he appears before the general and says that he's taken a burr out of the general's paw—something that happens in a fairytale. When Dick realizes what has happened to him, he begins to weep, thinking, Oh boy, I've got it made—I'm going to have enemies, I'm going to be lonely, I'm going to suffer. That is the theme of that book.

Do the characters in your novels, then, have rather conventional notions of what exceptional is?

Elkin: Yes, I think so.

James Boswell says that there are "only two kinds of intelligence, the obsessive and the perspectual" and goes on to praise the obsessive while living an obsessed life. Could you comment on this interest in obsession?

Elkin: It's my notion—and I suppose it's a lot of writers' notion—that the thing which energizes fiction is the will. In the conventional fiction of the nineteenth century, it is the will to get out of one class and make it up into another class. We're no longer so interested in that, since everybody more or less has the things that he needs. The conventional drive toward money has been replaced. At least it's been replaced in fiction, and what we read about now—and what I write about—are people whose wills have been colored by some perfectly irrational desire. In the case of Boswell, it is the will to live forever. In the case of Dick Gibson, it is the will to live the great life which is the trite life. In the case of "The Bailbondsman," it is to know the answers to questions that no one can know. In the case of Ashenden in "The Making of Ashenden," it is the desire to find an absolutely pure human being—someone as pure as himself. In the case of Feldman, it is to sell the unsalable thing and to make the buyer pay as much for it as possible. Now these are options that define the characters and that the characters choose as options to define their lives. Their obsessions drive them. Feldman has all the money in the world. He doesn't need to make more. My characters—with the exception of Boswell, who marries money—are well off. This liberates them to do the kinds of things which people don't really do in real life but which they do do in fiction—to follow their own, irrational—but *sane*—obsessions which, achieved, would satisfy them. Alas, these guys never catch up with their obsessions.

Their obsessions also give you an interesting perspective on the world, don't they?

Elkin: Yes, I let them stand back and take potshots at the world and make commentaries on this or that, but I am not so much interested in those potshots. It's just that I admire their intelligence. I find it impossible to write about dumb people. While they may be misguided in terms of their obsessions, they are not unintelligent and, by permitting them intelligence as I permit them wealth, I have it both ways.

It seems to me that the metaphor of economics is important in your fiction—Boswell's "turnover, turnover, turnover," Feldman's "unsalable thing," the give-and-take on Dick Gibson's programs, the buying of time in "The Bailbondsman." Does this sound reasonable to you?

Elkin: Yes. A man named Dave Demarest has said that the major fact in my fiction is the transaction. I would agree with him. Feldman someplace says a sale lost is lost forever, irrecoverable. A profit not made is a profit never to be made—and is irrecoverable. My people do buy and sell, if that's the question you were asking. And I myself in my own personal life am not so much a seller as I am a buyer. I love to buy things. I love being in stores. I love things themselves. I love having money to spend and buying things which are not perhaps the most utilitarian things in the world and may even be vulgar. Department stores, not museums, are the first place I go to in a new city, and I love the position of purchase. My characters tend to be salesmen although, as I talk to you like this, it occurs to me that perhaps I should write a novel about a purchaser instead of a seller.

A reviewer of The Franchiser *called you America's "eminent vulgarian" and meant it as a compliment. You seem to find beauty in popular culture, in what you call "the multitudinous slag of the ordinary." How?*

Elkin: I don't necessarily find "beauty" in popular culture. What I *do* find is immense energy. Just consider how complicated the world is, what an immense task just to get the messenger from Aix to Ghent. How much more complicated it must be to organize fast food joints, to mastermind or even just participate in any ordinary human enterprise.

Would you comment on the germination of Boswell?

Elkin: A man named Phil London used to teach here at Washington University. Phil was at my house one evening and was telling me how Boswell got to meet Voltaire. He had sent Voltaire letter upon letter, and Voltaire ignored them. Boswell was having none of this, so he travels to Ferney, and he knocks on the door and tells the servant, "My name is James Boswell and as I happen to be in the neighborhood and have been writing your master, I am here to meet him." The servant goes upstairs and tells Voltaire that this nut is at the door, and Voltaire, who had been besieged by all these letters, none of which he had answered, comes down and gives an audience to Boswell. Boswell says, "Hi, Voltaire!" Now, London did not tell the anecdote as I told it to you, but that's in effect what happened. It struck me as being so funny that I thought a modern Boswell, on the make for all the great men of his time, might be the source of an amusing novel.

Why did you decide to make mortality the driving fact of his life?

Elkin: That's the driving fact of my own life. There isn't a day that goes by that I don't think, "Jesus Christ, how many more months do I have left?" or years, I hope. I am totally preoccupied with death. I mean my own death. Barth, for example, has said that he comes from very good stock and expects to live a long time. Bill Gass thinks that one of the reasons he takes so much time writing his novels—it took him ten years to write *Omensetter's Luck*—is that he has an infinite amount of time left to him. I don't believe that I have an infinite amount of time left to me. Probably I would be a healthier man if I did believe it.

Is this a matter of concern to you as a writer, as it was to Faulkner: that idea of making a scratch on a stone?

Elkin: I know what you're talking about. No, I don't think I am making scratches on stones by writing. Whatever happens to me in my career I hope happens before I die. And screw the libraries.

Could you comment on the immense power of your protagonists within their novels? Does it reflect the novelist's power over his characters?

Elkin: I don't think it has anything to do with the novelist's power over his characters, but it is clearly a pattern in my fiction. To have each protagonist his own novelist—if that's what you mean—yes. Each protagonist moves the other characters around as though they were pawns, or tries to.

Very near the end of the novel Boswell starts thinking about enclosing all other people; he wants to internalize them . . .

Elkin: That's in the penultimate chapter of the novel. The death of everybody else in the world is what validates Boswell's life. He grows immense, becomes the ultimate bodybuilder, by destroying other bodies. Boswell is no sycophant; Boswell is a total egocentric.

I like him because he has the energy of ego. I think his is a jerky way of living one's life, but I think a novelist has to like his characters. If you establish a distance between yourself and your character, then that distance is magnified once it gets around to the reader and the reader is, in effect, looking at a character across the Grand Canyon and can't possibly care for him. So, all characters, all protagonists, are ultimately sympathetic. If they aren't, the novel fails, becomes silly. This is precisely the failure of Alison Lurie's *The War between the Tates.* Miss Lurie clearly despises her characters.

Boswell is a perpetual outsider, and the only thing that gives any vitality to his life is trying to get inside those doors and up those goddamn stairs. At the end of the novel, he could have knocked down that barrier, could have produced credentials that would demonstrate that he's Boswell, could have gotten into The Club. But once he's done that, then, by God, he has to die because he's got nothing left to do. Since the thing that keeps him alive is running scared, he has to start all over again. So "Down with The Club."

Would you tell us how A Bad Man *began?*

Elkin: Again, with a friend. Al Lebowitz was telling me about a lawyer here in St. Louis who had been caught out in some shady deal and had been sentenced to a year in jail. It struck me—What must it be like for a man of the upper-middle class to have to spend a year with pickpockets? The mixture of classes is a very attractive theme. There is a basic fascination in the situation—what it must be for a man who never split a Republican ticket in his life, as Feldman says, to be thrust into a jail with lowlifes. But that itself would not make a novel, so I upped the ante philosophically and asked, what would it be like for a man to be sentenced for his character? To do time for his character? You see, Feldman is perfectly innocent of the charge that actually got him into jail. It was a machine error—an error in the IBM accounting system. They don't put him in jail for doing those favors. They put him in jail for something that, in fact, he is innocent of. And the real thing he is in jail for is his character, as the warden knows. Yet Feldman is not the bad man in that novel. The bad man is the warden. Feldman ain't exactly a sweetiepie; he is capable of all kinds of cruelty in the name of energy. But as far as I am concerned, the *real* son-of-a-bitch in the book is Warden Fisher.

What about the setting? It's no real prison.

Elkin: No, it's no real prison. As one character says, "It's a whole country of penitentiary we got up here." After I was about a hundred and fifty pages or so into the novel, I tried to get into a prison to see what a prison was like. That's very hard to do, unless you commit a crime. I wanted to see how far off I was, so I went through the Walpole State Penitentiary in Massachusetts, and it was one of the most boring after-

noons I have ever spent in my life. I am surprised that men can come out
and still be sane creatures because they have absolutely nothing to do. I
was in one room, for example, where the prisoners were all assigned to
bristle brushes. That would be perfectly terrific if it weren't for the fact
that they had a brush-bristling machine in the room that could bristle a
hundred brushes a minute. They had these ninety prisoners and just this
one machine, so eighty-eight of the prisoners are sitting around the walls
of the room and just two prisoners get to work the machine for an hour,
and then the others get to work the machine. They aren't allowed to talk to
each other. Though I was very bored with that prison experience, I went
back thrilled with the notion that my prison was so much better than their
prison. If I were a penologist, I would make the prisons more like mine
because at least the prisoners wouldn't be bored.

I was aware of the Kafkaesque tone of some of this stuff, and I wanted to
short-circuit that by suggesting that Feldman was aware of it, too. That's
called cheating. I tell myself this for my own good.

Did you do research for The Dick Gibson Show, *or have you been a
long-time radio . . .*

Elkin: I'm a radio listener. I have more radios in my house than you
could imagine. And I was just saying to Joan yesterday, "By God, Joan,
there's a new radio out. We've got to get it. It gets nothing but television
stations." You weren't upstairs when you were at the house yesterday, but
I have every conceivable kind of radio, and I *listen*. I really listen to the
radio.

In The Dick Gibson Show *did you set out to qualify the romantic heroes
in* Boswell *and* A Bad Man?

Elkin: No, but in fact that's what happens. Dick can't stand anybody's
obsession but his own, which is largely the plight of myself and yourself,
probably, and everybody. He's opened a Pandora's box when he opens his
microphones to the people out there. When they find the platform that the
Gibson format provides, they just get nuttier and nuttier and wilder and
wilder, and this genuinely arouses whatever minimal social consciousness
Dick Gibson has. The paradox of the novel is that the enemy that Gibson
has been looking for all his life is that audience. The audience is the enemy.
Dick builds up in his mind this Behr-Bleibtreau character. That Behr-
Bleibtreau is his enemy. That's baloney paranoia. The enemy is the amorphous public that he is trying to appeal to, that he's trying to make love to
with his voice. Dick Gibson is a bodiless being. He is his voice. That's why
the major scene in the novel is the struggle for Gibson's voice.

*Is radio in the novel an index to social change, perhaps the devaluation
of language?*

Elkin: That was not my intention. I could make a case that once upon
a time there were scripts, a platform and an audience out in front of Jack

Benny and Mary Livingston, that radio then was a kind of art form and now it is an artless form in which you get self-promoters and people with theories about curing cancer by swallowing mosquitoes or something. Language, since it is occurring spontaneously rather than thought out, is devalued. But actually, in real life, modern radio talk shows are much more interesting than *The Jack Benny Show* ever was because you are getting the shop talk of personality.

Dick is a professional word man, and by the end he is reduced nearly to silence. Is this your "literature of exhaustion" that Barth talks about, a comment on the futility of language . . .

Elkin: No. Certainly not.

He does say less and less as the novel moves along.

Elkin: Right. And the other people say more and more. That is intentional. But Dick makes an effort to get his program back from the sufferers. He starts hanging up on people. Then he gets the biggest charlatan—Nixon—at the end. Wasn't it clever to invent Nixon before Nixon did?

In bringing together so many stories and storytellers, did you have a thematic unity in mind?

Elkin: I had in mind, as a matter of fact, *The Canterbury Tales*, particularly in that second section where the journey to dawn is the journey to Canterbury. Although there are no particular parallels, when I was sending out sections of the novel to magazines, I would call the sections "The Druggist's Tale" and so on. There is that choral effect of the pilgrims to Canterbury.

Do you still write short stories, or do you feel your gifts are best suited to the expansiveness of the novel?

Elkin: Probably the best story I ever wrote, "A Poetics for Bullies," was written for *The Saturday Evening Post* in 1964 (although the *Post* rejected it and *Esquire* picked it up). They wanted to do a children's issue, and they asked me to write a story about kids. Joan had made a bow and arrow for my son Philip. A kid who lived behind us said to Philip, "I can do magic; I will give you two arrows where there is one." The kid then broke the arrow, and that gave me the initial idea to do a story about bullies. Actually, it is a companion piece to "On a Field, Rampant," the first story I wrote which I felt was any good. The character in the earlier story is unnamed but thinks he is a king, and he really is the John Williams of the bully story.

Are the stories in Criers and Kibitzers *collected consciously as studies in heroism?*

Elkin: No. Collected consciously as studies of complaint and *utzing*, a Yiddish word for troublemaking, getting people to do things they don't want to do. There are two kinds of people, according to the title: the troublemakers and the troubled.

What's a Jewish-American novelist who says he loves Bellow's work doing writing The Living End? *You said before you were not a "thinker," but the book seems your crack at the Problem of Evil.*

Elkin: I'm a Jewish-American reader who loves Bellow's work. I'm *not* a thinker. That is to say I have to have pen or pencil or word processor in order to think. Real thinkers don't need tools but operate like mathematicians and never get chalk on their hands because they don't even need chalk. Maybe they don't even need hands. I've *known* thinkers. They're mostly a distracted lot and either do not listen or hear what you're saying to them. *The Living End* is my crack not at the problem of evil but at the problems of myth and convention. *Honi soit qui mal y pense.*

"The Bailbondsman" is my favorite in Searches and Seizures. *Alexander Main seems to me to be the representative Elkin man.*

Elkin: I would agree with that—because he gets the best of other people. And he is a great salesman. He talks people into taking bond, or he decides not to give them bond, purely on whim. He is truly a master not only of himself but of absolutely everyone else who comes in contact with him. He is a scholar, and he is a rat bastard. But I admire him for his rhetoric. I, myself, am closer to Main than any other character.

Closer to Main than to Ben Flesh in The Franchiser?

Elkin: I'm probably closer to Main than to Ben Flesh, since he and I share a considerable awe about the world while Flesh and I share only this dumb disease.

Do you—or would you—want to say anything about the M.S. or disease in general?

Elkin: Some diseases are worse than other diseases. M.S. is relatively benign since it takes years to kill you. As I said elsewhere, it kills you by yards but you suffer by inches.

Do you read academic criticism on your fiction?

Elkin: On mine, yes. But I don't read it on anybody else. If you write an article about me, believe me, I'll read it because I am profoundly interested in myself.

If you were going to write an essay on your own work . . .

Elkin: I did. I did write an essay on my own work when I wrote the introduction to *Stories from the Sixties*. That contained most of what I think about writing.

If you were going to write this essay in a somewhat less indirect form than that introduction, what would you talk about?

Elkin: I couldn't do it . . . I suppose it would be a retaliatory essay. Some reviewers, particularly Christopher Lehmann-Haupt, are hung up on this notion that I do routines, that I do *schtick*. I do not do *schtick*.

What I do are organized routines and connected *schtick—schtick* upon *schtick* upon *schtick* until we have a piece of carpentry. I am not a stand-up comedian, and what I would try to do in such an essay would be to demonstrate the form that exists in the novels. Reviewers write about the hilarious passages—who gives a shit about the hilarious passages? Hilarious passages are easy to write. There are passages that aren't so hilarious that I like much more. And metaphor: Feldman is talking about a girl lifeguard in a white bathing suit, and he says that he sees "the dark vertical of her behind like the jumbo vein in shrimp."

What kind of a mind does a writer have that "the jumbo vein in shrimp" is present and available for him to get down on the page?

Elkin: I don't have it here in my office now, but if we were over in my carrel, where I do my writing, you would see a J. C. Penney catalog, an enormous J. C. Penney catalog and its big supplement. Now this guy in *The Franchiser* has a Radio Shack franchise. He is describing what these radios, phonographs, and stereos look like. A speaker is black as a domino, some damn thing like that. Of course I invent that, but I invent that by *studying* the photographs of those speakers. I try literally to look at what I am writing about. In "The Bailbondsman," I didn't make up a single thing in the descriptions of teeth. All those teeth are right there to be seen in the Victoria and Albert Museum of Natural History. I went with a pad and pencil and copied down the shapes of those teeth. I'm not a very good artist, but I could get the rough structure and by God there was a tooth with three holes that looked exactly like a goblin's face. It would look like a goblin's face to you. There was another thing that looked like a piece of cork. That's the *only* thing it looked like. So it's not a question of making imaginary leaps or having a third eye. It's a question of using the two eyes I have—and looking hard and close at things.

In The Living End *God is a frustrated artist who destroys the world because he never found his audience. Reading the reviews, I thought it ironic that with this book you had found a larger audience than before. Do you think that's true, and if it is are you pleased?*

Elkin: In a way, *The Living End* turned my "career" around. As a result of its publication all my books suddenly came back into print. *The Living End* itself probably sold three times as many copies in hardback as any previous book of mine. But we're still talking the minor leagues, Triple A. We're talking drop in the ocean, spit in the bucket. But I'm pleased. I'm easily pleased.

I've heard that your novel in progress, George Mills, *is different from your other work. Would you talk a bit about it?*

Elkin: I'll talk in terms of length. *George Mills* is certainly the longest book I've ever written. Right now I have 472 pages and need to write two more chapters to finish it. Which should make the book over 550 pages long. Roughly, and very superficially, it's about a man whose family has been cursed with blue-collar blood for a thousand years and finally realizes that the meaning of life is to live long enough to do something well.

An Interview with
Raymond Federman

The following interview took place at my home in San Diego on March 18, 1980. Raymond Federman had actually arrived in San Diego from his home in Buffalo, New York, four days earlier, but our schedule had left no time for an interview. Within forty-five minutes of the moment when his plane touched down, we were standing on the first tee of a local golf course, arguing about handicaps and the size of the bets (Federman is a nine handicapper and notorious gambler). The next few days' activities included more golf, poetry readings, two late-night poker games, class visitations, and several informal readings by Federman from his recently completed novel, *The Twofold Vibration.* (Come to think of it, there must have been another round of golf in there.)

Despite the frantic pace of his visit, Federman remained (very typically) energetic throughout nearly six hours of tapings. Chain-smoking French cigarettes, he would excitedly stride about the living room while answering questions, his incredibly thick French accent often making it nearly impossible to completely understand his replies. Dressed in stylish pants and a golf shirt, he looks a great deal like a fortyish French movie star; although he appears to be in remarkably vigorous shape for a man of fifty-two, it is Federman's face, with its prominent laugh lines and penetrating dark eyes, that immediately catches one's attention. In responding to questions Federman's tone shifted rapidly from serious to humorous, with playful digressions often interrupting lengthy, serious observations.

Raymond Federman is the author of two books of poems (*Among the Beasts,* 1967; *Me Too,* 1975), four novels (*Double or Nothing,* 1971; *Amer*

Eldorado, 1974; *Take It or Leave It,* 1976; and *The Voice in the Closet,* 1979), and numerous short stories. A professor of comparative literature at SUNY–Buffalo, he is also the author of various critical studies, including *Journey to Chaos: Samuel Beckett's Early Fiction* (1965) and *Surfiction: Fiction Now and Tomorrow* (1975). Federman was born in Paris in 1928. His parents and sisters were exterminated in the concentration camps, a fate which Federman escaped only because his mother placed him in a closet which was never searched. After arriving in the United States in the late 1940s, he eventually received his B.A. from Columbia University in 1955 and his Ph.D. from UCLA in 1962. Federman's fiction is perhaps best known for its typographical experimentation, its complex narrative structuring, and the frantic, almost delirious energy of its language unfolding upon the page. Constantly circling, evading, and storifying the traumatic events of his youth, Federman self-consciously projects himself into his narratives even as he spins forth new versions of his fictional self. He has recently completed a fifth novel, *The Twofold Vibration,* which Indiana University Press is publishing.

—Larry McCaffery

Could you talk a bit about your creative process—your writing routine, if you have one?

Federman: I always work in the morning, six days a week, never on Sunday (Sunday it's football-watching, or hockey, or whatever), six days a week except of course when I don't work and sometimes I don't work for weeks, I just sit and wait for something to happen in my head, but that's work, too. But normally breakfast around seven-thirty, then at the typewriter by eight.

What happens once you're actually at the typewriter?

Federman: First I always reread a good chunk of what I have written. I read it aloud to get the tone, the voice, the timbre back in my head. Then I work, which in my case is type, since I always work directly on the typewriter. That does not mean that pages are flowing out. From eight to about one, which is my usual writing séance, sometimes if I manage to produce one clean (supposedly final) page I'm doing well. So I usually work from eight to one, unless things are going so well that I forget the time. Sometimes I walk away from the typewriter (especially when there is no one at home), look at the clock and realize it's five in the afternoon and I have totally forgotten to take lunch, I feel dizzy, my throat hurts from all the Gauloises, but somehow time has vanished into the text. Part of the working process is also the time you waste doing other things (like writing letters to friends) and fiddling around with papers, books, rearranging your books, simply not to work on the novel or whatever in progress, what I call the scratching of the head and the picking of the nose, but that too is part of the creative process. But somehow the pages get written.

No, I do not drink coffee when I write; no, I do not smoke dope; I never get drunk. But lots of cigarettes, sometimes three at the same time burning in different ashtrays. And yes, I listen to jazz while I write, or at least jazz plays while I write. And let me add that I can write with all sorts of disturbances going on, it doesn't bother me. I learned that, I suppose, while I was writing *Double or Nothing* on the kitchen table in our little apartment in Paris in 1966–67, and the kids were running around, and Erica (my wife) was cooking, and life was going on. In other words, like everyone else, I get disturbed all the time while I am writing—the phone, the wife, the kids, the mailman, the doorbell—but I can get up from the typewriter and still get back to what I was typing and not feel like things have stopped forever. One learns to live a double life while writing, not only double, but simultaneous lives.

How does a book typically begin for you—or is there any consistency?

Federman: All my books literally come to me in the form of a sentence, an original sentence which contains the entire book. *The Twofold Vibration* began with the sentence: "If the night passes quietly tomorrow he will have reached the twenty-first century and be on his way . . ." That doesn't mean that this sentence will be the opening sentence of the book when it's finished, but that's how it began in my head, during a sleepless night in fact, and was continued on paper. The first sentence that came to me and became *Double or Nothing* was: "If the room cost eight dollars a week then it will have to be noodles . . ." As for *Take It or Leave It*, it was this sentence: "The easiest of course would be to blow my brains out (BANG!) this way I wouldn't have to begin . . . but suppose . . . Yes suppose . . ." And the book went on from there, moved on while cancelling itself. But I insist that these first sentences are not necessarily at the beginning of the book; often they are displaced into the text, and very often repeated to keep the text going. I suppose the most important thing for me in these sentences—these threshold sentences—is that they establish a tone for the rest of the book.

I notice that most of these first sentences are set in some form of the conditional—"If . . . Suppose . . . Let's say . . ." This isn't just a coincidence, obviously.

Federman: Certainly not. One could say—there I go again—that the major tense, the governing tense of my fiction is indeed the conditional tense. The supposition implied in the opening sentence already undermines the truth, the reality, the validity, the permanence, the totalization of what follows in the book. Basically what I'm saying with these first sentences determines the entire condition of what's to follow. The book is always written to find out somehow what would happen *if* the room cost

eight dollars, . . . *If* the night passes quietly, and so on, blah blah blah
and whatever. My fiction emerges out of that unfinished, unsettled conditional statement, which means then that the fiction cannot pass for
remembered events but is truly invented, even if some of the facts in the
fiction belong to the past—my past. I would say that if one were to study
this carefully, one would indeed come to the conclusion that the governing
tense in my fiction is the conditional tense, but one could extend that further for an analysis of much of contemporary fiction. I read Márquez's
One Hundred Years of Solitude as a novel written in the conditional, even
though the dominant tense in the book may not seem to be conditional.

*You've placed a great deal of emphasis on this "threshold sentence."
How do you proceed once you have this sentence?*

Federman: Once I have that first sentence, I continually examine it,
scrutinize it for its implications—not only of meaning, but of tone, tonality, structure, temporal twist, etc., for in fact the entire novel is already
contained there. I begin to detect in that sentence some of the details of the
plot—well, the story, the anecdote, since I do not write plots—and even
though I basically know what will happen in the novel, since it is usually
loosely drawn from my own experiences, nonetheless what I am looking
for in that sentence is the structure, the rhythm of the entire book. My
stories are usually based on a journey of some sort. This doesn't have to be
a physical, geographical journey from one place to another—I say
"journey" simply in terms of movement. And whenever there is movement in a story, then there is also displacement, discovery, loss, and
mystery. But after I have found all that, drawn out this movement from
my first sentence, I still have to find the image, the metaphor which will
sustain the novel. That too is crucial to my writing, or to much of so-called
postmodern fiction: it relies strongly on a central metaphor. While the fiction seems to be telling a particular story, it is really telling another story,
for in a metaphor you always have two terms—very often terms that are
seemingly incompatible—and while you are looking at the one term of the
metaphor you are also seeing the other term. *The Twofold Vibration* is
constructed on that principle, and I mean rigidly constructed. And of
course *The Voice in the Closet* as well. My role, once I have set up the
metaphor, is to decipher the meaning of that metaphor and write its symbolic meaning. That will be the novel. Perhaps rather than use terms like
"metaphor" or "symbol," one should speak of "snapshots." We all have in
us such snapshots, and we draw the meaning of our existence by interpreting these—very much the way we try to interpret our dreams, which
are also complex systems of metaphors and symbols.

*So this is actually a visual image or picture—a "snapshot," as you
say—and not just some abstraction or thought?*

Federman: Yes, absolutely a visual image. That's the only way I can work, and I'm sure it's true of most novelists. One does not work with abstractions, ideas (whatever these may be) to write fiction. You work with concrete material, and I mean "concrete" almost in the sense of "cement."

Could you provide a "concrete example," then, of what you mean?

Federman: Certainly. Obviously the central image in *The Voice in the Closet*, for example, comes from a real, a very visual image or snapshot—the image of the boy in that closet crouching to take a shit on a newspaper. That's the snapshot around which the entire book is constructed. Of course, I have to *imagine* (or invent) what is in that box, in that closet—the clothes, the box of sugar, the empty skins, the hats—and beyond that the fear, the apprehension, etc. The real closet (if there was a closet) may not have been like that. But once I have the snapshot, it's simply a matter of looking at it as though I were looking at a painting and deciphering its meaning, its symbolism. Isn't this how we look at a great painting? We stand there, and inside our head (or wherever we speak to ourselves) we entertain a dialogue with ourselves—we discuss the subject, the color, the geometry of the painting, etc., etc. And when we walk away from the painting we have explained it to ourselves, and it is this explanation which gives us pleasure, moves us, makes us feel that we have gained some understanding not only of the painting but also of the world around us and ourselves in that world. Of course, there are people who prefer to have others explain paintings to them, or books, or poems—thus the need of critics, explicators, psychiatrists for personal mental snapshots. My good friend Ron Sukenick always says to those who say that his novels are unreadable: use your imagination, my friend, lest someone else use it for you.

In discussing your creative process, I haven't heard you mention revision very much, even though I know that you work and rework every page that finally appears.

Federman: To me there is really no such thing as revision. There is only writing, and more writing, and more writing on top of more writing, between the lines, through the lines, between the words. The real writing for me is this rewriting. Not revising, but rewriting. My books grow from the inside, not necessarily growing from left to right, in one direction, but also from right to left, up and down and sideways. All I need is a few words scribbled here and there, and I can make these words grow, explode into pages. A slow, painful but joyful process. This is probably why my books never look like finished products—because more could be written between the lines of what is finally published. And of course more could be removed, too, because the process goes in either direction. It has often bothered me that publishers want to publish only the finished, polished product. It would be interesting to publish the entire writing that goes into making a novel. Everything. All the drafts, complete or partial, all the notes, scribbling, doodlings, etc. All the labor, in other words. Imagine that. In a way that's what you see when you look at a painting, especially a modern painting. All the paint that went into the process is there on the canvas. I wish one could see all the words that went into the making of a novel.

Does that mean you have no sense of where you're going when you begin a novel?

Federman: Absolutely not! I nave no idea where I'm going. No idea whatsoever. Otherwise what would be the point of writing? I write not to transcribe something, but hopefully to invent something which was not there before.

Do you ever listen to jazz when you write?

Federman: Yes, jazz. The moment I walk into my study, I turn on the cassette player, or the radio, and the music blares during the entire time I'm working. Jazz establishes a rhythm for the day, so all day long I play jazz while I work, old stuff, bebop, new stuff, and if there is something really good on the radio, I turn it on. A friend of mine once described my books to me in a letter as long tenor sax solos. The language of my novels just goes on and on, improvising as it goes along, hitting wrong notes all the time—but, after all, jazz also builds itself on a system of wrong chords that the player stumbles upon and then builds from. So there are a lot of wrong things in *Take It or Leave It*, for example, that are useful to the reader. It's jazz.

Is this parallel with jazz really accurate to draw, since you rework and rewrite your fiction so painstakingly?

Federman: But that's what improvisation is! What do you think is going on when jazz musicians are working in a recording session? The musicians start searching for something, stop and go, repeat the same stuff, but each time with slight variations, until they think they have stumbled on the right stuff, the right combination. I have a recording like that of Charlie Parker where there are six or seven different takes of the same piece. And we can hear him revising, or trying to get to that little breakthrough that will generate the piece, that one chord on which he can build his next set of improvisations. That one chord which the pianist is feeding to the sax player, or the rhythm section searching in the background while the soloist is trying to work his way in. What they are really trying to do is come together (and I mean "come" in its double meaning), and each attempt takes them a bit further. Well, what I call "revising" is basically the same thing. Perhaps the term is not right—as I told you, I usually simply call this "rewriting," which in this case simply means writing on and on. In any case, it's a constant reshuffling of things until you find the right combination, the right aggregate. It works the same way with writing, at least with my writing. What you finally read in the published text is what's been collaged and montaged (can one use these words like this?) from all my various improvisations. In other words, writing for me is also a way of splicing stuff together. That's real writing for me, and not that initial spontaneous flow of words. That's in the final text, too, but buried inside the other levels of improvisation. It's in the various re-working and re-writing sessions that the real elements of improvisation (and not inspiration) come, because improvisation is always something that builds on something else. Perhaps this very interview is, has been, pure improvisation. It has built itself on itself.

When you were talking just now about the musicians trying to come together—in the musical and sexual sense—I was reminded of that incredibly vivid scene in Take It or Leave It *where the jazz musicians go back to that garage to play and then masturbate collectively. Could you explain your intentions in that scene?*

Federman: I was trying to show several things, but especially the relationship of jazz with sex, and of course the sexual act as a creative act. That jazz scene has offended certain people, but at the same time it has moved a lot of people. As you know I was a jazz musician myself for a number of years, in Detroit, and later in New York. I played with many curious but wonderful people. I was not that good; otherwise I would still be a jazz musician. In any event, the key to that scene has to do with what it means to spend a whole night improvising jazz. If you've played jazz and improvised, you know that you can never get to the end of yourself, to the essential. You want to play that one great perfect solo that's going to blow it all, say it all, but you never do. So when you walk away from those jam sessions where you've been playing with a group of people you respect and who feel as you do, where you have really been interacting, you always walk away feeling depressed. You don't want to go home, you don't want to be alone, but at the same time you really don't want to go and screw the woman who was sitting there listening and making eyes at you. No, you want to stay with the cats. You see, the first part of that jazz scene in *Take It or Leave It* merely describes the jam session, the excitement of that great evening when Charlie Parker himself plays Frenchy's saxophone. The second part is, metaphorically, a repetition of the first part, but now instead of playing their instruments the musicians are playing with their sex. They are masturbating collectively in order to ejaculate, you might say, what's left of the music in them, in order to get to the end of themselves. And that you can only do yourself, to yourself, and with those who participated in the jam session.

Masturbation plays an important metaphorical role in all your works, it seems. I'm interested in why you choose masturbation so often, rather

*than other sexual metaphors—doesn't it take two to get it on and create
something, to keep life going?*

Federman: Remember, you always have to read masturbation in my
work in its purely metaphorical or symbolic form. For me the act of
masturbation is a positive act, even if most people think of it as ugly or dirty. There is a crucial passage in *The Voice in the Closet* that no one has yet
caught and which came to me directly from Proust. Somewhere in his
work Proust raises a most interesting question about masturbation: the
first time a child masturbates he/she doesn't do it in order to *reenact* the
sexual act, since he/she doesn't know what that act is. It is therefore a pure
act, an act of discovery, of invention, or creation. Therefore there is
something beautiful about this first masturbatory gesture when it is performed without any memory, without any mental images. Later the act of
masturbation becomes a substitution for the sexual act itself, performed
because one is deprived, frustrated, horny, or whatever. It is between
these two acts that I'm working in my fiction. It is not because one has
discovered sex that one cannot masturbate the primary way. There are indeed moments of masturbation which are strictly substitutional, and
others which are creative, original, pure and free of all imitation. The
masturbation moments in *Take It or Leave It* play with both types, but
usually it is the original, primal act that is implied, especially in relation to
the discovery of America. The young man who hasn't screwed America
doesn't know who she is, has no memory, no experience of it. Of course,
there are other moments when the masturbation is merely the substitution
for the original purity of the act. Between these two types of moments we
have a symbolic possibility which helps us read the book, and one must
grasp the implication behind the act. And I don't mean to suggest here that
there are all sorts of psychological implications. For me, masturbation is
simply a gesture which may carry symbolic or metaphorical possibilities.
It's in this sense that one must read the masturbation scene that follows the
jam session in the jazz scene. In other words, masturbation, whether performed singly or collectively, can be symbolic of heroic gestures, just as it
can be an act of cowardice or escape.

*A bit earlier you spoke disparagingly about ideas by saying "whatever
these may be"—and somewhere I recall your saying that you "don't give a
shit about ideas" in your fiction. And yet readers invariably discuss all fictional works—no matter what the author says about the fact—in terms of
ideas. This tendency on the part of readers and critics often seems beside
the point with a lot of postmodern fiction—with the works of Barthelme,
Katz, Gass, Sukenick, and Federman. What's your idea about this issue?*

Federman: This whole issue of ideas, writing ideas, is very
troublesome to me. There are not too many ideas in the world. Ideas are
not little birds that fly around which a writer grabs and then puts into his

novels. No. The language of a novel may create some ideas, inadvertently perhaps. But a novelist does not sit down to write ideas. A novelist is not a philosopher. Most of us never have original ideas. There's really no such thing, especially if you're a novelist. Novelists aren't interested in ideas, they are interested in stories. I always come back to Beckett on this question of ideas—Beckett because he is undoubtedly among the three or four great novelists of this century. Well, if you read the entire work of Beckett—and it's been over fifty years since he published his first piece of fiction—you'll find only one idea, repeated over and over again. An idea in the form of a question in fact: What the hell am I doing here writing this stuff? This is the essential question, the central idea of Beckett's work—a question that all human beings should ask themselves, the guy in the factory, the guy digging ditches, the guy behind a desk. They all should ask themselves, What the fuck am I doing here in this life? That is the essential idea of life and of writing. My own writing is always about that.

Some critics and readers have suggested that it's egotistical or narcissistic for you to always write about your life story. How do you answer such charges?

Federman: I don't think these critics and readers have the courage of their own narcissism. I have a story to tell, which is basically the story of my life. We all want to tell our life's story. But the more crucial question is: Why would readers want to hear it? Mine may have been strange, curious, dramatic even from the beginning—the closet, the Germans, the concentration camps, the farms where I worked during the war, my coming to America, the factories in Detroit, the years I spent as a jazz musician, the people I loved, my sexual adventures, my intellectual adventures. I could go on and on and scribble all that down, but finally it's not that interesting, that unusual. No more so than the life of another guy. What *is* interesting is not the story itself, but *how I tell you that story*. It's the only reason you want to listen to me, or read my books. Not because of the story per se but because of the way I'm going to tell you what happened to me. In a way you are more interested in the lies, the exaggerations, the disguises I'm going to use to tell you my story and which are going to make you believe in the truth of my lie. Even if a story is great, if the teller is poor, you won't listen to the story. In all fiction you have the teller and the told. The told is the story, the action, the material, but usually we are more interested in the teller, the voice, the tone, the language. In fact, I think what interests us most in storytelling is not so much the main line of the story as the digressions, the necessary digressions of good storytelling.

You just said that most readers are usually more interested in the teller, the voice, the language, rather than the tale, the story. Do you really believe this has been the case during the history of fiction?

Federman: The authorial voice has always been present in fiction. It has to be. Otherwise it's not fiction. Of course, there is always a matter of degree—degree of presentness of that authorial voice. But even the fact of pretending to write a piece of fiction which doesn't reveal the voice of the author is a way of pointing to that voice, or to the absence of that voice. The so-called omniscient author in realistic fiction is a question that needs careful reexamination.

I guess what I was trying to ask is whether or not you feel that your own emphasis on the teller at the expense of the tale (that may be a bit too strong) or on a voice which is always at the center of the reader's interest—isn't this a break with the usual traditions of fiction? What do you see as your literary "line of descent"?

Federman: To begin with, I don't think of myself as breaking with tradition: on the contrary, I think I'm working within an important tradition. Of course, one must emphasize that there is not only one tradition, but many traditions. Each novelist works within one of these many traditions, or several. In my case, the list of writings which my books have an affinity with goes way back—it starts with Homer (but I suppose everything starts with Homer), but then it goes on with *La Chanson de Roland*, Rabelais (Rabelais, who was doing what most of us are doing today—much better, perhaps), then *Tristram Shandy*, then Laclos' *Liaisons dangereuses*, and Stendhal, but perhaps not Balzac, not Tolstoy, not Zola for sure, but certainly Dostoevsky, and into the twentieth century, Proust of course, Céline, Camus, Beckett. As you can see, my line does not go through a certain type of realistic novel, or what I would call a novel which functions on the basis of a closed form. Most of the novels which form the tradition within which I work are novels which in one way or another reflect upon their own form—all have within themselves images of the writer inside the text, more or less visible. So, as you can see, I have not invented anything new, nor do I pretend to have invented anything new. I am simply exploring, pursuing a way of writing fiction which has been around for a long time, as far back as the days of Homer, who is one of the most self-reflexive writers imaginable. In Homer's work you see all sorts of writers (storytellers) telling little stories (one could almost call these essays) which reflect on the main story. By the time you get to Rabelais' work you confront pure extemporaneous fiction, pure improvisation. Rabelais is the first great jazz fictioneer. And of course with Sterne all the "gimmicks" of experimentation are there, including the blank page and Chapter 17 where the author tells us: I have nothing to say in this chapter. That's the tradition within which I work.

Let's pursue this issue of "voice" and "author" a bit further. In all of your fiction—but especially in The Voice in the Closet—*you deliberately blur the usual distinctions between narrator, author, and voice, as well as between language as product and language as a active, self-ruminating pro-*

cess. To an extent this tendency can be found in a great deal of postmodern fiction: the works of Sukenick, Gass, Katz, Barth, even Vonnegut. I suppose related to this is the general confusion that often develops in these works between reality and illusion, fictional versus supposedly "real" selves. Would you talk about this tendency a bit?

Federman: You have to accept the kinds of confusions you're talking about all the time in contemporary fiction—I mean the confusion that exists between real selves and real objects and fictional selves, fictional projections. When Kurt Vonnegut introduces himself in *Slaughterhouse-Five,* is it the real Vonnegut who is there in the story, or a fictitious one? Same thing with Sukenick, I mean the name Sukenick, in Ronald Sukenick's fiction. How can you tell? I have said—and many other contemporary writers agree and have said the same thing—that there's no such thing as reality, only fiction.

What exactly do you mean to suggest by this?

Federman: OK, obviously there is a reality "out there." I mean the trees, the grass, nature, people, etc. All that exists. But it's the way we deal with reality that makes it fictitious. For example, I know that you have seen the Eiffel Tower; I once stood with you in front of that monstrosity, that phallic symbol of the twentieth century that rises over the City of Light, as Paris was once known. It is ugly. It is fun. I don't know, you may even have climbed to the top, maybe even climbed the stairs and counted the number of steps, perhaps even eaten in the restaurant up there on the second floor (not a bad restaurant, but expensive!). Anyway, we both know that there is that thing out there which we call the Eiffel Tower, we have seen it, even touched it. But when I say "Eiffel Tower," anyone, even someone who has never seen the damn thing, has a mental image of the Eiffel Tower. So now we have *two* Eiffel Towers—the real one that you and I saw, and an image, a mental image of the thing that the rest of the people who have never been to Paris have never seen. There is, then, in all of us, a mental Eiffel Tower. Traditional fiction worked on the principle that there is this real thing—let's call that "experience." Some of us have experienced the Eiffel Tower, climbed up and down that thing. That's the original experience. But then there is the mental experience of the Eiffel Tower, remember, the mental cinema we all play in our minds when someone says "Eiffel Tower." Traditional realistic fiction does not make any distinction between the real experience and the mental cinema. It confuses the real thing with the illusion of the real thing. Or if you prefer, it makes the illusory mental image pass for the real thing. Well for me, and for most contemporary writers, the mental image is more interesting, more important than the real thing. There is more to that, however. If I were to ask twenty people to take out a piece of paper and *write*—I don't mean describe it, but write, invent their own Eiffel Tower on the basis of what they know of it, from directly experiencing it or from the mental image they have of it—the result would be very interesting. We would now have twenty Eiffel Towers. Not twenty physical descriptions, but twenty fictitious Eiffel Towers, twenty *verbal* Eiffel Towers, which, for me at least, would be much more interesting, perhaps even much more *real*, than the real thing out there. The actual object is nothing, an ugly construction, a useless thing. In other words, even if you have seen it, touched it, experienced it, what really counts is what you *say* about it. The Eiffel Tower is *words*, the words we say about it, and as such it's a fiction.

But to come back to your original question more specifically. When you read a novel which plays with the dichotomy of external object and the mental image of that object, you are in fact only dealing with one entity that abolishes that dichotomy, that split. You are dealing with a verbalized object and that's all. You have to realize that author, narrator, character, all the voices in a novel—all these are part of this verbalization, part of this third dimension of experience: the written or spoken form of the original experience. It is what hides behind, inside these original experiences that is what fascinates me. And I don't mean inside these things physically, but symbolically. If we talk about the Pyramids, we must talk also about the history, the mythology, the fiction, drama, tragedy that is connected with these monuments. In other words, what interests me about the reality of the Pyramids is less the monuments themselves (except of course for their architectural forms) than the catastrophes, one might say, that are contained, implied in them. That's how we must read and write novels also, less for the reality/realism than for the catastrophe/drama that hides behind the imposture of realism.

Since you consistently downplay the importance of the "realism" or the "ideas" in your fiction, what is it that you are hoping your readers will get out of your writing?

Federman: Several things. But perhaps the most important thing I can say about my writing is that it is a form of liberation. For myself first, but hopefully for the reader, the potential reader of my books. For me writing and reading are means of liberation—you liberate yourself, in the process of writing (and reading), from all sorts of misconceived and preconceived notions. You liberate yourself from the conditioning that our environment, our educational system, our social institutions, our background, including our parents—all these things impose on us. I hope that my books will help readers step out of this. Perhaps it is the language, the looseness, the irrationality, the delirium of my langauge which will help them, and perhaps even its vulgarity, its blasphemous aspect. In a way I think of my novels as disrupting a certain form of logic. Whether we like it or not, or even admit it, we are raised on logic, raised with a sense of rationality and coherence. I believe there is as much value in making *non-sense* as there is in making sense. It's simply a matter of direction. Suppose Descartes, and the rationalists, had formulated *ir*-rationalism instead of rationalism, we would now be living in a delightful culture of irrationality, and it would work just as well—or just as badly. So I believe that one of the functions of my work, and of most work being done today in fiction, is to offer other alternatives, and thus to liberate us from preestablished and preconceived notions that still govern us.

Another thing that contemporary fiction does for the reader—and I include my own fiction in this—is that it reinvents the world for us, and allows us to look at it in a different manner. The world, as we received it when we reached consciousness, or what Sartre used to call the Age of Reason, was all spoiled, saturated with crap, with shit. It looked dead. Full of clichés. Beckett and his generation of writers realized that the world was dead, that it had closed upon itself, and in a way Beckett in his work gives us the final vision of that world. Though Beckett has been going on for years now talking about that dead world, to some extent he closed it for us. After Beckett there is no possibility of writing about the world again, at least not that old dying world. However, there are writers today, and I would name Gabriel García Márquez as the most important, who are reinventing the world for us, showing us new possibilities, possibilities that anything can happen. These writers lie, they exaggerate, they surrealize the real; and yet somehow they captivate us, they make us believe in the world they are reinventing and make us wish we could live in that reinvented, magical world. Well, I hope my fiction also reinvents if not the whole world, at least a little piece of it.

I also want to put my readers in touch with a certain personal experience I had with the world and with history—recent history. And that I can only do with *language*. I want you to read me not just for my story but mostly for the language, because, ultimately, that's all we *are*, that's what keeps us together, language. What differentiates us from animals and plants is our language. Animals may have their own language, but that's their business.

Although I'm not personally sympathetic with this view, a lot of critics and readers have suggested that most postmodern fiction is "useless"—or less valuable than previous fiction—because it fails to provide the kinds of solutions and models for behavior that fiction used to provide. It therefore becomes "immoral" in the sense that John Gardner is talking about.

Federman: I'll accept that. But at the same time, why should I, or any writer, be held responsible for furnishing replacements, ways out, for his fellow man? We don't ask painting, music, and even poetry to give us better worlds, better conditions of living. Poetry, music, painting are, to some extent, nonfunctional arts. Why should the novel be functional?

In 1857 (or maybe it was 1859) Baudelaire published *Les Fleurs du mal*, and at about the same time Karl Marx published *Das Kapital*, and Darwin *The Origin of Species*, and immediately poetry was declared useless. Before the middle of the nineteenth century, before the bourgeoisie took over the moral, social, and political control of our lives, people would read poetry simply for the pleasure of reading poetry. They would go out and sit under a tree, near a lake, on top of a mountain, and read books of poetry. But somehow the new social class found that poetry was useless. I'm serious—they didn't need it anymore, it served no useful function. And so poets became alienated, discarded. They were considered either lazy or crazy. What happened to poetry then? It turned inward, became hermetic, started talking to itself. It cut itself off from the moral and social concerns of the new ruling class. And yet, between 1860 and 1940, some of the greatest poetry in Western culture was written. Sure, there was some great poetry written before that, but think of Baudelaire, Rimbaud, Lautremont, Mallarmé, Rilke, Yeats, Pound, Eliot, Valéry, and the list goes on and on. These poets wrote great work which spoke mostly to itself. But don't kid yourself, nobody today goes about reading books of poetry, goes to a bookstore to buy a book of poems saying to himself, "Oh, I'm going to buy a book of poetry and go home and read it." You might read a few poems, two or three, here and there, maybe poems written by a friend of yours because he sent you his latest book, or because you have to for a course, but in general we don't read much poetry, and rarely for the pleasure of it. Those who do read poetry these days are poets. In other words, poets speak to themselves, and in fact have lost their audience. Yes, they come out once in a while and read to groups of people in order to peddle their stuff, but even that is not too good for poetry because soon the poem must function like a joke, like an anecdote, with a neat punchline, otherwise the people who listen will fall asleep. And yet fantastic poetry is still being written, even though no one really listens to it. For the last hundred years (one hundred years of poetic solitude), poetry has been examining itself.

In the nineteenth century the novel served a real purpose — it entertained, it told stories, it gave knowledge, it was a social, historical document. Indeed, the novel became functional in the nineteenth century. When one read Balzac, Dickens, Zola, Tolstoy, one was not only reading a story, or seeing what happened to the characters, one was finding out about all sorts of things, about banking, about coal mining, about the slums of London, about life in the country, or in the city, and so on. In a way this was necessary — there was no radio, no television, no real mass media to give information about the world and about human activities. The novel served that purpose; it was and had to be informative. As we move closer to the present, to the so-called postmodern period, we discover that the novel gradually loses its function in relation to society. In the past twenty years it has not only been declared useless, sometimes unreadable, but even *dead*. Yet this moribund thing refuses to die! It keeps coming back at us in bigger and bigger forms—John Barth's last novel, eight hundred pages of what most people consider unreadable stuff; William Gaddis's *JR*, more unreadable stuff; Pynchon's *Gravity's Rainbow*, and many others. It seems that all these so-called unreadable novels continue to be written (and published, for some strange reason) while saying to the potential unreaders: Fuck you all, you don't want to read me, that's OK, nonetheless we'll go on being written (and hopefully published).

OK, what has caused this development of "unreadability"? I assume you are saying that the novel's function has fundamentally changed in relation to its audience, so that the older virtues—providing information, readability, and so on—now seem not worth pursuing.

Federman: Exactly. There are good reasons why the novel has become as useless and unfunctional as poetry has been for over a hundred and thirty years. Television, radio, magazines, and newspapers have taken over much of the novel's function. Mass media have taken over what I would call the documentary aspect of fiction—they give the information which in the past was given to the reader by the novel. Then you have this curious type of information book which is called "New Journalism," or the nonfiction novel. These books deal with social and political events. In a way these types of books are bastard children of the old-fashioned realistic novel. They refuse to give up the documentary aspect of fiction, and as such turn into pseudo-journalism—or is it the reverse, pseudo-fiction? Consequently the serious novel (whatever that means, which for me really means the playful novel) is suddenly forced to ask itself, What is left for me to do? How can I survive, if survive I must? And why? In a way my first novel, *Double or Nothing*, is simply a long interrogation of what the hell that book is. It was once described in an article as "a manual for writing novels." Perhaps that's what novelists, serious novelists are really doing today: writing novel-manuals about how to write, how to continue to write novels.

But I sense that in the past few years writers have begun to turn away from the extremely self-conscious, self-reflexive works of the late '60s and early '70s. Don't you feel as if writers have decided, to an extent anyway, that experimentation in this direction has gone far enough, and that it's time to look around in other directions for the solution to how to write novels?

Federman: Yes and no! Yes, in the sense that I agree that too much self-consciousness in fiction can undermine the work; and yes, because of what has been happening recently. In a number of recent novels it seems that the consciousness is becoming more prominent, while the self is gradually diminishing. For a while we had something like *self*-consciousness, and now we have more of a self-*consciousness*. The two terms are not yet separated, but they have achieved a different kind of balance, so that we are going to have much more *consciousness*, much more *reflexiveness* (in the sense of thinking), much more awareness in the novel, with a lesser emphasis on the self. In this sense the novel will reconnect with the outer world, not necessarily with reality, but with history—history which is, of course, also a form of fiction, "a dream already dreamt and destroyed," as John Hawkes once put it. I think this is already evident in a number of recent novels, those of Márquez and other Latin American novelists such as Cortazar, Fuentes, and others. *The Public Burning* by Coover is also a novel where the consciousness of a specific historical moment is central to the text. I suppose Barth's *Letters* is another example, quite different in approach and style, but still a more conscious than self-conscious novel. I think that my own *The Twofold Vibration* works like that, too—it reconnects with a certain vision of history, and the self-consciousness of the text emerges only when it is necessary.

As for the No: I believe all great fiction must have an element of self-consciousness. It's its only defense, and it's also its only justification as fiction—if a justification is needed. So I feel we are going to witness an interesting change in the novel within the next ten years. Not that it's going to go back to realism—and remember, even realism is just an extremely sophisticated system of illusions—not even to hyper-realism, as painting has done after abstract expressionism. No, not back to reality, whatever that may be. But the novel is going to reconnect with what is often claimed to be missing in my novels—not ideas, but actions.

Could you clarify what you just said about realism being a system of illusion?

Federman: Certainly. I was in Paris last summer and I went to the Louvre. I don't go to the Louvre very often. It's a flea market of art. And dusty, too. Anyway, I went there just to see some Rembrandts. But as I walked through one of the long corridors, my eyes caught two huge paintings by David, certainly one of the ultimate realists. Huge paintings which usually represent life-sized human figures—Roman soldiers standing with spear in one hand above the head, and a shield in the other, a panached helmet. The body half-naked. Perfect anatomy. Beautiful body. All the muscles, the veins in the legs and arms are there, precisely painted, and so real. Incredible! What details, what reality! I stood there and I was totally *floored*! I couldn't believe it was only a picture of a man. I was so convinced, so fooled by the reality of this picture that I approached the painting and touched the veins in the leg of that Roman soldier. Of course, I only touched paint. Old dried-up paint. But David had entrapped me in his system of illusions, and made me believe that what I was seeing was a real human being. That system of illusions had been refined to such an extreme that I couldn't even see the paint, the medium. The realism of the figure had made the paint vanish, had rendered the paint itself irrelevant. Therefore this raises an important question — what we call realism, in painting or in writing, is really a perfected system of illusions. Much of the work of the twentieth century, in all forms of art, is an effort to unmask, to destroy that sophisticated system of illusions, that veil which makes us believe that what we are seeing or reading is reality, and thus allows us to play our little mental cinema.

How far can artists take this process of unmasking illusion before new illusions start to develop? I think of this process as being akin to politics—the reformers overthrow the old regime only to begin instituting their own forms of oppression.

Federman: A good point. Naturally you can't ever truly destroy illusions; you can only go so far when dealing with works of art, and then you start rebuilding a new screen of illusions. Part of my work is to keep pushing that screen of illusions as far away as I can, to remind the reader or viewer that words or paint do not necessarily represent reality, but are realities themselves. The Roman soldiers in David's paintings are not real people, they are paint. The same with characters in fiction: they are words, word-beings. When you hold *Take It or Leave It* in your hands, the book itself calls your attention to the fact that it is made of words, and that it is not the world. But as soon as you start reading you rebuild the world through my words and create a new system of illusions. It's inevitable, because we really don't want words only, or look at paint only. Let me make this clear: I'm not destroying illusions simply for the sake of destroying illusions. I'm destroying illusions in order that we may indeed face up to reality, and now what passes for reality. Especially in these days of mass media and television which perpetuate illusions for us and mystify the real and the illusory, it is necessary to clean up the world, push aside the illusions that make this world livable for us. Unless we constantly question what passes for reality, challenge it, defy it, we will always exist in falseness, in a system of twisted facts and glorified illusions, and we quickly become lobotomized by it.

Is the effect of pushing through illusions that of reaching some sort of deeper reality—or does such a thing exist? I guess what I'm really asking is whether you feel that this whole issue of "illusion versus reality" isn't false, since everything man thinks is "illusion" on some basic level.

Federman: I'm not sure what you mean by "deeper reality." I'm not looking for reality in the sense that I'm looking for truth. I'm looking for the essential—the essential of life and of my work, of course. I'm looking, for example, to write the essential of the closet experience of my childhood. It is that essential, and not the story itself, which may mean something to my readers. I think *The Voice in the Closet* comes close to that essential. But of course to write the ultimate book, the perfect book would be like one long cry in the dark. Imagine, if someone were to come along and explain the meaning of the universe in one sentence, then I wouldn't have to search anymore. But then what would be left for me to do? Of course, that's what we are all after. So as for myself, I'm looking for the essential of *my life*, not of the world at large—Why does my life mean anything? After that, after I find that meaning, then maybe I'll turn to the meaning of the universe. Meanwhile, I keep working with my personal snapshots and trying to make sense out of them.

But I often get the sense in your books that, somewhat like Stencil in Pynchon's V., *you are more interested in the process of the search than in actually finding this essential you are describing. That is, your books seem to emphasize digression, repetition, evasion, and procrastination to such an extent that, almost by definition, they can never arrive at the place they are supposedly heading for.*

Federman: If indeed the process of telling "the" story is an effort on my part to come to terms with a situation. which I have really never understood, then I want to keep telling that story so that in the process I might stumble onto the meaning of that story—the right aggregate. So there is a deliberate system of repetition in my work, a going over the same stuff, just in case I missed something. I mistrust those writers who tell us they understand themselves, the world, everything. The writer begins to understand only in the process of writing. The more you write, the more you rewrite (even the same thing over and over again), the better you stand a chance of understanding what you are doing and who you are. Ask Beckett. That's his method.

Of course, if I knew what the essential was, I wouldn't be looking for it, I wouldn't be trying to write it. In a way, it is because I *can't* find it that I keep looking for it. If I could say it all in one word, I would; but I can't, so I have to put down all these words, thousands of them, millions of them, which in a way prevent me from getting where I want to go. Remember that great statement, by Beckett again, yes, he's the one who said: Language is both what helps you get where you want to go and at the same time prevents you from getting there. But then if I were to write the essential, it would be the end. What else could I do? I would be dead, perhaps not physically, but as a writer.

Apparently the essential moment in your life—the moment that your fiction constantly circles and evades—is that moment when you were thrust into a closet by your mother to escape the Nazis. What do you understand about that moment? What have you remembered about it, learned about it in the intervening years?

Federman: When the Germans came to arrest my parents and sisters in

July, 1942, and my mother pushed me into that closet on the landing, out-side our little apartment, I was in my underwear, and I had no idea what was happening to me. I just sat in there, in the dark, and waited, for almost twenty-four hours, before I dared sneak out. I was only thirteen years old, and I didn't know what the hell it all meant. I was just there. Scared. Perhaps it was a game, but I was not lucid enough to realize that. Later, years later, and still today when I reflect on that closet and see that figure, that boy sitting in there on a pile of newspapers, it sounds, feels like a game. But I cannot tell how I felt then. Except that I was scared. And on top of that, in the middle of the afternoon I had to take a crap. And why not? So I unfolded one of the newspapers and took a shit on it. Made a neat package of it and later, when I left the closet, I placed the package on the roof. This is all in the book, in *The Voice in the Closet*. But this experience meant nothing for me for years, except that it was what one might call one of those snapshots I was talking about earlier—we all have these stored in our minds—that I kept looking at and trying to make sense out of. That picture has haunted me all my life, and I knew that someday I would have to sit down and deal with it, not necessarily *write* it, but somehow come to grips with that snapshot. So what I finally did—because the writer must always do this—is to analyze this space, this closet. I began to see this little boy, and I replayed, you might say, his gestures, the way he placed that package on the roof. If you wish, I was trying to understand the sym-bolism of that scene. *The Voice in the Closet* is the deciphering of that pic-ture and its symbolic implications. Obviously the closet becomes a womb and a tomb—the beginning of my life, but also its end—metaphorically speaking. It is this kind of question that the book raises. The central ques-tion, however, is perhaps not stated but implied throughout the book: Why did my mother push *me* in that closet and not my sisters? Why me? This gets to be a very complex question—in the Jewish mentality the boy must survive, the girls are irrelevant. Therefore my sisters are deported to Auschwitz and I survive. Here I am today, trying to make sense out of my mother's gestures. These are questions that somehow are still in that closet, and I have not yet found the real answers.

Could you talk a bit about how The Voice in the Closet *got started? Its voice, tone, and typography seem very different from your other novels.*

Federman: When I finished *Take It or Leave It* I found myself in one of those empty periods where I was waiting for the next book to come, and then to fill the gap, the void, I started writing something. Without know-ing it I had started *The Twofold Vibration*, though it was not called that at the time, it was called *Winner Take All*. But that stuff was depressing me, perhaps because the tone of it was all wrong. Or perhaps because I had started it too soon, before October 1st, the day on which, for some curious reason, I've begun each of my novels. So I put it aside and started fiddling with something else, *The Voice in the Closet*, in which I had in mind to write a story, or perhaps a short novel. I ended up with a twenty-page novel.

What do you mean by a "twenty-page novel"?

Federman: I mean that in order to produce those final twenty pages, I wrote something like four hundred pages. Yes, the manuscripts for that text are something like four hundred pages, and all I had left when I was finished was twenty pages. And contained in every page are twenty pages or so of the stuff that has been removed from the text. The process of writing the thing was to write a page as though I was shaking the page—not adding to what I had, but reducing them, taking out the words. The words there that were superfluous disappeared.

Did you have the peculiar form of the novel—its rigid, boxlike structure, the absence of all punctuation, and so on—in mind from the outset?

Federman: No. When I started it I thought of it as a novel where two voices would be speaking simultaneously, one of which would be the voice of the little boy in the closet, and the other the voice of the writer (in his own closet) relating the first voice. So first I put a piece of paper in the typewriter sideways—horizontally—to have more space for the two voices, and I started writing the text in two columns. On one side was what I called "the voice" and on the other "the closet." The voice was writing/speaking a very incoherent, fragmented discourse without any punctuation, a kind of crazy syntax; on the other side of the paper the story of the closet was written in a nice, neat, coherent language—the kind that still respects grammar and punctuation, the grammar and punctuation one learns in school.

I kept going like that for a while, with two separate voices, two columns, two forms of writing sort of coexisting on paper, until I realized that some of the lines in one column wanted to move across the page into the other column. There were lines which wanted to move into other lines across the page. So I started playing with this idea of allowing one of the voices to speak into the other voice, or vice versa. And soon I had all sorts of criss-crossing lines/voices messing up the neatness of my system. I wasn't pleased with this—it didn't come together. Then I said, hell with it. I mean I didn't say that exactly, but I must have thought it, and I put the paper back in the typewriter the normal way, vertically, the way it's supposed to be. Though I'm not sure there is a correct way to put paper in the typewriter. Anyway, I started writing the two voices together, but using two different types—two different little Selectric balls. I was mixing the voices but still showing a difference, a visible difference between the two, so that what was relevant to the closet was in one type of character, and what was particular to the writer's voice in another. After a while I realized that even this distinction was not necessary. Why do I need these two types of characters (I mean, of course, typing characters)? Let them mix. I didn't say that in those words, but I must have thought something like that. I started all over again—ah, the number of false beginnings when you're starting a new book! So I let the voices speak within one another without showing any distinction in characters. That was a real discovery for me.

Am I right in assuming that the narrative voice in this book is not really you so much, or a "character" in the usual sense, but is actually the voice of all your earlier fiction?

Federman: Exactly. It's the voice of fiction, the voice of all of Federman's fiction—everything in our lives is fiction, as I mentioned earlier—and this voice is saying to Federman (the real one or the fictitious one doesn't matter much): Federman you fucked up, you messed up the story completely. All these words, millions of words, and you've never managed to tell the *real* story, I'm really pissed at you. That's what the voice in the closet is saying. That voice could also be the voice of the little boy who was left behind in the closet, but then that's the voice of fiction too. All of Federman's fiction comes out of that voice, so that you have echoes of earlier works, as when the voice remembers the first name it was given, Boris, who is the protagonist in *Double or Nothing*. This voice remembers, or perhaps one should say re-calls, all those earlier names, and how Federman (the writer—Hombre della Pluma, Homme de Plume) was trying to tell that story and always failed, or at least cancelled that story before it could be told. And so now the voice is accusing him, denouncing its own creator. The author. It's a curious reversal of roles, reversal in terms of how fiction usually works. When you read or write a text you supposedly stand (physically and metaphorically) on this side of the text—by "this side" I mean the side that goes from the eyes to the hands which are holding the text. But somehow *The Voice in the Closet*, if I'm correct about it, forces you to stand (metaphorically speaking) on the other side of the text, as though you've gone right through the story, through the paper itself, and are reading it from the other side. It's a breakthrough, you might say, but let me quickly say that I didn't invent it. This breakthrough was done once before, only once I believe in the history of literature, and of course it was Beckett who did it when he wrote in 1950 *Texts for Nothing*, a magnificent work, somewhat neglected by most readers, even fanatic readers of Beckett. In the *Texts for Nothing* the voice of fiction speaks back, not directly to the author, but to the hand that is writing the words. Or, if you prefer, the words of the text are watching themselves being written and comment on their own existence, their own being as word-beings while they are being scribbled, from the reverse of farness, as they say. This, in my opinion, was an amazing breakthrough in terms of how fiction could be conceived. My own *Voice in the Closet* uses a similar technique.

You told me once that Amer Eldorado *is a "version" but not a translation of* Take It or Leave It. *What did you mean by that?*

Federman: I started writing *Take It or Leave It* on October 1st, 1976, when I was spending a few months in Paris. I was living alone in a little crummy hotel (Hotel des Deux Continents, it was called—how appropriate), and it was there that I began writing this new novel in English and French simultaneously. I would work on the English one day and the next day I would write the same thing, more or less, in French. So that each day the stuff I had writen in one language the preceding day became the material for what I was writing that day. It was a maddening process, but I thought that this way I would finish two novels at the same time—basically the same book, but in two different languages. I even had visions of that book, that twin book being published as one volume. I don't think anyone had ever done that before—written the same book, at the same time, in two different languages. And why not? So I would work on the French one day, on the English the next, and the two texts kept growing, but curiously enough not necessarily in the same direction. In fact they were pulling away from one another, feeding on one another, devouring one another, contradicting one another. Also each text progressed at a different pace. I finally realized that even though I was writing basically the same story, I was in fact writing two different books. The two books were fighting each other; they wanted to come together, and at the same time they were pulling away from each other.

After about six months of that, I showed what I had written in French to a friend of mine in Paris, a poet, and he liked it so much that he told me, Why don't you finish this thing and I might be able to show it around to some publishers? I went back to the States after that and, encouraged by my friend's reaction, I set aside the English text and finished the French, which became *Amer Eldorado*, which was published in Paris (Editions Stock, 1974). That book received a lot of attention and did extremely well—I mean, being what it is, and what the French novel does these days. But *Amer Eldorado* is basically the same story as *Take It or Leave It*, and yet it is only half of that book. *Amer Eldorado* is about two hundred pages, where *Take It or Leave It* (even though the pages are not numbered) runs about five hundred pages. The French novel is written in the first person, and it is that first-person narrator who tells his own story, with digressions, of course. But that narrator speaks directly to a group of French intellectuals—the Tel Quel group, in fact. When that book was published, I returned to the English version that I had set aside, but instead of just finishing it as it was—in the first person, etc.—I introduced another dimension, another narrator in the texts who speaks of the original narrator in the third person. In other words I complicated the narrative structure, and in the process I wrote not only an entirely different book, but I wrote another book on top of *Amer Eldorado*. In a way *Amer Eldorado* is inscribed (in a free English adaptation, by the author) inside *Take It or Leave It*. You might say that there is a book within a book. The essential difference, however, is structural. And also there is a difference of tone: the French first-person narrator, as I said, tells his own story to a group of French intellectuals, and he does it with a rather shy, somewhat intimidated voice, whereas the narrator (the second-hand teller, as he is called) of the English novel is much more arrogant, sarcastic, playful too, and he addresses, from his platform, a group of American listeners—probably some typical New York Jewish intellectuals. In other words, you can say that *Amer Eldorado* is contained in *Take It or Leave It*, but not as a translation, more as a free adaptation.

The subtitle for Take It or Leave It *includes the phrase "an exaggerated secondhand tale." Is this because the novel is, in a sense, "secondhand" due to the fact that you had already told the story in* Amer Eldorado?

Federman: No, that is not really what I had in mind at all. Basically what I meant to suggest with that subtitle was that telling a story, recounting a life, is always presenting the experience "secondhand." So I used the phrase "a secondhand tale" to suggest how a real or imagined experience passes from one hand—the actual experience—to the other hand—the telling of that experience. So *Take It or Leave It* becomes a story already told, not in the sense that it was told in *Amer Eldorado* but in the sense that my life is my story, the story is my life. Living the experience is, then, having already written the story; when I write it in a novel, I am really writing a secondhand story.

You talked a bit earlier about your literary "line of descent." But who are some of the writers you feel have specifically had an impact on your work?

Federman: Perhaps curiously, I would say that much of my formation as a writer remains tied to French writing—Stendhal and Flaubert in the nineteenth century, but not Balzac or Zola; perhaps poets like Rimbaud and Lautremont. But the real impact begins with Proust. Somehow in reading and rereading Proust I have discovered something crucial about writing—that is, if you write a novel, the writer must always be present. Another way to put this is to say that to write a novel is not only to tell a story, it is to confront the very act of writing a novel. Since the writer is always interrogating the creative process, he must be present somehow in the text—sometimes merely as a metaphor, but also often as a direct figure, the fabricator or creator. In Proust you have this everywhere in the novel.

Next I would mention Céline. Of course, Céline's work insults me personally as a Jew, but that's irrelevant. When I discovered Céline I found myself confronting pure verbal delirium, and when I write fiction (as you know) deliriousness is a crucial aspect of it. There are other aspects of Céline's work which have intrigued me as well. For example, the closer Céline got to our time, the older he became, the more he removed all fictional pretenses from his books—the pretenses of point of view, characters, plot, even the phony names for his protagonists (finally the protagonists are all named Louis-Ferdinand)—until we find that he is talking directly to us about himself. But yet we are reading fiction, and not autobiography. What fictionalizes this material is the tone, the rhythm, the madness of his language. There is a statement from Céline which I often quote, or misquote, in my books: "One invents one's biography after the facts." And in a sense all my fiction is trying to come closer to the truth of my own self by writing myself into existence.

And then, naturally, there is Beckett. Of course I don't write like Beckett, though there are some similarities between some of my writing and Beckett's. What I learned from Beckett, both from reading his work and talking with him, is that as a writer who writes because he has to—because not to write would mean death—you must never compromise your writing, never give an inch, especially to economic demands and desires.

As far as more contemporary influences, I can't really name them all, but I admire all contemporary writers who do not compromise their work either economically or intellectually. I have already mentioned Márquez, and his novels have indeed affected me, especially *The Autumn of the Patriarch*, with its incredible stream of language moving across the page. Ron Sukenick's fiction, which I always read in manuscript form, always does something to me, especially the way in which he uses and abuses language, the way he breaks up the flow of his sentences so that they never seem to end. I myself have tried to fragment language in my fiction through typography (a process which also taught me a great deal about how language functions—indeed, my interest in typography is as much an interest in exploring the way in which syntax can be distorted and manipulated as it is in the shape or design of words on the page); but my typographical experiments remain somewhat artificial, whereas Sukenick's linguistic distortions seem very natural. Another writer I have recently come to admire is George Chambers, who manages to infuse a bit more emotion into his experimental texts, more feeling. A few other names I would have to mention are Steve Katz, Clarence Major, Walter Abish (ah, the control in Abish's fiction!), the list could go on and on.

Throughout this interview—and in other situations as well: golf, poker, late-night discussions—you often seem to be deliberately distancing yourself from yourself: you sound a bit like a critic talking about somebody else when you talk about yourself. Have you thought about why you do this so much?

Federman: That's an interesting comment because that distance, that distance from the self of the writer, is what writing fiction is all about. Most writers claim that one should write about one's own experiences, but experiences as such are irrelevant, unless you have created a distance, an aesthetic distance between the original experience and the fictionalized experience. It's a matter of reinventing yourself as a fictitious being. Say that the experience I went through in the closet as a child, which in a way allowed me to survive by not being deported to a concentration camp, was to be told without that aesthetic distance; then all you would have is the story of my life repeated over and over again, and the repetition of that story then becomes a kind of whining, of self-pitying about the experience. It merely sentimentalizes it. However, if you can create a distance, whatever you call that distance—formal, aesthetic, illusory—then I can talk about "Federman" as though he were some other guy, a totally fictitious being.

One final question. Except in a very general sense, The Voice in the Closet *has no real story in it, or let's just say it's a story in a very oblique way. Do you think writers can push fiction much further in the direction of storylessness, the way painters eliminated representation?*

Federman: Even Beckett, who went as far as you can go without story, knew that someday he would have to tell stories again. He had erased all the junk connected with narrative fiction until by *The Lost Ones* all you have are words totally empty of their story. So Beckett knew that story was essential, but in a sense it was too late for him. Because he refused to compromise, he had reached the erasure of story completely. Maybe Gass or Coover or Barthelme will get to that point and also go all the way with it. But for me *The Voice in the Closet* is as far as I want to go in this direction. Many contemporary writers have wanted to go as far as we could go with this erasure, the same way that painters did when they went to the limits of abstraction. But finally writers cannot do this because they're still dealing with language—unless they decide to give you the white page. If you look at Stein, Beckett, and many others (including myself), we were all at one point or another in our careers working our way toward the erasure of language. Like the painter wanting to erase the scene or the portrait, we wanted to erase the words, the story, the people, from our writing. But how far can one go with that? Beyond is the white canvas, the blank page. Some painters tried this, but you can't fake it and give readers the white page. Beckett contemplated this: the Unnamable says, "I could simply say blahblahblahblahblah . . . " But that's not the blank page, either.

So Beckett (and I suppose myself and others) were all leading to this white page, but we stopped. We saw that once we get to that white page, we're finished, we can't write anymore. Beckett saw he had gone as far as he wanted in this direction, and then he promised us that the story will rise again. *He* doesn't write these stories, doesn't want to, doesn't need to. He saw that once you got to that white page, the ultimate fiction, the ultimate poem, you can start writing with ink again, with words again. Let me read you something out of Beckett's *Stories and Texts for Nothing* [goes to my bookshelf, picks up a copy of the text, immediately finds the desired passage, and softly reads]: "I'll close my ears, close my mouth and be grave. And when they open again it may be to hear a story, tell a story, in the true sense of the words, the word hear, the word tell, the word story, I have high hopes, a little story, with living creatures coming and going on a habitable earth crammed with the dead, a brief story, with night and day coming and going above, if they stretch that far, the words that remain, and I've high hopes, I give you my word."

That's a beautiful, fantastic passage which Beckett wrote in 1950 when he knew where he was heading. It's a testament of Beckett for me, but it's also a lesson to all of us. You *have to tell stories*, Beckett is telling us, don't follow me, I'm leading you on the wrong path, I'm closing the door. That's my life, what I've chosen to follow, but you guys . . . And Márquez heard that—and so did a lot of other writers, myself included. Beckett *loved* story, but Beckett—like the great painter Clifford Still—knew he had to pursue what he was doing as far as he could. Like Clifford Still said one time (I'm paraphrasing, of course), If you're going to go abstract, go abstract—don't fuck around. Beckett went abstract and eventually won the Nobel Prize.

An Interview with

William Gass

Although William Gass had talked cordially with me at a college appearance, I thought he might be difficult to interview, certainly imposing
and perhaps impatient with mere conversation. In one of his essays he
describes the pressure he had felt as a graduate student when asked to
think of a question to put to Wittgenstein. Driving to St. Louis in July,
1976, to interview Gass, I was feeling a similar anxiety about questioning
this philosopher–artist. But when I parked in front of his home near the
Washington University campus, Gass was waiting at the door. Although
deliverymen were in the house, and his small twin daughters wanted to inspect the visitor and his tape recorder, Gass was ready to talk. We went
immediately to his second-floor library just off the bare room where he
writes when at home. Dressed in cut-offs and a T-shirt, Gass is a small,
compact man who reminded me of the poet John Shade in Nabokov's
Pale Fire. Sitting in an easy chair, sipping a bottle of Ballantine ale, Gass
seemed relaxed, but when the tape and questions began his voice became
highly inflected and aggressively rhetorical—even, as he describes his best
working mood, "combative." This combativeness was directed not at the
interviewer but toward himself and the language he must give his own
sound and shape to. Later, at dinner with his wife, Mary, and Joan and
Stanley Elkin, who live nearby, Gass was any Saturday-evening
academic. The next morning, though, when we taped for another two
hours, the intensity returned as soon as his speech became his work.

"I am not a writer of short stories or novels or essays or whatever," says
Gass. "If I am anything as a writer, I am a stylist." His books, whether fic-

tion or criticism, are elaborate discourse, what Roland Barthes calls in *The Pleasure of the Text* "writing aloud." Until recently, when Gass's second collection of essays, *The World within the Word* (1978), was published, he had written only one of anything, but these performances most often mix genres. *Omensetter's Luck* (1966) does work at telling a novel's story, but its four sections are formed according to the kinds of consciousness—historical, poetic, rhetorical, and dramatic—within them. Gass's collection of stories, *In the Heart of the Heart of the Country* (1968), includes a long, almost plain narrative, a small meditation on insects, and the mock autobiography of a poet and his small town. Probably Gass's most influential book is his first collection of essays, *Fiction and the Figures of Life* (1970), which brings together reviews, philosophical essays, and highly metaphoric theories of character and language in fiction. *Willie Masters' Lonesome Wife* (1971) is a mixed-media experiment, a metafiction that uses photographs, different colored pages, and typographical irregularities. Gass calls *On Being Blue* (1976) "A Philosophical Inquiry" into sex in literature, but it's also a lexicon and theory of reading. Parts of his work-in-progress, *The Tunnel*, have been appearing since 1969.

—Tom LeClair

Do you feel you are writing full throat now?

Gass: I hope so, but if I am a hound, at what am I baying? I am basically a closet romantic, a tame wild man. When I was in college I closed the closet door behind me. Then, for all sorts of reasons, some artistic if you like, but at bottom personal as bottoms are, I became a formalist: I became detached; I emphasized technique; I practiced removal. I was a van. I took away things. And I became a toughie, a hard-liner. When I was in high school, I chanted Thomas Wolfe and burned as I thought Pater demanded and threatened the world as a good Nietzschean should. Then at college, in a single day, I decided to change my handwriting . . . which meant, I realized later, a change in the making of the words which even then were all of me I cared to have admired. It was a really odd decision. Funny. Strange. I sat down with the greatest deliberation and thought how I would make each letter of the alphabet from that moment on. A strange thing to do. Really strange. And for years I carefully wrote in this new hand—I wrote everything: marginal notes, reminders, messages—in a hand that was very Germanic and stiff. It had a certain artificial elegance, and from time to time I was asked to address wedding invitations, but when I look at that hand now I am dismayed, if not a little frightened, it is so much like strands of barbed wire. Well, that change of script was a response to my family situation and in particular to my parents. I fled an emotional problem and hid myself behind a wall of arbitrary formality. Nevertheless, I think that if I eventually write anything which has any enduring merit, it will be in part because of that odd alteration. I submitted myself to a comparatively formal, rather rigorous kind of philosophical training. I stuffed another tongue in my mouth. It changed my tastes. It wasn't Shelley any longer, it was Pope. It wasn't even Melville, it was James. Most of these changes were for the better because, being a little older, I saw more in my new choices than I had in my old ones. But now, after maybe twenty years of not going near Nietzsche—of even being embarrassed by my youthful enthusiasms—I find him exciting again. My handwriting has slowly relaxed and is now the sloppy kindergarten scrawl I had as a child. I suspect the same kind of thing is happening in my work. I am ready to go in any direction. But I hope I've learned that the forms are inherent, that the formal discipline is inherent, so that when I want to start improvising I won't have forgotten how to dance. It wasn't until I was ready to come out of my formal phase that I began to read Rilke. Once I took my thumb out of my mouth—well—soon there was no dike. So now I try to manage two horses: there is one called Valéry and another called Rilke. I remember I once compared writing to the image of the charioteer in the *Phaedrus*. Intellectually, Valéry is still the person I admire most among arists I admire most; but when it comes to the fashioning of my own work now, I am aiming at a Rilkean kind of celebrational object, thing, *Dinge*.

How much did this change have to do with your family?

Gass: I think a lot of it was deeply personal. Every powerful reason is a cause, accounts for a condition. When you decide to change your handwriting, and when you sit down and spend a day or more making new characters, you've got to be in an outraged and outrageous state of mind. I simply rejected my background entirely. I decided, as one of my characters says, to pick another cunt to come from. Did I come out of that hole in the wallpaper, Rilke has his hero, Malte, wonder. I just had to make myself anew—or rather, *seem* to. So I simply started to do it. And I think it very obvious now, though it wasn't obvious to me then, that I should pick the way I formed words to be the point where I should try to transform everything. The alphabet, for Christ's sake—I would have changed that, if I'd been able. So all along one principal motivation behind my writing has been to be other than the person I am. To cancel the consequences of the past. I am not the person who grew up in some particular place, though people try to label me as a Midwestern writer; but I never had roots; all my sources (as a writer) were chosen. I chose to be influenced by this or that book or chose to be defined as the author of this or that. I think that for a long time I was simply emotionally unable to handle my parents' illnesses. My mother was an alcoholic and my father was crippled by arthritis and his own character. I just fled. It was a cowardly thing to do, but I simply would not have survived. I still hate scenes unless I make them. My situation certainly wasn't more severe than most people endure at some time in their lives, but I was not equipped to handle it. What is perhaps psychologically hopeful is that in *The Tunnel* I am turning back to inspect directly that situation and that means I haven't entirely rejected it. On the other hand, I am taking a damn long time to write the book. But I don't know. What is psychologically best for a writer is what produces his best work. I suspect that in order for me to produce my best work I have to be angry. At least I find that easy. I am angry all the time.

Have you spent a good part of your writing life getting even?

Gass: Yes . . . yes. Getting even is one great reason for writing. The precise statement of the motive is tricky; but the clearest expression of my unwholesome nature and my mean motives (apart from trying to write well) appears in a line I like in "In the Heart of the Heart of the Country." The character says, "I want to rise so high that when I shit I won't miss anybody." But maybe I say it's a motive because I like the line. Anyway, my work proceeds almost always from a sense of aggression. And usually I am in my best working mood when I am, on the page, very combative, very hostile. That's true even when I write to praise, as is often the case. If I write about Colette, as I am now, my appreciation will be shaped by the sap-tongued idiots who don't perceive her excellence. I also take considerable pleasure in giving obnoxious ideas the best expression I can. But getting even isn't necessarily vicious. There are two ways of getting even: one is destructive and the other is restorative. It depends on how the scales are weighted. Justice, I think, is the word I want.

Isn't there a line in Willie Masters' Lonesome Wife *about the pencil moving against the page with anger?*

Gass: Something like that, sure. I am developing a theory about that in an essay I'm writing on creativity. One doesn't want to generalize from what might be just a private psychology, but it seems to me the emotion is central. There is another sentence from *Willie* that should be mentioned here, though: "how close in the end is a cunt to a concept; we enter both with joy." That's the other line of mine I remember with pleasure. And both express something very close to me. If someone asks me, "Why do you write?" I can reply by pointing out that it is a very dumb question. Nevertheless there is an answer. I write because I hate. A lot. Hard. And if someone asks me the inevitable next dumb question, "Why do you write the way you do?" I must answer that I wish to make my hatred acceptable because my hatred is much of me, if not the best part. Writing is a way of making the writer acceptable to the world—every cheap dumb nasty thought, every despicable desire, every noble sentiment, every expensive taste. There isn't very much satisfaction in getting the world to accept and praise you for things that the world is prepared to praise. The world is prepared to praise only shit. One wants to make sure that the complete self, with all its qualities, is not just accepted but approved . . . not just approved—whoopeed.

Did your years at Kenyon College have much influence on your later aesthetic positions?

Gass: Not directly. I was already very fascinated by Ransom's stuff when I was in high school. I wrote an article on Ransom and sent it to him at the *Kenyon Review*. It was godawful, but he was very sweet and returned it with a nice letter. I'd never met him, but I was so in love with the man's "manner" I scrawled his initials in the books of his I owned and pretended to others that he'd signed them. When I got to Kenyon he did remember my essay, or was polite enough to pretend to. And that "manner" was real. When I was going to school there, the faculty were very much under the influence of Ransom and the New Criticism, but I think that influence was so widespread you'd have found it most places. I did audit a few courses that Ransom taught, but I didn't take any courses in English while I was at Kenyon. I was busy taking philosophy and other things of that sort. And I found that I fought English classes. I was such a smartass I thought I knew much more than the instructor. No, my pretensions got ground beneath another heel. I couldn't get published in the literary magazine—not a colorful fart, not a thumbprint. The students were very good writers; some of them were publishing in the *Review* already. And I held a small limp pen; I was terrified and crushed; I couldn't get anywhere; I was unbelievably bad; I was lousy. I knew the formalist ideas were in the air, of course, but I didn't really come face to face with them in any extensive way until I went to grad school, so I think that the influence of Kenyon was predominantly philosophical.

What was your orientation when you were working on your Ph.D. in philosophy at Cornell?

Gass: I wanted to work in aesthetics, but they didn't have anybody who was interested in the area, and I didn't take any courses in the subject. They had a nice elderly man the students called "Bedsprings" because he rocked from his toes to his heels all the time and stared at the girls. Most of my courses were in language analysis, philosophy of science, logic, and the theory of meaning. The faculty finally settled on allowing me one wild paper a year which they would be agreeable about and not grade. What I eventually ended up doing was working with the philosophy of language and the theory of metaphor with Max Black. I had to learn to write analytical stuff for all these people, and it is not my natural manner. I hated it in lots of ways because I was working against the grain all the time. But it was very good for me. It was a superb faculty.

Do you still retain that rigor?

Gass: I can still use it, though it isn't easy. I still admire it. I hope I can recognize its many fakes. Now I don't have to be what one would call "rigorous" very often anymore, except in some classroom situations, because when I'm writing I find it very difficult to harmonize a desire for a certain kind of style with the rigor and precision appropriate to a certain kind of subject. The only compromise I can manage is expressed by the hope that I've done a reasonably thorough job on any philosophical issue before I start to write, so that beneath that fluffy flamboyant style and all that sweet sugary rhetoric there is some real cake—some sense at least of the complications of the problem. But I don't pretend to be treating issues in any philosophical sense. I am happy to be aware of how complicated, and how far from handling certain things properly I am, when I am swinging so wildly around.

It seems that the style, no matter how flamboyant, is always very precise.

Gass: Well, I hope so, and you are a kind person to suggest it. Rigor is achieved by pushing things very hard and trying to uncover every possible ramification, nuance, and aspect, and then ordering those things very, very carefully. I think that's always valuable. Still, the kind of ordering you get in philosophy is quite different from the kind you try for in literature, although there is a similarity—an analogy. That's one of the reasons why I admire mathematicians, I guess. You found beauty listening to Austin give a lecture—he presented a beautiful landscape of the mind. Everything was so crisp and beautifully drawn. It was like watching a good draftsman. It wasn't as profound or original as Wittgenstein, for instance, but it was really a pleasure to hear such a careful disposal of ideas: a trash bag anybody'd be happy to plug on TV.

You described the most important intellectual experience of your life, seeing Wittgenstein, as almost wholly without content. How important is the notion of activity to you?

Gass: That was Wittgenstein's famous definition of philosophy: it was an activity, a certain way of doing which was without end. That notion is very similar to the one Valéry had about poetry. He was interested in the activity of writing, the consciousness in the art of composing, creating, and less so (he said) in the final result—which wasn't for him final, only the sign of an absolute weariness. Well, I'm very interested in the process, of course. I can become my subject. But I am interested in the process because of what I want it to lead to—the story, the poem. Perfection. But the process is a great lure, and you can postpone failure by dallying along the way, like Ulysses. I can hardly get from one sentence to the next.

Is that why you write so slowly?

Gass: I write slowly because I write badly. I have to rewrite everything many many times just to achieve mediocrity. Time can give you a good critical perspective, and I often have to go slow so that I can look back on what sort of botch of things I made three months ago. Much of the stuff which I will finally publish, with all its flaws, as if it had been dashed off with a felt pen, will have begun eight or more years earlier, and worried and slowly chewed on and left for dead many times in the interim.

Is Austin's and Searle's notion of speech acts of any use to you as a writer?

Gass: If you start talking about speech acts, what you are doing is connecting the notion of writing with a concept of performance. I think contemporary fiction is divided between those who are still writing performatively and those who are not. Writing for voice, in which you imagine a performance in the auditory sense going on, is traditional and old-fashioned and dying. The new mode is not performative and not auditory. It's destined for the printed page, and you are really supposed to read it the way they teach you to read in speed reading. You are supposed to crisscross the page with your eye, getting references and gists; you are supposed to see it flowing on the page, and not sound it in the head. If you do sound it, it is so bad you can hardly proceed. It can't all have been written by Dreiser, but it sounds like it. *Gravity's Rainbow* was written for print, *JR* was written by the mouth for the ear. By the mouth for the ear: that's the way I'd like to write. I can still admire the other—the way I admire surgeons, broncobusters, and tight ends. As writing, it is that foreign to me.

But in Willie Masters' Lonesome Wife . . .

Gass: Oh, sure, there I'm playing around with it . . . Yes, I was trying out some things. Didn't work. Most of them didn't work. I was trying to find a spatial coordinate to go with the music, but my ability to manipulate the spatial and visual side of the medium was so hopelessly amateurish (I was skating on one galosh), and the work also had to go through so many hands, that the visual business was only occasionally successful, and most of that was due to the excellent design work of Larry Levy, not me. Too many of my ideas turned out to be only ideas—situations where the reader says: "Oh yeah, I get the idea," but that's all there is to get, the idea. I don't give a shit for ideas—which in fiction represent inadequately embodied projects—I care only for affective effects. I'm still fooling around with visual business, but I am thinking of a way to make them *sound*. One problem, for instance, is trying to get the sense (in print) of different lines of language being sounded at the same time, or alternately, or at different speeds or pitches, as in music.

How have visual art and music influenced your practice of fiction?

Gass: The kind of aesthetic necessary to comprehend the modern movement in painting up through, let's say, abstract expressionism is one which I find very congenial. In great part, it preceded the development of a

similar kind of theory for literature. I think the impact of formalism, con-
structivism, and so on was very great in the visual arts, even though music
had been free to go its independent way for some time. Painting, though,
had seemed to be about things, had seemed to be mimetic in a basic way,
and now it was possible to see how such vulgarizations might be abandoned and real purity achieved. There were great paintings which didn't
get their artistic value from some sort of statement they were making
about the world. Then we could begin to wonder whether it was Fra
Angelico's piety or his genius as a painter that makes his painting so
wonderful. For him, of course, piety and painting were one. Not for us,
though. There's nothing new about non-representationalism, of course,
but it is still very much misunderstood and very much opposed.

*There's a lot of theorizing now about silence. Are you ever tempted by
silence?*

Gass: Obviously not. No. I think I am perfectly aware of the dangers
and limitations of language. But the people who are talking about
language running out as if it were the oil supply, or of reaching beyond
language, as if there were a better plate of peaches just beyond the
pears—well, that's just cheap romanticism. Beckett likes to work with
silences the way a musician works with rests, though he works within a
linguistic context, and even if he lowers and restricts his vocabulary, it is
all language, nevertheless, and language is all he is basically interested in.
Then this glorious emptiness is employed as a romantic cliché by people
who persist in using language all the same. They say they are going beyond
the limits of language toward something or other and this excuses their execrable style. No matter. They will pass away.

The fact remains that we are moving away, in terms of science and other
communications systems, from what one ordinarily calls "language." I remain interested in what we are going to use to talk to ourselves with. One
of the fundamental problems with film is not simply its easy effects and its
conceptual poverty. That may in time be overcome. Film may be able to
carry universals in a useful way. But you can't show films to yourself.
There is no way of communicating inside your head but speech. And if
you can't talk well to yourself, who can you talk to? You simply aren't
anybody. I frequently imagine people who get bored with their own talk,
who don't talk to themselves very much. Talk is essential to the human
spirit. It *is* the human spirit. Speech, not silence. That's also Beckett's
point.

*You've said that the love of the word as a resonance or shape is the least
understood of all aesthetic phenomena.*

Gass: One of the things which children do early on is discover the
ability they have to surround themselves with their own sensory world.
Shit, piss, and bellow, kick and wiggle: that's it! I think that what often

makes writers is a continued sense of the marvelous palpable quality of
making words and sounding them. My god, how Beckett has it. I have a
very strong feeling about that love of making sounds. I think it must have
been very enjoyable—in the old days—to form letters with your quill or
pen and hand. I, for example, still have an old typewriter. An electric takes
away from the expressiveness of the key. It was very important for Rilke
to send a copy of the finished poem in his beautiful hand to somebody,
because *that was* the poem, not the printed imitation. Writing by hand,
mouthing by mouth: in each case you get a very strong physical sense of
the emergence of language—squeezed out like a well-formed stool—what
satisfaction!—what bliss! That's another reason why I like the metaphor,
in *Willie Masters'*, of cunt and concept. As an artist you are dealing with a
very abstract thing when you are dealing with language (and if you don't
realize that, you miss everything), yet suddenly it is there in your mouth
with great particularity—drawl, lisp, spit. When the word passes out into
the world, that particularity is ignored; print obliterates it; type has no
drawl. But if you can write for that caressing, slurring, foul-mouthed singing drunken voice . . . that's a miracle. Gertrude Stein said poetry was
caressing nouns, and I think she was right, only I wouldn't leave out verbs
or prepositions, articles or adverbs, anything . . .

As a writer you are, of course, aware of the arbitrary relationship of
symbol sounds to their meanings; but no real writer wants it that way. In
doing *On Being Blue*, I was struck by the way in which meanings are
historically attached to words: it is so accidental, so remote, so twisted. A
word is like a schoolgirl's room—a complete mess—so the great thing is to
make out a way of seeing it all as ordered, as right, as inferred and following. Now when you take language out of the realm in which it is produced
and put it in poetry and fiction, you transform it completely. Maybe *that*
is the least understood aesthetic phenomenon. That process of transformation is perhaps the essence of creative activity. And if you take really
bowel-turning material, from the point of view of its pragmatic importance in the world, and surround it like kitty litter with stuff that is there
purely for play, then you can get an electric line between the two poles
clothes would turn white simply hanging on. The electricity of Elizabethan
drama is total. They are talking always of life and death matters, but they
are standing there playing with their mouths.

Do you sound words over and over to yourself at the typewriter?

Gass: Yes. One time, two times, three times, times, times, times
. . . That's the final test. When that goes well, all's well—well, nearly all's well. And it stands. A bad line or a missed start will get scratched
down so deeply in my head like a schoolkid's desk he's trying to carve
"fuck," "cunt," and his name on, that it becomes extremely hard for me to
start over and go at the sentence in a different way. I am almost never able

to do that. If I've a botch at the beginning, I have to keep fiddling around until I have somehow fiddled it into a squeak, the squeak into the score. This damn imprinting is one of the hardest things I have to overcome. But I also appreciate Valéry's account of how a poem came to him because and while he was walking the meter. When work is going well for me—which is rarely—I have a clear metrical sense of sound and pace. This whole problem is vital. When one section is singing, it sings the rest. I've heard many of the speeches in Elkin that way. The song began and sang itself. Prose gives you flexibility, and you want to use it to shift the whole mode or manner of voice within a paragraph or within a single sentence. So you must have a notion, some clues, which will do the job. Joyce fiddled around with a lot of things trying to get that done, but I didn't get those clues of his until I heard him on records. Then I realized how he should be sung and that he had in mind a notation which isn't present in the book.

One problem is that the reader isn't conditioned, hasn't the time, intelligence, patience, to perform the work. When you think of being a good reader, you tend to think of yourself or somebody as having a sharp eye, quick intelligence, who pays attention, follows this resonance of meaning or that, and has a good memory for what happened before, and all that admirable true crap. But who thinks of the reader as an oral interpreter? When I read a traditional novel, I never remember anything except language, the rhythms in the language patterns, and I do have a good memory for that. I think I forgot the basic plot of *Middlemarch* hours after I read it, and it was of course a terrific book. But the impression, the quality of its style—that I think I shall remember forever. One used to read Henry James aloud. It's the only way to read him. But it takes time; you've got to figure out how to do it, and all this alters the temporal reach of the work entirely. Beckett is our best example. You look at the text and you see all those pauses. You say to yourself, yes, there are pauses, but you don't pause. You don't perform it. If you don't perform it, you ain't got it. In music, you can't *think* the rests, pretend the silences. There happen to be some splendid Beckett manuscripts at Washington University, and they taught me a great deal. I went over a little story called "Ping" one day with the idea of reading it aloud. It's about six or seven pages, but it is a half an hour or more in the reciting. If you do it properly, well spaced, larded with silence, then it's overpowering. You gotta wait, you know, and wait, and wait, and wait, and we just don't do that sort of thing—the world turns—who has time to wait between two syllables for just a little literary revelation? A lot of modern writers, I remember saying, are writing for the fast mind that speeds over the text like those noisy bastards in motorboats. The connections are all spatial and all at various complicated intellectual levels. They stand to literature as fast food to food.

Have you considered giving the reader some kind of extra-textual directions on how to read, as Barth does in Lost in the Funhouse?

Gass: "The Pedersen Kid" has some. *Willie* is full of them. I keep fussing around, trying to find ways to symbolize what I want. But notation . . . notation . . . what a difficulty! The myth is that Joyce tried to indicate that the speed passages in *Finnegans Wake* should be taken by variously spacing the words. In the novel I'm working on now, I want, for instance, a certain word to sound like a bell the whole time the reader is reading certain lines. I want this bong going bong all the bonging time. I'm trying to figure out what device will work—on the page—not only to give the proper instruction to the reader, but to make him begin to hear it—dead dead dead dead—the way it's supposed to go. But as soon as you try to note it the page goes crazy and you get a dozen other things you want no part of.

A character in The Tunnel *is writing a limerical history of the world. Why don't you write poetry other than your limericks?*

Gass: I can't. I would love to. When I was young I tried, but it was awful. Not just bad, but monumentally so. I tend to use the word "poetry" as a generic term for everything I approve of, but I am unable to manage those narrower forms for any length of time or with any success. I can explore prose sentences and prose paragraph structures. Those can be pretty tight sometimes, and certainly as formal as a poem. But when it comes to the damn poetry itself—well, I don't really know why I am so bad. Maybe I'm just a big dog and need a lot of room to turn around in. I can get away with a limerick because it is a very short form. I can turn out couplets, too, but not enough of them to make a whole poem. I have to be constantly discovering my form while I am working. In poetry, when you write the first two lines you have to have flung out the form fourteen or twenty-five lines ahead of you, but it takes me more than twenty-five lines to find the form I should have flung out ahead of me in the first place.

You've said that when you first started writing you wrote only sentences. Was this the result of your philosophical skepticism about language, or a program of exercises?

Gass: Experiments. I have no skepticism about language. I know it can bamboozle, but I am a believer. No. My experiments were stimulated by my reading of Gertrude Stein. I didn't really get to know her work until I was in graduate school. Talk about having your head tipped. I suddenly realized that I didn't know anything about the basic forms that I was supposed to be managing. Nothing. So I studied her very carefully. I am still studying her, and I have always learned a lot. She made me understand how little I knew about what could be done with the basic units of all writing. And she raised philosophical questions about what the basic unit really was, or whether there was one, and about the functions of grammar. In philosophy we were interested in some of the same things then, but we weren't then raising important aesthetic issues. Now, every issue is aesthetic. I don't know which is worse. But one of the wonderful things about Gertrude is that her repetitions rearrange the aesthetic grammar of the sentence and impose this new or special grammar upon the ordinary syntax of English. When I started to examine what she was up to, I realized that I had to begin to get a feel, the way a painter would, of what happens when you try a sentence this way or try it that. To write sentences out of context is a fool's business, but I set about doing the fool's business. You can't really talk very sensibly about the content of a sentence out of the context of its use, but you can talk a lot about the form of the sentence and how the forms are interlaced and how they interact within a sentence. I practiced a long time, I mean a long time, writing sentences and connecting sentences and generally fiddling around. I think I learned something. But not enough. I'm still doing it.

How do you define the aesthetic difference?

Gass: Much of it is musical, most of it is defined by the gut, and theoretically—well, it gets "defined" by negation. Most sentences are *formed* for the sake of communication. For efficiency, clarity; but rhetorical forms are there for the sake of effect, for persuasion. There are poetic forms, too. Of course you end up simply feeling that things are going right or, alas, that they are not.

Does it have to go against the grain to be right for you?

Gass: I don't think so, but it's true that I'm unlikely to trust anything that isn't against the grain. I am unlikely to trust a sentence that comes easily. I should love to be able to write with ease, but I can't, and when I do push ahead or rush on, the result is invariably poor. I have a bad attitude toward things which come easy—wine, women, work, or song—an attitude quite false to the facts, of course.

Is the reader an adversary?

Gass: No. I don't think much about the reader. Ways of reading are adversaries—those theoretical ways. As far as writing something is concerned, the reader really doesn't exist. The writer's business is somehow to create in the work something which will stand on its own and make its own demands; and if the writer is good he discovers what those demands are, and he meets them, and creates this thing which readers can then do what they like with. Gertrude Stein said, "I write for myself and strangers," and then eventually she said that she wrote only for herself. I think she should have taken one further step. You don't write *for* anybody. People who send you bills do that. People who want to sell you things so they can send you bills do that. People who want to tell you things so they can sell you things so they can send you bills do that. You are advancing an art—the art. That is what you are trying to do.

What is the proper relation of fiction to the world?

Gass: What you want to do is create a work that can be read nonreferentially. There is nothing esoteric or mysterious about this. It simply means that you want the work to be self-contained. A reader can do with a work what he or she wants. You can't force interpretations and you can't prevent them.

In *Omensetter's Luck*, I wanted to take on the nature-culture cliché because I knew that it was one of the basic themes of American literature, and I wanted to have my go at it. I set *Omensetter* back in that particular period precisely because I didn't want my writing to be influenced by reality. I didn't know a thing about the period. Still don't. I wanted to put the locale somewhere where I wouldn't have to pretend to do a lot of research to create an environment. If anybody looked at the book carefully, I think they would see that it really says nothing at all about the 1890s, nothing about the Ohio river towns, of which I have no knowledge whatever. Fiction, goddamn it, is fiction. When will that simple truth be acknowledged?

The same thing is true of most of the stories. The only one of which it isn't quite true is "In the Heart of the Heart of the Country." Once upon a time I decided that my tendency to work as far away from my real life as possible might be a kind of neurotic defense, and that it might be good for me to write as close to home as possible for a change. I learned that by writing close to home I got further away. Now I realize it was my worry which was neurotic. The novel I'm writing now is set in Indiana, its protagonist is a professor, has a name beginning in Bill. I set it in Indiana rather than someplace else because it seemed silly to set it in Maine.

Is it ironic that "In the Heart of the Heart of the Country" is probably your best-known work?

Gass: Typical. Typical. There's a whole world of people out there waiting like sharks to devour this sort of stuff. Our Town. How horrible. I don't get a lot of mail, but every once in a while somebody will write me from Texas or Iowa, places quite different from this little Indiana town, I should imagine, and they write to tell me that their town is the same, their lives are the same, their apprehensions are the same. I don't worry about readers when I'm writing, but it does annoy me, because apparently what they do when they are reading the story—and what must move them—is to put themselves in the narrator's place. They say: "Gee whiz, this *is* what it's like to live in this shitty little town: this *is* the way my shitty little life is," and so forth, and on, and on, and on. This means that they are not paying attention to themselves. If the story were an account of how it is or was to live in Brookston, Indiana, it would have to be much more extensive and much different. But of course the story isn't about that at all. It's about a mind with very severe limitations, about a psyche whose feelings are full of self-pity, about an eye that's been driven back in. So what happens is that a lot of in-driven and self-pitying people identify with the narrator and think this is the way to look at the Midwest (as if the Midwest were a bibelot on a coffee table). What, for Christ's sake, is positive about the narrator? The language. He has language. That language is unique. No one can claim it. That is the only accomplishment of the story. When people use literature to interpret the world, they are saying that the language of the work is theirs—they are Ahabs, Hamlets. Not only do they falsify the world, they lie to themselves. If you cannot speak this language, you cannot be these people, for that is what they are.

Is it also a mistake to see you as the narrator?

Gass: Sure it is. The story is less autobiographical than anything I have ever written.

This is going to disappoint a lot of people.

Gass: Well, only those who deserve to be disappointed. Such folks are really not interested in literature. They are interested in folks. Now folks are interesting enough, but they aren't literature. People who will never read a poet's work will go to hear him read. They want that presence. They want the gossip. They want what they regard as the truly real: the poet's goddamn body. When only his words are real.

That narrator of "In the Heart" is limited, full of fatal flaws. I spent a lot of time building those flaws into him. Some of the flaws I put there, the limitations, are mine. Some are not. Any writer has got to see more than his or her narrator, a hell of a lot more, otherwise they have no story. Plato warned us about the seductions of the poet. Take any opinion, any feeling. If I could write a few sentences that were good enough, then they will be convincing about those thoughts, those feelings. Convincing to the readers. It is a terrible thing, but people allow literature to dictate how they are going to think and feel about non-symbolic life, rather than about literature.

You are now willing to give more personal traits to a narrator?

Gass: I am taking more risks in that direction—yes. I found that it wasn't a risk. Except for the cheap effects the method makes possible—that is certainly a risk. I happened to be reviewing a book about suicide once, and uncustomarily began it by talking about my mother. While what I said about my mother was true, that wasn't the point: she had to be another datum. In *The Tunnel* I am going to use a lot of homemade material, but I am mainly interested in how I can transform that material until it will have the same status as stuff found in an encyclopedia. Or a newspaper. Or invented out of that fabulous whole cloth. It's the true-confession I suspect. The ME. I was THERE. And what was THERE? ME! Wholly unprofessional. Totally inartistic. The so-called confessional mode has an immediate rhetorical power (is he/she really telling me that?) which is fake, cheap. In these works the subject matter does your work for you, but the aesthetic qualities are all left out. So the problem is to get *in* the confessional mode, take *away* the confessional power, and reclaim that power in the language.

You mentioned "playing around with form" before. How does that work in, say, "In the Heart of the Heart of the Country"?

Gass: Suppose somebody says, "Why don't you write a piece of journalism about how it is to live in the Midwest?" It is not an interesting suggestion, and I don't think I am going to do it, but I nevertheless get curious. I take a few notes. I take a lot of notes. The notes are of themselves a kind of form. Here are a lot of little headings: under this, such and such, under that, so and so. Then you begin to see that you've got these little blocks of information, and you start thinking, maybe I could harden these up and move them around. So you start thinking what kind of pattern of presentation would achieve the best effect. It is like establishing a kind of very large sentence. You ask yourself what kind of existing form your notes are closest to. Notes! of course! you cry out. You can hear me, I imagine. And so word resemblance leads you on, not form. So you've really got a musical problem, certain paragraphs you are arranging, and you imagine you are orchestrating the flow of feelings from one thing to another. You want each note to have a certain integrity, but of course you are already thinking of how notes fit together. And you've got this private metaphor of notecard and note in music. Once you get your key signature, the theme inherent in the notes begins to emerge: the relationship between art and life and all that. And the town you've started to describe is called Brookston, but you don't want to call it that, and in a moment the B you've reduced it to is reminding you of Byzantium, which goes with the theme, so you decide to explore Byzantium poems, though with an ironic twist. You start out with "So I have sailed the seas and come . . . to B." Have I really come to be? No. Certain themes are developed that parallel themes in Yeats. The story moves through a series of suggestions, of formal relationships. And eventually what you want to do is take account of the kind of formal relationship that begins to emerge simply from a set of notes—simply from an accumulation of data—from the flow of commentary and the appreciation of a set of poems. For me any piece is a play of various forms against one another. When I am playing with forms, it is often simply to find a form for something odd like the garbage. I love lists. They begin with no form at all . . . often, anyway. A list of names is very challenging. There is one right order and the problem is to find it.

You are doing this damn thing on the floor of your study, shuffling and threading these cards—or forms. The reader is reading the story once, ten times, twenty times. He will never catch up with you.

Gass: He doesn't need to. If you convey, in the kind of story I've been going on about, if you convey a certain note-taking quality, a little crude sociology, that's all that's necessary. All these other devices are primarily for the psychological side of the creative process, not for the reader. The reader has to feel a certain set of moves. He doesn't have to know the calculations. Still, if you took the trouble to label the sections of "In the Heart . . ." as you would describe a rhyme scheme, you'd find a pattern. I played with lots of different patterns before I found one that suited me. But what suits ultimately is not the fact that something fits an abstract pattern. You have to feel a resolution and a movement in the fit, otherwise it's no good. Most of these formal tics are private.

Is much of the activity of your writing simply to amuse you or interest you as an exploration with no hope that the reader will catch any of this? Is it necessary for you in order to keep writing?

Gass: "Amuse" may be the wrong word because it hurts so much, but in essence what you are suggesting is correct. Psychologically these games are necessary. Every writer plays them, though what they are varies a good deal. It is also a protective device which can be dangerous. You may feel that certain things which you have put down on the page are justified because you know how they satisfy your blessed apparatus. That, of course, won't do. I think for most writers there are little private projects which each work undertakes, and that these are best studied by people who are interested in the psychology of the writer. The Homeric parallels in *Ulysses* are of marginal importance to the reading of the work but fundamental to the writing of it. Proust had to be suckered by Bergson. And so on. These beliefs and these forms have to do with the security and insecurity of going forward into the void. Writers have certain compulsions, certain ordering habits, which are a part of the book only in the sense that they make its writing possible. This is a widespread phenomenon. Certain rituals have to be gone through, in cooking, for example, which don't affect the final product at all.

Sometimes a writer, Nabokov for example, will engross the reader in his little games. What then?

Gass: I'm in favor of fun. Nabokov surfaces a lot of his game, however, and forces the reader, or the assiduous commentator, into paper chases. I don't think much of that, though I guess the assiduous commentator gets no quarter. Nabokov wants people to follow his private games with the same kind of interest he takes in them himself. Sometimes the intricacies and the little secrets and the codes really work for the reader; things open up and then it is really quite wonderful. Powerful private symbols are related to this. Lowry, for example, was obsessed with certain things. All great writers are. Lowry put down those obsessions on the page and because they are there, he believes they will have an effect. It is the kind of error the beginning writer makes, too—all this stuff that is so important to him never really gets to the page at all.

It seems to me that a number of the voices in your fiction are obsessional.

Gass: That's an impression which may come from my methods of construction. A particular piece is likely to be the exploration of a symbol or a certain set of symbols, and this constrains the text. No meaning can go away without returning. If you're writing an ordinary naturalistic novel, you would be normally interested in the range and extent of experiences and responses and other people. I'm not. You'd want to give the impression of a large world, as if the land was larger than the feet of your fiction. Like Lowry, I want closure, suffocation, the sense that there is nowhere else to go. Also I think the voices tend to reinforce the impression because I often locate the work in a single consciousness. Solipsism is one of the risks of the letter "I." If we were really listening in on any person's subconscious talk, it would sound pretty obsessional. One is consumed by one's self.

How important is it to you to establish some verisimilitude of character to release language?

Gass: Not terribly important. But what you are suggesting is. What I want to do is establish the legitimacy of the verbal source, which is sometimes a character, but it is sometimes a situation or some other kind of excuse. It must seem the right source. You mustn't turn on your tub tap and get crankcase oil. But this has little relationship to how people actually might talk or how oil might actually flow. People tell me that my characters are going crazy, and perhaps they believe that because I don't pay enough attention to verisimilitude. I don't think they are crazy, but the heightened language, the rapid shifts of feeling, the kind of construction I am fond of—these do make readers think that the mind they are experiencing is not an ordinary one, that the consciousness they've been made conscious of is unusual, and that therefore it must be unhinged, extreme. I have a problem with dialogue because it is difficult for me to envision the total context in which the heightened language I sometimes want to use for conversation is justifiable.

Is "Icicles" a kind of sport for you? It does create a voice—the real estate salesman—we might hear on TV.

Gass: The central images I wanted to develop led to that—basically the idea of the icicles as a kind of property, then as part of real estate. And pretty soon I was into the real estate business. I couldn't give this language to the main character, but I did want to carry a certain notion of property forward as far as possible. I sort of backed into that, starting—as I usually do—with a concrete symbol that I wanted to explore: What can I do with the image of the icicle? I ended up deep in philosophical materialism.

That is the way a lot of your stories start?

Gass: Almost invariably now. The only story that didn't start that way was my first one, "The Pedersen Kid," which had its story line first.

All the others have begun with a very concrete everyday image—insects, icicles—or in the case of the novel subordinate suns circling the larger theme of luck—skipping stones, and so on. That's what the unity, if you can find it in my work, comes from. I am exposing a symbolic center. When I think the exposure is complete, I am finished with the story. It's more than peeling a peach.

I used to collect names as possibilities. Certain characters in a sense emerged from their names. I never conceive a character and then seek to christen it. I always have to have the words. I can't even get a story going until I have the title. The title, though, is a direct statement of the central image. If I try to think out in outline some linear structure, then I start pushing my material in that direction like a baby in a pram. When you arrive at your destination, all you still have is a baby in a pram. I want the work to write itself, every passage to emerge from the ones which have come before, so I have to keep looking at what I've done to see what will come out. Usually nothing does, and I have to rewrite my beginning until something does suggest itself.

Do you like the stories still?

Gass: As soon as I finish something it's dead, so my writing a preface about it, as I've just done, is very hard. I rarely read things that are in print when I give a reading somewhere. I publish a piece in order to kill it, so that I won't have to fool around with it any longer. The best I can say is that when I have to look back on the stories I am sometimes not too terribly ashamed. *Omensetter's* got more passages which make me blush. There is one story in the collection which still suits me in the sense that when writing it I did fundamentally what I wanted to do. That's "Order of Insects." I think that's the best thing I ever wrote.

Is it representative of your work?

Gass: Yes, I think it is the heart of it: style and theme and subtlety. But I prefer it because it is much shorter than the others. Less chances to go bad. Like a kid who has a short life. Dies before becoming a gangster.

You said once that a sentence can contain more being than a town. Have you changed . . .

Gass: No. I am every day more persuaded that that is the case. "More being" is rhetorical and designed to set the idea in motion against the opposition. The division that is commonly made between life on one hand and literature on the other isn't tenable. Certainly literature and the language it contains is a quite different thing from things; but experience, even the most ordinary kind, contains so much symbolic content, so much language. For a great many of us in our society, now, a great part of what we encounter every day is made of symbols. We are overrun with signs. Some would say that the experience provided by a book is somehow artificial, not as profound or important as some other experiences. But I think the testimony of everybody who is interested in literature—or painting or film or what have you—science—is that this is not the case. Our experience of signs can often be the most profound and important of our life. In a way the point of getting control over the things of the world, non-symbolic nature, if you like, is to begin to surround yourself with the things which man is most interested in, and those are symbols. In the broadest way, one's aim in existence is to transform everything into symbols—and many of these will be signs, as in literature.

But from the sections of The Tunnel *that I have read, I'd say it is less pure, less impersonal, and yet more demanding. Do you see it as a change for you?*

Gass: Well, it combines my interests in the kind of continuous rhetoric which characterized the Furber section of *Omensetter's Luck* with the nonlinear development of a story like "In the Heart." I am finally finding what kind of mode I can work in best. Well, I hope that's true. It is a change, however, in lots of other ways. I am working closer to my own concerns, but that's not necessarily closer to me. I am deliberately taking on a subject that is highly charged—none more so, really—and one which has a lot of referential meaning. The challenge is to disarm that subject, to tame it, make it purr. I guess where it differs from my earlier work is in my desire to replace the reader's consciousness the way Lowry did in *Under the Volcano*. Once I get the reader captured in the book, I really want to do things to him. Still, I can entice him in like a whore. And I hope to write about certain kinds of objectionable attitudes and feelings in such a way that the reader will accept them, will have them, while he's reading. In that sense the book is a progressive indictment of the reader. If it works.

You know, one effective teaching method is the bail-tail trick: you take some set of ideas the student is inclined to accept rather uncritically, and then you steadily pull the consequences out like a magician who begins pulling silk out of his fist and ends with lengths of intestine. By pitting the reasoning processes which the student has been conditioned to follow against his emotional bias, you can either overthrow his intellectual hold on an idea or make him look at his feelings about what led him to say yes to this and no to that. I want to get the reader to say yes to Kohler, although Kohler is a monster. That means that every reader in that moment has admitted to monstrousness. So my point of view in writing this book is less detached for me than normal. It does involve the manipulation of the reader, and I am not sure about it. Well, not exactly the manipulation of the reader, either. I want to give grandeur to a shit.

You've said you would like to think up a new form for The Tunnel. *At least try not to borrow it from some other source.*

Gass: It's not going to be as new as all that. In the first place there is the metaphor which the book is supposed to correspond to. The book is a tun-

nel; the writing of the book is the digging of the tunnel. So it has to have
characteristics of tunnels which somebody might be digging, out of a
prison or concentration camp, say. Don't you feel surrounded by camp
guards? Anyway, some places are going to be damp and wet—
metaphorically. Some places will be easy going, some places hard. Some
spots will be narrow squeezes, some wide rollovers. My character starts to
dig a tunnel in his own basement. Maybe he is not digging a tunnel, maybe
he is just talking about it, wishing it very hard, dreaming it, imagining
very vividly. They'll all do. I've got to have it every way. But he is digging
a tunnel in his own basement, so he has to hide the dirt. If the book is itself
a verbal tunnel, then it is the depository: he dumps the language of the day
in this place. So instead of being a book in the ordinary sense, it is a dump
ground, a place, a location. The text is both a path through time and a pile
of debris.

   But a tunnel is just a hole.

   Gass: I want to twist that truth. A tunnel is a hole surrounded by
earth. This tunnel is going to be a hole surrounded by the words that the
narrator puts there. There are two ways of making a tunnel: one is to
hollow out a hole and take everything away, and the other is to use earth
to mold a tube. A tunnel is an escape route, a way of crossing over things
by going under. In my narrator's so-called referential life he is taking dirt
out, but in terms of the construction of the book he is bringing it in and
molding it. He is building two kinds of tunnels, then, one from the outside
and one from the inside. In the verbal tunnel the reader is on the inside. My
problem is again to find the symbols that will give the reader the analogy
for the shape of the book.

   Are there other problems?

   Gass: I wrote *Omensetter's Luck* over a very long period of time, during which I changed a good deal both as a person and as a writer. I think
the book's chief flaw is just there: that it wasn't written by one person, but
by a series of them. I have the same problem with *The Tunnel*. It, too, is
taking a lot of time. But I'm not changing as rapidly as I was when I was
trying to write *Omensetter*, and so I have a better chance of holding it
together. I have another advantage now. I work with a set of very open
possibilities, which is a nice way of saying that I don't know where I'm going, but this allows change more easily than the much more rigid design I
had laid out for *Omensetter's Luck*. Some writers write several books in
what is usually called their early manner. Well, I'm afraid I wrote several
books in that one book. I don't think of myself as having "early work"
precisely because each idea takes so long and because every work is a
pileup of persons and modes.

   Did Jethro Furber take over Omensetter's Luck *because of this
methodology?*

Gass: He certainly did. Furber went through a lot of midwives being born. When I first wrote the book, Furber wasn't even in it. That was the version that was stolen. Then I rewrote it to get the stolen version back. Furber was still not there. I looked at what my memory had regained from the thief and concluded that the book, although it was now much better than the original, was really no good. It was then that Furber began to emerge. The book began to be the book I should have been writing all along. Now a lot of people find that the Furber section is where the book goes to hell. As far as I am concerned, it is the only justification for that book.

Is Furber the hero of Omensetter's Luck *because he has the best rhetoric?*

Gass: Yes. In my books, if anybody gets to be the hero, he's got the best passages. Hamlet has the best lines. Milton's Satan has the best lines. Furber is what the book turned out eventually to be all about. That's not quite right. It's rhetoric the book is about, and *The Tunnel* is about rhetoric, too. It's more completely, more singlemindedly about rhetoric, about the movement of language and the beauty and terror of great speech. Omensetter is certainly not the major figure because he is basically a person without language. He is a wall everybody bounces a ball off. Now anybody who emerges in my work with any strength at all is somebody who has a language, and that's why he's there.

Two words recur throughout your criticism—"model" and "metaphor." What is their importance to you?

Gass: I love metaphor the way some people love junk food. I think metaphorically, feel metaphorically, see metaphorically. And if anything in writing comes easily, comes unbidden, often unwanted, it is metaphor. *Like* follows *as* as night the day. Now most of these metaphors are bad and have to be thrown away. Who saves used Kleenex? I never have to say: "What shall I compare this to?" A summer's day? No. I have to beat the comparisons back into the holes they pour from. Some salt is savory. I live in a sea. But that's why I am so lost in the Elizabethans, because they seem to have sunk in the same ocean. What is not metaphorical, is not.

"Leave nothing well enough alone" is my motto, and I have been studying the phenomenon of language called metaphor since graduate school. Metaphor has been thought to be a pet of language, a peculiar relation between subject and predicate mainly: unhealthy, odd. But you can make metaphors by juxtaposing objects, and in lots of other ways. Suppose the relation between literary language and the world were itself metaphorical? Suppose the relation between language and life is like the relation between the subject and the predicate in a metaphor? If the analogy held, then one might find in it a way to express the relationship between literature and the world which wouldn't be quite so severe as the formalist position I once took required, and yet avoid the imbecility which makes it into some "meaningful" commentary. I've been principally interested in establishing the relationship between fiction and the world. If we can see that relation as a metaphorical one, then we are already several steps in the direction of models. Theory, in science, is frequently conceived as that which flows from a model. Indeed, making the model and constructing the theory are not always two different activities. The kinds of misinterpretation which arouse my wrath—not to say contempt—are paralleled, one finds, by misinterpretations of scientific facts-theories-laws which lead to paradoxes and confusions of every kind.

If fiction is a metaphor, what is a good metaphor for fiction?

Gass: I have thrown out a number of them and I wouldn't regard any of them as much good. A fiction is certainly not a mirror dawdling down a road. If I could think of a good one, I would put it in a novel. It's not an emotional model of the world—that's too narrow. It's more like a phenomenological model.

You've mentioned the word "discourse." Are there models for this kind of anti-genre discourse that you find useful?

Gass: I am not against genres exactly. But I am interested in their intersections and limitations. It's a common interest, and I suppose everybody is aware of that genre stew which Borges serves up. What I'm concerned about has already been done to a turn by Sir Thomas Browne. I'm thinking of the kind of meditative essay which really is designed to exhibit the play of the mind over a subject in such a way that all its attitudes and interests get equal but never exclusive time. *Urn Burial* isn't scientific; it contains no extended philosophical argument; it is certainly not fiction. On the other hand, who would hold Sir Thomas Browne to the facts? It's not a sermon; it's not poetry; nevertheless, it is essentially a very elaborate linguistic enterprise.

Who are some living novelists you respect?

Gass: Well, the question leaves out so many dead ones who are more alive. I think Barth is one of the great writers. I have admired his work since I first encountered it. I think he is incredible. Several of his books, in particular *The Sot-Weed Factor*, are the works which stand to my generation as *Ulysses* did to its. His habits of work are wholly unlike mine, and the kind of thing which engages him is quite different, too. He is a great narrator, one of the best who ever plied the pen, as they used to say. He has been accused of being cold, purely mental but I find him full of passion and excitement. And what I like about his work in great part is the unifying squeeze which that great intellectual grasp of his gives to his work, and the combination of enormous knowledge with fine feeling and artistic pride and energy and total control. I really admire a master. He's one.

A lot of the work of Hawkes is extraordinary, breath-taking. Everybody likes Beckett. Now. It's silly to mention Bellow, Borges,

Nabokov—so obvious. And of course Stanley Elkin's work I like enormously. Some of Coover's, too, I find extraordinarily interesting. Control again. Gaddis. Control. Also Barthelme—a poet. A great many South American writers write rings around us. Infante's *Three Trapped Tigers* is a great book. I taught *Hopscotch* once. I'll never get over it. Márquez, Fuentes, Lima, Llosa . . . It is always an exciting time to be a reader. Lots of European writers are overblown, especially some of the French experimentalists, but Italo Calvino is wonderful. Thomas Bernhard's *The Lime Works* is impressive. In general, I would think that presently prose writers are much in advance of the poets. In the old days, I read more poetry than prose, but now it is in prose where you find things being put together well, where there is great ambition and equal talent. Poets have gotten so careless, it is a disgrace. You can't pick up a page. All the words slide off.

If you were going to write an essay on your own work, what would you concentrate on?

Gass: I think I would immediately start talking about the manipulation of language, and I'd end writing just another essay on style. If I am anything as a writer, that is what I am: a stylist. I am not a writer of short stories or novels or essays or whatever. I am a writer, in general. I am interested in how one writes anything. So if I were to write about my own work, I would write about writing sentences.

What kind of philosophy courses are you teaching now?

Gass: I teach aesthetics mainly. I have a number of different courses on the books, and one of them is contemporary aesthetics, in which I may trudge over structuralism, Russian formalism, Heidegger, Bachelard, Sartre, and so on. I have done seminars in Lévi-Strauss and I am interested in structuralism, but I like the Russian formalists. They ask the right questions: Why is this text literary? Unfortunately, their answers aren't as good as their questions. They aren't formal *enough*. The crucial question is always the one concerning quality: What is it, and why does this work have it when another work doesn't have it?

Do you teach any creative writing courses?

Gass: I resent spending a lot of time on lousy stuff. If somebody is reading a bad paper in a seminar, it is nevertheless on Plato, and it is Plato we can talk about. Whereas if somebody is writing about their hunting trip—well—where can one go for salvation or relief? Creative writing teachers, poor souls, must immerse themselves in slop and even take it seriously. Since I can't bear it, resent it, I shouldn't teach it. It is probably impossible to teach anyone to be a good writer. You can teach people how to read, possibly.

I am also aware of how little I can tolerate other people telling me how to write. So why should I do it to my students? I do not invite or accept this sort of personal criticism. I usually have poor to absent relations with editors because they have a habit of desiring changes and I resist changes. So why should I tell students to make changes? I also remember how bad I was. I wrote far worse stuff than I see from students. What can I fairly say to them?

You've said no decent sentence could come from a half-formed man.

Gass: I said that? I shouldn't have. Most writers are probably quarter-formed. Hopeless and helpless. One's complete sentences are attempts, as often as not, to complete an incomplete self with words. If you were a fully realized person—whatever the hell that would be—you wouldn't fool around writing books.

Photo by Shyla Irving

An Interview with

John Irving

Of all the novels to appear in America during the 1970s, John Irving's *The World According to Garp* was probably the one which most captured the public's imagination. Perhaps just as remarkable as its commercial success is the fact that *Garp* is much more than a highly readable potboiler peopled with dozens of engaging and memorable characters—though it *is* that, of course. Like Dickens and Gunter Grass—two writers mentioned admiringly in the following interview—Irving is a natural-born storyteller who transcends the categories of "academic" and "popular" fiction-writer. In all his fiction, though most effectively in *Garp*, Irving sustains a rich and entertaining narrative momentum without sacrificing attention to the rigorous demands of the *craft* of writing. *Garp* may be, above all, a funny and poignant family saga, but it is also a sophisticated metafictional investigation into the writer's relationship to his work, the nature of art and the imagination. In addition, it speaks to us forcefully about the dangers and hatreds lurking in our modern-day society, about the mortality we all must face, and about how art and love assist man in dealing with death.

I met John Irving for our interview on November 9, 1979, at the Harvest House, a fashionable restaurant just off Harvard Square in Cambridge, Massachusetts. When Irving arrived in the bar where I was waiting for him, it was easy to spot him—I had seen his picture staring out at me from countless magazines and dustjackets, and he possesses the kind of Robert Redford good looks that make him stand out in a crowd. Over a lunch which extended through most of the afternoon, Irving's responses to my questions were forceful, full of self-confidence, and often punctuated by laughter.

Those familiar with Irving's literary career know that his life has not always been a series of bestsellers, television appearances, and pictures on the cover of *Time*. His first three novels—*Setting Free the Bears* (1968), *The Water-Method Man* (1972), and *The 158-Pound Marriage* (1974)—all received good notices from reviewers and critics, but they were virtually ignored by the reading public. As Irving explains, each of these three novels anticipates various aspects of *Garp*; in fact, together with *Garp* they can almost be regarded as a four-book continuum. All four combine humor and terror, each examines the role of sex in human relationships and the relationship between literature and reality, and each contains the familiar bears and trips to Vienna that have become Irving trademarks.

Although in this interview Irving speaks out against fiction which emphasizes style at the expense of content, it is interesting that each of his first four novels relies on rather complex and sophisticated narrative approaches—as with his handling of the unreliable narrator convention in *The 158-Pound Marriage*, the subtle interplay and juxtaposition of different historical eras in *Setting Free the Bears*, the elaborate time displacements and montage effects of *The Water-Method Man*, and the book-within-a-book technique of *Garp*. Irving insists, however, that even in his most extreme formal experimentations—as in *The Water-Method Man*—his fiction retains accessibility and readability, two qualities he feels are missing from most contemporary "serious" fiction. Having early on developed an image as primarily an academic writer whose works had little public appeal, Irving decided to move from Random House to Dutton before finishing *Garp*. The enormous success of *Garp* permanently changed Irving's image, of course, and also allowed him the luxury of giving up full-time college teaching so that he could write full-time. He feels that his fifth novel, *The Hotel New Hampshire*, will begin a new direction in his work.

—*Larry McCaffery*

You obviously transformed a lot of the materials of your life into the fictional lives of Garp and some of your other major characters. And yet you seem to share with Garp a fundamental disdain of autobiographical fiction. Isn't this a contradiction?

Irving: I don't really mean to imply that fiction can't have a basis in autobiography. My fiction certainly does. I know from talking with Jack Hawkes about this issue that in a most tangential way a very visual scene "appeared" to Jack which began the novel *The Blood Oranges*. Elements as removed from the realm of fiction as perfectly ordinary moments in your life or things you see on the street can indeed provide the autobiographical beginning of a novel or story. What I really mean to say is that although I feel that all the things that have happened to me are fair to use in my fiction, *use* them is what I do. By that I mean I really use them very ruthlessly; I don't ever feel obligated in my fiction to tell the truth. The truth of what's happened to me is mostly irrelevant to what I write about.

What's wrong with relying on autobiographical material for a writer of fiction?

Irving: My years of teaching have helped me see that frequently the worst or weakest thing in a student's writing is what "really happened." Whenever I find an appallingly bad scene in a story and confront the student with this—"Why does this woman say this dumb thing at this moment in the story?"—the student invariably replies, "Well, that woman is my mother and that's what she *really* said." This, it seems to me, is the worst reason possible for something remaining in a work of fiction. That's not to say that you can't utilize the tactile, visceral, physical sensations that you're most familiar with. All good writers do this.

People quite consistently say to me, "You say that *The World According to Garp* is not autobiographical, but Garp was a wrestler and you're a wrestler; right?" Grinning, they go on to say, "He's sort of short and you're sort of short, right?" Well, one can be as naive about this issue as one chooses, but in the big matters *Garp* is a novel about how perilous and fragile our lives can be. My life is neither perilous nor has it been especially fragile. All the serious things that happen to Garp are invented from the point of view of my trying to imagine all the best and worst things that can happen to someone. But, like most real-life human beings, neither the best nor the worst things have happened to me. So I view autobiography as being merely a stepping-off point in fiction; it's something to use up and get over.

It's also perfectly true that most of us have not had lives interesting enough that we can sustain writing about them into our third or even fourth novel. The first novel is traditionally the one that is most autobiographical, and after that most of us have used up whatever traumatic experiences we have had in our lives. I honestly don't think I could have eked out even one novel from the experiences of my own life. In fact, I feel at an advantage as a writer in that I have *not* had a very interesting life, because it's a danger to a fiction writer to have had a significant number of things happen to you. Such things might create in you a sense of your own self-importance.

There's a scene in *Garp* that I particularly like on this issue of autobiographical fiction. It occurs when Garp is telling an interviewer that anything that's happened to her he can make better, if better is what he wishes to make it, or worse, if worse is what he wishes to make it. At that moment in the interview, the interviewer shuts off to Garp because, unfortunately, he is being interviewed by a woman who's just gone through a divorce and been left with four or five children, one of whom is dying of cancer. Garp stops trying to make his point to her when he sees "how much her unhappiness means to her." It seems to me that most autobiographical fiction is tyrannized by how much our unhappiness means to us. This unhappiness becomes an indulgence in our fiction.

It sounds like you're bucking a long tradition in American fiction: the idea that a writer's experience and memories should provide the basis of his fiction. The Hemingway dictum—"You want to be a writer? Go out, hunt big game, go to war, attend bullfights. Then sit down and write."

Irving: The whole basis of art is selectivity. There's nothing very selective about memory, especially when we remember traumatic events. I frequently say to students that if something very traumatic happened to them it is, of course, vital that they write about it. The occasional interesting things that have happened to me I have indeed wanted to write about and, in a way, I have. But what I suggest to students is that if they have been in a terrible automobile accident that compels them to write about how devastating the effects of an accident can be, they should put the accident in a train or plane or boat, or maybe make it happen to a pedestrian. Why? Because they then somehow become responsible for making up all the details. They don't lose the viscera of what that accident means, but they are forced to choose their details selectively, aesthetically.

The stories and novels that Garp writes, especially the "Grillparzer" and Bensenhaver *pieces, seem good examples of what you're talking about.*

Irving: Yes, they are. Without his personal experiences, Garp couldn't, or wouldn't, have written "The Pension Grillparzer" or *The World According to Bensenhaver*. We see exactly how he uses his experiences with death and with the prostitutes in Vienna and his experience with feeling impotence, rage, and frustration when he writes the rape story. And yet neither of these stories is strictly autobiographical because neither really happened to Garp.

When did you decide that you wanted to be a writer?

Irving: I was so young that it wasn't really a conscious decision. When I was fourteen or fifteen I found that I needed to tell stories. I was always writing stories and when I finally got to prep school I realized that this was not only a legitimate but an encouraged activity. So very early on it seemed to me the dream of something I might one day do. But I didn't feel I was very good at it. For one thing, I was not a very good student. I did all right in English and history courses, where I could simply read and write. But I was terrible at math, science, and language courses—a kind of C plus, B minus type of student.

I saw a comment once that when you were a kid you had a terrible sense of being different from everyone else. Did this contribute to your need to tell stories?

Irving: No, I don't think it was related to my sense of being an outsider. When I was a kid I was troubled by the fact that I didn't seem as happily sustained as my friends were by all the ordinary activities. I found I needed a lot of time to myself every day, and when I first started going to private school—I was living at home at the time—I began to think I was going a little crazy because I wasn't getting my necessary fix of time by myself. You're kept really busy at a good school, and it took me a couple of years to realize that there were places to go and be by yourself even when you weren't really alone. I'd go to a library and read for three hours, not noticing anything else going on around me. I found I could discover an empty classroom at school and that once I opened a book I had a legitimate reason to ask people to leave me alone. So reading became a kind of found privacy, which was especially important since I was living at home with brothers and sisters.

You were working on Setting Free the Bears *while you were at the Iowa Writers' Workshop in the mid-'60s, weren't you?*

Irving: Yes, from 1965 to 1967.

In many respects—its tone, its odd structure, its use of European historical references and the absence of American cultural references—it seems like a very peculiar book for a young American to have written during this period.

Irving: Yes. It was the first novel I had tried to write, and it *is* a peculiar novel. To contradict what I said earlier and admit autobiographical influences, I think it reflects the way I had grown up and was living up to that time. I remember a review in the *Saturday Review* in which the reviewer said, "This novel isn't really an American novel and it isn't really a European novel either—it doesn't come out of any recognizable tradition." The review then concluded that it was an astonishing literary debut nevertheless, or maybe *because of* these things.

You have to remember that I didn't go to college like most people went to college. I was never a part of a community of students the way most people who went to college were, nor was I ever involved in the issue that really obsessed most American people my age—namely, the draft and the war in Vietnam. The reasons for these omissions in my fiction are strictly autobiographical: although I always wanted to be a writer, for a significant number of years—up through all my college years—I was devoted to being a wrestler. As a result I had the habits and lifestyle of a jock, and most of the people I saw with any regularity were on one wrestling team or another. The only common denominator among us was staying in shape and not getting injured and keeping our weight down. A very small world.

You seem to be saying that, in focusing so intensely on sports, issues like Vietnam were simply put aside.

Irving: That's it exactly. When you're in training like that, you're in a pretty myopic position. Writing a book is also a myopic condition. When the idea of a book seizes you and you get twenty or thirty pages into it and the book has begun and you're looking down the road at two or three years before the thing will come to fruition, you're also necessarily in a myopic state. There is a preoccupying thing in your life, and you won't be easily influenced or impressed by other things.

What about specific literary influences during these years?

Irving: I suspect that very few people would recognize my chief literary influence, since my sensibility is American and my chief influence was not. But the book that meant the most to me for the two years before I started *Setting Free the Bears* and all during the time I was working on it was *The Tin Drum*. There is no living writer of whom I am simply in awe, except Gunter Grass. Yet he's from such a different literary generation, a different country, using a different language that, in a way, he's a very safe influence to have because there's no way I can be very much or sound very much like him. What appeals to me most about Grass, though, is not his feats of language and his sense of place but simply the narrative quality of his imagination. From the time I was a child and first started reading Dickens, I've loved a narrative that can be sustained, one that can continually make new things happen. I love books that say "And then . . . and then . . . " and which keep on going this way; just when you think that something has got to come to an end, that we're going to have a break, this kind of work simply compounds and compounds. I still feel that a narrative momentum—this sense of movement and pace and rhythm—is what I most admire in fiction. Grass, among my contemporaries, is the best at this; there is no one else around to compare with him in this regard. His imagination is extraordinary.

Your fiction often returns to the notion of survival in a dangerous, violent world. I've wondered if your interest in developing this idea isn't why your fiction seems to be haunted by Vienna and the Nazi takeover during the '30s.

Irving: When I first went to Vienna in 1963, it was the first city I'd had my own apartment in, the first city where I was completely free and independent. I had gone to the University of Pittsburgh and dropped out; I had gone to the University of New Hampshire and dropped out. So I had applied to a program for studying abroad—the Institute of European Studies in Vienna—and had been admitted to several courses at the University of Vienna. But at that time, quite honestly, I didn't think I would ever finish college. I was taking courses solely out of interest and had gotten a couple of part-time jobs in the city.

Now I won't say that what happened to me in Vienna would have happened if I had been in Cleveland, but it almost could have been Cleveland. That is, I was of an age—I was twenty-one—to be dropped in a new city, with a place of my own, where I could absorb everything that was around me. I was helped in that everything around me was foreign. This is a very refreshing position for a writer to be in—to be in a foreign country where even common, everyday things suddenly possess a freshness about them: the matches come in special boxes, the traffic lights are different, and so on. When I went to Vienna and lived there, though, I never wrote about Vienna—I wrote about living in Pittsburgh. I had never noticed Pittsburgh when I lived there.

So when you return to Vienna in your fiction it's not so much to present the idea of Vienna as a heroic survivor, an emblem of death, Vienna's ability to bounch back after a struggle . . .

Irving: No, not really. Vienna in my fiction isn't a real place but represents a fictional realm where I can take certain liberties. In other words, I use Vienna as a security blanket; when I go back to Vienna in each book, I feel like I'm home free because when I'm back there, I know the kinds of things that can happen. So the Vienna of my fiction is separate from the real Vienna. There's a line in a popular song that says "legal to dream"—somebody dies, and someone says sarcastically that this guy has finally gone someplace where it's legal to dream. My sense of Vienna, whenever I get there in my fiction, is that it's legal to dream there. I can start taking advantage of another kind of reality which is not bound by the usual restrictions.

What about the inevitable bears that appear in your fiction?

Irving: Bears may seem more significant in my books than they really are. I would be embarrassed to claim any significance to an animal about which I know so little. My bears, for instance, are always domesticated bears. I know very little about bears in the wild; if I saw one, I'd run. But I do know a little more about bears in captivity, how they're trained, how they remain somewhat surly and unpredictable. I feel the way about bears in my fiction that the mystery writer John MacDonald does about guns: "When in doubt, have a man come into the room with a gun in his hand," he said—or something like that. In my fiction I've always felt that as soon as I get the bear on stage, everything is all right. I can focus the reader's attention in specific ways, maybe because most readers are quicker to show sympathy for animals than for other humans. Finally now, with my fifth novel, I've *started* with a bear instead of waiting to get him on stage. In fact, there are two bears in my next novel.

Your use of bears and Vienna seem to constitute a kind of literary injoke. In fact, in Garp *you have dozens of playful, Nabokovian self-*

*references to your previous novels and characters. What function did
these serve?*

Irving: Yes, it's true there's a lot of self-parody there, spoofs of my
earlier works, games I'm having fun with. I like the idea of these kinds of
self-references. To mention Gunter Grass again, I loved it in *Dog Years*
when little Oskar Matzerath with his tin drum makes an appearance as a
walk-on character, the way Hitchcock always likes to be one of the people
standing in a corner in his films. It may be simply an indulgence on my part
from having been such a widely unread author for my first three books,
but it pleased me in writing *Garp* to think there would be people who had
been reading me all along who would say, "Uh-oh, here comes a bear
again," or "Oh, here comes Vienna again," the way in some Fellini movies
he makes homages to his other movies and to the films of other directors,
like Bergman. It's just a tip of the hat.

For example, I could have done any number of things with the
lobotomized soldier who impregnates Jenny at the outset of *Garp*; he's not
really important in these scenes, since the focus is on Jenny. But I don't
think many people can fail to miss that there's a tip of the hat in my presentation to Heller's airplane scene, or to the Randall Jarrell poem "The Death
of the Ball Turret Gunner." That's why I created the soldier in that way. It
doesn't *mean* anything necessarily; it's just a way of saying that if you,
too, happened to have read these things, I enjoyed them as well. But if you
look carefully, there is very little relationship between Garp's writing
career and mine, if only because I never wrote a book in my early days that
is as good as Garp's "Grillparzer" story.

Is Garp *the best book you've written so far?*

Irving: Yes, *Garp* is far and away the best of the four published books.
There's no question about this in my mind. *Garp* seemed to bring together
a lot of things I'd only been getting started in my other books. It summarized the other books for me, finished the cycle I had started. I felt, for instance, the need in *Garp* to finish or redo things that I had begun in the
other books. Now, in writing my fifth novel, I feel that completing *The
World According to Garp* completed the first three books so that now I no
longer feel the need to make references to any of them. It's as if I'm finally
writing my second novel and the first one is finally over. Even when I was
only a couple of years and a couple of hundred pages into *Garp*, it felt like
a summary or culmination of the earlier books, a bigger book in every
way.

What specifically made it seem "bigger"? Obviously not just the length.

Irving: No. A breakthrough happened for me with that book. It occurred to me that I did not want to write a book about people I absolutely
did not *admire*. That seems like a simple thing, but it took me three books
to discover it. This idea was a personal aesthetic decision and not

something I would recommend for every writer. I certainly enjoy reading books about people who aren't loved by the author and aren't meant to be loved by us. But for me it was a lifting of the clouds. I did not admire Siggy or Graf in *Setting Free the Bears*; I knew them, knew what they were like, and I could tell you about them. I didn't enjoy Bogus Trumper in *The Water-Method Man*, either. He was an arch procrastinator, like a hundred people I've known; he might have been the end of the little finger of myself, a figure who, if all things were to go to hell, I might become. But I wasn't him and didn't admire him. I felt in *The 158-Pound Marriage* as if I were still writing about people I didn't like, especially the narrator. With *Garp*, though, I was creating characters I genuinely admired and cared for; this was a major breakthrough for me.

Although your first three novels share certain themes and motifs, they seem remarkably diverse in terms of their structural approaches.

Irving: Yes, and the second two books—*The Water-Method Man* and *The 158-Pound Marriage*—are particularly self-conscious about the way they are made. In *Setting Free the Bears* my priority, like that of most writers creating their first book, was to see whether I could finish it. To that extent it is still my most important novel in that it's the book that gave me the greatest amount of confidence. I thought, My God, if I can do just this well not knowing what I'm doing, what can I do if I set out with a plan and know what I'm doing next time? I think that technically, in terms of structure, *The 158-Pound Marriage* is still the best made of the finished books. It was the first short novel I had written and I was very pleased with its tightness. It was also the book which was most like a literary exercise in that it's the only one to come directly from other books; that is, it would not have been written without my having read Ford Madox Ford's *The Good Soldier* and Jack Hawkes's *The Blood Oranges*, two books that rely on unreliable narrators. *The 158-Pound Marriage* developed from my choice to tell a tale of moral complexity and ambiguity from the point of view of a character who I felt was most like a villain. So it evolved from a specifically literary idea—this notion of the unreliable narrator—and was a very writerly novel. *The Water-Method Man* is also a very writerly book, probably the closest thing to an experimental novel that I will ever come to doing in terms of all my manipulations of tense, settings, and point of view.

Your earlier books received good notices with critics but didn't sell very well. Was this mostly a matter of promotion? I notice that you changed publishers with Garp, *moving from Random House to Dutton.*

Irving: I suppose part of the reason for *Garp*'s success is that it is a better novel than the earlier books. But I think my earlier books were all quite accessible and available. The mid-section of *Setting Free the Bears* is still the most interesting thing I've ever published. I don't think my earlier books were very well published or promoted, although they were well edited; I had a wonderful editor at Random House, Joe Fox, who remains one of my closest friends. Yet it's an old story, a publishing rather than a literary story: each of my books sold fewer copies than the one preceding it until finally I began to hear from Random House that I had a "track record." This track record was described thusly: "John Irving can be counted on for some serious critical reviews and diminishing sales. He's a sort of arty-farty writer who's going to be read by other writers and by people at universities, but he's too hard to understand for people in the mainstream." I resisted that view, saying, "Hey, this is *your* track record, not mine." I felt I had never been given a chance.

You've gone on record in a number of places insisting that there shouldn't be any necessary distinction between being a serious and a popular writer.

Irving: Being popular and unpopular for a serious writer is largely a matter of misunderstanding. For example, when *The Water-Method Man* was published in 1972 several critics—most noticeably, Alfred Kazin's sister—noted that it was charming, funny, sad, wise, and well written but not "serious" because it was supposed to be set in our country during the 1960s but had not said a word about black people or Vietnam. Well, when you're dealing with that kind of horseshit, that kind of naivete in reviewing—that kind of sociological notion that the novel must somehow speak to the social issues of our day and time with a kind of comic-book relevancy . . . Jesus, I don't think any review of any of my books so angered me as that sleight of hand. We are *always* trying to reduce literature to sociology, history, or psychology; what a sick instinct.

That kind of reviewer response seems ironic, considering the praise Garp *received for being so "relevant."*

Irving: Ironic, indeed. Obviously now when people write about *Garp* and say that it's "about" feminism and assassination and the violence of the '60s, they're ignoring the fact that I lived half of the '60s in another country. I don't know anything about the violence of the '60s; it's meaningless to me. I'm not a sociological writer, nor should I be considered a social realist in any way. So if at one time I was a victim of a misunderstanding—i.e., that my books *weren't* relevant—certainly right now, to a degree, I'm the beneficiary of a different misunderstanding: that *Garp* is somehow a piece of relevancy. But if you know my other books and then read *Garp*, it's perfectly obvious that there are little "*Garp*-like" parts in each of my earlier books. *Garp* just comes off a little better because it's bigger, more ambitious. It's like an acrobatic or athletic thing: in *Garp* I simply threw more balls up in the air and managed to catch them. In the other books, I didn't get as many off the ground and I dropped a few of them.

Many books in the '70s that are highly regarded by critics—Pynchon's

Gravity's Rainbow, *McElroy's* Lookout Cartridge, *Gaddis's* JR, *Coover's*
The Public Burning—*are dense, difficult books that seem to be written for
a kind of "ideal reader." Do you feel this is a dangerous direction for fiction to be heading?*

Irving: I've always felt that the most difficult thing for anyone to be is
to be *clear*—clear about the way one lives one's life, clear about the way
one conducts relationships, how we handle our children, how we write fiction. I think it's extraordinarily difficult to be clear. It's no triumph to be
difficult to read or understand; in fact, I think it's a triumph to be readable.
I think *The World According to Garp* is readable by almost everyone,
even if they don't get all of it. I try to write sentences that lead naturally to
other sentences; I try to end chapters that will make you want to begin the
next chapter; I try to do all those basic, openly seductive things that will
make you want to keep reading. I don't find that an aspect of commer-
cialism, but part of the writer's responsibility.

Is this a responsibility to his craft or to his audience?

Irving: Art has an *aesthetic* responsibility to be entertaining. The
writer's responsibility is to take hard stuff and make it as accessible as the
stuff can be made. Art and entertainment aren't contradictions; in fact,
above all the responsibility of art is to be entertaining. It's only been in the
last decade, or twenty years, that there has somehow developed this rubric
under which art is *expected* to be difficult. Why? On the basis of some sort
of self-congratulation of the strenuousness required of us? This notion
seems to me to be, frankly, a way of congratulating the middleman, the
academic who might be necessary to explain the difficult work for us. By
creating a taste for literature that needs interpretation, we, of course,
create jobs for reviewers, for critics, for the academy. I like books that can
be read without those middlemen.

It upsets me, for example, that with much contemporary poetry
someone like myself, with a reasonably decent education, can't deal with
it. I went to good schools, was taught the rules of meter and rhyme, read
Paradise Lost, learned what a sonnet was. So I find it ludicrous that today,
not having been educated much beyond an undergraduate level, I can still
real Milton and Shakespeare, and even Chaucer, with more comprehen-
sion than I can read half of contemporary poetry. Here I am listening to
someone who's speaking the language of our own time and who is of my
own age, and who is telling me it's *my* fault that I don't understand his
poetry. Fuck him. He's wrong. It's terribly easy to be hard to understand;
it's always easy to speak a vernacular language that our friends will
understand but no one else. I don't find being able to appeal only to those
who already know you much of an achievement, artistically or
aesthetically. What kind of communication is that? That reduces us,
linguistically, to the kind of people who go out every Saturday night and

say, "You know?" "Uh, huh." Mere mumbles! Such writers are creating a kind of intellectual, college-educated mumble communication or short-hand. I hate the elitism, the preciousness, the specialness of so much con-temporary fiction. I hate what is turning the novel—once the most public of forms—into something like contemporary painting and contemporary poetry; namely, largely designed for other painters and other poets. I find that easy.

Would you care to align yourself with one side or the other in the recent Gass–Gardner debate about the necessity or irrelevancy of art's allegiance to morality?

Irving: I'd be much happier if John Gardner and William Gass were to devote themselves to making art and to making fewer polemics about it. But the easiest way to talk about their debate is to say that Gass has been a much more careful man about what he has said than Gardner has. Gard-ner has been very careless about a number of things he's said, so it's easier to pick on Gardner than it is to pick on Gass. On the other hand, it seems to me that Gardner has tried to say a lot more about literature than Gass, and I have to admire him for that. I'd also have to agree with Gardner that literature should be a sign of life rather than a celebration of death; and if a novel doesn't address itself to something of human value, I don't see much worth in it. So, to that extent, I'd have to say I'm definitely on the side of Gardner's "moral fiction," although I hesitate to use that term these days.

I assume you would take issue with Gass's charge that people want art that does not create a sense of uneasiness on their part—that they want art that entertains but does not challenge them.

Irving: That's selling people down the river, to a degree. Dumb people might want entertainment of a sort that won't upset them, but there are more smart people out there than we know. These smart people want entertainment but of a sort that *does* upset them; they want catharsis, they want to be stretched and tested, they want to be frightened and come through it, they want to be scared, taken out of their familiar surround-ings—intellectual, visceral, spiritual—and to be reexposed to things. The public is more adventuresome than the producers of crap art are usually willing to see. Television, for example, could be much more exciting and get away with it; but currently it does indeed speak to a mentality that is pretty well described by Gass.

Still, there *is* an audience out there that wants something that will upset them. I'm not such a fool as to believe that more people will ever prefer Bergman films over *The Sound of Music*, but the dichotomy between the degree to which serious art is admired in this country and the degree to which junk is consumed doesn't have to be *as* severe as it is. And there is a lot of serious work that is successfully encouraged. There are usually two or three books on the bestseller list written by writers who are treating writing as an art, who write every sentence as if it mattered and whose sentences demand to be read more than once. There was a recent piece of garbage written about me in *The Nation* by Richard Gilman. It basically took the premise that if something is popular, we had better smell out what the rat is that's in it. His conclusion was that most serious writers don't get the kind of popular attention that *Garp* did and that *therefore Garp* can't be serious. He perhaps didn't know about my first three books, which probably would have been the kinds of books he could have responded to—that is, unpopular ones.

Let's talk about your work habits. Do you find yourself approaching each of your books in a consistent way?

Irving: My approach has varied from book to book, although all of my books have a sense of epilogue about them. That is, there is always a last chapter, whether it is called an epilogue or not, that seems to direct itself to how things have turned out for the characters or projects their future. More and more I have begun books by writing the endings first. *Garp*, for example, began with an epilogue—not the epilogue that finally appeared, although it was close to it. With the next book, which I'm halfway through now [*The Hotel New Hampshire*], I started out by writing a sixty-page ending for it. I can already see that the book is not going to come out the way I originally thought it would, and when I write new chapters I have to continually change the ending a little bit. Henry Robbins, before he died, laughingly referred to my approach as the "Enema Theory of Fiction"—the longer you wait, the better it works!

Related to this notion of epilogue is the fact that I try not to begin a chapter of a novel until I can write the last paragraph of the chapter. It's important to me not only to think I know what's going to happen, but to know the tone of voice I used toward what's going to happen, because then I know how I'm going to *feel* toward the later material. A lot of the time I'm wrong, of course, about my original conception, and I've begun many last chapters and last paragraphs that I've had to change later on. But I believe that there is a consecutive, linear quality, a kind of "hurry-up" pace that I like in fiction that is only enhanced—even if it's only an illusion—by thinking that I know where I'm going. In working for the past year on two hundred pages of *The Hotel New Hampshire*, I've begun each of my chapters only when I've had a very firm picture of everything that is going to happen and what the sound of my voice would be when I got there.

All four of your published novels have very different narrative structures. Has your approach to this aspect of writing evolved over the years?

Irving: Especially now, after *Garp*, I'm very conscious of attempting to make my narrative as absolutely linear as I can make it. With my first four novels I was always troubled, particularly with *Garp*, about the convoluted flow to my narrative. Because of everything in those stories it seemed necessary for me to be continually interrupting the narrative with other narratives. But it was not really my aesthetic taste to have these interruptions of the linear narrative, to have these stories-within-stories, all those convolutions which reach their high point in *The Water-Method Man* with all of its formal difficulties and its showing off of its structural play. *Garp* was, in fact, a kind of minor breakthrough for me just in the sense that it was the first novel I managed to order chronologically. I remember thinking while I was in the middle of writing *Garp* that finally, one day, I was going to learn how to develop a narrative in a very linear way, a way that would be more fast-paced on the surface so that the narrative and the prose would seem, rhythmically, very direct. Right now I'm trying very much with *The Hotel New Hampshire* to create a narrative more in the nature of "The Pension Grillparzer" story—a first-person narration that goes in a linear, direct fashion without convolutions or any stories-within-stories.

This is going to disappoint some of Garp's *fans when your new book comes out.*

Irving: Yes, I know that kind of intricacy appeals to readers of my fiction, and I think I handled that intricacy about as well as I could in *Garp*. But that approach is not the kind of structure for a book I would willingly choose—I had no choice but to make it that way with any of my earlier books. I always resisted it, in fact. Now, after four novels, I think I'm finally writing the novel I wanted to write all along. *Garp* wasn't it.

From what you've been saying, I gather that when you begin a novel, you start with a sense of a book's character and plot direction, rather than beginning with something more abstract, like a theme or metaphor.

Irving: It's hard to separate the strands of this, but I always begin with a character, or characters, and then try to think up as much action for them as possible. A story imposed on people you don't know just isn't very interesting. A quality that distinguishes something truly moving or truly engaging from melodrama is simply our concern for the people involved. If you come into a house in midafternoon and turn on the tube and look at some of those soap operas, you may see a woman screaming on the telephone, "My husband has left me for his secretary, my daughter is going to marry that awful Freddy Pinn, and I think I'm pregnant!" At which point we laugh and turn off the TV. But if a woman we've known all our lives—and for whom we have the deepest admiration and affection—were to burst into the house and say exactly the same thing, it would no longer be melodrama. The trick is you've got to establish respect and admiration for the characters. And you can't be afraid of the emotional extremes—it seems to me that sentimentality is frequently avoided in the modern novel by having the author avoid subjecting people to emotional extremes. I don't think Dostoevsky or Flaubert or Hardy would have approved of this practice. *The Mayor of Casterbridge* would be daytime television—in the hands of a clod.

This seems to be your reply to certain critics like the one in The New Yorker *who wrote of* Garp, *"Scores of characters die violently and dozens are melodramatically (and unconvincingly) maimed." In fact, you seemed to be making the point in* Garp *that life is daytime soap opera.*

Irving: Absolutely. You can have the most sophisticated and controlled existence imaginable and be completely on top of your life. But if you, like some creature in the *National Enquirer*, back your car out of the driveway and run over your daughter or your neighbor's daughter, your life will change. There is, though, a way of presenting this view of life without sounding like you belong on afternoon television. Still, if you don't expose your characters to these dangers, you're not doing much with human beings, not putting them to enough tests. You're milking understatement for all it's worth, which is really another form of being easy.

The things that most deeply affect us, after all, are love trysts, birth trysts, and death trysts—all of the most emotionally wringing kind imaginable. If a writer is not creating these kinds of scenes—which most writers avoid—he's simply being more *sophisticated* as a writer, but not talking about the things we care most deeply about. These soap-opera things are the scenes that matter. Everybody's life is not safe. We may go three or four years before somebody gets cancer, gets hit by a car, has an affair, but these things are what stay with you and produce the wounds that stick. Writers are responsible for writing about our most important behavior, and if we are soft or easy on our own behavior, we are shirking as artists.

In the early '60s, Philip Roth suggested that the contemporary writer faces a much more difficult task than writers of previous literary generations simply because telling the truth of contemporary reality is harder for a writer today—that life today is more extreme and ambiguous than it was, say, in Dickens's time. Would you agree with that?

Irving: Yes, I would agree with that, because every time a writer creates a weeping-and-wailing scene in his fiction, he's competing with extraordinary events in the real world. How the hell can anyone call my fiction excessively violent, or excessive in *any* way, if they've picked up a newspaper recently and read about the boat people in Cambodia? Could someone read a novel about that? *That's* tough stuff. People who take exception to the so-called excesses in my work can point out the fact that there's an awful lot of screwing, rape, violence, and other stuff in it that is usually associated with cheap cinema and fiction. I maintain that the stuff of cheap-thrill fiction or film is at our throats all the time. And we all fear it—that's why, if we have the means, we take a cab at night instead of the subway and send our children to private schools so that they won't have to go to public schools. People have to be blind to say that certain things are taboo to write about.

Did you find Garp's fictions-within-the-fiction difficult to write?

Irving: I think they were the most ambitious things I've ever written. I would never have written those kinds of things if I hadn't been doing them for Garp.

So none of the pieces—I'm thinking of the "Pension Grillparzer" story in particular—were conceived of before you started Garp?

Irving: No. I could never have developed the "Grillparzer" piece unless it was for a purpose like I had in *Garp*. It was only about halfway through *Garp* that I finally decided I had to make Garp a writer. I had known all along that I wanted him to have an imaginary life, but I resisted making him a writer at first—originally he was going to just be a wrestling coach. After I made this decision I became very depressed when I realized that if I made Garp a writer I would have to give evidence of the fact that he's a good one. Even more difficult, I wanted Garp to be a dazzling prodigy. Henry Robbins used to say that the most unbelievable thing about *The World According to Garp* was that a nineteen-year-old wrote "The Pension Grillparzer." I agree.

Several reviewers criticized Setting Free the Bears *because they claimed they couldn't see a connection between Siggy's historical background sections and the action in the present time. However, I sense that they were closely connected—that you were establishing a parallel between Austria's fight for freedom and the need of the two boys to assert their own sense of self-definition and importance.*

Irving: Yes, I certainly intended to suggest a parallel along those lines. What Siggy feels, and what a lot of other young people feel today, is a sense that he's living in a world which he's had no part in creating, that all the great decisions and important consequences have taken place before he's had a chance to affect them. It's a feeling we have, especially when we're young, that we've inherited a world not only not of our own making but not even of our own dreaming. That kind of frustration frequently yields a futile reaction—futile because at that age you seldom have the power to affect any kind of change.

This sense of history having passed us by is what Siggy keeps referring to as "Prehistory" then?

Irving: Yes. This sense of Prehistory is what leads Siggy to his scheme of freeing the bears. This attempt is indeed futile in the sense that it won't be able to *really* change anything. I've noticed that as my fiction progresses and I continue to write new versions of that zoo bust story, the escape becomes more and more disastrous and fewer and fewer animals get away. This is probably the result of my growing older and becoming more pessimistic.

The main characters in your last three novels—Garp, Severin Winter in The 158-Pound Marriage *and Bogus Thumper in* The Water-Method Man—*seem to have a lot in common: their maternal instincts, their obsession with mortality, their paranoia about their children, and so on. Would you say that Severin and Bogus were early versions of Garp, or were the three fundamentally different in conception?*

Irving: Although all three share certain resemblances, I wouldn't say that they are as alike as you're suggesting. Obviously with Bogus and Severin Winter and Garp I am dealing with parents who are obsessed with the notion of protection. At one point Bogus says that he wishes he could raise his children in a corral—a kind of simulated natural habitat—and his friend points out to him that if children were brought up in this way they would turn into cattle. This sense of protection and obsession with what might happen to one's children is simply taken all the way to its logical extreme with Garp. But we're not supposed to admire and respect Bogus and Severin the way we do Garp; they both possess emotional and personality flaws that make us evaluate them in completely different ways than we do Garp. Bogus, for example, is not only an arch procrastinator, but he simply can't face up to the mess he has created for himself with Biggie and Tulpen. As the title of *The Water-Method Man* suggests, Bogus is the type of person who tries to treat the *symptoms* of his problems rather than facing up to their source.

Despite all their masculine trappings—their wrestling, running, aggressiveness, and sexuality—there is a strong sense of vulnerability about your male characters. In Garp *there's even a passage that says that women are better equipped than men in containing the anxiousness and violence of the world. Do you believe this is true?*

Irving: Sure I do. In a very real sense women *are* better equipped to endure fear and brutality, to contain their anxiousness about their loved ones, because they have had to be this way. They've had to endure so much in the way of rape, violations of all sorts, punishments and condescensions, if nothing harsher—much of these created by men. *Primarily* created by men. To use one of my wrestling metaphors, if you're going to prepare yourself mentally and physically for a tough match on the weekend, the best way to do so is if you can get the shit kicked out of you by one of your teammates on Tuesday or Wednesday. If you work with something that is brutal and demanding, day by day, you'll be better equipped to deal with the real traumas later on. That seems to me to be what happens with women all the time. Women do, in a way, have more savvy about how to deal with the outside world because they take so much crap and suffer so much more condescension and abuse in the process of growing up or living at home with men. The abuse they then suffer in the outside world perhaps doesn't seem too harse or unbearable to them.

I gather that you're using Bogus's doctoral thesis in The Water-Method Man *as a kind of metafictional commentary on what is happening in his real life, much the same way that you use Garp's fiction in* The World According to Garp.

Irving: Yes, that's a good way to put it—his thesis *is* a "metafictional commentary." The point of that old Norse epic that Bogus is working on is that at the end of the bloodletting, when the principals have all come to an end, the old war between men and women immediately starts up all over again. I meant to reflect by the kind of violence and strenuousness of the relationship between Akthelt and Gunnel that equally strenuous engagements are being taken, in more civilized terms, by Tulpen and Bogus and between Biggie and Bogus. There are basic things in human relationships, especially sexual relationships, that never seem to change. I think that the area of sexual relationships is one place where the efforts of the women's movement to actually alter the basis of male-female relationships is doomed to fail. Only by *contracting* some arrangements that are not natural, not human, can we alter some of these basic differences between men and women and their relationships.

All of your fiction tends to deal with people placed in the midst of extreme sexual situations. What advantages does this kind of situation provide for a novelist?

Irving: Sex is one of the most important things that happens to people. When you place characters in extreme sexual circumstances, you are able to reveal a lot about them and their natures. In these kinds of extreme situations—sexual situations or violent ones or whatever—the best and worst aspects of ourselves are bound to come out, the things we admire and despise about people. Basically I always try to place my characters under the most and least favorable circumstances to see how they will react, to test them. In *Garp* this strategy was very self-conscious: I wanted to create characters whom I greatly admired and then bless them with incredibly good fortune in the first half of the novel—Garp wants to be a writer and he turns out to be a prodigy; he even wins the girl of his dreams by wooing her with a brilliant piece of writing; Jenny wants her baby in her own way and she gets it; she decides she wants to write her memories and they instantly make her famous. Everything these people want, they get, for a while. But in the second half of the novel I visit all the worst kinds of extreme things on these people to see how they can deal with extremes of adversity, just as earlier they had to cope with success. If a writer doesn't create these kinds of situations for his characters to face, he's copping out. There's also a line in *Garp* about human sexuality "making farcical our most serious intentions," which is something I believe.

In The Water-Method Man *you—like your character Ralph in his movie—refuse to investigate the so-called deep-seated motives of your characters. In fact, I'd say that one characteristic of all your fiction is a distrust of psychology and of the impulse to create psychologically complex and "deep" characters. What is the source of this distrust?*

Irving: My fiction is like that because I feel that the phrase "psychologically deep" is a contradiction in terms. Writers have traditionally tried to create the impression that they can explain their characters completely—that their characters can always be understood to do X because of Y and that hidden motives can always be found to explain everything that happens to them. But this kind of sociological or psychological approach is so much crap. The title of Ralph's movie— *Fucking Up*—suggests that often people simply fuck up, make mistakes. They misgauge certain situations or ignore the dangers that lurk everywhere in the world. "Fucking Up," by the way, was the title I originally intended to use for *The Water-Method Man* but my publishers wouldn't go along with it. There's a wonderful passage in Kurt Vonnegut's *God Bless You, Mr. Rosewater* where a psychiatrist resigns after successfully curing Eliot Rosewater's wife. When asked why he resigns after curing this woman, he says, "Well, I took a deep and troubled and complicated woman and made her calm, happy, shallow, and uninteresting." I have always liked that.

The attempt to psychoanalyze literary characters, either by critics or, most of all, by the writer in laying out the lives of his characters, is terribly simplistic and unimaginative. Ultimately it is destructive to all the breadth and complexity in literature. Literature had best treat psychology with the due amount of scorn or suspicion that it very much deserves. I've always felt that writers who themselves need, or think they need, psychiatric help are in the greatest trouble—because, of course, the nature of what writers do is psychologically unhealthy. In a sense, writers pick at wounds and make them worse—that's the nature of imaginative exploration, that's the nature of really getting at the roots of people, of really finding all the ways that we contradict ourselves. For a writer to then put himself into the hands of someone who means to smooth this out is a denial of the complexity that good writers ought to have. I think psychological and sociological interpretations are largely responsible for diminishing literature and, in many cases, for championing the literature that is less imaginative and more plodding but which is more easily seen in light of doctrines. I have no use for psychiatry.

Although you refer to wrestling in all of your novels, it obviously plays an especially important metaphorical role in The 158-Pound Marriage. *Were you using this conceit mainly to suggest a sense of the combativeness that characterizes the relationships of the main participants?*

Irving: Yes, the wrestling metaphor is certainly intended to reinforce this sense of combativeness. But the title is also supposed to suggest the perfectly *ordinary* nature of the situation I was depicting. It is a "middleweight situation" in the metaphorical sense that Severin is always using when he goes around saying that so-and-so is "a 158-pound intellect" or that a book is only "a 118-pound novel."

Your characters often have a difficult time communicating with each other, getting to know each other. I recall that in The 158-Pound Marriage *the narrator says at one point, "I felt that the more we knew about each other the less we actually knew." Are you as pessimistic about human communication as your narrator?*

Irving: It's been my experience, unfortunately, that what my narrator describes is exactly the case with people. People simply can't always understand each other. And even if they *do* understand others, it doesn't necessarily help them sustain relationships or even make these relationships more happy in the long run. In *Garp*, to take another example, I tried to show that even between two people who are close and who presumably understand one another—like Garp and Jenny—there is always the possibility of people misunderstanding one another, as Garp and Jenny do about the whole Ellen Jamesian affair.

I was interested in why you made the narrator of The 158-Pound Marriage *a historical novelist rather than any other kind. Utch tells him once, obviously dripping with sarcasm, "You think history means something." Since you make this narrator so unreliable in other respects, I assume you were suggesting that history can't be analyzed in the way that he tries to do it, both in his fiction and in his everyday life.*

Irving: Mostly I was trying to imply the limitations that this kind of novelistic approach implies. A historical approach can be, in its own way, as limiting as the sociological or psychological approaches I was criticizing earlier. I'm suspicious of any *totalizing* system. I like to contradict myself. I like to see these human contradictions really make mischief and run rampant in a novel. I like to see life get out of hand, like vegetation in the jungle with all sorts of growing going on.

I guess another way to put this is that I don't like to see a *thesis* about life, or people, disguised as a novel. I don't think the greatest novels of our time or any other time *are* theses. Great novels succeed much better when they are broad expressions or portraits than when they confine themselves to the singularity of an idea. Of course, I'm not trying to categorically put down a type of novel that I myself have practiced to an extent—you could say that *Setting Free the Bears* is a historical novel of sorts—but I was suggesting that the narrator of *The 158-Pound Marriage* is limited in that he tries too hard to base his art on what has *happened*—on real things. This is just one aspect of what makes his reportage so unreliable.

"Words fail me," says Graf in Setting Free the Bears; Bogus, *during his amnesia period in Vienna, goes through a time where he can't read or speak properly; in* Garp *you create several people with speech impediments—Tinch, Alice Fletcher, the Ellen Jamesians; during his recovery period Garp even finds himself trapped in almost a parody of a communication dilemma. Obviously you share with many other contemporary writers a particular interest in this issue of the difficulty of communicating effectly through language, through symbols.*

Irving: Yes, I've been very conscious in my fiction of dealing with this idea of how difficult it is to express oneself, how precarious our hold on symbols is. In *Garp* I created that recovery scene to push this idea to a kind of extreme: here we have the writer, who deals with language in order to express himself, placed into a situation in which he can't make himself understood because the words he has at his disposal, on those slips of paper, are ludicrously inadequate to communicate his feelings. This is a problem we all face, but with writers the situation is magnified. When I teach I try to begin every workshop or semester's writing class with a passage from Flaubert that I have probably remembered too loosely. It's a kind of commiseration about how difficult it is to use our language well. It goes, "Human language is a cracked kettle on which we beat our tunes for bears to dance to, when all the while we wish to move the stars to pity."

Garp's decline as a writer seems to stem from his attempt to use his writing as a means of relieving his own personal anxieties, as he does in "Vigilance," rather than out of any real reaction to the viscera of life. Am I right in assuming that you created "Vigilance" as a deliberately mediocre work to illustrate this problem?

Irving: Yes. In "Vigilance" I was trying to create a simple, trivial story to show how Garp had gotten off the track of *creating* a reality, using the materials of his life to develop something with an aesthetic unity. But in "Vigilance" he had abandoned this approach to the point where he was simply trying to rely on art to help him solve his own personal problems. I hate to see art being put to that use. Art should always be something more than merely a vehicle to deal with problems. Art-as-therapy is fine as therapy, but it's an insult to see artists writing simply to relieve themselves. I am especially pleased with the novel I am presently working on because it seems to me to be the most self-contained work I've ever written, the most a world unto itself, the least reliant on the outside world to be completely visualized or understood. In that sense it has the completeness of a "Once upon a time . . . " fairy tale—a form that goes back to a root of narration which is completely whole and self-sustained. I wish more fiction were moving in this direction and less in the direction of exercising a social point or developing a psychological thesis.

After all of the popular success with Garp, *do you worry about what the critics are likely to say about* The Hotel New Hampshire?

Irving: I think the one thing of a critical nature that will be said about whatever I do next is that it's not "serious." *The Hotel New Hampshire* will be a very readable novel by my own *aesthetic* choice. It will be as quickly paced as I can make it, it will be linear, it will be an unconvoluted narrative, it will be about likeable people. And by being fluid and fluent, by moving in as resolute and rapid a fashion as possible from A to Z, it will be a book that goes down with the apparent absence of difficulty. What it *means* or what it says about us all may require more thought on my reader's part, but to *read* it will not be difficult. However, by being easy to read, I suspect I will be misunderstood as being simplistic, as other writers like Vonnegut have been misunderstood. Since my book will be easy to read, people will assume that everything I've said was easy to write—an absolutely moronic charge.

What do you think your greatest strengths and weaknesses are as a writer?

Irving: I think my greatest strength is also my downfall. What I feel I do best is keep a narrative momentum going, stretch a story or a joke out while keeping my readers interested in what will follow next. Sometimes I go too far with this, though, and probably tax my reader's patience.

In addition to Gunter Grass, are there any other writers, living or dead, whom you greatly admire or whom you feel you have particular affinities with?

Irving: John Cheever would certainly come to mind. I know those people he writes about better than I know some other people, and I admire wholly the grace and affection with which Cheever writes about them. Those two things—grace and affection—mean a great deal to me in evaluating other writers. You could apply those terms to Vonnegut. You could say the same thing about Dickens—grace and affection. Certainly one would be very hard put to compare the *styles* of Vonnegut and Cheever, Dickens and Virginia Woolf; and I'm not trying to say that *all* their characters have great affection heaped upon them. But there is basically a great fondness for the vibrancy of life in all those writers. The differences between writers' styles are much more important, it seems to me, to amateurs.

I think art should be beautifully made. I don't care for the consciously ugly or consciously mundane, those kinds of efforts made by artists who pooh-pooh the beauty of the craft. I like the bravura of the show-off, but to me the difference between the consciously chosen styles of a writer like Jack Hawkes and a writer like Kurt Vonnegut is not nearly so important as the fact that *what* they do, they each do exquisitely. They both have a kind of grace at using their own voice, which is not the voice of their friends but a voice unique to them. They use this voice gracefully and with warmth; they use it with a fondness for the humanity they're writing about.

I care much less for writers who don't like people. There are a lot of writers around who don't like people. I prefer writers who like people, but I especially like writers who can use the language. My tastes in this regard are pretty catholic. There's no one way to use a language; there are many wonderful ways. In that sense my "heroes," if you will, are people who have demonstrated an ability to be extremists with language in their own ways but whose ultimate structures are graceful and whose ultimate feeling for people is fondness: Hawkes, Vonnegut, Gunter Grass, Heller, and Cheever, among my contemporaries; Virginia Woolf and Dickens among figures of the past.

An Interview with
Diane Johnson

The following interview with Diane Johnson took place on October 20, 1980, at her home in Berkeley, California. My wife and I had spent most of the morning wandering around the Berkeley campus, noticing how the ranks of hippies and campus characters had considerably thinned since our last visit in the early 1970s. When it came time for the interview, we found that Johnson lives in a fashionable house on one of those narrow, winding streets that weave their way among the ravines which eventually ascend into the hills overlooking Berkeley. Johnson greeted us and we drove out for a get-acquainted lunch at the Chez Panisse, a French café and restaurant which has a justifiably fine reputation all over the Bay area. Over lunch the talk centered on Johnson's latest literary project, a biography of Dashiell Hammett which she has been researching now for a couple of years. Since my wife had written her dissertation on Hammett, the two women had plenty of insights and anecdotes to exchange. Now in her mid-forties, Diane Johnson is an attractive, brown-haired woman whose ready smile and striking gray eyes somehow seem to convey the same qualities of openness and vulnerability so often present in her female characters.

After lunch we drove back to her house and set up shop in her living room, which contains one of those views from the Berkeley hills that most tourists only catch glimpses of. While I adjusted my tape recorder, Johnson pointed out one of her paintings—an original Henry Wallis given to her by his relatives after she had written of his life and involvement with Mary Ellen Meredith in *Lesser Lives*. The interview itself took us the remainder of the afternoon and early evening, punctuated by occasional coffee breaks. The atmosphere was relaxed and Johnson talked easily, with the same clarity and conviction that has marked her regular contributions to the *New York Review of Books* during the past half-dozen years.

Diane Johnson has had a remarkably varied career. Her first novel, *Fair Game* (1965), was written while she was still raising children and attending school part-time. She received her doctorate from Berkeley in 1968, writing her dissertation on George Meredith—a project which provided the later inspiration for *Lesser Lives* (1973). A work which examined the lives of Mary Ellen Meredith and the unfortunate circumstances surrounding her life with Meredith and her later scandalous affair with the painter Henry Wallis, *Lesser Lives* was nominated for a National Book Award and won Johnson considerable acclaim as a biographer, despite the book's highly unusual form, which mixes objective fact, Johnson's own imaginative projections, and various works of fiction and poetry from the era. Meanwhile, Johnson was continuing to write novels, all of them dealing with the lives of men and women living in California. (Johnson says her books shouldn't really be considered "California novels" in any narrow sense.) *Loving Hands at Home* (1968) was the first of her novels to receive much national attention; the books which followed—*Burning* (1971), *The Shadow Knows* (1974), and *Lying Low* (1978)—were widely (and favorably) reviewed and began to earn her both critical acclaim and popularity. Beginning with *Burning*, her novels also began to move away from the domestic arena to examine more public issues such as race relations, the nature of guilt and evil, and the precarious set of myths and fictions used by people to create personal identity and sustain relations with others. Although her fiction usually focuses on women characters, Johnson insists in this interview that her fiction is not necessarily "feminist" in its implications; rather, she sees it as dealing with tendencies that are present in us all. Thus the images which dominate her fiction during the '70s—images of apocalypse, insanity, paranoia, misdirected passion which can suddenly flare into violence—are images which speak to us all of the nature of contemporary American life.

It was apparently *The Shadow Knows*, an often horrifying metaphysical detective tale, which brought Johnson to the attention of filmmaker Stanley Kubrick. After discussing various possible horror projects with her, Kubrick finally decided to ask her to coauthor the script for *The Shining* (released in 1980) with him. The work she did with Kubrick also led Johnson to write a script for a Mike Nichols remake of *Grand Hotel* (the '30s Garbo classic), a project which was unfortunately later abandoned. She is now completing the Hammett biography and is ready to begin a spy novel, a book which is already fully outlined. She is also a professor of English at the University of California–Davis, where she teaches mainly Victorian literature.

—Larry McCaffery

You observe in one of your essays that Lina Wertmüller has complained about being labeled a "woman director," rather than being called simply a director. Do you feel a similar irritation when people refer to you as a "woman writer"?

Johnson: Well, it depends. That term is used in a variety of ways, most often—at least, for a long time—in a patronizing way. So for a long time it *did* bother me. I don't think of myself as a "woman writer" in the sense of writing things that only women would read or like. But of course in the modern, feminist sense it is a compliment and places me in very good company.

One critic I read even went so far as to claim that your books should not be considered feminist in their orientation.

Johnson: I'd agree. I don't think my works *are* feminist works. Our times make it hard to say that without seeming to wish to disavow feminism—and no nice woman is not a feminist these days. It's just that most of my books have been about other things, so it's surprising and annoying to find them appropriated for one political use. I don't usually remember reviews, but some of them burn their way into the psyche. There was a review of *Lying Low* by Peter Prescott in *Newsweek* that began with a long diatribe against the feminist novel, saying how formless novels by women were and how they only wish to screech their ridiculous ideology and have no plots. I found this response to be stupefying, since *Lying Low* didn't seem to me to be a novel where the term "feminism" had any application. It's a novel about commitment, although it does, like most novels, have women characters. It just demonstrated to me how book reviewing in this country is controlled by odd preconceptions and how very little these preconceptions often have to do with the actual novel that the critic is given to read. Peter Prescott had heard somewhere that I was a feminist, and this signaled some sort of fear which impeded his reading of a novel whose plot is, if anything, a bit contrived.

I saw that review and reacted the same way. Doesn't he go on to accuse you of being misanthropic toward men?

Johnson: He does, yes.

Any truth to that?

Johnson: No, I really don't think so. I like to feel that I am a true observer of human nature and that I can say mean things about men with impunity—and about women—and still have truth on my side. But in *Lying Low* particularly, the male characters are all rather amiable. It was that kind of statement that so surprised me and showed me that there was an emotional set to the mind of a reader so that misreadings are almost inevitable. I could see how someone might have said this kind of thing about *The Shadow Knows*, for example, where all the men come off rather badly. But not with *Lying Low* or with *Burning*; in the others, some of the men are good and some not, as in life.

You've already implied that you don't feel that your books are necessarily books about women per se . . .

Johnson: We don't regard, say, *Robinson Crusoe* as a "man's" book. That idea that a book about men is "universal" and a book in which women have problems is "special" is, after all, only a convention and a reflection of a historical situation, not a universal law. For example, I think of *The Shadow Knows* as being about race relations, the evil in human nature, and social fear. At the same time N., the heroine, has problems, like too little alimony, child care, and on and on, which are peculiar to women, the way in another book we might find the hero down on his luck without money in some strange town.

Could you talk a bit about your work habits?

Johnson: Actually, I don't have a daily writing routine. I tend to be a rather intermittent writer, except when I'm working on something and really into the middle of it. Then I can work quite long hours. So my work habits are really a matter of how involved I am with whatever kind of work I have. Rather than sit in anguish before the blank page—which I think, in principle, I ought to do—I find that I sweep the kitchen floor or sew or go for a walk or fidget. In other words, I dream a lot about my work, I think about it at the kitchen sink, so that when something is finally at hand I can sit down and work hard at it.

What sort of things seem to prompt you to begin a book? Do you start, say, with the idea for a character, a plot, a metaphor, a theme you might want to develop?

Johnson: Most of them come from a sociological observation—from a feeling about society or about the way things are in a place. *Burning*, for example, began as a Los Angeles novel. *Lying Low* was a novel about the political climate of the '60s. *The Shadow Knows* was a novel about fear, about how things were between blacks and whites in the early 1970s. So I guess they usually start just from some wish to render a certain mood, a climate. Typically I am feeling oppressed about some feature of American life and I want to somehow capture it. Then I have to figure out how to embody these feelings and observations in characters and situations.

Once your books start, how do you proceed with them? Do you start with an outline, work straight through a draft before you revise, or what?

Johnson: I work straight through a draft and then go back and revise, move the chapters around, make a lot of structural changes. But I don't work straight through in the order in which things will finally appear; I write different parts of the book at different times. Starting with *The Shadow Knows*, I have also outlined my books very carefully before I begin. I used to begin more haphazardly. Even so, I collect envelopes of bits scribbled in inspiration on the bus, bits I wake up thinking about, and then have to find out what they mean and weave them in.

I know it's difficult to separate the strands of the process of writing, but is there any single aspect of creating a book that you find especially interesting?

Johnson: You're right about it being difficult to divide up your preoccupations, but if I had to place a priority on what really interests me it would be on the *form* of a novel. As I just mentioned, I now usually work with outlines, and in these I work with formal principles of various kinds. I think of my books as having shape, as having parts which I move around. I even envision the process in a spatial way, in three dimensions somehow.

So your goal is to create a pleasing shape to these elements . . .

Johnson: Yes, exactly.

Your first novel, Fair Game, was written while you were still in graduate school. Could you talk a bit about your academic background and how your career in academia is related to your career as a fiction writer?

Johnson: As a matter of fact, my academic interests didn't relate to my career as a writer. It was simply that I had dropped out of college during my twenties and began to have babies, and one of the ways I found I could get out of the house in the afternoon was by taking courses at UCLA. But before I began to do that I was trying to write at home, which is a good kind of cottage industry for mothers of small children. Anyway, writing was what I had always been interested in—I'm not really an academic by temperament.

What was your academic field?

Johnson: Nineteenth-century British literature. My dissertation was about the poetry of George Meredith.

Could you explain what led up to your writing Fair Game? Were you trying your hand at short fiction while you were writing at home, for instance?

Johnson: No. Short stories are too hard. I've always just written novels except when I was in college. *Fair Game* was actually my second novel—I had written an earlier one which wasn't published. I was teaching myself how to write novels during this baby-having period, and then I actually wrote *Fair Game*. *Fair Game* just happened to come out while I was taking graduate courses in 1965. My fourth child was born in 1962, so I must have begun it in '63. But going to graduate school had to do with getting out of the house, not with writing novels. I'm very interested in literature and I love taking courses and talking to others, and there were wonderful people at UCLA in 1967—Ada Nisbet, the Dickens scholar; John Espey, the writer, and others.

Karen, the main character in Loving Hands at Home, *says at one point that she "was doomed by my smallness of spirit to a life of prim convention." And in* Lying Low, *Theo claims that the biggest risk of all for women is to take a chance on leading a plain, ordinary, unsung life. Is this the biggest danger facing women in contemporary life—the risk of leading a "lesser life"?*

Johnson: I'd say that's true for people of both sexes in connection with life in general. Most people are condemned to lead plain lives; coming to terms with this, finding some kind of philosophy or metaphysical position in regard to it, is something that almost everyone must face. I'm not sure everyone *does* face it, because I don't know to what extent people mind this situation. Specifically in the case of women, though, their general problem is that they do accept plain lives. They are apt to tell themselves that a plain, ordinary life is best and provide themselves with a lot of excuses for not trying things they might find interesting. Theo's remark about taking a "chance" on leading an ordinary life is self-deceiving on her part, a bit of sophistry. She opted out of being a ballerina.

It was interesting to me that in Lying Low *the situation is the reverse of what we find with most of your women characters. Theo and Marybeth are both women who've begun adult life by leading a daring existence and now are forced into leading a dull life. Was this a conscious reversal on your part?*

Johnson: Exactly. I was interested in newspaper articles that would come out about activists when they would turn up and give themselves up. These girls would almost always describe having led a life of utter banality while lying low, so I could imagine making this early attempt at breaking out of becoming a Weatherman or Weatherperson or whatever, but I felt that the reality would be that the life you created would be very much like the life you would have had to lead if you had just married your old boyfriend from San Jose—maybe even worse, even more stifling.

In one way or another, nearly all the major characters in Lying Low *seem to be doing exactly that: lying low. At least all the people you bring together under that one roof . . .*

Johnson: Yes, and maybe that aspect of the book is too patterned. They were parallel cases—each was disillusioned in some way with the prevailing ideology of her most passionately committed political time. This is true of nearly everybody, don't you feel?

It's certainly true of a lot of my contemporaries who were politically committed during the '60s. There's a lot of disillusionment among them.

Johnson: Yes, I've noticed the same thing—or the way fans of the Spanish Civil War still feel that it was the meaningful conflict of our time. I find it hard to write about the '50s and the McCarthy business with any sense of sympathy for, say, the Hollywood people, since they were all so cowardly compared to the people in the '60s who really went to jail.

All your books are set in California—one critic has even labeled you a member of the "California Gothic" school of fiction. How do you view the role of California in your work? Is it a mere backdrop for the main action, or is its function more important than that?

Johnson: It's mainly a backdrop. I happen to live here and it's easier for me to write about California than to try to imagine somewhere else. I'm not from California but I have lived here a long time. I'm going to try a different setting for my next novel, though, just to avoid the California label. It's puzzling to find yourself being categorized as a regional writer of some sort from a region not your own.

Still, I notice that your books are often populated by what many Easterners would probably regard as "kooks." Do you think there's something about California life that actually produces *these kinds of people? Or do they simply wind up out here somehow?*

Johnson: I think they just end up out here. I used to feel irritated when critics would say about my characters that they're not real people *because* they live in California, and so it doesn't matter what they are doing. This is a very shortsighted way to look at things. After all, with a California president we might have a complete California government. So Californization is probably going to be accelerated. California trends travel eastward.

But you did say a minute ago that you felt Burning *is specifically a Los Angeles novel. In what sense did you mean that?*

Johnson: It was about what I saw around me in L.A.—about despair, I suppose, and people creating certain terrible types of illusion. Max, for example, has to go to that charlatan psychiatrist, and the other people have their own different styles of illusory self-preservation. But I also wanted *Burning* to be just about the daily life of Bingo and her husband Barney and the ways in which they were completely separated from each other even though they lived together—the separateness we all live in, I guess. I like to write novels about where I am and what it's like, about how I'm feeling and about the people who are around me. All of this got lumped together into *Burning*.

Loving Hands at Home is similar to most of your other novels in that it is filled with symbolic moments or epiphanies which your characters analyze as such—they almost seem like literary critics, the way they think in terms of symbols. Do you yourself—English professor and woman—see the world this way? Or is this just a convenient fictional device?

Johnson: I suppose I probably see the world this way, but that form of symbolic thinking probably results from a literary imagination. I don't know if other people do it. I have noticed that a lot of people behave as if they're on television. That is, they seek explanations or means of articulating their problems or concerns from people who can articulate them for them—from psychiatrists or soap operas or fiction. Men do this as much as women, but they have different sources of metaphor—they don't have soap operas, but they have that whole macho thing and its offshoots. So there is a very strong control over men's interpretations of their lives by a sort of mythology. And many people read fiction for this. In fact, it's hard to think of another reason why people want to read fiction except for this kind of articulation. This is true of all art: it articulates our concerns and anxieties, it provides solutions.

As I recall, you took Toni Morrison to task a bit in your review of Song of Solomon *for not providing "solutions" to her characters' lives, for providing such a negative view of black life. Do you feel, with John Gardner, that great art needs to provide* answers *to fundamental questions, that it needs to be "moral" in its outlook?*

Johnson: No, I don't. Great art never advocates anything. It sometimes may *represent* evil or immoral things. One can go along with Gardner in a certain way, in matters of *taste*—there are certain things that appear to me to be gross and to which I respond with "Uck!" But I don't think I would want to elevate a condemnation of those things into some sort of aesthetic principle. I don't feel that art can be so programmatic as Gardner seems to want it to be.

As to my review of *Song of Solomon,* I wasn't trying to complain about her presentation of black life at all. She *does* present a horrid view of blacks and of their relationships, and presumably she was presenting what she felt was a true, accurate view. What I *was* objecting to—and evidently I didn't make this ultimately clear, since I was timid about saying it directly—was the *critical reception* of the novel. It was so dopey; reviewers kept saying, "Wow, that wonderful Toni Morrison, she's written such a warm and loving novel with all those darling blacks." I thought *that* was patronizing. Nobody was really facing up to the terribleness of her view and all that it implied. But I wasn't saying that it wasn't a true view, or that it needed to be more positive to be a great work.

Karen, in Loving Hands at Home, *vicariously obtains excitement and passion in her life—at least early in the novel—by means of her "secret life," which ultimately involves her imagination rather than any real excitement. Several of your other heroines—Bingo, N. Hexam, even Theo—also have fantasy lives that are important to them. Do you feel that fantasy or the imagination is more important for women than for men, due to the nature of women's lives?*

Johnson: I suppose there are some sexual differences which cause people to have different kinds of secrets, different kinds of fantasies, but clearly it isn't only sex related. Smart and dumb people, for example, would have different secrets. I assume that there are male things that men don't tell women and vice versa, but these aren't necessarily things to do with sex. Among women these secrets are often shared jokes about the male character, and I assume that men have the same kind of thing. And there are always a few little things that you don't wish to tell your partner about—things you've done, or wish to do, or may do. The mystery of personality. But as far as having a fantasy life, I would think that most people have these sorts of things; probably it's not a sexual thing that men or women have or don't have, but just something that some people have while others don't. I myself, for example, don't have much of a fantasy life. Having novels to write, which is just an extreme form of fantasizing, perhaps takes away my need to fantasize over the breakfast table.

I was wondering, though, if in your early novels you didn't create women who were particularly vulnerable to the pleasures of a fantasy life because of their situation as women and mothers.

Johnson: You mean because they're stuck at home with the kids?

Yes—and because they don't seem to have any real outlets for their creativity, or even their emotions.

Johnson: If I had a job as a man—a job as a bookkeeper or working as a television repairman or whatever—I would probably find *that* boring as well, and perhaps I would want to escape mentally from that sort of thing. In fiction, one of the ways that one can know the other sex—if one *can* ever know them—is by daydreaming about romance.

Could you talk a bit about what you had in mind in developing the central metaphor of "burning" in your novel of that name?

Johnson: What I wanted *Burning* to be about was people's private passions—their wish to burn, to generate heat, warmth, the Paterian phrase about burning with a hard gemlike flame and all of that. And how people's efforts to do that, or even to sustain a passionate commitment to life, are fraught with difficulties. *Lying Low* is about this, too. There's a lot of false fire around, a lot of stuff passing for emotional warmth and commitment that isn't really. You know, I haven't read *Burning* in a long time, but I actually liked it pretty well—much better than the critics did. I think people found it cold somehow, despite its title.

What first got you interested in the life of Mary Ellen Meredith, the subject of your biography, Lesser Lives?

Johnson: It was mainly my dissertation on George Meredith, but it also involved that business we were just talking about: the relationship between art and life. I was reading about Meredith's life and I was struck by how casually the biographers always referred to this episode in his life—about how he and his wife quarreled and then she ran off and then she died—as though there were a connection between her running off (and therefore being the "erring wife") and her dying. This connection was, as you know, very much a fictional convention of nineteenth-century literature.

You mean that all women in those days who had sex outside marriage didn't die or go crazy?

Johnson: Apparently not all of them. But in literature, anyway, if a woman erred sexually in some way or flaunted convention, she was almost always punished.

*I gather from your title—*Lesser Lives, *rather than* A Lesser Life *or some other alternative—that you view Mary Ellen's situation as being representative of other women's lives in some sense.*

Johnson: Yes, but I was also thinking about the lesser lives in that book—Henry Wallis, the lover; and Thomas Love Peacock, whose life wasn't really so lesser; and Mrs. Peacock, who really did go crazy. I got interested in all of them, and for none of them was there enough material for a whole book. My general interest was in the idea that, to the person involved, his own life is always of major importance.

You ask the readers on the opening page of Lesser Lives *to join you in pretending to freeze time, and in the rest of the book you do a lot of other novelistic "pretending" of your own. Why did you take such an obviously novelistic—I hesitate to use the term "New Journalistic"—approach? Was it mainly this lack of factual material that you just mentioned?*

Johnson: Yes. There was simply a lot that I had to infer from events. There were some known facts but very many gaps which I had to fill in somehow. But I never make things up without saying I have done so; and I never made up speeches or anything like that because I don't approve of that approach in biography. But I had to do a certain amount of imagining in this case.

Let's pursue this a bit further. You comment in your notes that you take the relationship of the writer to his work to the logical extreme by using the literary works to comment on the life of the author without any qualifying commentary of your own at all. You say, "This can be more easily justified on artistic grounds than on sound biographical methodology." What did you mean by saying it could be justified on "artistic grounds"?

Johnson: In using, say, some questions from *The Egoist* which seem to very closely duplicate what appears to have been going on in Meredith's life, I felt I was making my book better, more vivid. Meredith wrote the scene. But strictly speaking you could quarrel with that whole approach by saying, "You don't know that that was what he was thinking about when he wrote that scene—this is an unwarranted association of life and art." I decided to go ahead and use this approach, but I thought it was only fair to admit that I was vulnerable to this objection.

In a review of Families *by Jane Howard, you say that "there is something about the author's presentation of herself that is vital to the book's success." I felt the same thing about your role in* Lesser Lives—*that you were deliberately projecting yourself into the book almost as a kind of character.*

Johnson: Yes, I know the sense that you're referring to. I saw myself as the overviewer, a narrator who was a puppet master, the person who was drawing together all the materials and making all the inferences. Again, the reason for this was just that my materials were so sporadic that they needed a kind of organizing consciousness. Also the book had to cover a long period of time—almost seventy-five years by the time Henry Wallis died, even longer if you count Peacock's life. So there had to be one form of continuity provided, and in this case it was the narrator's voice. That voice was my voice.

You also say somewhere that you don't understand why the serious reader of today feels more trustful of reality than of the imagination "which is often so much truer." What do you mean by that?

Johnson: Sometimes I probably talk a lot of nonsense, but I think I meant there that often one's imagination or intuition can get to what really happened in some sort of truer sense than a mere examination of the objective facts. I know that in *Lesser Lives* and in other places I've made the case for biographers being novelists of sorts. A good biographer should have the intuition and the narrative skills of the novelist. Objective reality shows what happened; intuition or imagination can see why.

Are you developing the biography of Dashiell Hammett that you're currently working on in the same way?

Johnson: No, not at all. With this book there is no "me," no narrator. Hammett himself is really always the narrative consciousness, since I try to use as many of Hammett's perceptions, taken from his letters, as I can. So I don't have to make as many guesses.

What originally got you interested in Hammett? Were you a fan of his work?

Johnson: Yes, I've always been a fan of Hammett's, although I didn't originate the idea of the biography. But when somebody else suggested that I take over from Steven Marcus, the Columbia professor who had for some reason gotten bogged down with the project, I was intrigued with the idea. And living here in San Francisco, I thought that working on it would be a lot of fun, since so much of Hammett's work deals with this area.

Have you contacted Lillian Hellman for assistance?

Johnson: Oh, yes, she and I are certainly in touch. She has told me a lot of things about Hammett and has also given me his letters, which span a period of thirty years. I find that these letters are my best source of information about Hammett. There's simply not a lot of other reliable information. The records of his Pinkerton days, for example, are gone. Also, I'm not a very good detective myself—I can never think of ways a person might find out about the Pinkerton records. Real detectives haven't been able to find out much either, though.

I didn't realize that. What have you learned about Hammett so far? Was he a different man than the character most of us think of him as being?

Johnson: My overall presentation will, I think, differ from the myth that he was a more strange, violent, doomed person, all that, than he has seemed. But I haven't found out any really unforeseen and unexpected facts, no secret secrets. Alas. Or perhaps I have lost track of the public mythology, and it will seem to others than this is an unexpected presentation. I don't know.

Of the forms you've worked with—novels, biographies, essays, filmscripts—which have you found to be the most challenging or interesting?

Johnson: I guess I enjoy writing novels the most. They're the most interesting to me, probably because I think they're the most complex. It involves your mental life and transforms day-to-day life; everything seems to bear on what you are writing. Somewhere Colette compares novel-writing to dowsing. When you get near underground water, the stick twists in your hand. I love that strange leap into life of the stick. Essays are what you think; dramatizations are more like novels, except you get to leave out the descriptions. And descriptions are always the hardest part for me; I have to go back and put them in. Stories are like—what?—a sneeze, over too fast. I'm not assured enough to be good at stories.

Doctorow told me that he felt he had learned a great deal about fiction-writing from having worked with filmscripts and simply from having grown up with the cinema; Coover and Barthelme told me much the same thing. Would your experiences with writing filmscripts confirm this tendency?

Johnson: I've only written two filmscripts—the one I did for *The Shining* and one with Mike Nichols, *Grand Hotel*, which wasn't made—and I had written all of my novels before I wrote either of them. But I think nonetheless that I have learned something about writing fiction from working on these scripts, though time will tell. What I learned was something I had started working out myself—mostly about outlining, about the shorthand form of manipulating the narrative materials by means of which you are provided with a scheme that allows you to visualize the shape of the narrative. As I've mentioned, I had made quite careful outlines of *The Shadow Knows*, and then I found that Stanley Kubrick very much works this way. He convinced me how very valuable it is to work that way.

How does this outlining process work?

Johnson: It's working with narrative units, bits and pieces which could be represented as A-B-C or as a single word or symbol. This is basically what you do when you're making a filmscript. Working with a script also taught me something about suspense, theme, and very much about creating scenes.

Do you think your fiction has been influenced by any of the other arts or media other than the cinema—for example, by television, painting, music?

Johnson: Probably not. It's interesting that you should ask that, though, because I am very interested in other art forms, especially painting and the decorative arts. You would think there would be some carryover to my own work, but except in some kind of general effect on my sensibility I can't see much influence.

The Shadow Knows *has affinities to different versions of the detective novel—it is, on at least a very obvious level, a kind of whodunit. What did you find intriguing or useful about this genre?*

Johnson: Yes, it is a kind of detective novel. I was intrigued with this form because I'm getting more interested in plot as I go along. I got tired of character, in fact, as a major consideration in planning my books. The detective novel seemed to be a genre which already existed, so it had a certain number of rules which specifically defined the nature of its plot—that is, where the resolution would be immanent in the plot, in the events, rather than in the characters. I'm sure you know the old cliché about the novel's action arising out of character. But *should it?* What about exigency, what about fate, what about arbitrary happenings and all of these other things that seem, in some ways, to be a truer representation of modern life? This is something I've just begun to think about, really, in regard to a spy novel that I've just begun to outline.

It's obvious, though, that The Shadow Knows *doesn't really follow either the classical or hardboiled detective pattern, because instead of clarity being created out of ambiguity and mystery, quite the opposite occurs—the possibilities seem to proliferate as the book goes on. Even the conclusion seemed to me to be fraught with different possible interpretations. Did you stucture your book this way simply because you—like Dashiell Hammett, I guess—don't believe that life's mysteries can be resolved?*

Johnson: Yes, that was my game—to make the mysteries proliferate, as you say, which I felt would be true to life and fictionally interesting. I still stand behind these reasons. But people have complained a lot about this, and I've found that you don't tamper with conventions or that you *can't* tamper with them without creating a lot of reader irritation. However, I did feel that I had solved the mystery in the novel for the reader. One of the things that I thought of while I was working with

Kubrick was that I had, in fact, gotten some of the events in *The Shadow Knows* in the wrong order. If I were rewriting it today, I would change a couple of things and these would make a great deal of difference in clarifying a certain explanation, although I would hope they wouldn't remove the general aura of ambiguity.

What kind of changes are you thinking of?

Johnson: In the novel as it is now, N. has a miscarriage in the parking lot and while she's laid up for the night she discovers that her friend Bess has a knife—which suggests that Bess may have done some of the things to her. Then afterward she finds an ashtray in the washroom which explains another mystery. I can see now that if the ashtray scene had come first—so that she had solved to our satisfaction the mystery of who had bashed Ev in the washroom—and then *later* she had had her bleeding episode, we would have already known who had bashed Ev and that Bess was somehow implicated. I'm sure you can't follow that, but the point is that it would have felt like she was getting closer and closer to the central mystery by solving the lesser ones first. Where I had seen a series of almost unrelated mysteries, each needing to be cleared up, the reader, perhaps because of the conventions of the genre, appeared to assume a connection, an unraveling of one ball of twine.

But isn't one of your major points the idea that, as N. says in the book's opening words, "You never know"?

Johnson: Yes, that's right, although I do feel there should be an optional, potential explanation if you choose to take it. That's why I put in the book the possibility that Osella bashed Ev, that Bess was really crazy and doing the vandalism. The rape scene was meant to be a final symbol of ambiguity and everyone's complicity in evil. I wrote that last scene lightly, before my consciousness was raised about the political implications of rape. I've had so much criticism about the scene, probably justified, and about having N. seeming to like being raped—which I didn't mean to imply at all; I meant that she was simply in on all this, too—that I might now choose another metaphor. I also felt that you might suspect that the famous inspector was the rapist.

I recall N. saying that she doesn't "quite trust the angel of order"—something that seems to relate to what you said a minute ago about fate, exigency, and randomness being perhaps more a part of our lives than the well-made novel has suggested all these years.

Johnson: Exactly. I think this is something my fiction often tries to deal with. One of the sad things about fiction is that it's so organized and unambiguous. It is facile and inauthentic for fiction to suggest that things *are* organized and can be wound up as neatly as they are in most novels, and yet the novel must impose form on random experience.

Although it's usually for very understandable reasons, most of your characters seem, if not paranoid, then obsessively worried and fearful about things. Do you think this is because they are women—and hence in a more vulnerable position in the world—or is this simply a fact of life for all of us today?

Johnson: I'd say it's a bit of both. I do feel that women worry about different sorts of things than men do. In the same way that men and women both fantasize but have different kinds of fantasies, so too with worries. I am sure that most women worry about things more than men, but in a different way. Everyone has noticed that men sleep very soundly while women sleep lightly and listen for the baby, to take a very obvious example. This is clearly a sociologically determined thing which we are all subject to. I know it's a real aspect of my life and of other women I've known.

When I talked with John Irving, he mentioned that he felt women were more aware of the brutalities and dangers of life—and ultimately more able to cope with them—simply because they had been subjected to more bullshit.

Johnson: I don't know if this is innate or conditioned, but I do feel that women are more aware of these kinds of things. Just the fact that we're physically smaller and weaker tends to make our responses to situations different than men's. I know that my husband, who is six feet five, is very untroubled by certain things that I can directly ascribe to the fact that he's never been threatened or annoyed by them. Nobody has ever leaped out of a car and threatened to punch him in the nose. Such things give one a different attitude toward life.

I take it that the title "The Shadow Knows" comes from the old radio program . . .

Johnson: Yeah, "Who knows what lurks in the hearts of evil men? The Shadow knows." So the shadow represents simply the evil that lurks within all men—again, not meaning men as males, but mankind.

Am I right in seeing both Osella and Ev as being different kinds of "dark doubles" for N.?

Johnson: Yes, that was my intention. Osella, huge, fat, out of control, enacts the thin little N.'s rage or whatever; Ev, I'm not sure, but something about goodness and doomedness. Incidentally, they were also quite real women who happened to work for me in Los Angeles. This is probably hard to believe, because in many ways they're the most fantastic characters in the book. But all those qualities which are balanced around N. as her "double," as you put it, were literal qualities. There was this woman I based Osella on who used to be a sort of mammy for my then-husband when he was a boy. She came to work for us, went mad, and left. Then we separated and everything blew up. Although I didn't move to a housing development, as N. did, I did get Ev to work for me—her name really was Ev, I couldn't think of another name for her for some reason. Ev was very wonderful and victimized, like Ev in my novel. Now that I'm talking about this, I can see that *The Shadow Knows is* quite an autobiographical novel, probably my most autobiographical.

I was rather puzzled by the witch imagery you employ in the novel—N. Hexam's name, Osella's accusations, N.'s references to herself as a witch, and so on.

Johnson: I'm not sure I thought out the witch business very well. Its origin was that, in the course of going mad, the real Osella accused *me* of being a witch. Her reasons for thinking that seemed to focus on some pictures on our bedroom wall. They were pictures made of bark that we had brought back from Mexico. She said, "And them *witch* pictures, man, I know you're witchin' me with them pictures." She burned them in the course of her final mania and frenzy. It was very scary. Later on, though, I started thinking that one of the things I found interesting was how these poor women *were* in my power just because of the fact of American life and them being black and me being white—how your situation gives you power. So it struck rather forcefully that one *does* experience people and the power they have over you as a kind of menacing magic.

*Your most recent books—*The Shadow Knows, Lying Low, *even your work on* The Shining—*seem to concern themselves increasingly with what N. calls "the terror of the real beneath the form." And they deal with increasingly violent, frightening materials. Any explanation for this?*

Johnson: I see what you mean, and I've wondered about this myself. I've noticed that as my material life improves and my family relationships become more stable and I'm more middle-aged and calm, my books become more hysterical, brooding, preoccupied with violence. But I don't really know why this is so. Maybe you have to organize one part of your life before you dare explore these other things. The first novel I ever published, *Fair Game,* is a miracle of cheerfulness, but I wrote it when I was probably most unhappy. I'd like to change this pattern, and that's one of the reasons why I'm working on this spy novel—that, along with the fact that it's set outside the United States.

Let's talk about your work with The Shining. *How did you get involved with this project?*

Johnson: Stanley Kubrick called me up and we met during the time when he was thinking about various books with the idea of making a horror movie.

Was he interested in filming The Shadow Knows?

Johnson: Maybe. He had read it, and although he never said so—and I never asked him—that was my impression. So we talked over dinner in London and about six months later he called back and said, "I've bought this Stephen King novel and would you read it?" I did, and when he got started with the project he suggested that I work with him on the script.

How did this collaboration work?

Johnson: I was in London altogether for eleven weeks, although at different times. Each time we went a little further with the script, went into different drafts. I had a flat in London and I would stay at home in the morning and then he would spend the mornings, say, working on the sets—he was doing everything simultaneously, so the sets were being designed and he had a lot of things to oversee. I would arrive in the afternoon and we would spend the afternoon and evening together talking a lot about fictional problems—he's very literary—and about the story itself, of course.

So the actual script itself would evolve out of these talks.

Johnson: Yes. From time to time I would stay home and actually write up a scene. First we would do an outline, and then another outline, and then another. Then I would write out the scene and bring it to him and he would also work on it. He's quite a good writer, as well as a great director, and he really improved my version a lot.

So you were basically creating a rough draft and then the two of you would work up a final version together.

Johnson: Sort of. After I would bring something in he would say, "I don't think that will work," or come up with a trenchant line. He was very good at lines. He wrote Jack's part, more or less, and I wrote Wendy's. I was interested to see that finally the Wendy that came out on the screen was much quieter than the Wendy I had written, who was more like a female character in my novels, I suppose, in that she had a lot to say.

In adapting King's book, what did you feel it essential to keep in your script?

Johnson: The horror, of course—the whole atmosphere of growing fear within the domestic circle was the core, I think. The thing that was more interesting to us, though, was *why* this situation was horrifying, if it is horrifying. There was something very basic here, with the father trying to kill the son and the son trying to kill the father. That and the feeling of powerlessness. So it was an archetypal situation, and that was what was most interesting—more interesting, say, than the business about the ghosts. But we did try to work out a rationale that would give an explanation for the magic. Time, of course, dictated that certain things would have to go, and the physical limitations of the cinema dictated some other changes.

What's your opinion of the final movie version? I assume you've seen it a number of times.

Johnson: Actually I've just seen it once. It hadn't come to France this year while I was living there, so I saw it with the Kubricks in London after it was out. When I got back here it had already moved on, so I only got to see it that once. My first viewing, though, was very much taken up with technical matters, listening to the dialogue, and seeing how it really is to see the words that you've written being spoken by a person on the screen. So I had no appropriate response.

What was it like to work with Kubrick?

Johnson: I liked it very much. He's extremely smart and I felt very comfortable working with him. We developed a harmonious working relationship, and I think I learned a lot about film from him. Even though he's very much a perfectionist, he has a kind of professorial side to him that makes him patient and willing to teach.

Did he ever explain what it was about The Shadow Knows *that made him feel you would be a good person to work with on* The Shining?

Johnson: I think it was mostly his opinion that I had shown the ability to create the feelings of dread and fear.

Thomas Edwards in his review of Lying Low *claimed that you were unsuccessful in developing a credible male sensibility. Do you find it difficult to portray male sensibilities—more so than those of your female characters?*

Johnson: It's hard to say. I wouldn't try to refute Edwards, but I wasn't really very concerned with the male characters in *Lying Low*, who both happen to play rather minor roles. The only book I've written mainly from the point of view of a man was *Fair Game*, although *Burning* is half male point of view and half female. My assumption in doing both works was that one's inner thoughts would be much the same in males and females, as long as I stayed away from certain sex-related subjects that I couldn't quite render—specifically male sexual attitudes, I mean. I don't know if people would feel that I was successful or not, but you have to assume that there is some kind of core level that can be developed by women authors about men.

Who are some of the writers you most admire or feel some affinities with?

Johnson: I was raised in a small town in Illinois where for some reason Victorian writers were read as if they had just come out. I mean, modern literature had somehow not arrived there; at least if it had, my family didn't know about it, and the librarian at my school didn't know about it. So what really influenced me were the Victorian novelists in particular, but not George Eliot for some reason; in fact, I'm going to talk about this in New York this weekend—why *not* George Eliot? But certainly Jane Austen, Dostoevsky, Kafka very much, Dumas and Flaubert—probably those kinds of European writers even more than the English writers. I loved Trollope but never cared much for Dickens. Now I don't read very much fiction. I like the work of people I know. I admire Doctorow very much, and Joan Didion. And Alice Adams, Alison Lurie, who are friends of mine. Susan Sontag, her essays, but I also like her fiction a lot. Don DeLillo, Don Barthelme, Elizabeth Hardwick, Grace Paley. A very wonderful Welsh poet named D. M. Thomas. And of course, V. S. Pritchett, absolutely, and especially *A Cab at the Door* and Malamud's *The Assistant.* More than with writers, I fall in love with books: *Henderson the Rain King* was once a passion, for example.

What's your opinion about the kinds of experimental fictional approaches that were so evident in American fiction during the late '60s and early '70s? As I recall, you've stated somewhere that you don't think that contemporary fiction's preoccupation with formal innovations and the processes of language precludes reader identification or character development.

Johnson: Of course it doesn't. I was just now thinking, in connection with Toni Morrison, that she does have such a very rich language and that it was precisely this wonderful language that, in her case, distracted critics from what she was saying. But it seems silly to me to suggest that you *can't* have a representation of reality and still have all those wonderful metaphors and colorful black speeches. But that's not exactly what you asked.

Not exactly, but you've more or less answered what I was wondering about—your opinion of experimental fiction, whether or not you felt it was self-indulgent or unable to create satisfying characters.

Johnson: I would say that the *really* inward, self-indulgent, and ultimately not-so-satisfying writing of our time was produced by all those '50s New Yorkers who were writing very autobiographical stuff. I don't find that true of Barthelme, for example. He's sometimes difficult, but for formal reasons, not because he's wallowing around in his own psyche. I find Doctorow to be very interesting in the same way—he's projecting a reality. I do think that the turn away from realism into abstract fiction is a reaction against self-analysis that began to be popular in the '50s and which continues to have a large following, especially in the popular press.

What about you? Why haven't you tried your hand at more abstract, experimental forms?

Johnson: I haven't because I still believe that I have a certain obligation to readability and suspense. From the point of view of writing, I find it more interesting to take a situation and prolong it, which is, I suppose, *plotting* in the old sense. So I wouldn't find it as interesting to write something quite so spare and unplotted—"painted," you might say—as something by Barthelme. Still, I think what Barthelme and some of the other minimalists have done is wonderful. But for me, considering that I've got to sit down and write 120,000 words or something, it's got to interest me in whatever way fiction interests me, or otherwise it's just a lot of work. So I am very sympathetic to experimental writing; it just doesn't seem right for me. I wish it did. I admire Joan Didion, for example, someone who seems to be working along an experimental rather than a strictly traditional woman's way. And Alison Lurie's last novel, which didn't get much attention, is a very lovely, quite strange evocation of childhood, which is unrealistic, that is surreal, experimental in some sense.

An Interview with

Steve Katz

Most of the following interview took place on Halloween, 1977, while Steve Katz was in San Diego in conjunction with a writers' program at San Diego State University. Katz is a barrel-chested man in his early forties, and in answering questions there often emerged the same ready humor and sense of absurdity that is so evident in his fiction. Knowing that Katz's fiction often deals with the mask of personality and the thin line which separates illusion from reality, I had instructed students in my graduate seminar to wear Halloween costumes to our session. Katz, who was unaware of these plans, had decided to outfit himself for the occasion—he eventually came to the seminar wearing two masks, one on top of the other. After Katz strode into class, there was a few moments of silence and then laughter; eventually one student (dressed as the Cowardly Lion) pointed a paw and said, "Mr. Katz, I've noticed that you are wearing what appears to be a mask—are you afraid to answer our questions, to reveal yourself for who you *really* are?" Katz replied that he was not in the least afraid and ripped off his Clark Gable mask—which revealed a Marilyn Monroe mask underneath. Thus we were all treated to an apt metaphor of the mystery of personality.

Beginning with his first novel, *The Exagggerations of Peter Prince* (1968), Steve Katz's fiction has consistently focused on the way in which the imagination can free man from stale, pre-packaged systems of organizing experience. His highly experimental works of fiction and poetry have often been compared to jazz music and with the works of Kafka and Raymond Roussel. Displacing and disrupting words, ideas, and images from their usual meanings and contexts, Katz's fiction transforms the elements of fiction into new codes for and contexts of experience. The newborn, newly formed fictive creations do not represent the world as it is usually seen, but explore the creation of experience and assert the power of the imagination to control our understanding of reality.

In addition to *Peter Prince*, Katz's work includes *Creamy and Delicious* (stories; 1970), *Saw* (a novel; 1972), *Cheyenne River Wild Track* (a poem; 1973), and *Moving Parts* (stories; 1975). Currently Katz is teaching in the creative writing program at the University of Colorado–Boulder; he has just finished a play and a novel entitled *Wier and Pouce*.

—*Larry McCaffery*

Writers obviously write for many different reasons. Why do you write?

Katz: I've been asking myself that question every time I finish one project and get into that kind of limbo that exists between one book and another. But I guess I write because I'm interested in exploring. Here I am in this consciousness, whatever this "I" is, and I find it to be enriching to try and explore what this is.

Then do you really write more for yourself than for an audience?

Katz: No, I write for both. If you take yourself seriously and you're exploring yourself and you do this with intensity and perception and insight, somebody's liable to be interested in your work. And the extent to which I'm successful in examining myself is the extent to which other people will be interested in my work. Now I don't mean in terms of being a bestseller. I can't imagine *Moving Parts* arriving on the bestseller list. Can you see me appearing on Johnny Carson with that book? It would be like continually being on "This Is Your Life." But even though I think that book is best for a small audience, I do think it is a good book as far as sharing my experiences of living and getting to know myself and other people.

Obviously your books are very nontraditional. Since your writing seems always to have been so formally unusual, so uninstitutionalized, I wonder how much luck you've had in trying to operate within the publishing institution.

Katz: Surprisingly enough, I've been lucky. In the 1960s, you know, there was a time when it seemed like reputable publishers and weird writers were thinking in much the same way. About that time I had written a very straight novel called *Kulik in Puglia*, which I still think is really a beautiful book. The novel is very lyrical, and I like to think that a lot of readers would enjoy it—they'd sigh and empathize with the characters and would all wonder if the guy was going to get the girl. But my chances to get it published eventually fizzled out, and then I decided, what the hell—I have this idea for a book, *The Exagggerations of Peter Prince*, and so I wrote it, bringing in material from everywhere. And, weird as that book was, it eventually got published, while *Kulik* withered on the vine. So who knows about these things?

What seemed to spark the radical change in your approach to fiction-writing when you started writing Peter Prince? *Were you trying to abandon "straight" approaches deliberately?*

Katz: I don't generally think about straight or innovative forms when I'm composing my books, but I find that different modes of experience require different formal approaches. *The Steps of the Sun* is the first novel I wrote, finished when I was twenty-one, and it was, I suppose, relatively "straight," with a lot of Faulknerian grotesqueries. My next book was *Kulik in Puglia*, which was a love song of sorts to Southern Italy, particularly to Salerno, where I lived for a while. As I've said, it's a straightforward, lyrical story, with characters, a modest plot, conflict and interaction, empathy requested. Malcolm Cowley read it at one point and liked it, and Viking was even supposed to publish it. Knopf said, after I showed them a recent revision of it, that it wasn't a Steve Katz book. What commercial publishers would like is for you to produce a uniform product that is easy for them to market. I understand their position, but it doesn't allow much latitude or creativity. It makes a lot of good writers produce later in their lives bad imitations of their commercially successful books.

So innovation per se has never been an important motivation when you sit down and begin writing a book?

Katz: Innovation doesn't interest me as much as exploring, discovering, maybe inventing the forms appropriate to my understanding of the world. The things I write that are successful seem to have that quality of innovation. The conventions of character development and psychological verity in fiction were depleted very early for me. That approach seems to coat the art with a residue of romanticism, and to give it an anthropocentric bias that makes me feel like I'm fibbing. So I enjoy playing with the mechanics of and approaches to storytelling, investigating my own function as storyteller, and I come up with configurations that I hope are as interesting to everyone else as they are to me in the process of making them. But the point for me is what I'm learning from doing it; there's no reason for doing it except to grow with it. If I were doing it just to make *the* Steve Katz product, as defined by the publishing industry, it would get pretty discouraging for me. And imagine not growing—can you imagine how boring it must be to be a musician who at sixty is still sitting around singing the same songs? Bob Dylan in some twenty years, singing "Creaking in the Wind"?

Have you been discouraged by the Steve Katz product, as defined by the publishing industry? I've heard you've had some bizarre experiences with your publishers.

Katz: Sure, I've been discouraged about that aspect of my work. I've learned that even if you get your books published you're not always going to be happy with the results. The biggest hype I ever put myself through was when I published my first book, *Peter Prince*. My publishers, Holt, Rinehart and Winston, were going to do a big promotional campaign for it, with a big advertising budget. But at the last minute they withdrew the advertising budget because CBS had taken over and they wanted to wipe the slate clean. So while the changeover took place, my book was being published. As a result my book didn't get advertised; they had already put a lot of money into the production of the book, but none went into promotion. I was left stranded and feeling lonely because I had trusted this function of collective greed to handle my work. That made me realize that I had to reorganize my own thinking about what I was doing as a writer. If that kind of success—becoming famous, making a lot of money—comes my way, that would be fine; but it is highly unlikely in this system.

What about your novel Saw*? It was published by Knopf and seems like the sort of wacky, science-fiction book that might do well in today's market.*

Katz: Yeah, *Saw* should be fun, and I had a good publisher for it. But what happened here was that Knopf didn't put enough glue in the bindings of the first two thousand copies, so the pages came off and started showering down over the heads of the reviewers. Once that happened, they didn't go back and redo it. So a little mistake like that ruined the promotion of that book. Now I don't think my books are particularly accident prone, but when *Creamy and Delicious* came out, I opened the first couple of copies they sent me and bound inside the covers of my book, *Creamy and Delicious* by Steve Katz, with a book jacket on it, was *Beggar in Jerusalem* by Elie Wiesel. My book jacket with Elie Wiesel's book was going out to reviewers all over the country. So how can you depend on that kind of incompetence? I thought I was playing in the big leagues with Random House and Alfred Knopf.

Did any reviews of Creamy and Delicious *ever come out? Borges would have loved to hear about this kind of screwup.*

Katz: *Creamy and Delicious* was never reviewed anywhere except maybe once. And with *Saw*, the reviewer in the *New York Times* said, "Was it the author's intent to let the pages fall where they may?"

Rumor has it that when you were an undergraduate at Cornell you were originally in the veterinary school, and that somewhere along the way you switched into English. What caused this switch?

Katz: I went around for a while with the vet and I had to hold the hoof of a cow while he was scraping out the foot rot. So it was mostly my sense of smell . . . But Cornell was a great place for a would-be writer in those days—1952–56. I rubbed against Sukenick, Pynchon, Farina, to a minor degree each. And I spent time with Peter Dean, now a painter.

In The Life of Fiction *Jerome Klinkowitz compares your works to jazz, emphasizing their improvisational nature. I can see how this applies to the stories in* Creamy and Delicious, *but does it work with your other books?*

Katz: Jazz was my childhood. Whenever I could I snuck out to Birdland, sat on the wooden chairs in the No Minimum gallery, getting closer and closer with every set to Bud Powell, Charlie Parker, Zoot Sims, Miles Davis, Max Roach, Clifford Brown, Lennie Tristano, Lee Knoitz, Thelonius Monk, all my heroes—John Coltrane, Eric Dolphy. I would whistle "Round Midnight," or "Jumping with Symphony Sid," while waiting for the subway, hoping that someone, preferably a beautiful girl, would pick up on the second chorus. Or while waiting in line at Yankee Stadium. Or while going through the Museum of Modern Art. I think jazz had a deep influence on all my work; but it wasn't a love for the "freedom" of improvisation that drew me to it. Rather, jazz was the first art in which I began to perceive what *form* was, and that thrilling tension between the freedom of blowing and the imperatives of order. And I began to realize that art has a formal influence on the emotions, and is permitted through form to enrich the intellect. It's instantaneous at the moment that the form is perceived. I got that from jazz, and it opened the way for me to understand form in all the other arts. The way jazz is voiced by different individuals within one framework surely freed me to write my individual works in a manner I'd call multidirectional.

Do you make yourself write every day? And do you enjoy writing?

Katz: I try to write every day, and I find it a great pleasure to write every day. You know, I've written three novels that have never been published, and one of them is about eight hundred pages in manuscript. I think the Tibetans say that a man who can organize his life is happy anywhere. I find that one of the pleasures of writing is to get up every morning and have this thing to do, to write a novel. I think that's one of the differences between novelists and poets—a poet is a poet all the time, but usually a novelist is a novelist only when he's writing a novel.

What was the background of your own "epic poem," Cheyenne River Wild Track? *Had you written much poetry before that?*

Katz: I wrote a lot of poetry before *Cheyenne River Wild Track*, but that was the first book of poems I wrote in that particular "journalistic" way. I was working as a scriptwriter on a movie set on an Indian reservation in South Dakota. It's very difficult for a writer to figure out what the hell he's doing on a movie set. I was supposed to produce "pages," though the script was already written. But I suddenly found myself directing traffic at an incredible intersection of the many vectors of American culture—the rednecks, Henry Crow-Dog, the Sioux holy man, hippies, money, drugs, motorcycles, the movie industry dream machine, artists compromised and not, animal trainers, South Dakota land/spacescape, the wind, the Missouri River, the ripoff—all these elements and more were plunged together right in front of my eyes into the incredible pressure-cooker of a movie-making experience. I felt obliged to testify to my experience there, and *Cheyenne River Wild Track* were the "pages" I produced. A great pleasure to put that book together.

Have you been writing much poetry since then?

Katz: I've since done a book similar in approach to *Wild Track* called *Journalism*, which I've finished this fall [1977]. *Journalism* is drawn from eye- and ear-witness accounts, and retellings of stories to which people have made me privy, and which I have redecorated slightly for rhythmic purposes. I think of that poetry as "the news" from the Steve Katz News Service. It differs in process from my fiction because it's a record of daily events and feelings, though not a diary. Writing the fiction, I dwell in a fictional space of its own duration, dictates, and dimensions. It's not the immediate processing of my daily experience that the poetry is. I love doing the poetry because it keeps me grounded and tuned.

Were the so-called poems in Creamy and Delicious *simply "throw-away" items, or was there any serious literary intent behind them at all?*

Katz: Those poems are absolutely serious in intent, and once you begin to understand them you will be on your way to unlocking the secrets of the universe. Good luck, Mr. McCaffery.

You say when you write your fiction that you begin living in a sort of fictional space. How do you begin a book like, say Moving Parts? *Does it come to you line by line—do you just start writing until something begins to sustain itself—or do you have an outline or at least a plotted narrative in mind?*

Katz: I think there's a hint about how I went about writing *Moving Parts* in the structure of the book—I think you can pretty much trust the things you read there about my writing. I really did wake up in the middle of the night with that parcel of wrists in my mind; I really did become obsessed with that woman; I had been collecting, for no reason that I could understand (except for the reasons that I give in the book), information about the number 43. After I wrote that first piece, "Parcel of Wrists," I thought, God, I've got to take a trip to Tennessee, I've got to go there—it was a mini-calling. And I did it because I'm an artist, which generally means that you do things that nobody is going to pay you for. I felt that those things—the story, my trip, trying to re-create the story in reality—created a resonance that was really spooky. And I thought if I could ever get all these pieces together, it would make a nice book. I've written other books, though, that started out with a narrative line, a story from beginning to end. But that's the way I did *Moving Parts*.

So you really did take that trip south and visit the commune?

Katz: Yes, and the whole experience was amazing. When I left I didn't realize that there was this very famous commune near Nashville called The Farm—there was even a special on "60 Minutes" about it. But first I did all the things on my trip that my character in Nashville did, or I tried to; of course, reality has a way of correcting your fantasies, though not as much as you'd think. My idea of Nashville was surprisingly close to what I found. Then I thought, I've got to get to a commune, so I went to the Chamber of Commerce. I was a little worried about what they were going to do—were they going to arrest me because I'm asking to see a commune? But, no: I walk in, talk to a receptionist, and she says, "Oh, yes, there's a very famous one nearby," and she gets on the phone and immediately calls the commune. So I went down there and it was an extremely interesting place, with people of all ages. You just go in there and put in a certain amount of work and live with them for a while. I didn't stay there long, but I would like to go back there. The most interesting thing about the whole experience, though, was discovering that my fantasies were occasionally corroborated.

So there were times when your fiction and your real life did intersect?

Katz: Yes. It was coincidence, but it was curious, especially when I saw that Route 43 going through there, what with 43 being the number I was writing about.

That image you develop in "Female Skin" of you surgically removing Wendy Appel's skin and then walking around in it both shocked and amused me; it later occurred to me—I was listening at the time to the old Frank Sinatra classic, "I've Got You under My Skin"—that your image served as a nice metaphor for getting deeply involved with someone.

Katz: Sure. Haven't you ever been involved in a relationship with someone, when you become so obsessed with the person that it feels like you're wearing that person all the time? When your involvement with her is much greater than the other person could imagine it to be, for reasons of your own, because you're so vulnerable? The greatest literary example, of course, is in Proust, with Swann and Odette.

It seems that nearly all your works involve the idea of an individual searching for an identity, creating himself and creating masks behind which to live. Each of the stories in Moving Parts, *for instance, seems to contribute a different aspect to this kind of search.*

Katz: Yes, the stories in *Moving Parts* should suggest this if they work. Identity *is* a series a masks; it can't ever be known. Looking for it in my fiction and in my life helps keep me from being bored.

This whole question of the relationship of the real and the imaginary, fiction and reality, seems to be at the center of nearly all your fiction.

Katz: It's certainly one of the things I'm interested in exploring. Reality itself is a mode of description of whatever your experience is. The reality expressed in, say, "Female Skin," although fantastic, is just an extreme expression of the kind of experience I find myself occasionally having in a relationship. And the description I create there is as much an honest description of my experience as any other—it is as much a "realistic description" of my experience as are the kinds of reality that are described in what are represented in the journal sections of the story. Those journalistic sections are a kind of day-to-day, blow-by-blow account of what seems to be happening.

Were all those journal entries, then, "real"?

Katz: Yes. Didn't they sound pretty maudlin and sugary?

Didn't you retouch them at all?

Katz: No, I just cut them—there was quite a bit in between. Basically I just cut anything that seemed irrelevant to the action of *Moving Parts*.

In going over your works from Peter Prince *on, you seem to appear as yourself pretty directly in nearly every one of them—I remember that in* Saw *you claim that the Astronaut is you, for instance. Why do you do this—aren't you worried that people will start gossiping about you?*

Katz: Gossip has always bored me to death, though I like everyone to be in the room with me when I expose myself. The author of a work of fiction always lurks as the stupid mute in each of his characters. Some have a great mastery for creating the illusion of separation. Tolstoy never admitted to being Anna, but Flaubert did confess to being Emma. Melville is all over *Moby-Dick*. I confess out front that I am all my characters; then there's no doubt in anyone's mind what instrument is being used to look at the world. It's the Steve Katz, with all its limitations. Though I love to create the illusionist's space, I also enjoy disrupting those illusions, so there's no attachment to them. To accomplish that end I have employed Steve Katz to patrol my books.

Do you think there's a difference between the way you use yourself in your works and the way that Ronald Sukenick uses himself in his books such as Up *or* The Death of the Novel?

Katz: Well, for one thing I think Ron uses himself more as a purely invented literary character than I do. But I have a deep admiration for Ron Sukenick's prose. Everything he writes has an immediacy that invents the moment you read it, so he's as real in his books as I am in mine. Reading him is like opening telegrams every minute. When I used Sukenick in *Peter Prince* I tried to make him stupid and irresponsible, but he wouldn't cooperate; in fact, he is so uncooperative that I don't understand how he can use himself as a character in his own books. He's a very busy man. He doesn't have the time. He must appear in his own work at great sacrifice. I use my own self in my own work because I don't demand a large fee, and my emotions are an open book.

How do you account for the fact that so many good fiction writers—I'm thinking of you, Sukenick, Ray Federman, Barth, Coover, even Vonnegut—seemed to develop a similar innovative blend of fiction/biography/metafiction at approximately the same time in the late '60s? Were you aware of each other's work, for example, or were these methods simply "in the air," ready to be developed?

Katz: I don't think you have uncovered any conspiracy; in fact, I see more differences in our work than I do similarities. I knew Sukenick when he wore white bucks in college, but I wasn't aware when I was writing *Peter Prince* of the approach he was talking with *Up.* I didn't meet Federman until much later. I don't think the ideas were "in the air" as you say; rather, all of us found ourselves at the same stoplights in different cities at the same time. When the lights changed, we all crossed the streets.

From what you've said, you seem to imply that your fiction just sort of "comes" to you. Do you see yourself as a sort of vehicle for your fictional expressions?

Katz: That's a very complicated question. Yes, I do feel that I'm the vehicle for my stories; I feel that's one reason I treated the stories In *Moving Parts* the way I did. That story "Parcel of Wrists" happened to me—the image of the parcel of wrists and the structure of the story, like an ineffable geometry, appeared all at once in my head. I woke up in the middle of the night and said, "Oh, God, do I have to write this one?" So I wrote it and then suddenly I had this story which I admired and which I had to live with. I'm not saying that I wrote it in a kind of blind fever, but that while I wrote it I wasn't thinking any thoughts—I was just thinking about the images moving in the story and the way the narrative evolved, and that's all. I certainly wasn't thinking, "Let's see, shall we make my character experience an existential dilemma?" I never have that kind of thought. So after I was done with it, I looked at it and I said, "Well, now I'm going to have to go there, I'm going to have to do the trip myself." Because it seemed like that was the next thing that was required. So, in a sense, I take orders from my work.

When you say that you woke up in the middle of the night with the parcel of wrists, are you saying that they came to you in a dream?

Katz: No, the image didn't come out of a dream. Sometimes I write as if I'm dreaming—like I dream the transitions. But I never specifically draw any of my images from dreams. For a long time my writing seemed to involve itself with images of dismemberment—it's obvious in *Moving Parts*—but I never felt it was physical dismemberment, but some sort of metaphor for the way we have given up parts of ourselves to technology, to the good life.

How long did it take you to write "43"?

Katz: About fifteen years. That was how long it took me to assemble the information and try to figure out what the hell to do with it. And I wrote the piece to get rid of number—I was really tired of seeing it everywhere after a while. And now I'm getting it from everybody—everybody has his own 43 story to tell me.

I noticed that you deliberately left page 43 blank in Moving Parts.

Katz: Sure, because what could I say on page 43? It would be like violating it to put anything on that page except the blank page itself. I just looked at that page and decided that there was no way I was going to screw around with that.

Do you use drugs to help you get your ideas when you write?

Katz: No, I don't. When I use drugs, I use drugs; when I write, I write.

But has using drugs had an effect on your writing?

Katz: I haven't used any drugs for a long time, but everything I've ever done has had an effect on my writing. Look, I enjoy drugs; everyone in this country enjoys drugs, whether prescription or not. I've always felt, though, that when I'm doing drugs, I'm getting information; and that's been a part of my total experience, so it has affected my writing. But I don't enjoy writing while doing them. I enjoy writing when I'm straight, when I'm clear. No, the weirdness in my writing, unfortunately, comes from something else, something inside me.

The stories in Creamy and Delicious, *at least the "mythologies," seem to have a deliberately "underwritten" quality about them that seems different from the rest of your writing. What was the background of those stories?*

Katz: I wrote those mythology pieces almost immediately after I discovered that Holt, Rinehart and Winston was going to publish *Peter Prince,* so I was very excited. I figured that the next thing for me was a ten-round bout with Norman Mailer. I was living in the east at the time, but I decided to come out west to Nevada where Pat, my former wife, is from. Her father was a prospector and they have a cabin up near Buckskin Mountain. So I went up to this cabin on Buckskin and I went to work for a man who was developing this quicksilver claim. And I realized as soon as I went to work for him that I really didn't want to work a full day — it's a lot of work with a jackhammer, things that writers aren't supposed to be doing. So I told the guy I'd work in the afternoon but that I wanted the mornings free to myself to write. And I set myself this task of writing a story every day. The limits of it were to write a story every day, and to spend only two hours actually writing the story—or three hours, because in a given timespan I probably cheated a little bit one side or the other. And these stories, the mythologies, were the result of that intention. I must have written forty of them. When it came around, to my surprise, to being in a position to publish them, I probably should have published them all as one book. Random House wanted me to do a book of stories, so I added a few stories of other kinds. But except for tampering with a few of the loose ends, I never revised any of the mythologies beyond those first drafts.

Would you say, then, that these mythologies were mainly exercises to keep you writing?

Katz: No, I really had these stories in my head. I would wake up in the morning and Boom! "Nancy and Sluggo" would come into my mind, or Boom! "Wonder Woman" would arrive so that I would sit down and write it. At the time I thought I could keep doing this forever. I thought, Wow, I'll be entertaining the world forever. But it stopped at a certain point. So my approach involved a certain kind of inspiration, with the format being a formal problem: to write a story in two hours. This kind of thing is not uncommon to other art, especially painting, you know. For instance, Jackson Pollock, the great postwar American painter, set himself time limits for a lot of his drip-and-splash canvases, and they are beautiful and lyrical. And it is a condensation of the deadline idea. Most people don't have two-hour deadlines when they write fiction; but Charles Dickens had deadlines. I thought the two-hour pieces, left alone without revision, would be interesting. I think they are.

Coover, Barth, Pynchon, and several other contemporary writers seem to share your interest in our society's "mythic residues." But you seem especially interested in the myths of popular culture—cartoons, movies, comic books, sci-fi movies, and so on. Why do you rely on these rather than on more traditional mythic elements?

Katz: If I had been born on the island of Lesbos, my work might have evolved differently; but I was born in several movie theaters, reading comic books between feature presentations. Captain Marvel is a fantasy more competent to deal with the cities in my life than Odysseus would be, though some of his tricks are handy to know. I admire the purity and simplicity of the Greek stories, but I know them as something I learned when I began to read "literature." Batman, however, and Wonder Woman, and Nancy and Sluggo, and the Three Stooges, and Laurel and Hardy, and the New York Yankees, and Veronica Lake, and the Camel cigarette package, are all working in the marrow of my experience, an American experience, which is the experience I'm here to testify for. I love Gilgamesh and many other ancient texts, but I don't need them to maintain the sense of continuity with my own culture.

Can you tell me something about what you were attempting with your remarkable dreamlike stories, "Three Satisfying Stories"? The repetition and transformation of the different elements reminded me of Raymond Roussel.

Katz: Yes, the story was closer to Roussel than anything else I've written. As far as the circumstances around the composition of the stories goes, in 1968 I had wanted to take a trip somewhere and I chose to go to

Istanbul. I got there and then wanted to follow the flow of hippies to Katmandu. But while I was sitting in a cafe one day in Istanbul, I overheard this conversation—the story about infanticide which is in the second of those stories. These people were the only people in the place who spoke any English—they had British accents—and as far as I could tell from looking at the Turks who were there around me, I was the only person there who could even understand what they were saying. And this conversation—the one that begins with "You still believe in the sanctity of human life"—dropped into the center of my mind like a stone into a still pool; it struck something in me about people, about nurturing, about progeny. So the first piece is about how we nurture children; the second piece has the conversation in it that I just mentioned and is about the social situations out of which the contacts are made which produce children; and the third piece is about the use of human beings. And obviously I was also very interested in using the same material in different contexts, somewhat the way Roussel had in some of his fictions. Roussel is very great, and the closest I have come to playing out one of his games is with "Three Satisfying Stories." But I am not organized enough to be Raymond Roussel.

In addition to Roussel are there any other writers that you admire or would say have had some influence on your work? I'm often reminded of Kafka when I read your work, for instance.

Katz: Kafka obviously made a great impression on me, but he has become something of a nuisance. I feel too attached sometimes to a "sound" that his work makes, a disingenuous note of everything going on normally, that clouds men's minds to make them believe in his extensions of reality. But at its core my work is not at all like Kafka's. It hasn't got that psychological bias. I feel that, formally, my work is more influenced by Pound and Williams, back then; and by Gogol and Lermontov. There is too much weight placed on literary influence altogether. When I was in high school I spent a lot of time at the Met and the Museum of Modern Art. The fantastic side of my work has as much to do with seeing Rousseau's *Sleeping Gypsy* once a week, and Hieronymus Bosch, and being around the Ensor, the Matisse, Picasso, Mondrian, Tanguy, Malevich, Soutine, etc., as with the influence of any writers. There's also an aspect of my work I see coming from my love for Italian Renaissance painting—Masaccio's *Tribute Money*, Piero's frescoes in Arezzo, Simone Martini, Pisanello. I admire the magic clarity of the space around all their figures. And then there's the influence of Mel Allen on my work. "Going . . . going . . . gone!" is a formula for success I learned from listening to hundreds of Yankee games. I'm sure I use it in all my work, maybe formally attenuated, but I do occasionally go for the home run. And listening to Charles Ives and Béla Bartók informed my work. Ives was using American popular culture at the turn of the century. And Joe Louis, when I was real

young. I often wanted to write a story that lands like the right hand he used
to flatten Tami Mauriello. Or to make art with as much continuous energy
communicated as in a fight between Rocky Graziano and Tony Zale.
Those events I witnessed in my childhood, so perfect in form and expression, such icons, informed my work, not for the sake of nostalgia or trivia,
but in helping determine its actual shape. The work, I always feel, has to
echo in its form the shape of American experience, the discontinuous
drama, all climax, all boring intermissions in the lobbies of theaters built
on the flight decks of exploding 747s. What I'm saying is that the literary
influences are the least interesting pressures that a writer feels in making
his work. All the rest of life around him has more bearing.

*Do you think that you'll try to explore the type of fiction that you
developed in* Moving Parts, *and to a lesser extent in* Peter Prince *and*
Saw—*I mean fiction which is directly about yourself and your personal in-
volvements?*

Katz: I don't know. I think I may have taken my fiction as far in that
direction as I can. For instance, I have just completed a three-hundred-
page novel which wasn't in the same vein, so it's hard for me to say what
I'm going to do next.

*Obviously you're aware that a lot of readers are shocked, confused, and
even annoyed by a great deal of what passes for experimental or innovative fiction today. What is your motivation for writing such highly
unusual stories? Is it to surprise the reader with unusual contexts?*

Katz: What I'm interested in is exploring the potential of storytelling. I
think storytelling, more than the novels as such, serves a function in
human intercourse. And I want to stretch the bounds of the potential of
storytelling, which always has to be refitted to the times, reexamined,
reinvented. In other words, the structure of the exchange has to be re-
imaged. I suppose some people want to go back to an oral tradition and are
playing with that possibility with public readings and tape. I'd rather look
to the possibility of adding to the tradition of the printed book. It seems to
me that reading habits are changing; the way people are receiving information in its parable forms, its most essential forms, its mythical forms, is
changing. That's one of the reasons why I'm really interested in the book
itself as a context. I'd like my books to be a certain kind of object, so I'm
very careful about the way my books look. I'm trying to make my books
look like *another* context than a novel, so that there's a kind of disparity
between the metalanguage which is the appearance of the book and the
content and language in the book. I don't think people look to the novel
anymore for a paradigm for their lives, the way they did when the novel
was king of entertainment, when the Victorian father sat around with his
family and read a chapter from Thackeray or Dickens every evening. We

get that kind of information from television or from popular music; if it's from reading, it's from science fiction.

I'd certainly agree that your books are among the most interesting, from a visual or technological standpoint, of any that are out today. What is there about this quality of the book as an object that interests you and makes you want to take advantage of these qualities that aren't really available to the "pure" storyteller?

Katz: From the time I was a kid I've always enjoyed the way books look and feel. There is a small world of delicious intimacy you develop, especially when you're young, with the books you love, that comes from the content, but also from the way the books are things. An illustrated *Tom Sawyer*. The heft of *War and Peace*. The whole world safe within the wonderful bindings of the encyclopedia. The thing itself is magical even before you read it, and it's something else again when it sits on your shelf after you've read it. It not only contains and stores the information, but it attaches your sentiments to itself and develops an aura of nostalgia. Computers can't do that; and that's why, although they're neutral, they can seem malevolent. I enjoy playing with and manipulating that quality of books to enrich the experience of my work.

Are you, then, aiming at the same types of effects that the concrete poets are?

Katz: No, I'd say my interests intersect only occasionally with what is called concrete poetry. In *Peter Prince*, for example, I was interested in the surface of the book, both in its language and in its visual qualities, and in exploring the tension and play that is created by continually pulling the reader out of the illusionistic space with references to typographical events, designs or columns or pictures, so the reader has to look at the surface of the page like watching a sea that calms enough so you can look deep into it, but is crossed by winds and currents that frequently make it opaque. The visual elements were chosen also for their metaphorical and emotional resonances.

And for their humor?

Katz: Yes, and to be funny. It's great to be funny. It's great to be American and give in to the influence of the Marx Brothers. So many writers in America work too hard to be French. I wish, though, that I was in the position with a major publisher again to do another book like *Peter Prince*, just to have that whole technology to play with again. I didn't know quite enough about it at the time to control it, so some unnecessary compromises were made, some things left out. A case of too soon dumb, too late smart. *Moving Parts* is a complicated book visually, though not as difficult to design as *Peter Prince*. I use the visual "authority" of photojournalism in that book to create emotional disjunctions and spooky reverberations. The visual and the verbal interact very strangely in that book, in ways I like but still don't totally understand.

Was it partly your freedom to do anything you wanted visually that made you decide to publish Moving Parts *with the Fiction Collective?*

Katz: It's unlikely that a commercial publisher would have done a book like this, so the Fiction Collective was perfect for *Moving Parts*. If I had given it to another publisher it would have been a hassle all the way through. As I've said, I'm very interested in the way a book looks, in playing with the possibility of communicating something just from the way a book looks, the way a face communicates. The Fiction Collective gave me total control of this aspect of *Moving Parts*, so it looks pretty much the way that I wanted it. The main problem with the Fiction Collective so far has been with distribution. It's hard to find bookstores that will carry serious books and keep them on their shelves long enough.

Do you see more organizations like the Collective developing?

Katz: I think it would be great. The idea behind the Fiction Collective was not to be *the* exclusive Fiction Collective, but to start the operation with six to ten authors and then have people start similar organizations all over the country. It seems obvious that commercial publishing houses are not publishing the work of serious authors.

Do you feel that many other writers share your interest in trying to bridge the gap between fiction and what's going on in some of the other visual arts? And are there any contemporary artists that you feel have helped you develop your own theories of fiction?

Katz: It's always amazed me how few writers study the visual arts very carefully. They tend to be very conservative in their appreciation of other arts in general. Henry Miller is one of the few who really spent a great deal of time with painting and then talked about it. I get a lot of my ideas and energy from watching what's happening in the recent visual arts. The '60s were a very exciting time. Carl Andre, Bob Morris, Charles Ross, Robert Smithson, Richard Serre, Mike Heizer—they've all been very important to me, probably more than other contemporary writers.

Have you dabbled in any other media yourself? Paintings or videotapes or anything like that?

Katz: Yes, I made some videotapes and then destroyed them. I also did some happenings in 1965 or 1966.

What went on in these happenings?

Katz: I did one which involved "Three Satisfying Stories." It was on a stage and I had three slide projections, one for each story. First I read the pieces live. I had a tape recorder, so then I read the stories over again, trying to keep in sync with the tape recorder and with some pictures that I had projected. They were very mysterious pictures—old postcards from Istanbul, where I had written the stories. One was of two proud Turks standing beside a heap of dead dogs, taken, I guess, right after Ataturk outlawed dogs in Istanbul. During the performance I sort of obliterated myself with adding machine tape, covered myself with it. Someone in the audience set fire to the tape, but that wasn't planned. I did another happening in which I interviewed a woman on tape as if she were Steve Katz, and played the tape. She was supposed to be Steve Katz reading these poems that I had written. They were very macho poems. About ten minutes into the show, I walked out on stage in pajamas with a big "E" on them which was supposed to stand for "Everybody," though nobody knew. I sat down and listened to her and when that stopped I had about twenty people planted in the audience with flash cameras who started getting up and taking pictures. Then I got up and started reading myself while a movie was projected of myself playing handball with a nude woman in the center of the court. I tried to get as close to her with the ball as I could without hitting her.

You've tried your hand at other unusual projects—like your pornography novel Posh. *Was there any serious intent behind that work, or did you write it purely for the money?*

Katz: I wrote that book in six weeks just to get the money. I enjoyed writing it, but I don't think it was really pornographic. It was really more of a satire on pornography, unfortunately; if it had been more erotic, maybe it would have sold more. But I did learn from *Posh* that I can't write eroticism without this satiric edge. So I learned from the book, but I didn't take it very seriously and I wrote it very quickly.

You mention in Moving Parts *that, once you find yourself put into a system, it's easy to become a part of that system's dogma. Evidently you've gone through some traumatic experiences with the publishing system, so do you see art as being just another system, or part of a system that should be avoided?*

Katz: Only if you define "art" very narrowly. But I do think there is a system that tries to consume artists, just like there's a system that tries to consume athletes, just like there's a system that tries to consume all of us. For example, the center of the visual art world is New York City, and there are people there, rich people, who use art products as a kind of metacurrency. Paintings appreciate in value a lot faster than anything else, so these people will use this currency on a level that we poor folks can't imagine. It turns art into fashion, and artists into designers.

An Interview with
Joseph McElroy

To find Joseph McElroy and his eighteenth-century farmhouse on Franklin
Pierce Lake in Antrim, New Hampshire, one has to know what a barrel of
nutmegs (a local landmark) looks like. To read McElroy's fiction, one has
to know—or be willing to learn as one reads along—neural physiology,
topology, cybernetics, and many more specialized disciplines. Before I
met this polymath, I worried that the disembodied brain launched into
space in his novel *Plus* might be an apt metaphor for the writer. But on the
August, 1978, day set for our meeting, rapidly leaking recently acquired
information, I found the nutmegs and soon after found Joe McElroy's
brain quite comfortably attached to a handsome, unlined face with dark,
direct eyes and a body of medium build dressed in denim shirt, jeans, and
sandals. In his late forties, McElroy is remarkably youthful in appearance,
voice, and bearing, very quick in his movements and responses. Far from
being disembodied, he is an extremely friendly and attentive man, a writer
with questions about, as well as answers for, the interviewer. We talked
through the morning and late into the afternoon before a smoldering
fireplace in his sparsely furnished living room, the formality of an interview quickly giving way to the intimacy of conversation in which
McElroy's wife, Joan, occasionally participated. As we talked, I found
McElroy's planetary knowledge matched by a planetary concern, a deep
belief that literature must grow beyond the merely literary if it is to exert
force in the world of the future.

Although McElroy's five novels have been regularly praised by the most
thoughtful reviewers, he has unaccountably failed to receive the critical

attention usually given to a writer of his ambition and achievement. Perhaps it's because McElroy does not compromise in his fiction, does not mix college humor with technology as Pynchon does. Although original, McElroy's novels can best be briefly described by comparisons with the works of other writers. *A Smuggler's Bible* (1966) has the mass, complexity, and father-son theme of Gaddis's *Recognitions*. *Hind's Kidnap* (1969) is a Nabokovian mystery story, full of linguistic leads and pastoral games. *Ancient History* (1971) and *Lookout Cartridge* (1974) begin as stories of detection, with echoes of Mailer and Pynchon, and end as elaborate fictional systems modeled on physics and cybernetics. In *Plus* (1977) McElroy uses a conventional science fiction situation to create a linguistic tour de force like Golding's *The Inheritors* or Burgess's *A Clockwork Orange*. In all of these novels, science and other nonliterary materials give McElroy new sources of metaphor to express themes that are Faulknerian in their emphasis on the past and family connections. When more readers come to know what McElroy knows and transforms into sophisticated fiction, he will, I believe, be recognized as a major writer.

—Tom LeClair

Could you say a bit about your working habits?

McElroy: Oh, I would be delighted to. I really would. I steal paper and pens and that gives my imagination a more disembodied feeling. My materials are like my time. I have stolen paper from the university where I have worked, from stationery stores in New York, Boston, New Hampshire. I write in longhand and type early drafts on yellow paper. Yellow paper with black type is pretty vivid it seems to me. I have stolen pens from real estate agents, insurance agents, banks, friends, children, and my daughter Hanna. As for working, I admire E. B. White's saying that the first thing he did was to have a martini in order to work up courage to write, because I have often felt that writers—various august American writers who will be nameless here—who would say things like "I never write after I've had a drink" were being a little bit too austere and pure. I write at almost any time of day or night. I prefer to write in the morning because I think my head is a little bit clearer. I feel, although it is probably not true, that my time is heavily fragmented and broken into, and therefore I like to think that I must be able to write in any odd fifteen-minute period. So theoretically I am a disciplined worker, but my discipline might ask to be interrupted; then I will have to work in odd little bits of time, almost anytime.

You grew up in Brooklyn Heights, and it is a setting in each of your first four novels. Could you say what you found special about Brooklyn Heights?

McElroy: It is a community, a community with enough variety to be interesting, at least in the '30s and '40s, and with enough snobberies and other limitations to be irritating and upsetting. Mainly I was a New York kid. I played on the streets of Brooklyn Heights, but I was always very much aware of what lay beyond Brooklyn and the city because we were right on the harbor. I used to sit at my window and stare at it, and my father would take me out on ferryboats and I'd go down to the docks. Some of the details in *A Smuggler's Bible* are right out of my childhood in Brooklyn Heights. I didn't realize when I finally got down to writing novels in London in 1962 and '63 that my books would be about disintegration and reintegration, would be psycho-philosophical mystery stories about the self putting itself back together again. But I found myself writing about Brooklyn Heights as a place that had a communal integrity, a wholeness, almost as if I had lain down on a couch and started talking to a psychiatrist and there suddenly came Brooklyn Heights. By the time I started writing novels I was pretty unhappy and felt that I had no home and was increasingly finding my home in friendships and in myself. Brooklyn Heights suddenly loomed up to me as not only a place I didn't want to go back to but also a place which had a kind of coherence and beauty while I was growing up.

In Hind's Kidnap, *the protagonist's father wanted him to be a scientist. Did your father want you to be a scientist when you were in school?*

McElroy: My father majored in chemistry at Harvard, where he was a scholarship student from Boy's High School in Brooklyn. His family had been poor. He was somewhat puritanical and a high achiever, but when he came out of college, instead of going on with this specialty in chemistry, he got pulled into another line of business because he had a chance to make some money. I think he should have been a professional chemist and possibly even taught chemistry. He was an excellent teacher and something of a polymath, certainly interested in everything, especially good at mathematics and sciences. He was also a good writer. I grew up feeling that I could never be as good in science as he. But I don't think that he would ever have been—if he had lived longer into my life than he did—presumptuous enough to have wanted me to be a scientist. However, he certainly would have been doubtful if not unhappy when I was seventeen or eighteen if I had said I was going to be a novelist. But I was very much aware of being in my father's shadow. In the first couple of years after he died, when I was fifteen, I had it up to here with his old friends saying to me, "Your father was the nicest man I ever knew. If you turn out like your father, that should be good enough for anybody." I think that I wanted to in some way satisfy or equal my father, but at the same time I was also painfully aware that my father was less lucky than I, that he hadn't had advantages like mine. Later on I found myself drawn to scientific subject matter and to scientific method as elegant ways of getting at the truth, more because I wasn't always good in science than because I had ever been distinguished in science. I know that I am drawn to geology at the moment partly because I had an excellent geology course at Williams—and did very poorly in it. I think, though, that the technological strain in my work is derived indirectly, haphazardly from the world that I am living in, rather than from my studies.

You seem at ease handling scientific materials. Can you say why, and why so many novelists are not?

McElroy: There is a resistance to technology as being the instrument of our destruction, an activity which is fundamentally dangerous. I would agree with Doris Lessing's vision of the planet exterminating itself in *The Four-Gated City* and with Peter Matthiessen in *Far Tortuga*. But it also seems to me that many writers don't let themselves take science and technology seriously because they see these areas conflicting with the human imagination. They see science as anti-human. I don't. Science and technology offer forms by which we can see some things clearly; their experimental and measuring methods, their patterns larger than life or smaller than sight, beckon us out of ourselves. If you assume your assumptions are only one of many possible views, maybe one day you find a way to drop, say, the reassuring habit of scale models and conceive distorted models, a model you can visualize only in fragments that the mind must leap to unite.

Could you reconstruct some of the reasons why you decided quite early that you did not want to write what you have called the "sensitive American novel"?

McElroy: I think I said in "Neural Neighborhoods" that I came to a point of confidence or ego at which I decided that some of the near chaoses of my dreams and the turning consciousness in some of my sentences weren't wrong, weren't bad, might be extreme but had to get free play, room to jump, to wander, to sweep. My short story "The Accident" is a last effort to write a packaged, settled sort of well-behaved fiction. It wasn't me. I guess I side with the Hamsun of *Mysteries*, the Céline of *Journey*; I don't mean their politics but their will to bust loose in order to hold fast to a self that might get lost in blandness and closet imitation. Though with Céline, who at times seems to become the age, an open secret from himself is that he's afraid to give equal time to all the love and strength you can't help knowing he's seen in people. To go on—single books: Stendhal's *Charterhouse*, Gogol, Mailer when all his stars are out, which isn't often enough. Kleist's *Kohlhaas*. Miller's *Colossus of Maroussi*, a moral book. Grass's *Dog Years*, history as the obsessed, uninhibited voice flowing out of broken memory. That's one side of me. That says no to, partly, that conditioned response built into the sober pluperfect and past-tense sound of sensitive objectivity that comes out like soap opera—though God knows Robbe-Grillet can be pompous enough even in *Jealousy*, a fine book that represents I guess a desire that's another side of me, to turn microscopic seeing into meditation—to be truthfully precise. But to what and through what? I'm sick of this dogma, a platitude supporting the virtue of concreteness without ever asking why concreteness, what philosophical conclusions does it rest on?

There are very strong paternal figures in the early novels; could you talk about them?

McElroy: I grew up in a household full of books, with loving parents who encouraged me to do pretty much whatever I wanted, although there was a very strong superego presiding. In *A Smuggler's Bible* and *Hind's Kidnap* there is a strong sense of a father loved, protective, somewhat forbidding, and even some father role which I take on myself, maybe in order to exorcise. I was dimly aware when I was writing *A Smuggler's Bible* that the hedonistic, yet also strangely homosexual, homogenitive, voice in the interchapters who was urging Davey to have more, to take more, to be more, had something to do with a drive in me that I was afraid of. The desire in *Hind's Kidnap* to protect, to pacify, to soothe, to take care of others, which is one strain in my being, I now believe covered or sublimated the other feelings—aggression, ambition, pleasure-loving, even wild desires to have everything, to have it all.

One of the slightly bewildering and strangely relieving pleasures of looking back on what one has written is to see a pattern. As I look back, I see my books as a cryptic autobiography. The most articulate this has become is toward the end of *Plus* when I began to see that this adventure in consciousness which had intrigued me, partly as science fiction, partly just to see whether I could do it, was really about the same old subject my books are always about—getting myself into an awful trap in order to feel more real, then figuring a way out. Someday I will write a short novel about a happy man.

After your four realistic novels, Plus *could be read as a sport, but it seems to me a kind of coda to your work.*

McElroy: Someone said to me he thought it was a funny book; I guess I was pleased to hear that, because it seems to me a somber and rather threatening book. I saw *Plus* as a more personal extension of technological and scientific themes in *Lookout Cartridge* and in the slightly kitsch preoccupations of the main character in *Ancient History*. I also saw in *Plus* the good old theme of reintegrating the body and the soul, a dynamic drama of growth, unexpected growth. That was very important to me, because the more I write the more I feel that books can't be researched. The important experiences that you write about have to ambush you. Suddenly you wake up one morning and you see that something has happened to you.

You have been writing prose all your life, and now you have lived through something. So I wanted the growth theme in *Plus* to involve an unexpectedness which was somehow related to the collaboration process, in which it is partly the solar energy experiment and partly some mysterious, residual will in the main character and in the universe, which Imp Plus ties into, that cause the growth. The process, you know, is worked out exactly if the reader wants to find it, to follow electromagnetic cascade and the rest to that void point of converging causalities. I wanted to create something tragic but beyond tragedy, a space idyll in which the body and the mind are reintegrated into a whole, organic substance. Although I don't think of *Plus* as science fiction, except insofar as "science" might mean "knowing," I did want to use scientific materials which seem to me to be modern and not to be as easily dismissable as liberal intellectuals like to dismiss the space program. To use these materials as means of insight—but in a way that was more private, more personal, more intense. I also set out to write a book of a hundred and fifty pages partly because I had been goading myself and partly because so many people have said, "You are a long book writer; you couldn't write a short book."

Did you have to research brain anatomy for the writing of Plus?

McElroy: I did do some reading but I was more interested in some kind of transcendent anatomy which never claims that the anatomy you can find in books is not true but moves beyond that physical anatomy to some of the possibilities which are associated with our word "mind." If mind emerges from brain, it certainly is also true that mind changes brain. Mind can actually change the physical thing that we call brain. I also feel that there is something not individual—more collaborative—called "will" which arises from the anatomy of our zoological self but which transcends it, and I was trying to find a dramatic image of some life force in *Plus* that to me would be more important than any amount of dissective neuro-anatomy that could be done on the brain. What I had in mind was a more transcendent, visionary, even simple book. While the book arises out of materials that are scientifically observable, it is more inclined toward the visionary or the religious.

Some of the earlier books, Hind's Kidnap *for example, are very tightly structured and seem to be researched. Has your method of composition changed as you have gone along?*

McElroy: Everything in the forms and rhythms that I feel in my narratives could be seen to bear upon organism, the growth of organism. *Hind's Kidnap*, which I like for its traditional mythic narrative force but which I grant is the most artificial of my books, is a contrast in formalities. On the one hand, the mass of material that is gathered into the book is rigidly organized into three parts, the first and third being mirror images of each other. On the other hand, the titles of the three sections suggest that each section is part of an independent sequence which is going on. The novel is rigidly formal about something which can be only partially known, so the independent parts are seen also as parts of systems which no doubt interpenetrate. But you can only have intuitions of this.

The method which has remained constant is the writing of the individual sentence, and I increasingly feel that I want the sentence to be a paradigm of everything. I see myself as writing one sentence, then writing another sentence, but the rest of the method, if one can even use the word "method," has been staggering, haphazard, informal, dishonest, painstaking, and it has necessarily involved information. I use the word "information" as a big word in the twentieth century. We collect information. I feel sometimes like the character in *The Golden Notebook*, Anna, who feels herself a center being besieged by information from all corners. I have needed information for my books, and sometimes the information has been in my head and sometimes it has not, so I have gone out and studied up to acquire information to fill a gap. I have done various things to make this less reprehensible because it does violate a principle of mine, which is that any book you write should be something that you could write just by writing in a bare room without books—just a table and a chair. But I violate that. One of the ways in which I have made this research or search process less reprehensible is by associating my ignorance with the ignorance or neophyte status of the character, as I believe I do in *Lookout Cartridge*. I feel that Cartwright's information about cinematography and so forth can be acceptable to the reader because Cartwright is not a professional. He has suddenly found himself involved in a plot that has to do with filmmaking, and he has had to acquire a lot of information fast. You add that to the fact that his temperament is sometimes a rather excessive collector's temperament, and you have the beginnings of my attempt to excuse my need to acquire further information in order to elaborate and work out my fundamental conceit in the book.

What was that fundamental conceit in Lookout Cartridge?

McElroy: Knowing is Not-Knowing. I knew that I wanted to write a story a sense of being between, of being caught between what is known too well and what is known too little. About being caught between wanting to be free, independent, and wanting to be secure, protective. I had had, years before, a dream of being a lookout at a construction site where there was something valuable in which a band of people of whom I was a member were interested. They were involved in some kind of theft—that was all that the dream told me. I was the lookout, and increasingly in the dream I felt in between those I am looking out for and those I am looking out against. That was one main source of *Lookout Cartridge*. I knew also that I wanted to write a story about a film that had been stolen and possibly destroyed, and I didn't really have any more than that to go on.

You knew you wanted to get the sense of between. You know it is going to be a "mystery-thriller," as you have described it. What is the next step in the elaboration of the conceit? How, for example, did you choose Stonehenge as a setting?

McElroy: Stonehenge was for me certainly a place for reunion in the deepest sense of the word. I think at some point David Brooke in *A Smuggler's Bible* is called a reuniac. I suppose this is not a very graceful word-image of the novelist's bringing a bunch of characters together like Fellini—picking them from here, here, here, bringing them all together and making them work coherently into a scene. So my imagination might naturally turn toward a place that would draw together a variety of people. Stonehenge also fitted into my plans as a place around which many hypotheses circulated for generations. It is a place associated with hokum, but it is also a very real place where you can feel deeply about the past and about the mystery of how much people knew about their universe a thousand, two thousand years ago. Its association with measurements and observation, what we might loosely call science, was inseparable from religion. So increasingly Stonehenge seemed to me to be a natural setting for some crisis event to occur in my story.

What is the next step in connecting materials?

McElroy: I have faith in a multiplicity of connections that any one magnetic point in the book will have. I have suggested some possibilities Stonehenge seemed to me to have. One can see *Lookout Cartridge* as a linear movement closer and closer toward some answer to the question "What happened to the film?" But you can also see the book as a rhythm of gatherings together and dispersions. I am using this even more in *Women and Men*. I have become particularly interested in the work on coincidence of the the Austrian biologist Paul Kammerer. He argues that there is a force in the universe parallel to—not excluding, but parallel to—causality which is like what we might call coincidence or convergence. The events of *Lookout Cartridge* are not only linear but also a collection of dispersions toward what you might call disorder or provisional transition and magnetic nodes or points at which everything comes together.

The elaboration or composition seems to move by analogue.

McElroy: What I have wanted to do is transcend metaphor and work toward homology, I suppose partly because I like to think of my books as being true rather than literary in some artificial sense. And I think that my books, up through *Lookout Cartridge* anyway, tried in a sane more than a paranoid way to create a collaborative network which human experience is. We can never know enough in order totally to understand it, but it is there as some kind of mysterious network. Maybe it is the image of God in the world. In the process of understanding the network, one sees innumerable correspondences, and these yield what we may call metaphor. Sexual relations between two people may be like telepathy. But always I wanted to make these comparisons, these analogies, these metaphors have a stronger status, so that my books would not seem to be literary artifices but would seem to be pretty desperate, sober explorations into what the larger network of the world really is.

What are the sources of this notion of a collaborative network?

McElroy: Sources? The City. The sense of hearing. Maps. The dictionary. The telephone in America. Memory. Hope. My body. Dreams—which I think Nietzsche said we spend so much of our artistry on that we don't have any artistry left for daytime. Also fear that I might be outside the network—therefore it exists.

How does this notion of network affect the relation of cause and effect that moves most fiction forward?

McElroy: I find in myself a wish to get to one side of or pass beyond sequential cause and effect. That's why I find David Hume's destruction of cause-and-effect assumptions entrancing, though he knows it's only theoretical. It supports a fiction writer's just showing events and not ascribing causes. *A Smuggler's Bible* has a temporal sequence and many histories through it, but formally it is to be seen also as a mandala or some other spatial form in which the eight chapters have a kind of equality outside of time. In *Ancient History* the narrator is increasingly overcome by thinking in twos—in dichotomies—and he wants to get beyond this, by moving not through some dialectic to a synthesis, but to some stasis which I associate with a physical field in which everything is at rest. Different entities in a field would have hierarchical relations because they would be at different distances which could be measured, but they would also be distributed in such a way that they are all equal.

My Cartwright finds himself in such a position at the end of *Lookout Cartridge*. He is alone at a center which is one of many centers. He has moved through his story knowing things which have to be partly why he moves and acts; but the more important causes are not behind but ahead of him, pulling him on, the action constantly reinventing, restating its track, which makes him seem more free at the same time that his power is that he knows better than anyone else in the book how much he's a mere part of a necessity partly seen. He's in the open, at the end, wonderfully free within the opening field. Sounds dumb, eh?

Do your suspicions about causality influence your conception of character and psychology?

McElroy: I guess I am interested in the present and the future and in action more than I am in its cause. I am interested in seeing as closely as I can see, and I find that the most I can do is to look at the phenomena or the scene in which people move. Psychological explanations of why some of my characters behave as they do can be easily deduced. It is just that I have not been especially interested in that, perhaps because the analysis of those chains and linkages has been done and done and done over and over again. That may be one reason why I am drawn to Castañeda, where the emphasis is upon finding some initiative or entry into action in which the inner dialogue is stopped and the inhibiting or distracting past is cast behind. Perhaps there is some anarchic romanticism in me that wants to break free of any psychological analysis or explanations which could be given for a person being as that person is.

You have spoken about fiction in spatial terms. Have you been influenced by visual art or by film?

McElroy: Not in any ways that would interest you. I toy with trying to see a view two-dimensionally, as if my eyes couldn't distinguish distances. I'm attracted to navigators' maneuvering-board plots of relative motion and to wind-vector diagrams—time or force seen in a spatial model. Painting is madly sexy. Visual arts? Blow-up color photos of marine life, what's going on on a coral reef, orange zoanthids, animals like plants. Film? I'm encircled by a wall of film; I'm audience and projector.

You once wrote about the "wonder and awe" the Apollo spacemen experienced. Would those two reactions be an appropriate aesthetic aim?

McElroy: I think at various points in *Lookout Cartridge* I presumed to effect something like that, and then this flickered out of my mind. There was a time when I thought of *Lookout Cartridge* as being a computer in itself. And I thought, that is grandiose and I couldn't honestly defend it. But I think I do at times rather grandiosely imagine a book as a human-made system that through elaborate, labyrinthine intricacy can bring us to a threshold of ravishment and wonder. To do everything I can do ambushing, analyzing, cracking open, acting, tracking, forcing—to be at last surprised, rewarded by the truth being not exactly earned by me but from a totally unknown and unexpected direction *given* to me. But the elements of it, you see, are all with me already; I'm carrying the message, I'm in possession of it, but I don't know it all until I'm *given* its meaning.

Who are some writers working now whom you have affinities with or admire?

McElroy: During the 1960s it was Nabokov more than any other who I felt was on the right track, and then increasingly I felt that he shouldn't be any different from what he was—generous of me—but I should be different from him. Now I have gone back to reading Doris Lessing, whom I was unable to read when I tried in the '60s, and I feel that she has a tremendous amount to say in spite of a style that I used to find an impediment. Names at random: Calvino, *Invisible Cities* (story beyond story into meditative plane). *t zero*, science without jokey undercutting. Butor,

Passing Time and *Degrees,* which I've said too much about in "Neural Neighborhoods." Harold Brodkey in his search for an absolutely right and natural language. Cormac McCarthy, who published a book called *The Orchard Keeper* in 1965 which I thought a very powerful work of American landscape, menace, and love. He is a writer I still look for great things from. I haven't read too much of Walter Abish, but his way of playing with the given energies of language so that language seems to be playing with the writer's mind has a gaiety and an independence; his is certainly one direction that I think literary art can take.

I read a lot of poetry. I admire Ammons for his beautiful reconnoitering into the structure and form of natural things. I love Kinnell's *Nightmares,* Levertov's touch where nature and person meet, Snyder's domestic poems, Ashbery's rhetoric as a unique image of the mind living its changes. While I try to keep up with writers like Updike or Iris Murdoch, the reading that matters most to me is in nonfiction and often philosophy. Eugene Marais's books on baboons and termites. He was an amazing, versatile, tragic man. I've been writing a play, quite an extravaganza, about him for three years. Philosophy I read because I am looking for visions and statements that have an unusual clarity, a clarity perhaps not so swarming with business and dread as Pynchon's *Gravity's Rainbow,* which I admire, or Gaddis's *The Recognitions,* an older, less well written book I admire much more. I have gone back to read Schopenhauer and Hume, whom I admire immensely. Hume would be on my list of six dead dinner guests. (That sounds like a poisoning.) I read and reread Nietzsche, and since my present book, *Women and Men,* turns upon economics in various forms I've reread Marx, Keynes, Schumacher's beautiful book, and Thorstein Veblen, who seems to me to have more to say about the relations between women and men than a lot of women have. In a different way the Buddhists and Ruskin tell me more about goods and services than all the rest of the economists put together. What about Keynes as a difficult fiction writer? Much as I admire the stories of all kinds of people from Eudora Welty back to Hemingway, from Isaac Babel to Flannery O'Connor, there is something about the crystallized definition in the work of many philosophers that appeals to me. Even when the philosophers' hypothetical visions of truth are shaky and subjective and open to criticism—heavy criticism, as in the case of Nietzsche and our moral mystic magic tourist Castañeda—I often find more inspiration from them than from big books like my old love *U.S.A.*; Gaddis's *JR,* a better big book; Mark Smith's *The Death of the Detective;* or a smaller, finer, but safer fantasy, Cheever's *Bullet Park.*

I also want to mention William Wilson, who has published a collection of stories entitled *Why I Don't Write Like Franz Kafka.* This is a man whose knowledge of philosophy and whose insight into science and the visual arts are enormous and whose mind is bewilderingly brilliant. Of all the people I have known over the last ten years, I would have to single him out first as an influence. He felt there was some distinctive strain in my notion of correspondences and phenomenal forms making up a network which was a field, and he encouraged me to have confidence in the rather haphazard intuitions that I had.

John Gardner has written a good deal about the immorality of contemporary fiction. How do you see this issue of moral fiction?

McElroy: *Great Expectations* and *Middlemarch* can't be done now. They don't feel to me like the atmosphere I'm living in now. I'm with William Carlos Williams and Joyce and others; whatever I'm "saying" I have to give the feeling of time now, the multiple disastrous world now, the world that came awfully and finally out of World War II. But *Great Expectations* and *Middlemarch*—they show people losing their true centers, going after money or status or displaced ideals, letting errors multiply, self-deception, self-punishment even. Great novels. I reread them. They move me. They add to me. I see how the whole thing works out (more maybe than any book can pretend to today)—*but* it is that whole *process* that adds to me, not an abstractable credo or assent. A novel isn't a sermon or a moral program—excuse the truism. My step-grandfather, who came from Maine, thought the old copybook maxims were the way to teach you how to live. I thought about this, this conviction of his; but the *fact* that it was a conviction of his told me more than any of the actual maxims ever could.

Fiction is a model of how life is and what its possibilities are, and the two are always somehow together, whether the artist has control or not. Aidan Higgins' *Langrishe, Go Down* adds to me, but not by encouraging me with a cautionary lesson—a lesson, say, on decadence or a woman trusting the wrong man. No; it's the wonderful merging of human energy flagging with some unarguable rhythm of Nature running down—all a part of the style—this is what I receive, right? And the whole of the experience enlarges me, but not so I then go to work the next morning and apply the lesson. And Beckett's *Molloy*—I don't know, what adds to me here is partly the leaving out of what most novels leave in, so that while I am Moran and Molloy, mainly I am in the sound of a self existing, reaching a model of a trip outward and back. I don't see life like Beckett, but I am increased by his braving his own peculiar limits. But how a work of fiction adds to me can't be judged by whether I approve of a character, or even love or hate. I mean, Céline and Burroughs are unique. They might *mean* one thing morally but as performers living their own limits and dreams they might *be* another. There's no morality in art unless there's art to begin with, in the sense of some successful passion for the medium, originality, radiance. So the message, for there *is* one, in *Pale Fire* is nothing without the life-

giving shock and delight and composition of the pieces forming and refor-
ming like parts of a model where the parts have no place without their
dependence on other parts that have no place without, et cetera—and
beyond to Jupiter—and back.

Sometimes a writer writes too much or too fast, a tale, let's say, of
tenderness, of compassion, or an ambitious drama debating good and
evil, order, disorder, but his righteous intent might be fundamentally corrupted by bad writing, dead, slick writing. On the other hand, I pardon
Doris Lessing for writing so awkwardly because what she's saying in the
two big books becomes almost a substitute for style, form, technique,
magic. Understand, I'm not temperamentally a maker of lists of moral and
immoral, who's on the index, who's just been taken off. I like a lot of
Borges, poems too, for the invention, the benevolent invention of another
reality which I guess owes something to a fanciful reading of Berkeley.
What he does is thorough, intriguing, elegant, enchanting; but then in the
end, for all the honor he gives to art in the brevity, the clarity, the surprise,
and that sense of a revelation being imminent, why I find myself regretting
his view of life, which seems to me a fadeaway.

I heard Grace Paley introduce Donald Barthelme as a journalist and a
poet. Sounded odd, but maybe she meant that Donald in a way records
daily life (reports back) while at the same time, in the midst of our debase-
ment of language and the feelings and thoughts that language is supposed
to help us to have, he leads us to hold to our language, like our honor. At
his best, his warmly demented, accurate criticism of life is a strong, clear
moral criticism of language. Turn that around—it works better the other
way: language first, then life. Did I mention *Ulysses*? I haven't said all I
wanted to say. Maybe someone should write a book on moral fiction. I
want to be true to the difficulty of what I see around me right now and get
to the end of each complex fable I think up so that some image of the
rediscovery of wholeness can seem really earned.

*"Attention" is a word that appears several times in your essay on
Wilson's fiction. You discussed Calvino's* Invisible Cities *as "models of intense and vital attention." Could you discuss the importance of
"attention" and "model" for you?*

McElroy: I picked them up from the language around me, which is
often pretentious jargon. "Model"? Model I guess I get from science and
social pseudo-science and some connotative shimmer, the General Motors
Futurama at the '39–'40 World's Fair, or maybe a home where my head
might feel comfortable. In science and social science the word for me implies our increased ability and temptation to draw from dread, from the
unquenchable traffic and the masses of power-out-of-control a simplified
structure upon which to think more clearly without ever losing the tension
between the model and the mass it came out of. Think more clearly, also

feel more clearly. Models are for me not just hypothetical systems to predict weather or nuclear attack—or economists' equations—or images like a planetarium ceiling—but maybe also, in the spirit of Marvell, Dante near the end of the *Paradiso*, Stevens in "The Snow Man," Donne in the "Sickness" hymn, condensed anatomies and paradigms, an escape into concentration which itself becomes a model of what might be true, the spaceman in *2001* streaming necessarily into the heart of things wondering (as *I* imagine him) whether God had any choice in creating the universe.

"Attention" is a rather cold word I use to suggest that the ways in which we embrace the world and embrace other people can be more precise and clear than we sometimes think. We can express allegiance with other people, whether or not this is love, by thinking closely about what they say. Look terribly closely but neutrally. Love is at odds with possessing. I think that *Lookout Cartridge* is about the relation between attention and love, paying attention to things and people around you so you know something about them at the same time that you are increasingly blocked from knowing enough about them. Maybe this comes partly from how people have misunderstood my eyes—a sharpness that isn't attack or surveillance at all. Just interest, reflex.

How do you get away with the abstractions you use in your fiction?

McElroy: By tying them as closely, even at times fanatically, as I can to phenomena, which is what I believe I do. Which abstractions were you thinking of?

The talk in Ancient History, *the language at the beginning of* Plus.

McElroy: I like books that try to push the reader into a strange state of mind in which everything has to be relearned. I like William Golding's *The Inheritors* for that reason. The language of *Plus*, especially at the beginning, is that of a consciousness that is discovering the world all over again. I set out to take everything away from a person and write a drama in which that person would begin with some essence which could not be taken away and rediscover the world and reconstruct the self. I do not like to speak of novels as being about language or even in a sense made of language, because it seems to me language always has to somehow refer to a shared world. That is why I can admire the work of Dreiser and of Doris Lessing. Still, *Plus* is an exploration or experiment in language, where I am moving more toward Beckett than toward Joyce, trying to establish a minimal language upon which one might build.

Can we talk about Plus, *or must we talk in the language of* Plus?

McElroy: That is in some ways a flattering question, because you suggest that there is something very distinctive about the vision and language in the novel. But what I resist in your comment is the notion that a work of art that is moving and has been felt and understood might be so strange that you couldn't talk about it. I can't think of any book I have ever read that I liked and knew anything about that I wouldn't enjoy talking about to somebody else who had read it also. This doesn't mean that I can make an adequate verbal image of it, but I can talk about it. The problem is that whatever point of departure you choose in talking about the book, you have violated your own secret whole sense of it.

As you say, a great deal is taken away in Plus. *But it seems to me that the more common tendency in your work is overload, giving the reader more than he can possibly process . . .*

McElroy: . . . because I want the reader to say, "You have offended me, you have wearied me, you have made me mad as hell because I spent ten bucks on your book, but I still love you." OK, that might be underneath it all, but I think we live in a world in which we are overloaded by information if we pay any attention at all. Just as I wanted to introduce a strain of chaos into *A Smuggler's Bible* and into *Hind's Kidnap*, in *Lookout Cartridge* there is in the sentences and in the information a vast amount of overload to give the reader a sense of teetering on the edge of not understanding. At the same time, he is tantalized by the sense that the information is all here if he just knew how to understand it.

Does your giving the reader more than he wants remind him of how little he knows or can know?

McElroy: That question hurts, but I think the answer is yes. I hoped to create ambiguities from excess—the need to know yet to have at hand too much—in order to have at least a chance of finding the key to it all. I knew that I was asking too much of the reader sometimes, but I persisted in doing it. If I had it to do over again, I would ease some of the identifications in *Hind's Kidnap*. Although I think that Updike hasn't been as adventurous as a person of his enormous gifts should have been, his notion of a compact with the reader is fair enough. I think he goes too far; I think I don't go far enough in that direction. I hope that I am writing for readers who would be willing to commit themselves to a strenuous, adventurous fiction, but I don't write fiction of deliberate difficulty. What I believe I am doing is being, possibly in some new way I'm not sure about, a realist. In the collaboration between the syntax of my sentences and the observation of phenomena that is contained in my sentences, I think that I am being faithful as much as I can be to the world that I find with my senses and feel in the forms that are my mind. I have a choice between going on as I have been or leavening and loosening and to some extent dissolving the surface obstacles that a reader finds reading me. I am trying to write easier prose because I don't think people have time for long books, and I am not even sure the human race has a great deal of time. So I want to write easier prose, but what comes out continues to be a sentence which is packed and convoluted.

I'd also like to think the overload of information is partly an act of giv-

ing, and that the obsessive attention which the writer seems to pay to the
world is not paranoid or defensive primarily but appetitive, an attempt to
say here the world is, to be loved and to be received. When I first started
writing, I saw myself being divided between a cornball and an iceberg. I
think now I am much more of a cornball than I am an iceberg, so I am
dismayed by people calling my books cold. I grant there is a cerebral,
analytic, even sometimes manipulative strain in my work, but I see this as
subordinate to the emotional, the impulsive and uprushing. I see the books
as emotional, almost too much so. I thought *Plus* almost got out of control. I see *Plus* also as a step beyond the despair and overload in *Lookout
Cartridge*. And *Women and Men*, which is number six, is my reentry, my
coming back to the world and attempting to understand relations between
men and women, women and men, in a way that will answer more honestly and fully questions which I only groped at before.

Are these questions close to being answered now?

McElroy: Not yet. In most of my books I knew where I was going to
arrive at the end, but I didn't know how I was going to get there. With
Women and Men I know how I am going to get to the end, but I don't
know what is going to be there. That sounds clever, but it is true. All I
know is that at the end I am going to look over the rest of the book and
somehow use that as a means of defining a relation between a man and a
woman that will be both ideal and possible. There are a lot of images in the
book, but the main image which I keep coming back to and which carries
us from New York to New Mexico, from New York to disarmament conferences, from Skylab in orbit all the way down into the depths of the
earth, is the image of a man and a woman facing each other but not on the
same line, as if they were on parallel lines, as if they were looking over
each other's shoulders. So they are looking toward each other, but they
are not seeing each other. And if the book were to be described in abstract
or structural terms, the narrative turns again and again upon variations of
this image, variations which can be abstractly seen as all the variations of
pivoting that are possible. If you see the man and woman as two arrows
pointing toward each other but on separate tracks, and pivot one arrow or
pivot them both, pivot them in various ways, that is an abstract way of
seeing all of the varieties of contact, of communication, of insight that
may be possible. The book is about intuitions that may be possible between men and women if they live together and know each other. These
can be destructive and can threaten separation. People knowing each
other too well. But because I am an optimist, they are also potentially a
secret means of living together.

Your wife suggested I might ask you what your M.A. thesis was on.

McElroy: It was on women in the novels of Franz Kafka. It was called
"The Secret Woman," and the secret gets larger and larger and larger and

the best I can hope to do is to find my way to the center of it and to live there. My relations with Joan and my daughter Hanna and some other women—some militant feminists, many other kinds, if that is the right word, of women—over the last ten or fifteen years have made me feel that relations between women and men are at the most interesting, potentially destructive, but potentially creative point that they have ever been. Living in New York among a lot of original, powerful, intelligent, imaginative women, I have increasingly felt that if I don't try to say what the possibilities are for men and women living together I will not have addressed myself to the most important thing in my life. *Women and Men* will be a way of putting into the deceptive coherence of English sentences some brief notion of what I have meant to myself and what other people have meant to me.

An Interview with
Toni Morrison

Toni Morrison's *Song of Solomon* was published in 1977 to unreserved praise; American readers had found a new voice. The plot of the novel, a young man's search for a nourishing folk tradition, was familiar from other Afro-American books, but Morrison's fireside manner—composed yet simple, commanding yet intimate—gives the novel a Latin American enchantment. Reading backward through *Sula* (1973) to Morrison's first novel, *The Bluest Eye* (1969), one sees her trying out different versions of what she calls her "address," rehearsing on more modest subjects the tone and timbre that give original expression to the large cultural materials in *Song of Solomon.*

How and why she arrived at that special voice were the questions that brought me to Toni Morrison's busy office at Random House (where she is an editor) just after she finished *Tar Baby* (1981). Although our interview was interrupted several times, when Toni Morrison started talking about writing she achieved remarkable concentration and intensity. This—not editorial business or author small talk—was clearly where she lived. No matter what she discussed—her loyalty to the common reader, her eccentric characters, her interest in folklore—her love of language was the subtext and constant lesson of her manner. She *performs* words. Gertrude Stein said poetry was "caressing nouns." Toni Morrison doesn't like to be called a poetic writer, but it is her almost physical relation to language that allows her to tell the old stories she feels are best.

—*Tom LeClair*

You have said you would write even if there were no publishers. Would you explain what the process of writing means to you?

Morrison: After my first novel, *The Bluest Eye*, writing became a way to be coherent in the world. It became necessary and possible for me to sort out the past, and the selection process, being disciplined and guided, was genuine thinking as opposed to simple response or problem-solving. Writing was the only work I did that was for myself and by myself. In the process, one exercises sovereignty in a special way. All sensibilities are engaged, sometimes simultaneously, sometimes sequentially. While I'm writing, all of my experience is vital and useful and possibly important. It may not appear in the work, but it is valuable. Writing gives me what I think dancers have on stage in their relation to gravity and space and time. It is energetic and balanced, fluid and in repose. And there is always the possibility of growth; I could never hit the highest note, so I'd never have to stop. Writing has for me everything that good work ought to have, all the criteria. I love even the drudgery, the revision, the proofreading. So even if publishing did grind to a halt, I would continue to write.

Do you understand the process more and more with each novel that you write?

Morrison: At first I wrote out of a very special place in me, although I did not understand what that place was or how to get to it deliberately. I didn't trust the writing that came from there. It did not seem writerly enough. Sometimes what I wrote from that place remained sound, even after enormous revision, but I would regard it as a fluke. Then I learned to trust that part, learned to rely on that part, and I learned how to get there faster than I had before. That is, now I don't have to write thirty-five pages of throat-clearing in order to be where I wish to be. I don't mean that I'm an inspired writer. I don't wait to be struck by lightning and don't need certain slants of light in order to write, but now after my fourth book I can recognize the presence of a real idea and I can recognize the proper mode of its expression. I must confess, though, that I sometimes lose interest in the characters and get much more interested in the trees and animals. I think I exercise tremendous restraint in this, but my editor says, "Would you stop this *beauty* business." And I say, "Wait, wait until I tell you about these ants."

How do you conceive of your function as a writer?

Morrison: I write what I have recently begun to call village literature, fiction that is really for the village, for the tribe. Peasant literature for *my* people, which is necessary and legitimate but which also allows me to get in touch with all sorts of people. I think long and carefully about what my novels ought to do. They should clarify the roles that have become obscured; they ought to identify those things in the past that are useful and those that are not; and they ought to give nourishment. I agree with John

Berger that peasants don't write novels because they don't need them. They have a portrait of themselves from gossip, tales, music, and some celebrations. That is enough. The middle class at the beginning of the Industrial Revolution needed a portrait of itself because the old portrait didn't work for this new class. Their roles were different; their lives in the city were new. The novel served this function then, and it still does. It tells about the city values, the urban values. Now my people, we "peasants," have come to the city, that is to say, we live with its values. There is a confrontation between old values of the tribes and new urban values. It's confusing. There has to be a mode to do what the music did for blacks, what we used to be able to do with each other in private and in that civilization that existed underneath the white civilization. I think this accounts for the address of my books. I am not explaining anything to anybody. My work bears witness and suggests who the outlaws were, who survived under what circumstances and why, what was legal in the community as opposed to what was legal outside it. All that is in the fabric of the story in order to do what the music used to do. The music kept us alive, but it's not enough anymore. My people are being devoured. Whenever I feel uneasy about my writing, I think: What would be the response of the people in the book if they read the book? That's my way of staying on track. Those are the people for whom I write.

As a reader I'm fascinated by literary books, but the books I wanted to write could not be only, even merely, literary or I would defeat my purpose, defeat my audience. That's why I don't like to have someone call my books "poetic," because it has the connotation of luxuriating richness. I wanted to restore the language that black people spoke to its original power. That calls for a language that is rich but not ornate.

What do you mean by "address"?

Morrison: I stand with the reader, hold his hand, and tell him a very simple story about complicated people. I like to work with, to fret, the cliché, which is a cliché because the experience expressed in it is important: a young man seeks his fortune; a pair of friends, one good, one bad; the perfect innocent victim. We know thousands of these in literature. I like to dust off these clichés, dust off the language, make them mean whatever they may have meant originally. My genuine criticism of most contemporary books is that they're not *about* anything. Most of the books that are about something—the books that mean something—treat old ideas, old situations.

Does this mean working with folklore and myth?

Morrison: I think the myths are misunderstood now because we are not talking to each other the way I was spoken to when I was growing up in a very small town. You knew everything in that little microcosm. But we don't live where we were born. I had to leave my town to do my work here; it was a sacrifice. There is a certain sense of family I don't have. So the myths get forgotten. Or they may not have been looked at carefully. Let me give you an example: the flying myth in *Song of Solomon*. If it means Icarus to some readers, fine. But my meaning is specific: it is about black people who could fly. That was always part of the folklore of my life; flying was one of our gifts. I don't care how silly it may seem. It is everywhere—people used to talk about it, it's in the spirituals and gospels. Perhaps it was wishful thinking—escape, death, and all that. But suppose it wasn't. What might it mean? I tried to find out in *Song of Solomon*.

In the book I've just completed, *Tar Baby*, I use that old story because, despite its funny, happy ending, it used to frighten me. The story has a tar baby in it which is used by a white man to catch a rabbit. "Tar baby" is also a name, like "nigger," that white people call black children, black girls, as I recall. Tar seemed to me to be an odd thing to be in a Western story, and I found that there is a tar lady in African mythology. I started thinking about tar. At one time, a tar pit was a holy place, at least an important place, because tar was used to build things. It came naturally out of the earth; it held together things like Moses' little boat and the pyramids. For me, the tar baby came to mean the black woman who can hold things together. The story was a point of departure to history and prophecy. That's what I mean by dusting off the myth, looking closely at it to see what it might conceal.

Do you think it's risky to do this kind of writing?

Morrison: Yes. I think I can do all sorts of writing, including virtuoso performances. But what is hard for me is to be simple, to have uncomplex stories with complex people in them, to clean the language, really clean it. One attempts to slay a real dragon. You don't ever kill it, but you have to choose a job worth the doing. I think I choose hard jobs for myself, and the possibility of failure is always there. I want a residue of emotion in my fiction, and this means verging upon sentimentality, or being willing to let it happen and then draw back from it. Also, stories seem so old-fashioned now. But narrative remains the best way to learn anything permanently, whether history or theology, so I continue with narrative form.

In the kind of fiction you have described, isn't there a danger that it will be liked for something it is not? Are you ever worried about that?

Morrison: No. The people who are not fastidious about reading may find my fiction "wonderful." They are valuable to me because I am never sure that what they find "wonderful" in it isn't really what is valuable about it. I do hope to interest people who are very fastidious about reading. What I'd really like to do is appeal to both at the same time. Sometimes I feel that I do play to the gallery in *Song of Solomon*, for example, because I have to make the reader look at people he may not wish to look at. You don't look at Pilate. You don't really look at a person like

Cholly in *The Bluest Eye*. They are always backdrops, stage props, not the main characters in their own stories. In order to look at them in fiction, you have to hook the reader, strike a certain posture as narrator, achieve some intimacy.

Song of Solomon seems to me a difficult book for a woman to write. Does the writer's risk become a subject of the novel?

Morrison: I know that I think about risk a lot. I know that what informed choices I make in life are frequently at a risk, being willing to risk and being willing to lose. Always. Coming to terms with death all the time so that life isn't your shroud, isn't something that you protect yourself with. I tried in *Sula* to suggest the outer limits of risk and freedom, where liberty becomes destructive because it is not informed by any sense of identification with other people, any responsibility. Sula is a pariah. In *Song of Solomon* I felt that that kind of risk is more accessible to men. Some women take a lot of risks, but I think there is something called masculinity which has nothing to do with sex or gender. It's the *idea* of masculinity, the courting of danger. And there is an *idea* of femininity. I think that Milkman Dead is whole at the end of *Song of Solomon* because he achieves both: he surrenders and controls. The last line is "If you surrendered to the air, you could *ride* it." To fly he had to exercise enormous control over his own body and, at the same time, be willing to drop. He had to cooperate with a wholly untrustworthy element, the air. Once all his information is gathered and selected and organized, he is willing to risk flying *for somebody else*. Personally, I think I am aware of this kind of balance. As head of a household, I have areas of my life where I cannot be safe, but there are also certain areas in which I am the safety. I suppose this spills over into what I write about.

As an editor, you look for quality in others' work. What do you think is distinctive about your fiction? What makes it good?

Morrison: The language, only the language. The language must be careful and must appear effortless. It must not sweat. It must suggest and be provocative at the same time. It is the thing that black people love so much—the saying of words, holding them on the tongue, experimenting with them, playing with them. It's a love, a passion. Its function is like a preacher's: to make you stand up out of your seat, make you lose yourself and hear yourself. The worst of all possible things that could happen would be to lose that language. There are certain things I cannot say without recourse to my language. It's terrible to think that a child with five different present tenses comes to school to be faced with those books that are less than his own language. And then to be told things about his language, which is him, that are sometimes permanently damaging. He may never know the etymology of Africanisms in his language, not even know that "hip" is a real word or that "the dozens" meant something. This is a really cruel fallout of racism. I know the Standard English. I want to use it to help restore the other language, the lingua franca.

The part of the writing process that I fret is getting the sound without some mechanics that would direct the reader's attention to the sound. One way is not to use adverbs to describe how someone says something. I try to work the dialogue down so the reader has to hear it. When Eva in *Sula* sets her son on fire, her daughter runs upstairs to tell her, and Eva says, "Is?" You can hear every grandmother say "Is?" and you know: a) she knows that she's been told; b) she is not going to do anything about it; and c) she will not have any more conversation. That sound is important to me.

Not all readers are going to catch that.

Morrison: If I say "Quiet is as kept," that is a piece of information which means exactly what it says, but to black people it means a big lie is about to be told. Or someone is going to tell some graveyard information, who's sleeping with whom. Black readers will chuckle. There is a level of appreciation that might be available only to people who understand the context of the language. The analogy that occurs to me is jazz: it is open on the one hand and both complicated and inaccessible on the other. I never asked Tolstoy to write for me, a little colored girl in Lorain, Ohio. I never asked Joyce not to mention Catholicism or the world of Dublin. Never. And I don't know why I should be asked to explain your life to you. We have splendid writers to do that, but I am not one of them. It is that business of being universal, a word hopelessly stripped of meaning for me. Faulkner wrote what I suppose could be called regional literature and had it published all over the world. It is good—and universal—because it is specifically about a particular world. That's what I wish to do. If I tried to write a universal novel, it would be water. Behind this question is the suggestion that to write for black people is somehow to diminish the writing. From my perspective, there are only black people. When I say "people," that's what I mean. Lots of books written by black people about black people have had this "universality" as a burden. They were writing for some readers other than me.

One of the complaints about your fiction in both the black and white press is that you write about eccentrics, people who aren't representative.

Morrison: This kind of sociological judgment is pervasive and pernicious. "Novel A is better than B or C because A is more like most black people really are." Unforgivable. I am enchanted, personally, with people who are extraordinary because in them I can find what is applicable to the ordinary. There are books by black writers about ordinary black life. I don't write them. Black readers often ask me, "Why are your books so melancholy, so sad? Why don't you ever write about something that works, about relationships that are healthy?" There is a comic mode, meaning the union of the sexes, that I don't write. I write what I suppose could be called the tragic mode in which there is some catharsis and revelation. There's a whole lot of space in between, but my inclination is in the tragic direction. Maybe it's a consequence of my being a classics minor.

Related, I think, is the question of nostalgia. The danger of writing about the past, as I have done, is romanticizing it. I don't think I do that, but I do feel that people were more interesting then than they are now. It seems to me there were more excesses in women and men, and people accepted them as they don't now. In the black community where I grew up, there were eccentricity and freedom, less conformity in individual habits—but close conformity in terms of the survival of the village, of the tribe. Before sociological microscopes were placed on us, people did anything and nobody was run out of town. I mean, the community in *Sula* let her stay. They wouldn't wash or bury her. They protected themselves from her, but she was part of the community. The detritus of white people, the rejects from the respectable white world, which appears in *Sula* was in our neighborhood. In my family, there were some really interesting people who were willing to be whatever they were. People permitted it, perhaps because in the outer world the eccentrics had to be a little servant person or low-level factory worker. They had an enormous span of emotions and activities, and they are the people I remember when I start to write. When I go to colleges, the students say, "Who are these people?" Maybe it's because now everybody seems to be trying to be "right."

How do you solicit the reader's sympathies for these eccentrics?

Morrison: I try to disarm him as we walk together into the book. The narrator—some participant or me, the author—is amazed along with the reader. The narrator doesn't understand, wonders, sucks his teeth. This again is my notion of village literature. In *The Bluest Eye* I used first-person point of view because I had originally written only about Pecola and her family and I needed a bridge between her strange life and the reader. I introduced her peers to help tell the story and give the intimacy I value. The "I" could function like a chorus. It was easiest that way, too, for you can cover up your fear, and the child's point of view can permit you to cover up lots of mistakes. In *Sula* Nell is not just an observer, but because her friend Sula is so wildly different Nell seems more like us, the readers. She was the only one who could express what the friendship had meant because she would be the last one to learn how important Sula had been in her life. Friendship is thrown into relief because of the extreme nature of the people who are friends. *Tar Baby* employed the whole benevolent world of nature as the chorus, the community. They gossip, wonder, observe fear, and they hurt. They do it for and with us—as the village does it for and with us in the other books. Sharing those feelings with clouds and butterflies elicits sympathy.

The tense of the novels also helps draw the reader in. The action has already passed, and while what is about to be described may be terrible, the reader is not to worry because it's already happened.

What is the difference between these first two novels and Song of Solomon?

Morrison: *Song of Solomon* is driven by male presence rather than female presence, I could not rely on certain kinds of language, metaphors, colors. *The Bluest Eye* and *Sula* are hermetic, enclosed; they have the feel of a room or a shut-door place. The rhythm of *Song of Solomon* had to be different. The first third of the book is storytelling, which Milkman simply hears and doesn't pay any attention to. I thought of this as a train being steamed up. Then the train and the novel take off, moving faster and faster, high-balling until the end with its terrible screeching of brakes. I equated the force that was driving the book with what I wanted to say about how to become a civilized human being: how Milkman gets his information, how he uses it, what he learns. Like my first two books, *Song of Solomon* ends happily, which is to say that a character learns something of overwhelming importance, something he or she would never have learned had it not been for the first part of the novel.

Naming is an important theme in Song of Solomon. *Would you discuss its significance?*

Morrison: I never knew the real names of my father's friends. Still don't. They used other names. A part of that had to do with cultural orphanage, part of it with the rejection of the name given to them under circumstances not of their choosing. If you come from Africa, your name is gone. It is particularly problematic because it is not just *your* name but your family, your tribe. When you die, how can you connect with your ancestors if you have lost your name? That's a huge psychological scar. The best thing you can do is take another name which is yours because it reflects something about you or your own choice. Most of the names in *Song of Solomon* are real, the names of musicians for example. I used the biblical names to show the impact of the Bible on the lives of black people, their awe of and respect for it coupled with their ability to distort it for their own purposes. I also used some pre-Christian names to give the sense of a mixture of cosmologies. Milkman Dead has to learn the meaning of his own name and the names of things. In African languages there is no word for "yam," but there is a word for every variety of yam. Each thing is separate and different; once you have named it, you have power. Milkman has to experience the elements. He goes into the earth and later walks its surface. He twice enters water. And he flies in the air. When he walks the earth, he feels a part of it, and that is his coming of age, the beginning of his ability to connect with the past and perceive the world as alive.

How do you discriminate among the different kinds of magic in the novel? What is nourishing, what is harmful?

Morrison: Black magic and white magic [*laughter*]. Black magic as healing—white magic as earth destroying. It's knowing the roots that are not objectively tested. We should try to perceive by all the senses, explore other ways of knowing. It may lead to accidents and error, but that may be necessary. What is healthy is a distrust of scientific objectivity. I was born with tuberculosis. The doctor said I had to go to the sanitarium. My mother said no, because nobody ever came out. Any well-educated scientific person would have said yes. But she trusted some other way of knowing, and she was right. She had courage. I do know that in the '40s the way of treating TB patients changed; no more fattening them up, sitting them in the sun and killing them. Now so many functions have been handed over to institutions that my mother's kind of courage is rare. I don't recommend that people live like Pilate in *Song of Solomon*, but I do believe we have a lot to unlearn as well as to learn. Pilate is the embodiment of ignorance in its pristine form, but she's also incisive.

You mentioned the importance of sound before. Your work also seems to me to be strongly visual and concerned with vision, with seeing.

Morrison: There are times in my writing when I cannot move ahead even though I know exactly what will happen in the plot and what the dialogue is because I don't have the scene, the metaphor to begin with. Once I can see the scene, it all happens. In *Sula*, Eva is waiting for her long-lost husband to come back. She's not sure how she's going to feel, but when he leaves he toots the horn on his pear-green Model-T Ford. It goes "ooogah, ooogah," and Eva knows she hates him. My editor said the car didn't exist at the time, and I had a lot of trouble rewriting the scene because I had to have the color and the sound. Finally, I had a woman in a green dress laughing a big-city laugh, an alien sound in that small-town street, that stood for the "ooogah" I couldn't use. In larger terms, I thought of *Sula* as a cracked mirror, fragments and pieces we have to see independently and put together. In *The Bluest Eye* I used the primer story, with its picture of a happy family, as a frame acknowledging the outer civilization. The primer with white children was the way life was presented to the black people. As the novel proceeded I wanted that primer version broken up and confused, which explains the typographical running together of the words.

Did your using the primer come out of the work you were doing on textbooks?

Morrison: No. I was thinking that nobody treated these people seriously in literature and that "these people" who were not treated seriously were me. The interest in vision, in seeing, is a fact of black life. As slaves and ex-slaves, black people were manageable and findable, as no other slave society would be, because they were black. So there is an enormous impact from the simple division of color—more than sex, age, or anything else. The complaint is not being seen for what one is. That is the reason why my hatred of white people is justified and their hatred for me is not. There is a fascinating book called *Drylongso* which collects the talk of black people. They say almost to a man that you never tell a white person the truth. He doesn't want to hear it. Their conviction is that they are neither seen nor listened to. They also perceive themselves as morally superior people because they do *see*. This helps explain why the theme of the mask is so important in black literature and why I worked so heavily with it in *Tar Baby*.

Who is doing work now that you respect?

Morrison: I don't like to make lists because someone always gets left out, but in general I think the South American novelists have the best of it now. My complaint about letters now would be the state of criticism. It's following postmodern fiction into self-consciousness, talking about itself as though it were the work of art. Fine for the critic, but not helpful for the writer. There was a time when the great poets were the great critics, when the artist was the critic. Now it seems that there are no encompassing minds, no great critical audience for the writer. I have yet to read criticism that understands my work or is prepared to understand it. I don't care if the critic likes or dislikes it. I would just like to feel less isolated. It's like having a linguist who doesn't understand your language tell you what you're saying. Stanley Elkin says you need great literature to have great criticism. I think it works the other way around. If there were better criticism, there would be better books.

An Interview with
Tim O'Brien

Although Tim O'Brien spent much of his youth in the relative wilderness of Minnesota, he currently lives in Cambridge, Massachusetts, in a modest apartment building located just off of Harvard Square. It was a clear, crisp April Fool's Day in 1979 when I arrived to talk with him; greeting me in a flannel shirt and jeans, he led me past the small study where he does most of his writing, to an open-windowed living room that was bedecked with plants. O'Brien is an intense, handsome man in his early thirties with long, dark hair which is beginning to thin just a bit. While I set up my tape recorder, we chatted about his current work-in-progress, *The Nuclear Age,* a book which examines the balance between the paranoia and numbness of Americans toward the prospect of nuclear annihilation. Once I turned the recorder on, it became immediately apparent that O'Brien was anxious to speak out on the issues that he felt especially strong about—the lack of seriousness he finds in most contemporary fiction, his own commitment to substance in fiction, the things he's learned about writing over the past decade, his views about how writers have dealt with wars, including Vietnam.

It was when Tim O'Brien's novel about Vietnam, *Going after Cacciato,* won the prestigious National Book Award in 1978 over the much-praised and highly publicized *The World According to Garp* that the literary world began to pay serious attention to O'Brien. After being drafted and sent to Vietnam in the late 1960s, O'Brien had begun to write short, non-fictional anecdotes about what he was witnessing; these pieces were eventually expanded and collected into *If I Die in a Combat Zone.* This book achieved some notice from an American public confused about their disturbing experience in Vietnam and anxious to discover writers capable of examining the nature of these experiences. O'Brien's talents as a writer of fiction were first made evident with the publication of *Northern Lights*, a book set in the wilderness of O'Brien's youth which dealt with the issues of courage and bravery and how these qualities develop. Although O'Brien admits in this interview that *Northern Lights* is a flawed novel (it is too long and talky, he feels), it was nevertheless praised for the most part by critics, with O'Brien's sharp, crisp prose rhythms and fusion of setting and character development being frequently likened to the early Hemingway. This praise was, of course, greatly expanded in 1978 when *Cacciato* appeared, a book which was hailed by many people as the first truly significant treatment of Vietnam and the ways in which it affected the imaginations of those who served there.

—Larry McCaffery

Two of your three books to date have dealt directly with Vietnam, and your third—I'm thinking of Northern Lights—*might be considered a marginal case. At this stage in your career do you consider yourself to be primarily a "Vietnam writer"?*

O'Brien: No, I don't. It's true, of course, that I came to writing because of the war. When I returned from Vietnam, I had something to say: I had witnessed things, smelled things, imagined things which struck me as startling and terrifying and intriguing in all sorts of ways. At that point I didn't care much about technique or language or structure or any of that craft stuff. All I had was a body of acquired experience that impelled me to write. But since the publication of *Cacciato* in 1978, I've been working in entirely different ways. My new book, which will be called *The Nuclear Age*, deals with a new set of issues and concerns. So, no, I'm not a Vietnam writer. Although Vietnam was the impetus and spark for *becoming* a writer, I do not consider myself a war writer.

Could you clarify the chronology of your writing career up through Going after Cacciato? *I understand that in between writing projects you were also a graduate student and a newspaper reporter . . .*

O'Brien: I was drafted in 1968, went to Vietnam in 1969, and came home in '70. I arrived at Harvard to pursue a doctorate in government in September, 1970. During my first year in graduate school I began writing *If I Die in a Combat Zone*. I finished that book sometime in 1972. In 1973–74, I took a year off from Harvard to work as a reporter for the *Washington Post*—I was a general-assignment reporter on the national desk; I covered a lot of Senate hearings, the first oil boycott, some veterans' affairs. General politics. While a reporter, I wrote *Northern Lights* during my off hours. I wrote *Cacciato* in 1975, '76, and '77.

Did your graduate studies have any relationship to the ideas that went into Cacciato?

O'Brien: Sort of. I was studying American foreign policy, and my dissertation explored American military interventions. Equally important, though, was my reading in political theory: Plato, Aristotle, Marsilius of Padua, Aquinas, Locke, Dante, Machiavelli, and so on.

You actually wrote some of the pieces in If I Die *while you were in Vietnam, didn't you?*

O'Brien: I wrote tiny vignettes or anecdotes—little pieces of maybe four or five pages. For example, seeing a land mine kill some people, I wrote a piece called "Step Lightly" that appeared in *Playboy* and later in *If I Die*. Perhaps five or six of these things were written while I was actually in Vietnam. But even then I wasn't thinking of myself as a writer; I was writing in the sense that we all do it—in letters and postcards.

The figure of a strong, dominant father appears in both of your first two novels. Was this because of your own relationship with your father or due to an aesthetic choice?

O'Brien: It was a planned artifice. Given the themes, for example, of *Northern Lights*, which are essentially themes of courage—why one is brave and why one isn't brave, how courage is developed—and given that I was writing about two brothers whose personalities and viewpoints were so disparate, it seemed necessary to have some kind of integrating force present. A father. In the case of *Cacciato*, the father doesn't strike me as all that strong; he's a force in the book, but an underplayed one. In a sense he's a sentimental fellow—telling Paul to keep his eyes open, his ass low, be careful. He's a deeply caring father and not at all the tyrant who appeared in *Northern Lights*.

Were you active in opposing the war while you were in college?

O'Brien: I was active in the sense in which activism existed then. From 1964 to 1968, while I attended Macalester College, there were no wild demonstrations against the war. Four or five local activists might wave signs saying "End the War." I wasn't among those four or five people. I was, however, a big supporter of Gene McCarthy during the 1967–68 period. I knocked on doors for him, took trips up to Wisconsin to help out during the primaries.

In both Cacciato *and* If I Die *you devote several important passages to the issue of why one goes to war even not believing that the war is just. In* If I Die, *for example, you say, "I was persuaded then and I remain persuaded now that the war was wrong, it was evil"—but you go on to say that "in the end it was less reason and more gravity" that finally influenced you to go to Vietnam. What did you mean by the last part of that quote?*

O'Brien: In both of those books I tried to describe those forces which seemed, almost physically, to push me into the war. One was my background: I came from a very small town, a fairly conservative town. I was part of the prairie. My father was a sailor in World War II; my mother was a WAVE. I sensed that the people I cared for in my life — friends, college acquaintances, professors — would have looked askance at my deserting. There was also the question of living in exile. I couldn't face that. To live in Canada or Sweden for the rest of my life was a frightening prospect.

Philosophical questions also played into it. Although I did feel that the war was wrong, I also realized that I was a twenty-one-year-old kid—I didn't know everything. Our president and his advisers were telling us the war was necessary and right. It seemed arrogant simply to give them the finger and say, "No. I won't go." The "gravity" that I was referring to in that passage was a feeling of emotional pressure—a fear of exile, of hurting my family, of losing everything I held to be valuable in my life. In the end, questions of political rightness or wrongness succumbed to the emotional pressure.

One of the most vivid passages in If I Die *is your description of your preparations for deserting the army—preparations you later abandoned. I take it that this personal struggle was one of the germinating ideas for* Cacciato.

O'Brien: Yes. *Cacciato* was in essence the flip side of *If I Die*. That is, in *Cacciato* the premise I started with was, What if I *had* deserted? Would I have been happy living in exile? Would I be happy running? What would I experience? Would I be able to live with myself? Was it *right* to run? What about my obligations as a citizen? My conclusion was basically that Paul Berlin's fantasized run for Paris would have been an unhappy experience—it wasn't compatible with his background, his personality, his beliefs. But while I was writing *Cacciato* I tried to keep things open-ended, to allow for the possibility of a happy ending for the flight. I found I couldn't write my way into a happy ending, just as in my life I couldn't live my way into it.

I noticed that in the dream sequence near the end of Cacciato—*where Paul is asked to step boldly into his dream of escape—he bases his refusal on much the same principles as you describe in* If I Die.

O'Brien: There are two essential answers that Paul gives there. One has to do with this issue of emotional baggage—that constellation of emotional pressures we were just talking about. But of equal importance is his argument—and my own—that he can't mold his imagination to fit what ought to be there. The decision to run or not run is based on that process of the imagination. Those soldiers who actually did desert were able to imagine a happy end to it.

All of our decision-making—opposing a war, marrying certain people, the jobs we accept or refuse—is at least partly determined by the imaginative faculty. If I can't *imagine* breathing life into a man who's been shot in the head, messing around with the blood and gore, it's very unlikely that I would choose to become a doctor; similarly, it's unlikely that I would become a nurse if I were unable to imagine sticking someone with a needle. Our imaginative capabilities determine, in large part, the shape and direction of our lives. We often look at imagination as weird fantasy—a bunch of Hobbits running around, Alice in Wonderland stuff. But to me the most compelling aspect of human nature is its imaginative aspect—what we're capable of imagining, the modes in which we imagine, the impact of imagination on our daily behavior.

In Cacciato *the issue of whether or not Vietnam was a fundamentally different war for Americans is raised in a discussion between Doc and Captain Rhallon. You present both sides very persuasively, but it seems to me that you give Doc the upper hand when he claims that the common soldier has always had the same kinds of problems and that he's never given a damn about justice or the purposes of war. Do you agree with Doc?*

O'Brien: Yes, I do. It's not a very popular belief. Many of the correspondents who came back from Vietnam based their reporting and general attitudes on the proposition that Vietnam was fundamentally different from other American wars. Vietnam, they said, was an unpopular war and was perceived as being evil by many of those fighting it. My quarrel, I suppose, is that, based on my own experience, not many of the soldiers believed that Vietnam was an evil war. Most people fighting there—the ordinary grunts like me—didn't think much about issues of good and evil. These things simply didn't cross their minds most of the time. Instead, inevitably, their attention was on the mosquitoes and bugs and horrors and pains and fears. These were the basic elements of the Vietnam war, and the same elements were present at the Battle of Hastings or Thermopylae or wherever. Once a soldier is in battle, the rational and moral faculties tend to diminish. All we can hope for is that these faculties don't fail entirely.

Why do you think that several of the most important works about Vietnam—your book, Eastlake's The Bamboo Bed, *Michael Herr's* Dispatches, Apocalpyse Now—*have relied so heavily on surreal or fantastic effects? Is this a reaction to the type of war that was fought there?*

O'Brien: I think all good war novels have a surreal aspect. *All Quiet on the Western Front,* for example, has that wonderful scene in which the coffins are blown out of the ground. *Catch-22* deals with World War II in a great many surreal ways; *Slaughterhouse-Five*—again about World War II—has a strong surreal element to it. Even *The Naked and the Dead* in that long and really impossible march up the mountain was, if not surreal, certainly fantastic and improbable. *The Red Badge of Courage* also has a good many scenes that seem surreal. In war, the rational faculty begins to diminish, as I just said, and what takes over is surrealism, the life of the imagination. The mind of the soldier becomes part of the experience—the brain seems to flow out of your head, joining the elements around you on the battlefield. It's like stepping outside yourself. War *is* a surreal experience; therefore it seems quite natural and proper for a writer to render some of its aspects in a surreal way.

But don't you feel that the Vietnam war seemed especially chaotic and formless—in both a geographical and a tactical sense—so that writers might be even more tempted to deal with it surrealistically?

O'Brien: Every war seems formless to the men fighting it. Certainly if you read *The Red Badge of Courage* you get a strong sense that Henry Fleming doesn't know where he's at or where the lines are or where the enemy is. There's a lot of smoke and noise mixing enemy and friend together into one inseparable mass. Who's behind me, Fleming wonders? Who's in front of me? Battles as witnessed on the ground don't have that classic feel of strong, unbroken lines between friends and enemies, a strong sense of location, or that sense of here is where I am. This wasn't quite so true for World War I, obviously, because of the trench warfare, but the chaos and general absence of order were still present in World War I fiction. It's very nice and easy to say that Vietnam was special because it was formless and absurd. But certainly World War I must've seemed equally chaotic and absurd to Siegfried Sassoon or Robert Graves or Rupert Brooke or Erich Remarque. And it *was* absurd—men were slaughtered like cattle for reasons that no soldier really understood. We like to think our own war is special: especially horrible, especially insane, especially formless. But we need a more historical and compassionate perspective. We shouldn't minimize the suffering and sense of bewilderment of other people in other wars.

What's your opinion about the other books that have appeared dealing with Vietnam?

O'Brien: I like Herr's *Dispatches*. It's very good.

What about the movies?

O'Brien: Horseshit. Simplistic and stupid. *Heroes, The Deer Hunter, Coming Home, Apocalypse Now*—they all come across to me as cartoons, garishly drawn rhetorical statements. Some less so than others. *The Deer Hunter* was the best.

Do you have a daily writing routine?

O'Brien: I work seven days a week, six to eight hours a day. On weekends, I may only work five to six hours. I'm slow; I need big chunks of time. It's very regularized.

Do your books or stories begin in the same way for you each time—with a character, a plot, an idea, a metaphor?

O'Brien: Most often it starts with an idea. I want to stress here that I'm a believer in substance—that is, I feel the fiction writer should have something to say. I mean this in all sorts of ways—in terms of a body of witnessed experience, the physical things that are seen and felt. But beyond that, I mean "substance" in a philosophical and thematic sense. It's not enough to say, "Here's what I saw in Vietnam" or "Here's what I experienced on my peace march." The writer needs a passionate and knowledgeable concern for the substance of what's witnessed, and that includes the spiritual and theological and political implications of raw experience. All my fiction is governed by this concern for substance—ideas with philosophical meat to them. I begin my books with a search for a dramatic vehicle for an idea. For example, *Cacciato* started with an idea: the metaphorical and literal flip side of *If I Die*. What if I *had* walked away from Vietnam? What would have happened in terms of my psychological well-being? What were the moral implications of desertion? Next, I sought a way of dramatizing this cluster of ideas and questions. *Northern Lights* began almost precisely the same way. I wanted to explore ideas of courage; hence I looked for the proper dramatic vehicle.

Once you've found this dramatic vehicle, how do you proceed to develop your books? For instance, do you work straight through on a novel and then go back and revise? Or do you keep working on individual sections until you're satisfied?

O'Brien: I have a peculiar way of approaching books: I try to make chapters into independent stories—that is, I like my chapters to have beginnings, middles, and ends. There are two reasons for this. One is very practical: I can publish chapters as stories in magazines. This has the advantage of making money, and also of testing things out, getting responses from magazine editors and readers. The other reason, which is more important, has to do with why chapters are chapters. I've always wondered why so many chapters end arbitrarily. It's much nicer to have your chapters conclude with a nice mini-resolution. There should be a sigh from the reader at the end of a chapter, the sigh signifying that he's recognized a natural end and that the chapter has an internal integrity to it. Sure, the reader knows that the book will go on, but there has been a temporary resolution—not just a dramatic resolution, but also in terms of psychological development, suspense, or whatever. Again, I don't like novels that seem arbitrary. As a result, much of my time is spent trying to forge dramatic wholes, so that the first chapter of *Cacciato*, for example, is a story. The book could end there, with Cacciato up on that hill and Paul Berlin saying, "Go, go."

Are you happy with the way your first novel, Northern Lights, *turned out?*

O'Brien: The book is maybe eighty pages too long. Someday, before it's reissued, I'll go over it and cut it considerably, especially in the first two hundred pages. There's a lot of interior monologue material that's too set up, and there's a lot of unnecessary repetition. These are things that can be solved. I'm firmly convinced that style is not the most important element of good literature. Stylistic problems *can* be solved: by writing better, by recognizing your own faults and getting rid of them. What *can't* be learned, however, is passion for ideas—substance. Out of every forty books of contemporary fiction, I'm lucky to find one which gives the sense of an author who really gives a shit about a set of philosophical issues. I'm not saying that fiction should *be* philosophy, but I am saying that a fiction writer must demonstrate in his work a concern for rightness and wrongness. What I see instead is concern for style and craft and structure. I see concern for well-drawn characters, concern for plot, concern for a whole constellation of things which, however, seem peripheral to the true core of fiction: the exploration of substantive, important human values.

So you wouldn't agree with someone like Gass, who feels that style is its own reward in fiction—maybe the only *legitimate concern for the writer—or with other writers like Barth and Borges, who feel that in exploring the nature of language and fiction-making they are also exploring something fundamental in man's makeup?*

O'Brien: If these writers are interested in exploring language as a tool of human inquiry and understanding, then I'd say OK. But I would also ask: "Why aren't you doing linguistic philosophy? Why aren't you writing essays? Why use the camouflage of drama? Why do you need a plot of characters? Why do you need even the semblance of a story?"

Do you have a similarly negative attitude toward all the experimentalism that was so prevalent in American fiction during the early and mid-'70s?

O'Brien: Experimentalism, in various guises, has been going on since people started writing. In many ways I think of myself as an experimentalist. I'm always experimenting with new sentences, new structures, new meanings. I'm creating what seems to me to be brand-new people, putting new words in their mouths, finding a storytelling method which accomplishes new dramatic magic. Although my experiments aren't startling—I'm not expecting a reader to look at my books and say, "My God, this is really experimental"—I feel I'm experimenting all the time. But the difference is this: I am experimenting not for the joy of experimenting, but rather to explore meaning and themes and dramatic discovery. For instance, *Cacciato* is structured as a teeter-totter, with the "Observation Post" chapters as the fulcrum—the present of the book. The teeter-totter swings back and forth between reality (the war experience) and fantasy (the imagined trek to Paris). Devising this structure was fun, yes, but I did it for thematic and dramatic *reasons*. I don't enjoy tinkering for the joy of tinkering, and I don't like reading books merely for their artifice. I want to see things and explore moral issues when I read, not get hit over the head with the tools of the trade.

You must pay considerable attention to the sound and rhythm of your sentences—it's one of the most striking aspects of your style.

O'Brien: Absolutely. When I start a book, I try to figure out its "moral aboutness" and then how to dramatize it. This process takes seven or eight months or even a year. But when I actually get to the typewriter, my time is spent in only one way: trying to make sentences and combinations of sentences which sound right and then work toward the creation of a dramatic dream. Rhythm is a big part of that. Dreams have rhythm. Drama has rhythm. The language mustn't be monotonous or repetitive. I like to juggle compound sentences and complex sentences and straight, declarative sentences. I watch certain words. I watch "ands," for example, to be sure too many of them don't appear. I'm very keen on catching unnecessary or showy repetitions since I used to use too many of them—in *Northern Lights*, for example.

Am I right in noting the influence of Hemingway in your approach to the sound and rhythm of sentences?

O'Brien: Yes, although I don't know really how much of his style I have absorbed. I don't think *Cacciato* sounds much like Hemingway; *Northern Lights* probably has more echoes of Hemingway than any of my other books. But as to what specifically I learned from Hemingway: efficiency; drama; sentiment instead of sentimentality.

In Northern Lights, *Paul Perry is said several times to be searching for "the bottom of things," and in his last visit to the pond you say he was in "a final search for the start of things." It occurred to me that this interest is really the obverse of his father's fascination with the end of things, with the apocalypse.*

O'Brien: Yes, that's a good way to put it. The book revolves around the genesis of personality, the genesis of one's moral outlook. I want the reader to ask: "Why is Paul Perry so cowardly in many ways, a homebody, whereas his brother is an outgoing macho-man, a hero? What makes them so different? Consequently, I had to go back literally to the sources of personality: Why do people turn out as they do? There's no simple answer, obviously, and I don't think there *can* be. But there are interesting combinations of experiences, and interpretations of experience, which can be more or less formative. For Paul and Harvey Perry, these experiences and interpretations go back to their father, and *his* father, and finally to the Kalevalan mythology. A reader rightly demands and expects a dramatic, satisfying explanation for the behavior of people. These motives and sources needn't be spelled out directly, but the raw material should be there, built into the novel's drama and context. You can let the reader shape the material, figure out what is most or least important, but nevertheless you must have this material present. Nothing infuriates me more in reading a book than unexplained behavior. There can be many, many possible explanations—not just one—but there must at least be something.

Apocalpytic images abound in Northern Lights, *and from what you've told me about your new book it will deal even more directly with the notion of the end of things. What do you find so sustaining about these particular images or metaphors?*

O'Brien: I'd say these aren't images or metaphors—they're *real*. In *Northern Lights* when the father builds a bombshelter it's because he's afraid of dying. Dying in general, but also death by way of the Bomb. When I wrote *Northern Lights*, I didn't think critics would interpret the bombshelter as a metaphor. To me, it's a *real* bombshelter; this guy's afraid of war. There is a whole litany of things to explain *why* the father is afraid of real bombs—the whole Finnish mythology which underlies the book helps explain this, for example. Still, this fear is real. But when the book came out, a few reviewers remarked, rather snidely, that the bombshelter was a pretty crude metaphor. This upset me. It wasn't a metaphor at all—it was just a damned bombshelter. A *real* one!

In the book I'm writing now—*The Nuclear Age*—there is another real bombshelter. No metaphor, no image. Real, real! The book's themes revolve around two issues. One is the whole question of how and why we become politicized and depoliticized; the second issue involves the safety of our species, of our survival. We *won't* survive if we can't stop thinking of nuclear weapons as mere metaphors. My new book, although it's designed to be humorous in a lot of places, treats the nuclear age in very tangible, realistic terms. That is, I want to hit people over the head with real bombs, real dangers, real perils, real possibilities. I want to ask: "Why are we so *numb* to these realities?" What motivated me to write my new book—and what motivated *Northern Lights*, too, although it wasn't recognized—was this desire to treat apocalypse as a startling fact of modern life. Not as biblical backlash or absurd theater or *Dr. Strangelove.*

Although Vietnam doesn't appear directly very much in Northern Lights, *I felt you might be using it as a sort of muted presence, much the way that Hemingway used World War I in* The Sun Also Rises. *This connection seemed reinforced by the fact that just as Jake Barnes comes back from the war with an overtly symbolic wound, so does Harvey Perry come back blinded—a wound which seemed to be linked to what Vietnam did to many returning veterans.*

O'Brien: As far as Vietnam was concerned, no, it didn't occur to me that I was writing about it in that way. The action of the book occurs after the war, and I wanted some kind of dramatic demonstration of Harvey's macho tendencies. So I had him go to a war—you know, "There's this brave sonofabitch"—and he gets wounded as a result. I *did* intend Harvey's partial blindness as a symbol of a deeper personality-blindness.

The idea of escape, of running away, is obviously a central concern in Cacciato, *but it appears in* Northern Lights *as well with regard to Harvey and Addie. In your earlier book, though, you seem to be treating escape as more of a frivolous activity than you do in* Cacciato, *where you seem more sympathetic to the idea that escape may be necessary—at least imaginatively—in an intolerable situation.*

O'Brien: Actually I think this idea is treated equally seriously in both books. Because Harvey and Addie are unsympathetic characters in some ways, I suppose the reader is justified in feeling that their attitude about escape and running away is frivolous. To me, though, it doesn't seem so much frivolous as it is a common human failing. I have it. I'm always wanting to run away: run to Tahiti, to all those places Harvey talks about. In all my works, and in what I am writing now, running away plays a big part, perhaps because running away helps open up all kinds of plot materials. In *Cacciato*, Paul Berlin is escaping a war; in *Northern Lights*, Harvey is escaping himself and his own history; in *The Nuclear Age*, my chief characters are trying to outrun their own obsessions, to escape from the Bomb.

A few reviewers compared your style in Cacciato *with the magical realism coming out of South America. Had you read Márquez when you wrote* Cacciato?

O'Brien: Yes, and Borges, too, but just dabbling. To me, *all* realism should be magical. All reality *is* magical.

Cacciato *seems less obviously governed by realistic impulses than your previous works, mainly because so much of the book is devoted to Paul's fantasy. Was this a conscious shift on your part?*

O'Brien: I think you could argue that *Cacciato* is the most realistic thing I've written. The life of the imagination is *real*—it's as fucking real as anything else, especially if you happen to be a follower of Fichte, who says that *nothing* is real but what is inside our own heads. But even if we don't go that far, I know that if I'm sitting in a room by myself, daydreaming, that daydream is perfectly real. The so-called fantasy sections of *Cacciato* are no less real than a soldier's memories of the war. The war scenes aren't happening in the present; when Bernie Lynn is killed, when Sidney Martin is fragged, these are memories which Berlin is reliving in his mind. Still, they have an internal reality—a visual and emotional and moral reality.

The same principle applies to the imagination. An internal phe-nomenon—again, real, real!

"Soldiers are dreamers"—that epigraph begins *Cacciato*. Soldiers fan-tasize and daydream—they live in their heads. War is horrible, and you need to escape it. Any psychologist will tell you that retreat into fantasy is a means of escape. Albert Speer, when he was in prison, used to walk around a small courtyard during his exercise period, pretending he was walking around the world. He'd count each step and say, "Today I've walked a mile and today I'm in Hong Kong." Then next day he's say, "To-day I've walked three miles and now I'm on the road to Peking." He was pretending it. Imagining it. This same sense of imprisonment and stress ex-ists in war, only heightened by the fear of death. So you retreat into your own mind. You manufacture a new reality.

It's interesting that you're so insistent on this point, because I felt that most reviews of Cacciato *were imperceptive in their desire to treat the novel mainly as a "Vietnam novel." There was very little discussion of what I took to be a more universal and important issue—the transforming and ordering power of the imagination.*

O'Brien: Yes, that was my feeling. The book is primarily a book about the impact of war on the imagination. And the impact of imagination on the war. To me in the writing of *Cacciato* I was grappling with something that a person who didn't give a shit about war would care about: the life of the imagination.

Several of the characters in Cacciato—*notably Paul and Doc—share an almost obsessive need for order in their lives. Am I right in feeling that you tie this notion of order and control closely to the controlling power of the imagination?*

O'Brien: Yes, that's one important elaboration of my interest in the imagination. A concern for the ordering of experience—whether or not it's imaginative or remembered experience—seems to be an important aspect of psychology. Even in daily life, it is often hard to recall the events of an ordinary day; it's especially hard in a situation of great stress and peril. The ability to manufacture order out of seeming chaos is important to our psychological well-being. Humans are causal animals. We have an im-pulse to order events, to seek out causes and consequences. You can imag-ine a murderer who's just gone out on a rampage saying, "Why did I do it?" And he'd try to sit back and remember what series of physical and psychological events produced the killing spree. Similarly, in the case of *Cacciato*, one of Paul Berlin's compelling concerns is to figure out why his platoon murdered Sidney Martin; hence all the retracing of what happen-ed when, the fitting of events together: When did Frenchie Tucker die? What did Martin say? What about Bernie Lynn? What happened first? What caused what? How did the murder come about? The ordering provides a partial motive for Cacciato's eventual flight from the war: he had been an implicit conspirator in a murder. All of this feeds into the motives which prompt Paul Berlin to consider his own flight.

I found it interesting that you placed the catalogue of the men's personal histories and backgrounds—Chapter 22, "Who They Were, or Claimed to Be"—in the middle of the novel, rather than at the very beginning, as most writers might have. Why did you do it this way?

O'Brien: If that chapter has impact, it's because of what's implied in its title—"Who They Were, or *Claimed* to Be"—the disjunction between the two. So the chapter has to do with their nicknames, the lies they tell about themselves, what they pretended to be, the kind of images they tried to project. A lot of the important character information has already been supplied by the time we get to that chapter, so I decided it would be instructive to dramatize the disjunctions and discontinuities between the surface characters and the internal characters. Oscar is a good example: he claims to be from one place, but all his mail comes from another place; he pretends he's from Detroit but doesn't know the names of any contemporary ballplayers. The whole business with nicknames is a way of hiding a lot of things, covering up fears, trying to become what one is not. That's common in war.

Another structural aspect of the book that interested me has to do with the very opening page, which is virtually a litany of those who will die in the rest of the novel. I imagine some traditionalists would claim that this destroys some of the suspense you might have capitalized on . . .

O'Brien: Books can also work as magic acts. You go into a magic theater and *know* you'll see these little chests and you know someone is going to get into one while someone else sticks swords through it. You know no one is really going to die, but you still say, "I've got to see this." You know the outcome, the story, but the mystery isn't so much in *what's* going to happen as it is in *seeing it happen*. That's one response. The names of the dead are listed in a kind of threnody in the beginning and then, one by one, they are killed off. We *see* it happen. I'm hoping that the reader is taken up with the happeningness of it. But, beyond that, the real mystery of the novel isn't given away on page one. We don't find out what happened to Cacciato—in fact, we *never* really find out. We also don't know what happened to Paul Berlin. A good reader will know by the second chapter that Paul is going to survive all that follows, that what we're seeing is all history. None of the important questions, then, is answered on that first page. I sure as hell didn't know what was going to happen when I wrote that first page.

So you wrote that first page first?

O'Brien: Yeah. The first chapter was the first thing I wrote. Other chapters were written later in a completely different, random order.

Earlier you described the way you like your chapters to possess a kind of dramatic unity of their own. But when you're proceeding with your books, do you usually move around from section to section and then later arrange them into a final form?

O'Brien: Yes, none of my books has proceeded in the order in which it finally took form. *Northern Lights* began for me in the woods, when Paul and Harvey were snowed in. *Cacciato* happened to begin with that first chapter, but that was because I already roughly knew the story of the book. My new book is even more jumbled than anything I've worked on before—I'll write one chapter when my narrator is a kid, and then develop the next chapter when he's talking to his *own* kid. I'm not sure as yet how to get from A to B; they're just two scenes that have to appear in the novel somewhere.

Unlike most of the other Vietnam novels I've seen, Cacciato *doesn't seem to be fundamentally an antiwar novel.*

O'Brien: I don't believe any good book could be "antiwar" in its conception. It's like writing an antifeminist book—how would one do it? One could make a caricature of a feminist and make her so shrewish and awful that every reader would hate her. But this approach would just result in a bad book, full of stereotyping and easy straw targets. No sense of mystery. I can't think of a great piece of literature that takes an absolute, black-and-white moral stance about the rightness and wrongness of certain issues, drawing all the bad guys as really bad and all the good guys as really good. An exception might be the two Malraux books, *Man's Fate* and *Man's Hope*, but even there it's not a closed question as to who is right and who's wrong. A genuine concern for the issues and complexity and the sense of discovery is much more important. Let the reader settle things.

So a scene like the one where that absurd young pacifist girl picks up the men is partly designed to add enough complexity to your treatment of war to allow the reader to draw his own conclusions.

O'Brien: Yes, although there are really two simultaneous responses to that scene. One is to laugh at her. She *is* pretty grotesque. But at the same time what the men do to her is also grotesque—they steal her van and leave her stranded. I get a sinking feeling when I reread the end of that scene. What they do may be funny, but it isn't *good.* The scene has a moral edge, too.

Obviously we see violence and inhumanity outside the sphere of Vietnam in Cacciato. *The most memorable scene of this sort may be the beheading which takes place in Tehran. I assume you were using these kinds of scenes to widen the scope of the novel, to suggest that the violence we see in Vietnam is not something limited to the American involvement in Vietnam.*

O'Brien: That's right. It's hard to articulate precise reasons for placing particular material or scenes in a novel. Obviously these scenes don't just happen—the writer makes them happen—and yet the reader should have a sense of dreamlike spontaneity. In general, however, my purpose was to hint at the roots of war in peace. War *always* grows out of peace. Always. As the soldiers in my novel run away from war, they encounter many of the same evils which they had hoped to leave behind—avarice, injustice, death, brutality. Unhappy things occur on their own peace march, which is a way of saying that one can't just ran away and expect a happy, magical ending. There are consequences in the real world to any kind of escape. There is no utopia to run to. The so-called peaceful world is full of butchery and tyranny. A physical running does not have the promise of genuine escape, because wherever you run, you're going to find the same stuff: you'll find, if not butchery, then tyranny, even in a small town in America. There is no happy place. That's what Sarkin Aung Wan is arguing for—a kind of Aristotelian felicity where everything is just right, just in moderation. But running or escape is not a solution.

When Paul is in Paris, a tour guide tells him, "Paris is not a place, it's a state of mind." What was Paris in your conception of the book?

O'Brien: Paris was that utopia in the mind of Paul Berlin and Sarkin Aung Wan—the absence of war, the City of Light and goodness. It was the peace of Paris that was a conceived antithesis to all the brutality and un-civilized behavior of war. Of course, Paris isn't *really* that way. Paul Berlin's response is that he hopes the guide is wrong and that Paris is more than a state of mind. But the guide is right. A lot of us in Vietnam used to talk about coming back to "the World"—we called the United States "the World." The United States was also a state of mind for us—it represented civility, decorum, felicity, and the absence of violence. But the States weren't really that way, either.

Your use of nature—or "Elements," as you refer to it in Northern Lights—*creates much of the important symbolic framework in your two novels, although in* Cacciato *the rhythms of birth and decay seem upset because of all the destruction. Is there any aesthetic or private reason why you tend to anchor your books so firmly in nature?*

O'Brien: Because *life* is anchored in these things. Another, more prac-tical reason is that I have a hard time writing scenes which are set indoors. I feel liberated by a sense of space when I am writing; I like the sky, not a ceiling or a wall. My best scenes, the ones which seem to me to be most vivid and alive, are those which take place outside the confines of walls. I'm not sure why this is, but good novelists understand that there should always be motion in a novel, even during dialogue. In practice, though, this is hard to accomplish, because one's concern while writing is to get the scene done—getting the dialogue out, the problem set up, the next step taken. This often becomes very static and talky. Although conversation is a form of behavior, I would rather establish my characters less by what they say than the way they behave, the things they do physically. And that means getting them out of chairs, out of the living rooms and sofas where too much stuff happens in novels.

A good example of what you're talking about is the scene in Northern Lights *where Paul must kill the muskrat—a scene which parallels the earlier one where he confronts the rat. Paul's actions and reactions in these two scenes dramatize the change that has taken place in his personality.*

O'Brien: Yes, and these scenes do this without saying, "Look—my personality has undergone a metamorphosis. I'm really a different man now." In a way I'm pleased that you saw that in those scenes, but in another way I was hoping to hide this—I wanted the reader to retain not a memory of the rat scene so much as a subconscious feeling that this guy has changed without knowing why you have been made to feel this way. The book is studded with parallel episodes like that, which I thought out very carefully. The trouble with the damn book is that there is so much crap surrounding the good stuff.

You're still early in your career, but do you think you've learned something about writing since you started writing seriously?

O'Brien: I've learned that writing doesn't get easier with experience. The more you know, the harder it is to write. If you know that repetition can be gratuitous and self-defeating, then this makes writing harder, since you've got to find new ways to say things. If you know that you shouldn't be monotonous in the length and style of your sentences, this makes writing more difficult, it challenges your skill. The most important thing, though, is this sense I've developed that a writer's true value must be found in his substantive contribution. Thought is the critical element in writing. Hard, rigorous, disciplined thought. I've learned to pay closer attention to the dramatization of moral choices. I've learned to ponder those choices before writing a story or a scene.

When Cacciato *won the National Book Award for 1978, it got a lot of publicity, partly because it had beaten out* The World According to Garp. *Did winning this award have any impact on your career—bolster your confidence or anything dramatic like that?*

O'Brien: No, it didn't bolster my confidence exactly. It did have some practical impact. It got me money, for example. It got *Cacciato* reprinted into three paperback editions and generated some foreign sales. The award means the book will be much more widely read. That's the best thing that happened, and it'll also generate a larger readership for my next book. That puts some subtle pressure on me, but it doesn't make the writing any harder or easier. I've always wanted to write good books. When you face a page in the morning, you don't think about awards. You just think about sentences and story and characters and themes—the book itself.

Are there any contemporary writers you particularly admire or feel affinities with?

O'Brien: John Fowles. I think he's our best living writer. There aren't too many others. I did like *Garp* a lot and also what I've heard of John Irving's new book, *The Hotel New Hampshire*. I'd probably also include Graham Greene, John Updike, Walker Percy, Norman Mailer, Tom McGuane. But as I said earlier, most modern fiction seems to me to be frivolous and gimmicky and . . . well, *boring*.

In If I Die, *you say, "Can a footsoldier teach anybody anything important about a war, merely for having been there? I think not. He can tell stories." Do you still believe this?*

O'Brien: Absolutely. What can you teach people, just from having been in a war? By "teach" I mean provide insight, philosophy. The mere fact of having witnessed violence and death doesn't make a person a teacher. Insight and wisdom are required, and that means reading and hard thought. I didn't intend *If I Die* to stand as a profound statement, and it's not. Teaching is one thing, and telling stories is another. Instead, I wanted to use stories to alert readers to the complexity and ambiguity of a set of moral issues—but without preaching a moral lesson.

An Interview with
Ronald Sukenick

The following interview took place over a several-day period in early February, 1981, at Raymond Federman's home in Buffalo, New York. Sukenick and I, along with Robert Coover, Federman, Jerry Klinkowitz, and several other writers and critics, were participating in a conference on postmodern fiction which had been organized by the English department at SUNY-Buffalo. The week's events had included various panel discussions, readings by the writers, the inevitable late-night conversations over drinks, and even a raucous poker game to celebrate Coover's birthday. At any rate, by the time Sukenick and I settled down in Federman's living room to begin the interview, we had plenty of immediate conversational material upon which to draw.

Ron Sukenick—now silver-haired and in his late forties, but still possessing striking good looks—first began to draw the attention of readers and critics in the late 1960s, when his highly experimental *Up* (1968) and *The Death of the Novel and Other Stories* (1969) appeared. Like a lot of other postmodern fiction from this period, Sukenick's early works mixed fictional biography, metafiction, improvisation, typographical play, and various other nontraditional devices to produce startling interactions between life and art, reader and text. Borrowing compositional techniques from jazz, abstract expressionism, and the experiments of writers like Kafka, Beckett, Henry Miller, and Raymond Roussel, Sukenick's fiction not only toyed with the readers' notions of what a literary text should be but also powerfully reflected the age's rebellious energy and the social, political, and sexual disruptions that were occurring.

Sukenick had begun writing seriously while an undergraduate at Cornell during the early 1950s. His graduate work focused on the poetry of Wallace Stevens and his dissertation, somewhat revised, was eventually published in 1967 as *Musing the Obscure*. In the early 1970s Sukenick, along with a number of other nontraditional writers like Jonathan Baumbach, Peter Spielberg, and B. H. Friedman, became convinced that the publishing industry in this country was no longer willing or able to publish and promote serious fiction. Sukenick became one of the co-founders of the Fiction Collective, a nonprofit writers' cooperative in which all business and editorial decisions were left in the hands of the writers themselves. Begun in 1974, the Collective began publishing some half-dozen titles a year. Despite a relative lack of media and reviewing attention and ongoing financial problems, the Collective published a number of the most significant innovative works of the 1970s.

The decade saw Sukenick continue to write novels which challenged the assumptions of realism. His works included *Out* (1973), with its diminishing number of words on the page, the language receding until the final blank pages at the end; *98.6* (1975), with its vision of America-turned-Frankenstein, its peculiar poetic rhythms, its collage method of organization; and *Long Talking Bad Conditions Blues* (1979), with its mirrorlike formal structure and its musical analogues. During the 1970s Sukenick was teaching at various universities and eventually became the director of the Creative Writing Program at the University of Colorado in Boulder. Annoyed and even disgusted by what he saw as the insensitive, irrelevant, and incestuous methods of book reviewing in this country, Sukenick also decided to form an independent reviewing magazine. The result was *The American Book Review*, a magazine whose reviews are written mainly by practicing poets and fiction writers and which reviews a great deal of fiction and poetry ignored by traditional reviewing agencies.

—Larry McCaffery

Do you write every day?

Sukenick: Yes. Especially when I'm working on a long piece, it's almost necessary to work every day. In fact, I have the feeling that I should work every day of my life. Everything else is a big interruption: teaching, lectures, traveling, these all just get in the way. But what can you do? That's life, right?

You say in your book on Wallace Stevens that "writing poetry was for Stevens a way of getting along." Is the same true for you with fiction?

Sukenick: Yes, it's a way of getting along because I re-create my life as I write.

You don't mean that in an autobiographical sense, do you?

Sukenick: No. In fact, I was just having a discussion with Ray Federman about why we don't write autobiography.

Why don't you?

Sukenick: Because autobiography isn't that interesting. Ray and I are
both involved in actively re-creating our lives, not simply recording our
pasts.

*When you say that autobiographies aren't interesting, do you mean in a
formal sense? Or simply that it's a lesser form because you're recording
events, rather than imagining them?*

Sukenick: Both, actually. It's not interesting in a formal sense, and it's
not interesting from the point of view of the data involved. I mean, who
cares? You yourself care, but of what public interest is that data compared
to what happened to Marco Polo or any fairly adventurous traveler or
soldier of fortune? It's just of no intrinsic interest, and for that reason most
autobiographies are really a kind of forgettable escape reading. That book
Papillion is a good example of a wonderful read on that level, but I totally
forgot it the minute I closed it. It was trivial.

But your fiction—especially your early fiction, such as Up *and some of
the stories in* The Death of the Novel—*has a lot of trappings of
autobiographical fiction. Why did you use yourself as a literary character
so often in those books?*

Sukenick: Part of what I was doing then was just trying to get into an
honest writing position. At a time when the whole question of whether fiction can say anything true becomes problematic, you can at least get
yourself into a position where you can say, "Well, at least I can say
something about my own experience anyway, directly, without making
anything up." Of course, the challenge and conscious paradox there is that
no matter how hard you try to get down the data as they literally are, there
are almost no literal data. They are always filtered through the creative
mind, even if that mind happens to belong to the person from whom the
life data come. You can see this idea pretty clearly in my story "Momentum," which begins, in effect, "I want to get the story down just as it happened on the tape recorder." And then, of course, it turns out that you
can't do this. You should always *try*, though, to capture the data of reality.

*Why do you think so many of you guys were trying such similar
pseudo-autobiographical approaches during the late 1960s? I'm thinking
of you, Federman, Steve Katz, William Demby, John Barth, even Kurt
Vonnegut. This obviously wasn't just a coincidence . . .*

Sukenick: No, like I just said, people were trying to get themselves into a position where they could use fiction to say something true. The
whole idea of mimesis having been challenged, in my opinion successfully,
there are two alternatives. The first is the one that Barth took, the retreat

into literature. And I think that, despite all his talent and intellectual gifts, this was the wrong move for him; his works have gotten predictably claustrophobic. Barth's tack was to say that there is always the intervention of interpretation of some kind, so that you could never get at the "real data." So instead of talking about the data, he took the position—simply expressed in that essay, "The Literature of Exhaustion," which he published so long ago now—that since you are always looking at those data of experience through the interpreting mind, they are, in effect, *already interpreted*. No matter how you come at "reality," it is already interpreted before the fact. Then what you do is move into the interpretations and deal with the *interpretations*, not with reality, because that's what the really acute artist realizes he's dealing with. You become, then, a connoisseur of fiction, the expert in measuring and collecting and judging between and making distinctions among fictions. The other direction was to propose to yourself that fiction could tell some truth beyond your personal vision and beyond literature itself.

I take it from what you say about Barth that you feel you followed the second direction.

Sukenick: Yes, Barth's position—which I think is also Gass's and Coover's position—is one I've never agreed with. My feeling is that you have always to move in the direction of the data of experience in "reality," whatever the chances that you can't do this. There's a line in Handke's *A Sorrow beyond Dreams* where he talks about the effort to investigate and develop the psychology of a character—in this case, of his mom—and he says that he realizes he can't do it, that he can never successfully arrive at the reality of that character. But at the same time he says that you have to try. I think that's true: you have to try, because it is only in making that effort to deal with those data that you finally create a legitimate fiction. In other words, you don't create a legitimate fiction merely by dealing with other fictions. One of the main purposes of really good writing is to destroy other really good writing, to destroy all the old concepts and formulas that come out of the best of the past. You should destroy them lovingly and with great consciousness and awareness of them, but always with the end in mind of getting beyond them again. And knowing that they were also trying to do the same kind of thing.

I take it that your main goal in deconstructing these prior fictions is this process of "getting beyond." Otherwise you'd seem to be basically engaged in a similar kind of fiction-exploring—or destroying—game that Barth, Borges, and some of the other writers are playing.

Sukenick: But is what I was describing really deconstruction? If I were just deconstructing, that would be staying at the level of fictions. What I'm after is to deconstruct *not* back to other constructs, the way Barth does, but *to what lies beyond constructs.*

In your Wallace Stevens book, you have a passage that is frequently cited when critics talk about this issue: "The mind orders reality not by imposing ideas on it but by discovering significant relationships within it, as the artist abstracts and composes the elements of reality in significant integrations that are works of art." What this suggests to me is something very important: that there are significant relationships in reality that can be discovered, not merely invented and then applied.

Sukenick: No matter how much things are interpreted beforehand, there are still some kinds of data there. The main one is death, or maybe the main one is birth and the second is death, with a lot of others in between that are experientially there. It's not as if we're confronting a blank space. There's things out there that are undeniable and you have to find some way of dealing with them. There's an interaction going on between language and those data in which the effort is to get rid of old language formulas. What seems to happen is that you break down the language and, as you break down the language, since language can't be broken down any more than consciousness can (you can't confront a total blank, either in language or in your mind, unless you're dead or in a coma), you hope that language will break open and offer the opportunity to make new organizations that are appropriate to new situations out there. I'm not going to argue that language makes any direct contact with reality, but I think there's a changing metaphoric contact with reality, and the only way that change can occur is by breaking down the old fictions, the old constructs. When that happens I think you open up a new space. It's like cutting a log in a new direction: a new grain opens up, literally a new content appears when you cut something in a new way from the way it usually gets cut. You see different things; words then begin to surrender their meanings in different ways and begin to reveal all that huge amount of accumulated wisdom that language contains from the whole history of the culture.

Is this one of the sources, then, of your obvious interest in wordplay, puns, pangrams, and other language games? I mean, do these devices help the author with this process of opening up new spaces with language, forcing the words to yield new complexities and meanings?

Sukenick: Precisely. Language play releases the possibility of meaning that is inherent in language, that is built up in it through tradition. The wisdom of language only reveals itself, oddly, when you break it down. It's like breaking open a piece of fruit—if you can find a way of cracking it open, you can find a way of releasing its content, its energy, its suggestiveness, its possibilities. But in order to do that you have to deform it, or transform it, through puns or through arbitrary devices of the kind that Raymond Roussel uses—through the imposition of odd schemes, non sequiturs, even through improvisation. You have to do that kind of peculiar manipulation of language in order to release its peculiar *power*. You may, in the process, manage to startle or surprise the reader, but the important thing is to surprise *yourself*, to get out of the premeditated.

Gombrich says somewhere that wordplay unleashes a "preconscious idea" for both reader and author.

Sukenick: The only problem I have with that is the word "preconscious." I wouldn't characterize this process as preconscious at all. I would rather use the word "nonexistent." It's not as if it were there already in your consciousness; on the contrary, it's something that is totally beyond your consciousness, that you bring into your consciousness in that way, that you *create in language*. Of course, it can work both ways, the way that Freud used puns to reveal the unconscious. But *Finnegans Wake* uses wordplay in both ways: it reveals the unconscious and opens up the multiplicity of history that exists in language; and perhaps accidentally, as an inevitable increment given the way Joyce was writing, it had the effect of bringing into consciousness information that could not otherwise have been reached, information that was neither in history nor in the unconscious. It was totally new information.

I'm interested in what you meant just a minute ago when you said that your approach was seeking a truth "beyond literature." What is the nature of such a truth?

Sukenick: There is experience beyond language. There are things that go on in the sensorium of the body that are pre-linguistic—and also post-linguistic—and that may or may not get into the language system. There is a whole chain of these "feelings" in the sense of what you experience when somebody touches you or kicks you. And that feeling registers in varying ways. For instance, it seems as if people are amnesiacs about pain once it's over, so I don't know what form pain really takes in the language system. There are probably lots of things that you feel physically that don't get into the language system. Then there's that other sense of feeling—feeling/emotion—and there is a gradation here. That is, bodily feeling turns into feeling/emotion; and of course the basic physical feelings turn into emotions most easily. Maybe pain and fear, or pain turning into fear, are the best examples.

And sex.

Sukenick: Yes. In a way, sex is the most of all, because it is pleasurable and desired. The reason sex is so powerful is because it's where feeling turns into feelings more easily. That may be one of the reasons, come to think of it, for this explosion of sado-masochism that's been going on in some circles (maybe a lot of circles) in this country. It may be that there's a kind of perverse curiosity about getting beyond formulated emotions back to a undeniable *source* of emotion, if we can talk about emotions becoming worn out, conventionalized, and inappropriate. This may be the same sense we get in language or fictional forms—maybe the whole *root* of that may lie in the emotions; maybe we have this feeling that our emotional life is fossilized and that the way to get back to that authentic source of emotions may be to get back to that precise point where your emotions are totally out of control. Thus the idea of being *forced* to have pleasure becomes attractive. There is an apparent authenticity there, however desperate, because it is out of our conceptual control, out of our cultural control, out of our conventional control. *That,* for example, is experience beyond language as far as I'm concerned.

Is this one of the reasons why so many of your characters—especially in 98.6—seem to relate to each other, both sexually and personally, through violence or other means of heightening their reactions? You seem to be suggesting that this is a product of the age, a response to all the things around us which try to deaden our reactions, to conventionalize them.

Sukenick: In *98.6* I was very unsympathetic to these tendencies. I diagnosed the culture as lapsing into sado-masochism and suggested this was a kind of sickness. The idea I had there was that power and sex had gotten confused. I think this is still true today—that power and sex, or violence and sex, are often confused in our culture—and that they shouldn't be.

Are there any writers you could point to as having specifically influenced your first couple of books? Kafka and Beckett seem likely candidates, for example . . .

Sukenick: My big discovery during my college years was Laurence Sterne, who I discovered via a course with Meyer Abrams. I had never seen anything like Sterne but I immediately recognized him as a sympathetic type and source of support. But I was always heavily into the modernist tradition, even in high school. I was worshiping the modernist heroes like Kafka, Joyce, and Lawrence in those days. But my real reading discovery was Henry Miller, which came some years later, in the early '60s.

What about Wallace Stevens? What intrigued you about his work?

Sukenick: I found the sensibility and ideology behind Stevens to be very sympathetic. I think I was right. Stevens, more than any other writer, was into what turns out to be the main line of post-romanticism—that is, the relationship of the imagination to reality. He was the most cognizant of that problem, and he handled it in the most direct, pure way. In fact, this was partly his hangup, because he could barely talk about anything else. So his poems get very repetitive.

In the interview you did with Joe Bellamy a while back, you try to counter his suggestion that artists "work out" the public fantasies and that therefore these psychological reasons are the chief reasons for the existence of fiction. You say in response to this idea that there are "epistemological reasons" for fiction's existence before there are psychological reasons. What did you mean by that?

Sukenick: Stevens's poetry illustrates what I was talking about. I would call Stevens a psychological poet only if you intend the broadest definition of psychology—say, the psychology of the way the mind works. If you think of it that way, there are a lot of other ways to think of psychology than as emotional-hangup analysis or Freudian depth psychology. And in fiction there are a lot of other things that underlie the creative process before ego psychology, like the whole cognitive faculty and just how we make sense of patterns.

A concern with the two examples you just supplied seems to be one of the defining features of postmodern fiction—its emphasis on cognition, epistemology, pattern-making, rather than the ego-oriented fiction of, say, American fiction in the 1950s.

Sukenick: I agree, although maybe this issue is already established now as something we can take for granted, like the idea of the intrusive text (the text that is conscious of being a text). That's one of those issues that we don't have to concentrate on anymore. We assume that now, and are free to investigate other things.

When you say that "we assume that now," do you mean that writers to-day don't have to deal with epistemological issues anymore, in the same way that your generation of writers assumed that depth psychology, at least temporarily, didn't need further exploration?

Sukenick: Not exactly. Contemporary fiction still has to deal with this issue, just the way fiction always has to deal with ego psychology. But it doesn't have to *focus* on it necessarily. If you focus on that kind of abstract problem—and this is what happened to Stevens—you get hung up on it. Once you discover it, what are you going to do but say it again and again and again? And that's not the point of fiction or poetry. The point is to *use* the discovery to investigate experience and language, or whatever it is that you're investigating. But these are *ongoing things*. If you just stop with the idea that, to give a simple example, the whole world is a fiction, and just say this repeatedly, it stops being interesting.

You state in your "Twelve Digressions towards a Study of Composition" that "the form of the traditional novel is a metaphor for a society that no longer exists." What were you trying to suggest there?

Sukenick: I must have been talking about the idea of fiction as a model, especially a mimetic model. The mimetic model crystallized when the novel came to maturity in the nineteenth century and was based on the imitation of a certain culture, with its norms, ways of perceiving, ways of thinking, and so on. But we don't have that culture anymore. Life and society have changed, so that model is not appropriate to our kind of society any longer. The mimetic novel, then, was developed in a certain period and now it's become antiquated.

In that same essay you say that "the voodoo at the heart of mimetic theory is the idea that verisimilitude suggested the possibility of control over reality." In what sense does a mimetic view lead to this notion of controlling reality? Just in the sense that we understand reality better?

Sukenick: If you create a model of the circumstances you are in, then presumably you can deal with them better. A parallel is developing a scientific description through mathematics of the way a certain chunk of experience behaves. Once you get that down, you can predict behavior, you can move back to the source of behavior—and I'm talking about the behavior of things as well as people and their interactions—and change the source of behavior and therefore alter behavior itself. Or you can look ahead and see what's going to happen if you do something or other. What are the consequences in a moralistic society of having an illegitimate child? There is a cautionary side to *The Scarlet Letter*. Or, on a more subtle level, what are the power relationships among the rich and the aristocrats in Henry James? Or what is the place of morality in Céline?

So you feel that the realistic novel did provide readers with a kind of model of reality—that you can learn about life from reading novels?

Sukenick: I have learned a great deal about life from fiction, especially the fiction of Henry James. But the thing is that the world is changing, there are new circumstances that demand new paradigms. And you can't control these new circumstances the way the realistic model wanted to. It's like trying to hold together an armful of large balls—something's going to pop out somewhere. The effort at control is hopeless. What you have to do—and I hope that my fiction is exemplary of this process—is to learn how your fiction can *be a part of the environment*, rather than trying to control it.

This has nothing to do with the fact that contemporary society may be more out of control than the reality of the nineteenth-century realist?

Sukenick: Maybe that voodoo I mention is always at work for the serious writer. What he's trying to do is control his experience in some way, cast a spell on it, find ways of dealing with it. And what he leaves *behind* becomes, maybe, a model for the reader. But if it's control the contemporary writer is after, I'd say he has to modify this view, because I don't think the model is now control.

What is the model?

Sukenick: I'd say *participation*.

I recall that in your story "The Birds" you have a passage about how wonderful birds are because they "carve shapes from nothing, decorate the silence, make melodious distinctions to distinguish one moment from the next." Should this be fiction's main role today—to serve as decoration, to create distinctions in a world which threatens to obliterate distinctions?

Sukenick: Of course, fiction has a lot of functions. One of them is simply to give pleasure. That line in "The Birds" is really about that direction in fiction. It's like the way music keeps time: not retentively but just taking note of it, varying it, articulating it, and making it pleasurable. That's one function of fiction, but it has dozens of others. People are always saying, "What's the political function of fiction, what's the this or that function?" But fiction is so basic that it has many different functions simultaneously, all the time. I mean, what would you say if someone asked you, "Hey, what's the function of your mind?" It's like that.

What are your views about the so-called Gass–Gardner debate about the "moral nature" of art? Do you take sides in this affair?

Sukenick: Great art—whatever that is, whatever we finally agree on as being the great texts—*acquires* a moral value because it becomes normative. It says, in effect, "This is what consciousness should be like." But it's a very broad kind of moral value. It's not issue oriented, you might say. Now it's quite possible that fiction can be issue oriented—it can talk about moral issues, it can talk about love affairs, it can talk about all sorts of subjects—but if we say that fiction must be moral in its outlook, we are putting art on the same level as propaganda. In fact, what would Gardner do with a morally noxious writer like Céline, who is nevertheless great? There are immoralities at the level of subject matter that are overwhelmed by the broader moral concern of seeing a consciousness articulate itself in such incredibly eloquent terms. Just seeing this kind of access, this increase in consciousness that a mind like that of Céline gives to language as a form becomes, in itself, a moral consideration finally, although if you just had somebody you know die in a concentration camp you wouldn't want to read his books.

On the other hand, I'm not in favor of Yale having given Pound the Bollingen Prize. That was a very bad thing to do *at that time*; it was morally coarse, a crude thing to do. There was an aestheticism involved that was misfocused, because there was no way you could avoid at that point Pound's pro-fascist, anti-Semitic activities. To give him the Bollingen award amounted to social recognition and approval of that part of his writing. That is not to deny, of course, the larger value of Pound's writing. I wouldn't deny that remark made about modern art—was it by Flaubert?—"The only obligation of the writer is the morality of the right sensation." That's quite true.

One of the other charges made by Gardner and others against a lot of postmodern fiction is that it is narcissistic and irrelevant to the larger concerns of the world. How do you answer these charges?

Sukenick: I have several ways to answer them, but my favorite one at the moment is Jerry Klinkowitz's argument that narcissism is *good*.

Why is it good?

Sukenick: It teaches people how to play with themselves. Everyone should learn how to play with themselves more and better.

Why do you think this notion of the "play" of literature and language comes up so often these days? And why does it make so many people feel uneasy?

Sukenick: Literature *is* playful, like sex is. Literature is a pleasurable activity, and play is a component of many kinds of pleasure. Maybe that's the reason for people's uneasiness: despite all the talk about personal and sexual liberation, playfulness is still a kind of taboo that makes people nervous. There is nothing that enrages people more than the idea that an artist is narcissistic. But why is this? Should they care? So it's perhaps best to take the position that the novel should be narcissistic, maybe even more than it is.

There are, of course, other ways of answering this. One is to say that this type of literature is *not* narcissistic, that self-reflexivity is a path —maybe the only path—to great consciousness. Every implicit step to increased consciousness has to be accompanied by some increase of *self*-consciousness, just as the scientist needs to perfect the tools of the experiment before he can get results that tell him something about reality.

On several occasions you've said in print, echoing Robbe-Grillet, that the main job of the modern writer is to teach the reader how to invent himself. Is this a justification for the kinds of metafictional, self-reflexive strategies you employ in your early work—and that writers like Coover, Gass, and Barth regularly use?

Sukenick: Yes, this approach is an investigation of the creative powers of the mind, of the imagination itself, and of language. Its aim is to make people super-conscious—as conscious as possible of the way the imagination inevitably helps to shape reality around the self. The reason that this kind of approach becomes so important today is because of the pressure of the media, which is nothing so much as the manipulation of the mass imagination, a sellout of individual experience. The media impose manipulative paradigms on individual experience, so that it is almost as if people don't have any individual experience—they only have what they see being presented on television. Of course, that's not literally true, but things move ominously in that direction all the time. So I figure that one of the things that art is supposed to do is to teach people how to defend their experience and prevent it from being stolen from them by showing them how to use their own imaginations against that manipulative imagination which is not in their own interest. Oh, I suppose that the media sometimes present things that are in the public's interest, but if so it's probably an accident. The tendencies of mass manipulation are primarily in the interest of politicians and corporations or the consumerist society, which have to make and sell things in order to survive. It's directed by the profit-making mechanism in our society. It's not for the benefit of the individual, although benefits may accidentally occur—you see, I'm not a complete pessimist about conglomeratism.

In a metafiction, then, the idea is that the writer becomes a kind of exemplary person who can respond to the world through his own imagination—not an imposed substitute—and hopefully invent something that is personal and meaningful.

Sukenick: Exactly. That's the crucial *political* function of the writer: to resist that sellout of individual experience. And that's why a writer with a very individual voice can make a lot of people nervous. Maybe this is one of the reasons why the Fiction Collective is always enraging some segment of the culture—because they are the most uncategorizable voices around. A slick writer can say all sorts of uncomfortable, rabid things. Norman Mailer can say, "Bring down the establishment"; and as long as he says this slickly, it will slip into the scene and take its place with all the other discourse. But if somebody is intentionally crude, uncategorizable, rough, disorganized and yet is felt to be a quality writer with something to say, that, even when narcissistic, can make people nervous.

How do books seem to get started for you? Do you begin with an idea, a character, a plot, a sentence—or what?

Sukenick: They usually have geometrical patterns that occur to me, or sometimes arithmetical patterns. But it's usually geometrical patterns—the ones described in the titles.

Like "Up"? What configuration was suggested by that?

Sukenick: It's simple. *Up* goes up, *Out* goes out. *Up* really does go up: it's a flight of the imagination. There is literally a scene in the beginning where an astronaut goes up, and then he comes down again at the end of the book. And the whole novel goes up and down in that curve in a lot of ways. And *Out* does move out: out of New York, across the country, out into the Pacific, out of the text, out of the language as the language gradually disappears and the book moves out into the blank page.

It sounds like this is a conceptual or abstract notion that generates your texts—spatial relationships . . .

Sukenick: Yes, but it occurs to me as a *feeling*, not as a concept. You get a feeling of the way a book will be moving. In *98.6* a sense of triangulation occurred that is evident in the book's structure and in other ways. In *Long Talking Bad Conditions Blues* there is a mirroring effect. With that book it would be better to talk about reflection, rather than self-reflection. And "reflection" goes two ways—there's the pun on reflection as careful thought. That doesn't deny the notion of holding the mirror up to nature, but part of the reflection is the work reflecting itself: the book has two parts, with a blank space in the middle, which is like a mirror in that on either side the parts reflect one another, repeat one another.

You mean in a formal sense—the structural arrangement repeats?

Sukenick: Yes, it's the way Abish's *Alphabetical Africa* does: from A to Z and Z to A. My book is like that, not in terms of the letter arrangements but in its spatial organization into sections. These spatial sections are organized very carefully to repeat in the second part. Now the first part was generated by improvisation. I started writing a sentence and for some reason that sentence didn't want to stop—it went on for about fourteen pages without punctuation. Then I got bored with it; it seemed to lose its zing. So then I decided to use another rhythm, which was based on segments of a certain number of words. And then another and another and so on. Then for some reason I thought, "Well, this improvisation is getting too loose, I've got all these different rhythms which I'm doing basically off the cuff, by ear, winging it, and this is all getting too loose." I needed a formal structure imposed to bring certain things out and give the book some order. What occurred to me at that point, for mysterious reasons which may have grown out of the subject of the book—or which maybe *created* the subject of the book—was that what should happen next was that it should repeat.

In your fiction and criticism you repeatedly bring up the attractiveness of jazz as an analogy for your own process of literary creation, especially the improvisatory nature of jazz. What advantages does a truly improvisatory approach to writing have over the traditional approach, which emphasizes artistic control at every step of the writing process?

Sukenick: Improvisation releases you from old forms, stale thoughts, it releases things that are released only with difficulty on a psychological basis. It allows in surprising things that are creeping around on the edges of consciousness. It prevents you from writing clichéd formulas. It's a release, finally, a release of the imagination. Today, however, I think that the idea of improvisation itself has become a formula and it has gotten very slack as a result. The novel got tired of improvisation in the beginning of the '70s. At least it did for me. Presently I seem to be moving in the direction of formalism—the kind of formalism that I think Coover and Abish are using. Another example is the sort of thing Federman used in *The Voice in the Closet*, in which you simply impose a form on your materials, it not really mattering how this form was generated. Calvino does the same kind of thing in—what's that book?

The Castle of Crossed Destinies?

Sukenick: No, I'm thinking of *Invisible Cities*. But the important idea is that the *genesis of form* isn't important, whether it's traditional or untraditional. The important thing is to have a form. I would say, in fact, that for this approach you don't want to have a traditional form because there are too many associations with it already—in a way, the form is already exhausted. So a truly nontraditional form would probably be an arbitrary form. But then the interesting thing becomes to begin investigating the differences between different kinds of form. We have an interesting formal situation there. Perhaps writers will come up with some totally idiosyncratic forms which can be used only once—which is fine—or forms which other people may be able to pick up on and use again and again. If this occurs, maybe we'd have a more continuous formal tradition. I know that I'm continually drawn, by temperament, to use idiosyncratic forms. But I suppose even that can become conceptualized and overconceptualized and exhausted. In any case, right now the literary situation—for me and I think for fiction in general—seems to be that form is fruitful. Instead of improvisation, it now seems that form releases my imagination.

When you're starting out with a book, or even when you're in the middle of it, do these kinds of generalizations occur to you? You know, "Improvisation isn't working, I need formal structures," that kind of thing?

Sukenick: No. Most of what I've been talking about I realized in retrospect. Who thinks of these things while working on a book? While you're working there is a kind of fruitful chaos and ignorance—at least that's the way I work and the way most people I know work. When I start out with a book, the last thing I want to know is what the book is going to be like when it's finished. This is a very painful and risky approach, though, because while you're working on the book it looks like you're dealing with failure. In fact, you *are* dealing with failure, right up until the moment when the book is a success. *If* it ever gets there. But until that moment the book is definitely a failure. This is a very floundering, uncomfortable feeling.

Doesn't 98.6 end with the phrase "another failure"?

Sukenick: Yes, and I believe in the idea of failure at various levels. A paradoxical but familiar situation exists in America these days, in which an artist may be authenticated by failure or ruined by success. So in a sense I don't want to write books that are successes or to write "great books" in the old sense. Also, to write a book that is a total success would be to write a book that is totally inhuman. The closest thing I can think of to this is *Finnegans Wake*. An analogous situation, although it's not as great a book, is Beckett's *The Lost Ones* because it's totally hermetic and quite perfect in its own way. But there's an intentional flaw in its whole scheme, a way out of the text's hermetic world. It has to do with Dante: the way out of the Inferno is through the Devil's asshole. It seems to me that in *The Lost Ones* there is some similar way out, some flaw of human nature that becomes a virtue, as the flaws in human nature sometimes do, simply because they're characteristic. Anyway, the kind of book I most want to write is the kind of book that *fails* back into the experience which it is about. It emerges—and re-merges—with this experience, having added itself to it. But I'm not interested in creating a book that remains in its own perfect sphere, apart from experience. My work has to cancel itself out to do what it is trying to do. It isn't trying to transcend experience, but is trying to add to experience.

With your earlier books—the ones which were indeed inspired by improvisational techniques—were you literally improvising on the page, that is, making up the book without revision or prior planning?

Sukenick: I've always revised very little. Even, in fact, *Long Talking,* which was completed in ten weeks—extraordinary for me, because I've never written a book in less than two-and-a-half years before. I've never seemed to need revision. If the thing is going to come at all, it seems to come right. A little manipulation is needed, but not much.

Is there any aspect of writing you could isolate as being the most intriguing to you?

Sukenick: That makes me stop and think. There's a lot that is intriguing: the rhythm of the sentences, their sound, but probably what I find most interesting is the way I get into a fiction and it literally starts producing new experiences for me. It's like having a second life, simultaneously with the first one. Or it's like Wordsworth blanking out and having visions. So although I'm not a mystic at all, it's very exciting to see all that new experience coming at you out of your own mind, adding to your life.

*It was interesting to me that your last book—*Long Talking Bad Conditions Blues—*appeared to be using* blues *rather than jazz as its central musical analogue.*

Sukenick: As I was going along with that book I was conceiving of it as a long song that had rhythmic sections repeating, like blues songs. But I guess I didn't really consider this to be a significant break with what I was previously doing. Actually the distinction among various forms, including literary and musical forms, seems to me to be lessening. For instance, I feel that the distinction between the long poem or the epic and the novel is beginning to disappear. I was going to call *Out* "a long narrative poem in prose"—a takeoff on Fielding's subtitle to *Tom Jones.* Why can't a novel be like a long poem—or a long song—if it's rhythmic? Those spacings in *Out* are like the prose rhythms I use in *Long Talking.* Of course, a novel *isn't* a long poem; there are differences. But why can't it use some of the techniques of a long poem?

Are there any other art forms—television, the cinema, perhaps recent trends in painting—that have affected your writing?

Sukenick: Abstract expressionism seems to me to be the basic art movement of this half of the century because it was an investigation of the reality of art itself and established its reality in a non-puritan way. It got rid of illusion and all those other pejorative terms like "suspension of disbelief." Illusion traditionally is a pejorative term, yet it has always seemed in our tradition the center of art. So no wonder the puritans didn't like it. Abstract expressionism got rid of that whole notion that art is apart from life, that it is something special which is siphoned or partitioned off from experience—art as a vampirelike entity that sucks the juices out of life and puts it into this aesthetic place that is of greater value than life itself, and is put by millionaires into museums so that people can come in, look at it, and approve of themselves. That whole schizoid split between art and life was broken down in abstract expressionism by virtue of its discovery of a new locus of reality for art—it moved everything back to the art of creation, rather than the act of audience appreciation. It said that the reality of art is the reality of *making art*—everything comes from this, instead of taking the position that the reality of art is located in the act of receiving or appreciating it, something that denies or soft-pedals the process of creation. When you look at a work of abstract expressionism you're forced to remember that there was a hand there that created it. There is an attachment to life without any schizophrenia, without any alienation. Art therefore becomes a human act—you're forced to say to yourself, "This painting I'm looking at was done by a person," and take it on that basis. I hope that my fiction has applied some of these principles.

What you're talking about seems the opposite of the Jamesian or Joycean idea of the work of art with no creator present—the God paring his fingernails over a work.

Sukenick: Yes, and in fact abstract expressionism represented the sudden explosion or destruction of the modernist movement.

I agree—modernism seems to me to have emphasized the ability of the artist to put the discontinuous fragments of modern experience together into a work which could oppose our sense of chaos. You know, it offered a kind of example of unity and coherence to people who couldn't find these things anywhere else. But postmodern writers and painters seem to refuse to allow this to happen—they seem to want to remind us that reality is chaotic and discontinuous.

Sukenick: Yeah, an abstract expressionist painting is another fragment added to the pile, but it's an *intelligent addition*, not a transcendent object.

I've always thought that one of the most striking aspects of your fiction is your refusal to present your characters as consistent beings with identifiable traits. Rather, like clouds, your characters are always shifting into different shapes, different beings, with different names, contradictory attributes, and so on. Do you do this mainly to emphasize the difficulty—or even impossibility—of devising a unified notion of self?

Sukenick: If you drop the idea of imitation as the mainstay of fiction, then the idea that you need "characters" drops away pretty quickly. You realize that characterization is always simply a part of the text or part of the consciousness of the writer, depending on at what point you wish to start talking about character. Either way, it's a division of the whole into a dialectical fragment. The whole consciousness breaks up into its parts, and various energies can begin to flow because of that polarizing among the parts. The fragmentation can then alter the parts, or the parts can be combined into different ways, and the final consequence can be that an alteration can take place in the whole consciousness or the whole text. In any case, that willful fragmentation of the ongoing narrative—or of the ongoing experience of a given consciousness in the process of composition—creates energy, creates detail. What goes on beneath the ordinary idea of characterization—having characters interact and conflict within a fictional world, for example—is really not very unlike the ordinary process of the mind in any inquiry about anything. In this case, instead of the entities being concepts, ideas, symbols, points of view, they are called Frank, Mary, and Larry. In both cases, the entities involved combine, recombine, split up. They die, they loose validity, they gain a certain authenticity—all as a result of the larger argument of the text. More and more, as the idea of imitation drops away, the necessity for having these entities under the label of hard-and-fast, well-rounded characters also drops away. You begin to realize that the process of characterization is the process of fragmentation and dialectic that the mind ordinarily pursues—although this process is pursued within a particular context and toward different ends than in, say, philosophy. Madame Bovary represents one cluster of traits of the bourgeoisie, Huck Finn represents one side of the split of the frontier, Ahab and Moby-Dick (is Moby-Dick a character?) symbolize something, and so on. So even traditional characterization has always been doing this.

The other side of this—since I've only been talking about the literary or textual side of this issue—is the sense I have that individuals' personalities are becoming less and less important and less defined.

Do you mean less well defined, more fragmented, in comparison, say, with people in the nineteenth century—the people represented in the great realist tradition?

Sukenick: Yeah, even compared to the kinds of characters I would see in my father's generation or especially my grandfather's generation, who were very august, aggressively rigid personalities. It seems that people now, for better or for worse and for good reasons usually, are less defined—more "laid back," as they say, "going with the flow" and all that. I'm using these clichés on purpose to show that people think about personality, even their own, in this way. I also like to believe that you can have a more flattened out, flowing, less rigidly defined personality that is still not necessarily uninvolved on its own terms.

Any theories about what's creating this change in personality structure?

Sukenick: It has something to do with the change in the methods of political and financial organization, and the methods of communication. Obviously, for example, all over the world societies are moving more in the direction of collectivization instead of individualism. It may well be that the age of individualism of Henry Ford and George Bernard Shaw is dying out, and that the social, political, and economic conditions that made that kind of definition possible—or even necessary and advantageous—are gone. Maybe it's the end of a process that began with the Renaissance. But this idea of pursuing a job or career, with the individual succeeding through conflict and struggle; the idea that character—which is what Undershaft in Shaw claims runs England—was the thing that saw you through that process and was its driving force, man's most essential untouchable element—all that has been eroded by the sense of collectivity, by the sense that people's character traits can be drastically changed by drugs, by brainwashing, by the interchangeability of people in corporate slots, by the rate at which information comes at us. It's just very difficult to absorb and respond to so much information while having a hardened, brittle personality circumference, as opposed to one that is porous.

What you've said in your remarks here, and also what appears by implication in your fiction, seems to disparage this notion of "depth psychology." You seem to prefer—a bit like John Irving and Donald Barthelme—to keep your fiction "on the surface." What I mean by that is that you seem content to give us behavior but not motivation. Is this because you simply don't feel that people can be explained as easily as fiction usually suggests they can?

Sukenick: That's probably true. There is also a loss of faith in Freudian therapy, as opposed to what we might think of as *activist* therapies, which concentrate on behavior rather than on motivation. The idea of motivation itself may have decayed as a persuasive concept. It seems very complicated in that you may figure out a motivation, but the complexity may well be too much for the analyst to offer any opportunities for behavior change. Or, if it's a simple motivation, it may be too strong to alter in any case. So it has seemed more fruitful for me as a novelist to concentrate on behavior, or on inventive ways of dealing with whatever givens we are confronted with in the ego that come up in that kind of humanistic therapy. It seems more convincing to begin therapy with and through the body rather than with the mind, which is constantly outwitting itself. So for a whole lot of reasons the notion of depth psychology and Freudian motivation doesn't interest me much. Furthermore, these concepts have very much become attached to a doctrine, so for that reason it's not of interest for a writer. Because when you make a Freudian analysis, for example, and create characters out of that view, really what you're discovering is Freudian analysis and not anything about character or the text or your own imagination.

It would also seem that if you continue to focus on traditional methods of character analysis, you're slipping back into the realistic writers' game of pretending that characters in books are like people in reality.

Sukenick: Yeah, it furthers the illusionism that a lot of writers of my generation are fighting against. If we create rounded characters, motivated by depth psychology, we are just furthering the illusionism that we're trying to get rid of. There's also that sense you mentioned a minute ago that things related to character and personality are more mysterious than we thought. We don't understand them as well as we once thought we did. Perhaps we can never understand them on the grounds that the mind may not be able to understand itself. So pretending to fully understand a character is not one of the things that can be fruitfully done through fiction. We sure don't in life, so there's no reason why we should pretend to in fiction.

Are there any contemporary writers you especially admire or feel affinities with?

Sukenick: There are so many good writers around right now that I can't even begin to name them all. But I suppose the writers I feel closest to are Steve Katz, Ray Federman, Clarence Major, George Chambers, and Walter Abish. I'm sure I'm leaving out a lot of names, but these come readily to mind.

You talked earlier about the advantages a writer has in creating a certain type of literary "failure." Are there any advantages in being misunderstood?

Sukenick: Yes, there are some distinct advantages, strange and perverse as that may seem. When I'm at work on a book, I don't have the variable of wondering, "Is my next book going to sell? Will I get a large advance? What will my next book do to my reputation in the publishing industry?" I can just say, "Fuck it!" to all those worries and concentrate on writing my book the way I want to. That's a big advantage for an artist, because it gives his style the chance to gestate in his own peculiar ways. Odd things happen to book and writers when they become famous.

Index